PSYCHOLINGUISTICS

Psycholinguistics: The Key Concepts is a comprehensive and up-to-date guide to ideas and issues in this important field. Over 350 cross-referenced entries cover all the major areas, ranging from language processing to the nature of linguistic knowledge, from first language acquisition to language disability. They are written in an accessible, non-technical style so as to provide a clear introduction to the subject. Entries include:

- Bilingualism
- Brain
- Concept formation
- Dyslexia
- Lexical access
- Nativism
- Reading: bottom-up vs top-down
- Speech perception
- Syntactic parsing
- Working memory

Featuring suggestions for further reading and a full index, this easy to use guide is an essential resource for all students of English language, linguistics and psychology.

John Field writes and lectures on Psycholinguistics and on second language skills. He teaches at the Universities of Leeds and Reading, UK.

YOU MAY ALSO BE INTERESTED IN THE
FOLLOWING ROUTLEDGE STUDENT
REFERENCE TITLES:

Language: The Basics (second edition)
R.L. Trask

Sport Psychology: The Key Concepts
Ellis Cashmore

Semiotics: The Basics
Daniel Chandler

Key Concepts in Language and Linguistics
R.L. Trask

*The Routledge Companion to Semiotics
and Linguistics*
Edited by Paul Cobley

Fifty Key Thinkers in Psychology
Noel Sheehy

PSYCHOLINGUISTICS

The Key Concepts

John Field

Routledge
Taylor & Francis Group

LONDON AND NEW YORK

First published 2004
by Routledge
11 New Fetter Lane, London EC4P 4EE

Simultaneously published in the USA and Canada
by Routledge
29 West 35th Street, New York, NY 10001

Routledge is an imprint of the Taylor & Francis Group

© 2004 John Field

Typeset in Bembo by Taylor & Francis Books Ltd
Printed and bound in Great Britain by
TJ International Ltd, Padstow, Cornwall

British Library Cataloguing in Publication Data
A catalogue record for this book is available from the British Library

Library of Congress Cataloging in Publication Data
Field, John, 1945–
Psycholinguistics : the key concepts / John Field.
p. cm.
Includes bibliographical references and index.
1. Psycholinguistics. I. Title.
P37.F5 2004
401'.9–dc22   2003018035

ISBN 0–415–25890–1 (hbk)
ISBN 0–415–25891-X (pbk)

TO PAUL
WITH DEEPEST GRATITUDE
FOR HIS SUPPORT, UNDERSTANDING
AND SENSE OF HUMOUR DURING
THE WRITING OF THIS BOOK

CONTENTS

List of illustrations   viii
Introduction   ix
Acknowledgements   xiv
List of concepts   xv
A key to the English phonemic symbols used in this book   xx

KEY CONCEPTS   1

Bibliography   335
Index   350

ILLUSTRATIONS

Tables

L1 Six stages of first language acquisition (Brown, 1973) 145
O1 Operating principles based on prioritisation (adapted
    from Taylor and Taylor, 1990) 194

Figures

B1 The human brain 43
C1 Illustration of a movement rule 58
C2 Simplified three-level connectionist model of reading 74
F1 Simplified spectrographic pattern of the sequences [d]
    + vowel, showing marked differences in the second
    (upper) formant of [d] 116
P1 A propositional network representation of the sentence
    'This is the house that Jack built' 226

INTRODUCTION

Why this book?

Psycholinguistics goes to the heart of what we do with language. It provides insights into how we assemble our own speech and writing and how we understand that of others; into how we store and use vocabulary; into how we manage to acquire a language in the first place; and into how language can fail us. One might therefore expect it to occupy a central place in any course of general linguistics, applied linguistics, communication studies or second language teaching. Yet it often does not.

The reason is that it is traditionally a difficult area to study. This is partly because of its cross-disciplinary nature. Any linguist who forms an interest in the subject has to tackle certain areas of psychological theory, while a psychologist cannot approach it without an adequate knowledge of linguistics. And, as George Miller observed (1990: 321), linguists and psychologists tend to have different perspectives on language: 'Linguists and psychologists talk about different things... Grammarians are more interested in what could be said than in what people actually say, which irritates psychologists, and psychologists insist on supplementing intuition with objective evidence, which irritates linguists.'

To this, one must add that Psycholinguistics overlaps with many other domains: among them, phonetics, discourse analysis, language pathology, neuroscience, computer modelling and language teaching pedagogy. For those of us who know and love the subject, this breadth of scope is what makes it so fascinating; but to an intending student the eclecticism can be daunting, to say the least.

A second source of difficulty is the inaccessible nature of many psycholinguistic ideas and findings. They are usually reported in specialist psychology journals, in a form that requires a knowledge of terminology and a familiarity with theory that an intending student is unlikely to possess. There are indeed a number of handbooks which provide an overview of the subject; but they are mostly aimed at the Master's student or assume a basic grounding in psychology.[1]

Far from treating Psycholinguistics as an instructional challenge, British universities have tended to respond by sidelining the subject. It is often taught by non-specialists, who themselves find it difficult to access information or appropriate teaching material. There are Master's courses in 'Applied Linguistics', and even Applied Linguistics conferences, in which mainstream Psycholinguistics is virtually ignored. Worse, the term 'psycholinguistic' is occasionally used to give spurious respectability to ideas unconnected with the discipline and unsupported by evidence within it.

In the USA, the position is rosier: Psycholinguistics features prominently in many course programmes. But it is still no easy task to present it to undergraduate majors in Linguistics or to postgraduate students who have never been exposed to Psychology. And in the USA, as in Britain and in many other parts of the world, the important field of TESOL (Teaching Speakers of Other Languages) has barely benefited at all from the vital research findings that Psycholinguistics has uncovered – simply because bridges have not been built to its students and its practitioners.

It is hoped that the present volume will mark a small step towards rectifying these problems. Its purpose is to make Psycholinguistics accessible to all those who wish to find a way into the subject. In all, over 350 key ideas are identified, and a brief introduction is given to the thinking and the findings which lie behind each. The concepts are explained systematically, with basic principles leading to more elaborate issues of theory. The book uses a language that avoids technical terms; and does not take for granted any previous knowledge of the field. Some background in basic linguistics is assumed, but even here the more complex notions are glossed where possible.

Psycholinguistics: The Key Concepts is one of the first major reference works to make this important area of study available to the non-specialist reader. The target readership includes students at under-graduate or at Master's level who are new to the field; general linguists who wish to widen their knowledge of Psycholinguistics or are asked to teach introductory courses; teachers of first and foreign languages wanting to know more about the processes involved in reading, writing, speaking and listening; and all members of the public at large who are curious about the extraordinarily complex and apparently effortless faculty that we call language.

The concepts

Psycholinguistics is a domain with fuzzy boundaries; and there is some disagreement among those who teach it as to how widely they should set their sights. A broad view of the discipline might embrace all of the following:

a. *Language processing*: including the language skills of reading, writing, speaking and listening and the part played by memory in language.
b. *Lexical storage and retrieval*: how we store words in our minds and how we find them when we need them.
c. *Language acquisition*: how an infant acquires its first language.
d. *Special circumstances*: the effects upon language of (e.g.) deafness, blindness or being a twin; conditions such as dyslexia or aphasia (the loss of language after brain damage).
e. *The brain and language*: where language is located in the brain, how it evolved and whether it is a faculty that is unique to human beings.
f. *Second language acquisition and use.*

Many courses in Psycholinguistics choose to omit f. The study of Second Language Acquisition has developed independently, embraces sociological and pedagogical factors as well as cognitive ones; and employs a more eclectic range of research methods than Cognitive Psychology would normally accept. In addition, some courses prefer to omit c, for the very different reason that it is a large area of study in its own right. In some institutions, courses in Child Language or Language Acquisition are taught separately from those in 'Psycholinguistics' (i.e. language processing).

It was thus by no means a foregone conclusion which concepts were to be included in this volume. However, most introductory courses in Psycholinguistics pay some heed to first language acquisition as well as to language performance. Furthermore, the two areas are closely linked, with findings from the former inevitably influencing our understanding of the latter. It therefore seemed sensible to ensure that all of areas a to e above were adequately covered. The same coverage has not been extended to Second Language Acquisition, where entries are restricted to those notions which have clear links to mainstream psycholinguistic theory.

Strenuous attempts have been made to ensure that the range of concepts featured is as comprehensive as possible. An initial selection drew upon the author's own experience of teaching Psycholinguistics to those who were new to the subject. It was expanded by taking account of less central areas, cross-checking with glossaries in standard handbooks and recalling areas that the author found problematic when himself a student. However, any reference work such as this can never satisfy everyone. There will inevitably be complaints that some issues have been overlooked and reservations about others that have been featured. Since the whole purpose of the book is to plug gaps in knowledge, the author would be very grateful for any feedback that the reader cares to provide. Suggestions and comments from those who teach the subject would be especially welcome.

Accessing a concept

Psycholinguistics: The Key Concepts contains 358 entries, plus a number of cross-referenced terms. Some of the entries are short definitions or explanations consisting of only a few lines. But the book is an exploration of key notions rather than a dictionary, and many of the concepts are discussed as part of larger topics. The best way of checking understanding of a particular idea or issue is therefore to make use of the index at the end of the book. It lists the technical and semi-technical terms which are likely to cause problems for the student of Psycholinguistics, and provides references to the entries under which they appear.

The text for each entry provides a summary of principal issues and areas of controversy. Important technical terms are highlighted. They are chiefly shown in italics, but appear in bold where there is a full entry elsewhere for the term in question. For the reader who wishes to explore further, there are '*see also*' cross-references to associated topics. For those who wish to study a concept in greater depth, there are suggestions for further reading.

Choosing this recommended reading was something of a headache. So far as possible, the suggested sources needed to be those that a non-specialist would find easily comprehensible, and those which a student could obtain through a good library. As a result, most recommendations are secondary sources and most are books. On the other hand, a guide such as this needs at times to specify primary sources – for example, where a given theory or finding is closely associated with a particular researcher. Recommended reading therefore sometimes includes research papers which the student reader may find somewhat demanding. A rule of thumb is: where the reference is to a book, it is likely to be accessible; where it is to a paper in a journal, it may be less so.

A bibliography at the end of the book lists all the suggestions given for further reading, and includes references which occur within entries. To assist the reader who is new to the field, it also recommends several titles which provide uncomplicated introductions to various aspects of Psycholinguistics.

John Field
London, 2003

Note

1 Notable exceptions are the very readable books by Jean Aitchison and Altmann's *The Ascent of Babel* (see final bibliography). My own *Psycholinguistics* (Routledge, 2003) offers a basic introductory course.

ACKNOWLEDGEMENTS

The author and publishers are grateful to the American Psychological Association and to one of the original authors for permission to use Figure F1.

Writing any book is a lonely task, and I have lived with this one for some 18 months. I owe a great debt to my long-suffering friends for tolerating my frequent disappearances from view and for continuing to show curiosity about what must sometimes have appeared a sterile academic paperchase. I am very grateful to colleagues from the University of Leeds for their support and interest and to John Williams of the University of Cambridge for some stimulating discussions. Particular thanks go to those who commented on entries, including Philida Schellekens and three anonymous reviewers, and to Anne Cutler for ideas on possible topics.

Like all teachers, I owe much to my students, especially my former Master's students at King's College London, who responded constructively to some of this material in its early form as lecture handouts.

I would especially like to express my appreciation to Louisa Semlyen and Christy Kirkpatrick at Routledge, who conceived the idea of this project and kept faith with it throughout what has been a long gestation period. At a time when Psycholinguistics is sometimes undervalued or misrepresented, it was heartening indeed to encounter such belief in what the subject has to offer.

LIST OF CONCEPTS

Access code
Accommodation$_1$
Accommodation$_2$
Accuracy
Acoustic cue
Acquisition
ACT (Adaptive Control of Thought)
Activation
Ageing
Agnosia
Agrammatism
Ambiguity: lexical
Ambiguity: syntactic
Analogy model
Analysis
Anaphor resolution
Animal communication
Anxiety
Aphasia
Apraxia
Argument structure
Articulation
Articulation rate
Articulatory suppression
Artificial Intelligence (AI)
Association
Attention$_1$
Attention$_2$
Attrition
Auditory perception

Augmented Transition Network (ATN)
Autism
Automaticity
Autonomous
Babbling
Basic level
Behaviourism
Bilingualism
Biologically triggered behaviour
Birdsong
Blindness
Bootstrapping
Bottom-up processing
Brain
Brain: human vs animal
Brain imaging
Brain lateralisation
Brain: localisation
Broad-class transcription
Buffer
Capacity theories
Categorical perception
Child directed speech (CDS)
Child grammar
Chimp studies
Chomskyan theory
Chunking
Cluttering
Cognition
Cognitive psychology

Cognitivism

Cohort Theory

Colour systems

Communication strategy (CS)

Competition

Competition model

Componential analysis

Concept

Concept formation

Confusability

Connectionism

Context

Context effects

Controlled

Creolisation

Critical period

Cue trading

Deaf parent

Deafness

Delay vs deviance

Dementia

Deprivation

Depth of processing

Derivational theory of complexity

Design features

Deviance

Dichotic listening

Disorder

Down's Syndrome

Dual route

Duplex perception

Dysarthria

Dysgraphia: acquired

Dysgraphia: developmental

Dyslexia: acquired

Dyslexia: developmental

Dysphasia

Echolalia

Effect

Elaboration

Embedded processes model

Empiricism

Event-related potential (ERP)

Evolution of language

Exemplar models

Expert systems

Expertise

Eye-mind hypothesis

Eye movements

Family resemblance

Field dependency

Figurative language

Filter$_1$

Filter$_2$

Fluency

Focus

Foreigner talk

Formant

Formulaic

Fossilisation

Frequency$_1$

Frequency$_2$

Function word processing

Functional load

Functionalism

Fuzzy boundary

Garden path sentences

Gating

Gestalt Theory

Given/new

Goodness of fit

Grapheme-phoneme correspondence (GPC) rules

Graphotactic rules

Hard-wired

Hearing

Higher-level processing

Hypothesis testing

I-language

Imageability

Immediacy of interpretation

Implicit learning

Incidental learning

Indeterminacy

Inductive learning
Inference
Information processing
Information theory
Informativeness
Inner speech
Input
Instantiation
Intake
Intelligibility
Interactional view
Interactive activation
Interactive compensatory hypothesis
Interface view
Intonation
Knowledge
L1
Language Acquisition Device (LAD)
Language acquisition: research methods
Language acquisition: stages
Language acquisition: theories
Language universals
Latency
Learning style
Learning theory
Left-to-right processing
'Less is more'
Level of representation
Lexical access
Lexical effect
Lexical entry
Lexical recognition
Lexical retrieval
Lexical segmentation
Lexical storage
Lexical stress
Lexicon
Linguistic relativity

Listening
Listening: higher-level processes
Logogen
Long-term memory (LTM)
Lower-level processing
Mapping
Markedness
Masking
McGurk effect
Mean length of utterance (MLU)
Meaning construction
Meaning postulate
Memory
Mental model
Mental representation
Metacognition
Metaphor
Migration
Modality
Model
Modularity$_1$
Modularity$_2$
Morphology: acquisition
Morphology: storage
Nativisation hypothesis
Nativism
Neighbourhood
Neural network
Neurolinguistics
Noise
Normalisation
On-line process
On-line task
Operating principles
Order of acquisition
Orthographic coding
Orthography
Over-extension
Over-generalisation
Over-regulation errors
Paralinguistic features$_1$

Paralinguistic features$_2$

Parallel distributed processing (PDP)

Parallel processing

Paraphasia

Pattern recognition

Pausing

Perception

Perceptual magnet effect

Phonological awareness

Phonological bias technique

Phonological development: perception

Phonological development: production

Phonological representation

Phonological working memory

Phonotactic rules

Piagetian stages of development

Pidgin

Pivot grammar

Planning: speech

Planning: writing

Position effects

Post-perceptual

Predicate

Predictability

Priming effect

Principles and parameters

Probabilistic

Probability

Problem-solving

Processing

Proposition

Propositional network

Prosody

Prototype Theory

Psychologically real

Rapid Serial Visual Presentation

Reading aloud

Reading: bottom-up vs top-down

Reading: decoding

Reading development

Reading: higher-level processes

Reading: skilled

Reading span

Reading speed

Recursiveness

Redundancy

Rehearsal

Repair$_1$

Repair$_2$

Representational codes

Research methods: approaches

Research methods: experimental

Restructuring

Rhyme

Rime

Savant

Scaffolding

Schema theory

Search model

Second language acquisition (SLA)

Second language acquisition: approaches

Segment$_1$ (N.)

Segment$_2$ (VB.)

Selective adaptation

Self-monitoring

Semantic network

Sensation

Sensory memory

Shadowing

Short-term memory

Sign language

Signal detection theory

Slips of the Ear

Slips of the Pen (and Keyboard)

Slips of the Tongue (SOT)

Social-interactionism

Speaking

Speaking rate

Special circumstances

Species specificity

Specific language impairment (SLI)
Speech code
Speech mode$_1$
Speech mode$_2$
Speech perception: autonomous vs interactive
Speech perception: phoneme variation
Speech production
Speech signal
Speech: unit of processing
Spreading activation
Story grammar
Strategy
Stroop test
Stuttering
Subvocalisation
SW (strong-weak) pattern
Symbolic representation
Synaesthesia
Syntactic development
Syntactic parsing
Synthesised speech
T-unit
Tachistoscope
Task demands
Thematic (theta) role
Theory of mind
Thought and language

Tip of the Tongue (TOT)
Tone languages
Top-down processing
TRACE
Trading relations
Turing test
Twins
Typing
U-shaped development
Underspecification
Uniqueness point
Unit of perception
Universal Grammar (UG)
Verbal report
Verbal transformation effect (VTE)
Verbatim recall
Vocabulary acquisition
Vocabulary spurt
Vocalisation
Voice recognition
Vygotskyan
Williams Syndrome
Word primitive
Working memory
Wrap up effects
Writing
Writing: skilled
Writing system
Zipf's law

A KEY TO THE ENGLISH PHONEMIC SYMBOLS USED IN THIS BOOK

Consonants

Voiceless			Voiced	
	stops / plosives			
p	pin		b	bin
t	tin		d	din
k	cap		g	gap
	fricatives			
f	fan		v	van
θ	thing		ð	this
s	sip		z	zip
ʃ	ship		ʒ	measure
			h	hit
	affricates			
tʃ	chip		dʒ	gym
	nasals			
			m	met
			n	net
			ŋ	sing
	approximants			
			w	wet
			r	red
			j	yet
	lateral			
			l	let

Vowels

Short			Long	
ɪ	hit		i:	heat
e	head		ɑ:	heart
æ	hat		ɔ:	hoard
ʌ	hut		u:	hoot
ɒ	hot		ɜ:	hurt
ʊ	foot			
ə	a(head)			

Diphthongs

eɪ	hate		əʊ	boat		ɪə	here
aɪ	height		aʊ	bout		eə	there
ɔɪ	boil					ʊə	cure

Triphthongs

aɪə   fire   aʊə   flower

The values illustrated above are those of British RP. In addition, the symbol /a / is used to represent the General American realisation of the vowel in *heart, pot*.

The symbol ~ above a vowel indicates that it is nasalised.

ACCESS CODE

The form in which spoken or written material is submitted to the **lexicon** (vocabulary store) for a word match.

With written language, the notion of an access code is especially associated with **search models**. These assume that the words in our minds are grouped in sets rather like dictionaries. The sight of the letters ALO would open up a set which included ALOFT – ALONE – ALONG – ALOUD, and the reader would work through the set until a match was found for the word on the page. Such a search would be cumbersome when a set consisted of all the words beginning with a prefix such as PRE- or UN-. So one theory (Taft, 1979) proposes that the access code for readers is the first syllable of a word's root. This unit is said to form the word's *basic orthographic syllable structure* or BOSS. In the case of prefixed words, the prefix is stripped off before any lexical search takes place. Thus, the BOSS of *unhappy* is HAP- and of *international* is NA-. However, the BOSS hypothesis faces serious problems in accounting for *pseudo-affixes* (Does one have to strip off *dis-* in *dismay*?), *bound roots* (What does *-sist* mean in *insist, persist*?) and *ambisyllabicity* (Is the BOSS for *lemon* LEM- or LE-?).

With speech, one theory holds that it is the stressed syllables in English that trigger a word search. So the access code for *alTERnative* would be (or commence with) TER. This again overcomes the problem of prefixes of high frequency and low saliency. However, there is also evidence that, during the search, the access code does not distinguish between stressed and unstressed syllables. The code for pairs such as *FOREbear* and *forBEAR* appears to be the same since the listener appears to process them as if they were homonyms.

See also: **Morphology: storage, Phonological representation, Word primitive**

ACCOMMODATION$_1$

In a phonetic context, the way in which speakers modify the pronunciation of a word in the interests of making an easy transition from one sound to another: for example, they might turn the [n] in *green paint* into a [m], anticipating the bilabial [p] that is to come. Phonetic accommodation includes:

assimilation	green paint	→	greem paint
elision	next spring	→	neck spring
resyllabification	I like it	→	I lie kit

These modifications are optional; the consequence is that the same word may be said in different ways in different contexts. This raises difficult questions in relation to listening: if words are so variable in connected speech, how does the listener manage to recognise them – especially when the modifications involve word beginnings and endings?

See also: **Lexical segmentation, Phonological representation, Speech signal**

Further reading: Brown (1990); Gimson (1994)

ACCOMMODATION₂

The way in which a speaker, often without realising it, echoes features of the speech of the person they are talking to. A speaker in a conversation might use particular words or syntactic patterns which their interlocutor has recently used. Accommodation theory explores the way speakers adjust their accent and speech style towards that of their interlocutor (*convergence*) as a sign of solidarity, or away from it (*divergence*) as a sign of social distance.

Further reading: Giles and Coupland (1991)

ACCURACY

Certain language tasks demand a higher level of accuracy than others – and thus a higher allocation of **attention**. Factors here include the **modality** (writing vs speaking) and the formality of the speech event. Allocating extra attention to accuracy may affect language performance adversely by (1) slowing down the production of speech and thus reducing fluency or (2) giving rise to language **anxiety**, with the ironic consequence that accuracy declines instead of increasing.

See also: **Anxiety, Fluency**

ACOUSTIC CUE

One of a set of features, physically present in the speech stream, which enable a listener to recognise the presence of a particular phoneme, syllable or word or to determine where a word, phrase or sentence boundary lies.

See also: **Cue trading**

ACQUISITION

The process of developing competence in a language. The term is used for infants acquiring their native language (*first language acquisition*) and for those learning a second or foreign language (*second language acquisition*). In this general sense, it is unproblematic; but researchers run into trouble when they apply the term to the mastery of a specific syntactic structure or lexical item. Here, 'acquisition' is often defined as having occurred when the target form is used with 90 per cent accuracy or in 90 per cent of contexts which require it. However, this fails to consider the relative gravity of the errors in the remaining 10 per cent, or instances of avoidance, where the speaker substitutes another word or grammatical form in order to avoid using the most appropriate one. Nor does it take account of:

- systematic variation, where the infant or foreign learner uses a form which is different from that of the target language but uses it consistently;
- **U-shaped development**, where the learner appears to have acquired a particular grammatical form, but later begins to make errors again;
- category acquisition in vocabulary, where the acquirer may have mastered the form, but may not necessarily recognise the precise range of senses that the form represents;
- **task demands**. A language user (especially a second language learner) may appear to have acquired a form while undertaking a relatively simple language task, but may not produce the form consistently in relation to a more challenging task.

See also: **Syntactic development**

Further reading: Ingram (1989)

ACT (ADAPTIVE CONTROL OF THOUGHT)

A group of models of the acquisition of **expertise** (Anderson, 1983), whose principles have been applied to second language learning.

The theory envisages two major components of **long-term memory** (LTM). *Declarative memory* contains factual and conceptual knowledge while *production memory* contains sets of production rules which specify how processes are to be carried out. Both supply **working memory**.

A learning experience begins with pieces of declarative information which are relevant to the goals of a task: for example, the knowledge of what steps to take when starting a car. Declarative knowledge has to be employed step-by-step in order to achieve a goal. However, this makes heavy demands upon working memory. The learner therefore enters an *associative stage* where he/she economises on effort by simplifying the steps to be taken. Some of the steps become combined through a process of *composition*. Through another process known as *proceduralisation*, the learner comes to recognise the relevance of a particular piece of knowledge to a specific situation. Thus, instead of having to retrieve several pieces of information, a single automatic choice is made. At this stage, errors can occur when rules become **over-generalised**. However, the operation gradually turns abstract knowledge into a set of procedures which form the basis for production memory. Continuing the car example, the result is that the driver manages to start the car without having to focus attention upon individual steps.

Declarative memory demands a high level of **control**. However, in the final, **autonomous** stage of learning, established procedures become increasingly automatic and thus demand reduced levels of attention. At this point, the user may no longer be able to express verbally what it is that constitutes the skill.

Anderson himself has suggested that the speaking of a foreign language is a form of expertise like driving or chess-playing; and that ACT can model the acquisition of second language syntax. One has to question the assumption that language learning necessarily employs declarative knowledge in the form of grammar rules as its point of departure; this is to take no account of **inductive** or communicative teaching practices or of the situation of the naturalistic learner. However, ACT offers a useful insight into the way in which a language learner progresses towards fluency as painfully assembled sentences are gradually proceduralised into chunks.

See also: **Expertise, Knowledge, Second language acquisition: approaches**

Further reading: Anderson (1983); O'Malley and Chamot (1990)

ACTIVATION

An important metaphor in models of language processing, based on the way information is transmitted within the brain by electrical impulses. It is often employed in theories of **lexical access**. A word in the **lexicon** is said to be activated to the extent that evidence supports it. Thus, reading the sequence *fro-* would activate FROG, FROM, FRONT, FROST etc. for a reader. The items would not all be activated to the same degree: some (e.g. FROM) start off with an advantage (or perhaps a lower recognition threshold) because they are more frequent. If the next letter the reader encounters is *g*, this new information boosts the activation of FROG to a point where it 'fires': i.e. the word on the page is regarded as successfully matched to the item FROG in the reader's lexicon. At this point, the activation of the other words (known as *competitors*) begins to decay.

In many models of language processing (especially **connectionist** ones) activation is represented as feeding up through different levels of analysis. It is assumed that there is a sub-letter level of processing that deals with letter features (parts of letters). If the reader sees a vertical line, the result will be to feed *excitatory* (or *facilitatory*) activation upwards to the letter level, supporting the likelihood of the capital letters E, F, H etc. No activation (or negative *inhibitory* activation) is lent to C, S or X, which do not conform at all to what has been seen. If the next feature processed is three horizontal lines, then E will be boosted to the point where recognition occurs and will win out over F and H. In some models, there is inhibitory activation between competitors at the same level. As E clearly becomes the correct candidate, the result is to depress the activation of F and H.

A phenomenon known as **spreading activation** provides an account of the way words are connected in the **lexicon**. When the word FOOT is read or heard, it lends activation to a string of other words which are associated with it, making them easier to recognise. They might be associated by form (in reading: FOOT – *food, fool*) or they might be semantically associated (FOOT – *hand, toe, leg*). Activation is said to vary in relation to the strength of the connections.

Thus, the connection between FOOT and *hand* would be stronger than that between FOOT and *elbow*.

Note that these effects are **automatic**: they are not under our voluntary control, so we cannot turn them on or off. In this, they are different from **context effects**.

See also: **Association, Competition, Connectionism, Lexical access, Lexical storage, Priming effect, Spreading activation**

AGEING

Language loss in the normal elderly (speakers of 70+ and 80+ with no apparent brain damage) varies considerably between individuals. There is often a decline in the receptive skills. Sentence length does not appear to be a major obstacle; but sentence complexity does. The main reason would appear to be increased difficulty in co-ordinating syntactic and semantic processing. This is especially noticeable when older people are called upon to process complex syntactic structures such as subordinate clauses. Their recall of connective links between sentences may also be less precise than that of younger subjects.

The variation between individuals may reflect the fact that some are more successful than others in developing strategies to compensate for the reduction in syntactic information. They often appear to fall back upon context, using sentence meaning and world knowledge to supplement their understanding. This reliance on semantics leads to difficulty in dealing with sentences which are ambiguous in meaning.

Many aspects of higher-level comprehension appear unimpaired: for example, the ability to make **inferences**, to integrate incoming knowledge into a **mental representation** and to bring world knowledge to bear. But there may be a reduction in the number of factors which the older person's **working memory** can handle: hence occasional difficulty in retaining the information necessary for handling pronoun reference or negative sentences. Older people find it easier to recall sentences where the chronological order is the order of mention (*After locking the door, she turned off the lights*) than those where it is the reverse (*Before locking the door, she turned off the lights*).

So far as the production of speech is concerned, elderly speakers tend to produce more unfinished sentences than do younger ones, and appear to need more time to assemble their utterances. One suggestion is that there is a general decline in a speaker's ability to **self-monitor**, which causes problems with both production and comprehension.

This may be attributable, again, to changes in working memory which reduce the ability to perform multiple tasks.

The classic syndrome reported by the elderly is difficulty in finding words: they report more frequent **Tip of the Tongue** experiences than do younger speakers. However, they have a high success rate in finally locating the desired word, and there is no evidence that items are actually 'lost' from the **lexicon**. The chief change seems to be that the process of retrieving lexical items becomes slower, as does the process of making associative links between items. The results are seen in unfinished sentences and a higher incidence of 'general' terms (*flower* for *rose*, *walk* for *march* etc.).

There has been interest in a theory (the *regression hypothesis*) that language loss may replicate in reverse the order of acquisition by infants. The hypothesis has not been demonstrated. Though certain linguistic concepts involving space, quantity, temporal relations and subordination do appear to cause problems for some elderly speakers and listeners, there is no evidence of a systematic pattern of loss.

See also: **Attrition, Dementia**

Further reading: Maxim and Bryan (1994)

AGNOSIA

A condition, sometimes caused by brain damage, where a patient receives a signal but cannot recognise or classify it. They might see a familiar object but be unable to say what it is. Visual agnosia in reading and auditory agnosia in listening result in an inability to perceive that two identical word forms represent the same word.

AGRAMMATISM

Speech production in which many function words and inflectional endings are omitted – one possible symptom of the syndrome known as *Broca's aphasia*. Early studies of agrammatism associated it with damage to motor areas of the brain which prevented sufferers from assembling syntactic structures. However, it was discovered that many Broca's aphasics had problems in understanding function words as well as in using them. A theory developed that there may be separate stores for closed class items (those with a grammatical function) and lexical items (those where meaning has to be accessed). Agrammatism may derive, in part at least, from difficulty in accessing the former.

See also: **Aphasia, Function word processing**

AMBIGUITY: LEXICAL

Ambiguity at word level, as represented in a sentence such as *Tick the right box*. Early experiments discovered that subjects' reactions were slower immediately after reading an ambiguous word. This suggested that the processing of ambiguous words demands additional attentional resources because two senses of the word are activated rather than just one.

An important question is what happens when a potentially ambiguous word is disambiguated by the context in which it appears (*Turn to the right*). One view is that context influences the processing of the word, so that we only access the appropriate sense. The other, which has rather more evidence to support it, is that we cannot help but activate both senses. A much-quoted experiment (Swinney, 1979) indicated that hearing the word BUG triggered associations with both possible meanings (insect and spy gadget), even when the word occurred in transparent contexts.

A second issue is whether all interpretations of an ambiguous word are treated equally. Compare, for example, a *balanced* homonym such as RIGHT, where both words are highly frequent, with a *polarised* one such as SCALE, where the dominant sense refers to a set of numbers but a secondary one refers to a characteristic of a fish. Experiments have examined how readers process sentences where polarised homonyms are used in their secondary senses; they indicate that reading slows down even when there is a disambiguating context. This suggests that multiple meanings of words are activated in parallel, with priority given to the dominant one.

See also: **Ambiguity: syntactic, Context effects**

Further reading: Simpson (1994)

AMBIGUITY: SYNTACTIC

Syntactic ambiguity falls into two types:

☐ *local ambiguity* where the word class or syntactic function of a word is unclear at the moment the word occurs, but is made clear by subsequent context. Examples (slash indicates point of ambiguity):

The horse raced past the barn / fell.
John remembered the answer / was in the book.

☐ *standing ambiguity* where a sentence remains ambiguous even after it is complete. In (e.g.) *Bond saw the spy with the telescope*, the telescope might be carried by either Bond or the spy, and the ambiguity can only be resolved by the wider context.

Local ambiguity provides insights into **syntactic parsing** because it enables the researcher to investigate how a subject reacts both at the point where the ambiguity occurs and at the point where disambiguation occurs. The reactions of a reader can be monitored by tracking eye movements or by presenting sentences word by word and noting when a processing difficulty causes a delay in moving on to the next word.

In principle, the language user could react to ambiguity in several ways:

a. Adopt a single analysis, even at the risk of later having to abandon it (a '*garden path*' view).
b. Hold alternative analyses in parallel, but provisionally make use of the one that best fits the context and add it to the meaning representation.
c. Hold alternative analyses in parallel, where they compete with each other until one becomes so highly activated on the basis of new evidence that it is accepted (a *constraint-based* approach).
d. Delay commitment until the ambiguity is resolved.

Evidence suggests that one preferred interpretation is chosen and revised later if necessary. Eye-movement experiments show that readers experience processing difficulty not so much at the point where an ambiguity arises, but at the point where disambiguation occurs. This might appear to support a 'single analysis' view, but might equally reflect processes b or c.

An important issue is how the preferred interpretation is chosen. Early discussion focused on syntactic considerations. It was suggested that the listener/reader exercised a preference for a canonical

(Subject–Verb–Object) sentence structure: hence an initial assumption that *The horse raced...* consists of Subject + main verb. A more sophisticated theory proposed two strategies that are specifically syntactic:

- *Minimal attachment.* Build the simplest structure consistent with the rules of the grammar.
- *Late closure.* Where there is a problem of attachment ambiguity make an attachment to the clause that is currently being processed; ideally, assume that the current clause is the main one.

Later *lexicalist* accounts introduced a semantic element, suggesting that the preferred reading is based upon the **argument structure** of the current verb. For example, the pattern associated with DONATE involves a donator and a recipient. The preferred interpretation of *the man donated* would thus be: Agent + Past Simple verb. But animacy also plays a part. A cheque cannot BE AN agent, so the preferred interpretation of *the cheque donated* would be: object donated + past participle.

A third explanation is entirely semantic. The preferred continuation of: *The lawyer examined . . .* would be *the witness* rather than *by the judge*, simply because world knowledge tells us that lawyers tend to examine rather than be examined.

There is thus some disagreement as to whether we attempt to resolve ambiguity using purely syntactic criteria, or whether lexico-syntactic or semantic criteria play a part.

A criticism of some of the ambiguity data is that it is not based upon a natural parsing situation. **'Garden path' sentences** are often presented to subjects without any preceding context. It is therefore not clear at what point context might normally have enabled the reader to resolve the kind of ambiguity that has been studied. For example, the preferred interpretation of *The horse raced past the barn . . .* might be influenced by a preceding sentence which ran: *There were two horses.* A *referential* theory argues that contextual information will often ensure disambiguation.

'Garden path' ambiguity is more easily exemplified in written texts than in spoken – though, it is sometimes dependent upon the omission of normal punctuation. In speech, **prosody** provides important cues (intonation, pausing, shifts in pitch level, variations in articulation rate), which often serve to resolve attachment ambiguity by indicating where clauses begin and end.

See also: **Ambiguity: lexical, Garden path sentences, Prosody, Syntactic parsing**

Further reading: Aitchison (1998); Mitchell (1994)

ANALOGY MODEL

A theory (Glushko, 1979) that English readers attribute pronunciations to unknown words by tracing analogies with known ones. This is because the *opaque* nature of the English spelling system means that many words cannot be identified by using simple **grapheme-phoneme correspondence** (GPC) rules.

The most important area in a monosyllabic word appears to be the **rime**: the vowel plus final consonant(s). Evidence for an analogy effect comes from experiments where readers find it harder to pronounce a non-word such as VINT which has *neighbours* of varying pronunciations (PINT and MINT) than one such as TADE whose neighbours all rhyme (FADE, MADE, WADE).

Analogy is an important strategy in early reading. However, the extent to which young readers make use of it (as against whole word matches) appears to vary between individuals and may partly reflect the method of instruction. Furthermore, analogy cannot represent a complete alternative to GPC rules. Many multi-syllabic words do not have neighbours; and there are many monosyllabic non-words such as JOOV whose pronunciation is easy to infer but which cannot be matched to similar words. The analogy model has therefore been expanded to include parts of words: the pronunciation of JOOV might be determined by its resemblance to (GR)OOV(E).

See also: **Dual route, Grapheme-phoneme correspondence rules, Neighbourhood, Reading: decoding, Reading development**

Further reading: Goswami (1999); Rayner and Pollatsek (1989)

ANALYSIS

When a child is in the process of developing its first language or an adult is learning a foreign language naturalistically, much of the linguistic information that is acquired is *unanalysed*. Unanalysed knowledge includes **chunks** of language: formulaic expressions and phonological sequences which have been picked up by the listener but have not been deconstructed into their constituent parts.

In time, the constituents of these chunks are identified, and the child or language learner progresses towards more analysed forms of knowledge. Analysed knowledge is more capable of being expressed (i.e. more *explicit*).

Operating in conjunction with analysis is a second parameter, *control*. This refers to the extent to which a language learner has to apply attention when using the target language. The degree of analysis and control exercised by the learner may be affected by the language task in hand.

See also: **Automaticity, Chunking**

Further reading: Bialystok (1990); Peters (1983)

ANAPHOR RESOLUTION

An anaphor is a piece of language which refers back to a previously mentioned entity, action or idea. Examples are: personal or demonstrative pronouns (*she, that*), pro-verbs (*did so*), adverbs (*there*) and expressions like *the latter*. Anaphor resolution is the process that occurs when a listener or reader interprets an anaphor by linking it to its *antecedent*.

Anaphor resolution appears to be an automatic **on-line process**, but one that can slow down reading – especially where there is uncertainty as to what the antecedent is. Experiments using ambiguous anaphors provide insights into how an antecedent is chosen. Factors include:

- *Parallel position*. A pronoun in subject position is taken to refer to an antecedent that is in subject position. Example: *John phoned Bill. He said he was ill.*
- *Current topic*. A pronoun is taken to refer to a topic that has been thematised in the preceding sentence or is in current focus. Example: *As for children, they don't like them. Maybe they frighten them.*
- *Proximity*. A pronoun is taken to refer back to the most recent noun phrase. Example: *He held some bread over the fire with a fork. It grew hot.*

Sometimes these criteria (e.g. parallel position and proximity) may be in conflict. Further factors appear to be world knowledge, animacy and the **thematic roles** associated with a verb. The first of these accounts for the different resolutions of *they* in:

a. *They bought the apples because <u>they</u> were cheap.*
b. *They bought the apples because <u>they</u> were hungry.*

There has been much discussion of the kind of representation that an anaphor accesses. This is especially an issue in listening, where there is no opportunity to look back to check understanding. The listener has to carry forward a mental representation in which current topics are marked as likely subjects for anaphoric reference. One account represents items in the current mental representation as activated to various degrees, thus enabling an anaphoric link to be made to the most salient.

Those who include definite nouns within the class of anaphors point out that definiteness entails two different retrieval processes. With some noun phrases, the antecedent will be in *explicit focus* (see c. below), while with others it will not (see d.).

c. *Erica unlocked the door with difficulty. <u>The door</u> tended to stick.*
d. *Erica unlocked the door with difficulty. <u>The key</u> tended to stick.*

An important distinction is also made between *surface* anaphors which require an antecedent that is linguistically present and *deep* (or *conceptual*) anaphors which do not, as in:

e. *The car needs washing. Don't make promises – just <u>do it</u>.*

In e, the listener/reader has to interpret the anaphor *do it* by reference to the entire meaning representation rather than to a specific entity held in focus within it.

Children learning to read find anaphor resolution problematic and the ability to resolve anaphors has been shown to be an important factor distinguishing skilled from less-skilled readers. The distance between antecedent and anaphor is an important factor: resolution appears to become more difficult as the memory load increases. However, this effect is observed to some degree in all young readers. What especially marks out the less-skilled reader seems to be a tendency to link anaphors to the nearest possible antecedent rather than to a developing mental representation of the whole text. They may even make links to real world phenomena outside the text (e.g. assuming that *now* refers to the moment of reading, not that of writing).

Language acquisition researchers working in the Chomskyan tradition have concerned themselves particularly with *cataphora* (sometimes termed backwards anaphora), where a pronoun refers forward to an entity which has not yet been mentioned. At a surprisingly early age, children are capable of correctly attributing a referent to the pronoun *he* in sentences such as *While he was dancing, the Ninja Turtle ate pizza*. They also distinguish this type of sentence from one such as *He was dancing while the Ninja Turtle ate pizza*, where *he* does not refer to an entity within the sentence. Another area of research has been the processing of reflexive pronouns. At an early age, children are much more successful in interpreting a sentence containing a reflexive (*Cinderella's sister points to herself*) than a similar sentence containing an ordinary pronoun (*Cinderella's sister points to her*).

See also: **Syntactic parsing**

Further reading: Garrod and Sanford (1994); Singer (1990); van den Broek (1994); Yuill and Oakhill (1992: Chap. 4)

ANIMAL COMMUNICATION

The transmission of information between members of other species, including transmission by means other than sound.

Studies of animal communication attempt to determine whether language can be said to be **species specific** – i.e. peculiar to the human race. Examples are cited of systems of communication which resemble speech: for example, the calls of vervet monkeys and the dancing of bees. Both involve *displacement*, the ability to refer to entities not immediately present. But both are limited in the repertoire of signals involved, and it might be suggested that they are *indexical* (the signal relating physically to the message) rather than *symbolic*. More interesting examples are the clicks used by dolphins to communicate information, and the songs of male whales, which change from year to year.

In an attempt to specify what characterises language, Hockett (1963) proposed certain **design features**, which are often quoted when determining to what extent any type of animal communication is speech-like. No type satisfies most of Hockett's criteria.

A particular obstacle lies in the fact that most animals are not physically capable of producing the kind of **vocalisation** which occurs in language. This is not simply because their vocal apparatus is different but because the ability to vocalise depends critically on having air passages which are not given over entirely to reflex breathing movements. Most mammals have larynxes which are controlled by the brain's motor system, whereas humans have a much greater degree of voluntary control over the sounds produced in their larynx. They can thus utter speech sounds while breathing out.

While animal communication does not seem to resemble human language, the question remains of whether animals are cognitively capable of acquiring language if they have human models. A number of researchers have attempted to teach chimpanzees, bonobos (pygmy chimpanzees) and orangutans to express themselves, using keyboards. Despite strong claims about the cognitive and linguistic abilities of the animals studied, unresolved questions remain about the extent to which they use the keys symbolically rather than indexically, and the extent to which their productions manifest an awareness of word order and structure dependency.

See also: **Birdsong, Brain: human vs animal, Chimp studies, Design features, Evolution of language, Species specificity, Vocalisation**

Further reading: Aitchison (1998); Deacon (1997); Dobrovolsky (1996); Pearce (1997)

ANXIETY

General anxiety is one of several affective factors which can influence **attention** and hence lead to a deterioration in language performance. But there are also specific types of anxiety related to language which reflect the complexity or perceived importance of a language task and the extent to which the task places a premium on accuracy. An additional factor might be the individual's uncertainty about their ability to perform the task. This might result from introvert personality traits, from a lack of self-confidence or from awareness of limitations in a particular language skill area.

Anxiety manifests itself in speech in a greater degree of pausing, in a lack of coherence, in the insertion of fillers such as *you know* and in an increased number of false starts. This suggests that the planning function is affected. In the case of a foreign-language learner, anxiety may sometimes lead to greater **accuracy** as heightened attention is paid to form; but **fluency** may suffer as a consequence.

See also: **Accuracy, Attention, Task demands**

Further reading: Horwitz and Young (1991)

APHASIA

A disorder in the ability to produce or to understand spoken language. It usually results from brain damage caused by an accident, a stroke or invasive surgery; but some accounts include the effects of **dementia**. Evidence from aphasics provides possible insights into the location of language in the brain, and into the constituent parts of language processing, some of which may be lost by an aphasic and others retained. However, it is dangerous to rely too heavily upon evidence from these atypical subjects. We cannot assume that brain damage has wiped out a given aspect of language processing. Information may have been relocated; or a process may have switched to new (and less efficient) channels than those normally employed.

Well-established syndromes are associated with damage to the two language-sensitive areas of the brain identified by Broca and Wernicke. It is important to note that the characteristics of each type are merely *possible* symptoms: the exact effects vary considerably from patient to patient.

☐ *Broca's aphasia* is often characterised by **agrammatism**: an absence of syntactic structure and omission of function words and inflections. Articulation may be poor and speech is generally effortful, with many hesitations. Comprehension appears to be good, but it may be that the patient is using positional, semantic or pragmatic cues to puzzle out meaning, rather than relying upon syntax. Vocabulary is weighted towards concrete nouns, with verbs sometimes under-represented.

☐ *Wernicke's aphasia* is characterised by syntactically complex and well-structured speech, containing function words and correct affixation. Speech is apparently effortless, fluent and rapid. Indeed, many of Wernicke's patients claim not to recognise that they have speech difficulties. But there may be severe problems in retrieving vocabulary, with a reliance on general or inappropriate nouns and verbs. Comprehension may be markedly impaired.

Early accounts of Broca's aphasia associated it with impaired motor activity which led to difficulty in assembling utterances; while Wernicke's aphasia was said to reflect impaired access to stored lexical information. However, Broca's aphasics show signs not just of being unable to use functors appropriately but also of being unable to understand them.

The fact that the symptoms of aphasia vary considerably from patient to patient suggests that the language-sensitive areas of the brain may be differently located in different individuals. Alternatively, particular language functions may be so localised that a great deal depends upon the exact position of the lesion which inflicts the damage. Recent brain imaging data suggests a third possibility: the reason for the vulnerability of the Broca and Wernicke areas is that they constitute a major crossroads for the neural connections which transmit widely distributed linguistic information across the brain.

Instead of relating type of aphasia to the area of the brain in which damage has occurred, clinicians prefer to analyse symptoms. A first observation might consider the extent to which lexical-semantic processing is impaired, as against grammatical or sentence processing. However, a distinction is still often made between *non-fluent aphasia* of the Broca type and *fluent* or *expressive aphasia* of the Wernicke type.

Other less-discussed aphasias are:

- *jargon aphasia*, characterised by a large number of nonsense words in the patient's speech;
- *conduction aphasia*, characterised by an inability to repeat what has just been heard (though comprehension may remain unaffected);
- *transcortical aphasia*, where the best-preserved skill is the ability to repeat words and comprehension is often severely impaired;
- *anomia*, where the main or only symptom is the inability to retrieve words.

Features of these types of aphasia are observed to different degrees in different patients. They suggest that the processing of word form can be separated from the processing of word meaning.

See also: **Brain, Brain: localisation, Dementia, Disorder**

Further reading: Caplan (1992); Harris and Coltheart (1986); Lesser and Milroy (1993); Obler and Gjerlow (1999)

APRAXIA

Disruption of the ability to control the motor programming involved in an activity such as the articulation of speech.

ARGUMENT STRUCTURE

The syntactic pattern or patterns associated with a verb. The argument structures for GIVE would be *give* + NP_1 + NP_2 (*give Mary a present*) and *give* + NP_2 + *to* + NP_1 (*give a present to Mary*). The argument structure includes semantic information which specifies the appropriate **thematic roles**. With GIVE, NP_1 (Noun Phrase 1) has to be a Beneficiary and NP_2 is usually a Theme (an inanimate direct object).

See also: **Lexical entry, Predicate, Thematic role**

ARTICULATION

The physical production of the sounds of speech. Fluent articulation is a highly complex motor skill, involving the co-ordination of about 100 muscles at a speed that enables around 15 speech sounds to be produced every second. The process is also highly automatic: we can only produce speech at this rate because we do not pay conscious attention to the process.

An *articulatory gesture* involves co-ordinated manipulation of the respiratory system, the larynx and the vocal tract. The first of these regulates the flow of air; the second, which includes the vocal cords, determines pitch and loudness, and applies voicing where appropriate. The vocal tract serves as a resonator, with changes in the oral, nasal and pharyngeal cavities affecting the timbre of the sounds that are made. The *articulators* within the oral part of the tract (tongue, jaw, lips and velum) serve to constrict or facilitate the air stream.

Some commentators suggest that the smallest articulatory gesture takes the form not of a phone but of a syllable, with the adult speaker possessing a repertoire of gestures which cover all the syllables of their language. The reason for favouring the syllable is that the articulation of any individual phoneme varies according to its place in the syllable and according to the phonemes which occur before and after it (a phenomenon known as *co-articulation*). As part of planning for an utterance, the speaker thus has to weave phones into the phonetic context in which they will occur, and to pre-determine the appropriate duration of each phone relative to the others.

In Levelt's model of speech production, articulation is the product of an *articulatory* or *phonetic plan* which anticipates the forthcoming chunk of speech. The chunk covers one or more complete phonological phrases. It is stored in a temporary **buffer** in the form of a programme which specifies the neuromuscular operations that will be necessary to produce the desired sequence of sounds. The articulatory system then translates the programme into instructions to the muscles controlling the larynx, the articulators and the respiratory system.

A number of theories attempt to account for how we manage to produce speech sounds so consistently.

□ *A location-programming* account suggests that motor commands sent by the brain direct the articulators to a target position for each phoneme. This explanation does not accord with evidence that the operation of the muscles involved in speech is highly co-ordinated and variable: if any are obstructed in their movement (e.g. if the speaker is chewing gum), others compensate to ensure that the articulatory goal is achieved.

□ *An auditory theory* suggests that the motor commands are coded in terms of the phonetic features that the speaker knows as a listener. This view envisages a systematic relationship between the perception and production of speech. However, it entails that the speaker has to wait for auditory feedback until he/she can decide if the articulatory target has been met or if an error of pronunciation has occurred.

□ *A model-referenced* approach assumes that each speaker has an internal model of their own vocal apparatus. Tactile and kinaesthetic receptors in the vocal tract enable the speaker to build up a sensory image of the patterns in which the articulators are engaging. This image can be compared against the phonetic goal that the speaker aims to achieve. An even more rapid checking mechanism is provided by *proprioceptive feedback* in which part of the nerve impulse to the articulators loops back and is compared to the intended signal.

□ *A co-ordinative structures* theory holds that articulation is achieved by means of a string of tasks. Each task triggers a motor command to not one but a group of muscles which function temporarily as a single unit.

The attractiveness of the last theory is that it accounts for the way in which speech impinges upon other activities. The co-ordination involved in articulation is highly complex, not just because of the need to combine different articulators, but also because the vocal organs serve purposes other than speech. The demands of speech have to be balanced against those of breathing (by the respiratory system), chewing and ingesting food (by some articulators) and protecting the air passages from intrusive food (by the larynx). During speech, the speaker switches to a distinctive respiratory pattern (or **speech mode**), with greater air displacement and a more constant rate of outflow. Similarly, although the same muscles are used in speech as in chewing and swallowing, they are co-ordinated in a very different way.

Articulatory settings (the positions adopted by tongue, lips, palate etc.) vary from speaker to speaker. They do so partly because every individual has differently shaped articulators (vocal tract, tongue, mouth and dental structure). Settings also vary due to personal speaking style.

See also: **Buffer, Speech production, Vocalisation**

Further reading: Laver (1994); Levelt (1989: Chap. 11); Pickett (1999)

ARTICULATION RATE

The rate (usually in syllables per second) at which the actual sounds of speech are produced by a speaker. An important distinction is made between **speaking rate**, based on the overall length of an utterance including pauses, and articulation rate, based on the length of the utterance with pauses deducted. When speech is perceived as 'fast', the impression is often mainly due to a reduction in pausing (i.e. speaking rate is significantly reduced but articulation rate is not).

Articulation rate varies between speakers and between types of speech event. It also varies within the speech of an individual. When the same speaker repeats the same phrase several times, there are small changes in the relative duration of the syllables within the phrase.

It appears that listeners are very sensitive to the articulation rate of speakers. Indeed, speed of articulation has been shown to be a factor in phoneme identification: enabling us to distinguish /ba/ from /wa/. However, because articulation rate is so variable, it is difficult to incorporate into theories of speech perception. For example, one way of dealing with the unreliability of the phoneme as a unit of perception is to suggest that listeners analyse the signal in slices of (say) a tenth of a second. But the problem then is that any given slice of connected speech will contain different amounts of phonetic information according to how fast the speaker is articulating.

Articulation rate varies from one language to another, reflecting the type of syllable structure that a given language contains. Languages also vary in how a fast speaker achieves an increase in speed of articulation. English speakers prefer to shorten unstressed syllables, to shorten vowels rather than consonants and to reorganise syllable structure by means of elision, assimilation etc.

See also: **Normalisation, Pausing, Speaking rate**

Further reading: Laver (1994: Chap. 17); Levelt (1989)

ARTICULATORY SUPPRESSION

An experimental task that interferes with the process of **rehearsal** in **working memory**. It might require a subject to keep repeating a word such as *the*. Because this meaningless task involves speaking, it is said to prevent the subject from being able to rehearse (practise) information subvocally. It thus obstructs the learning of lists of words, which need to be rehearsed in this way if they are to be stored effectively in **long-term memory**. It also obstructs the processing of written material, since rehearsal enables us to recode such material into phonological form.

See also: **Rehearsal, Working memory**

ARTIFICIAL INTELLIGENCE (AI)

Psychologists and computer scientists have joined forces to create computer simulations of human cognitive processes. The processes studied in this way include the understanding of language and the nature of **expertise** and how it is acquired.

Researchers working within AI require a detailed information-processing model before they can simulate an activity. Hence the custom among psycholinguists of presenting theories in the form of **models** which resemble the step-by-step operations of a computer. The argument is not that a computer would operate in the same way as the human mind but that, in designing a computer program, we can obtain insights into the real-life process.

Sometimes AI researchers and psycholinguists have different goals. A distinction can be made between programs whose aim is to make computers 'intelligent' without regard to whether the processes involved resemble those of the human mind, and programs which attempt to shed light on human cognitive processes. For example, computer programs designed to parse written text can achieve their goals on the basis of *frequency* (the statistical likelihood of a particular word occurring in a particular type of text) and *transitional probability* (the statistical likelihood that word A will be followed by Word B). This ignores factors in natural comprehension (e.g. world knowledge and the existence of a meaning representation of the whole text) in the interests of efficient machine processing.

Another difference between many AI programs and natural language processing lies in the fact that linguistic information may have to be coded for presentation to the computer. Thus, some AI models of spoken word recognition depend upon the researcher transcribing the utterance into phonemes.

AI research explores a number of specific areas of human cognition which are relevant to language:

☐ *Knowledge representation.* Knowledge systems simulate the form in which knowledge (including linguistic knowledge) is stored in the mind; in particular, the relationship between *declarative knowledge* (knowledge that) and *procedural knowledge* (knowledge how).

☐ *Learning.* Learning systems simulate the way in which features of a first or second language might be acquired from the data that is available.

☐ *Inference.* **Expert systems** apply inference to a store of knowledge in an attempt to model the way in which the human mind analyses data and arrives at conclusions. This may in time assist our understanding of how listeners and readers impose inferences upon discourse.

☐ *Search.* **Problem-solving** systems attempt to trace the way in which thinking moves from an *initial state* to a goal state, choosing one or more paths and selecting sub-goals along the way. Here, there are potential insights into, for example, the way in which speakers construct a syntactic pattern to express a proposition.

A more applied area of AI research aims to develop speech recognition programs. These projects face a major problem in the fact that human voices vary enormously in pitch, in articulatory settings, in the shape and size of the articulators involved and in **paralinguistic features** such as breathiness. Some programs (e.g. phone answering systems) are designed to discriminate between a limited number of words uttered by a wide range of voices. Others (e.g. transcription programs) are designed to discriminate between a large number of words uttered by one voice.

Currently influential in AI is a computational approach to lexical recognition known as **connectionism** or **parallel distributed processing** (PDP). It is based upon the transmission of activation between different levels of processing. Connectionist models often include a learning process, *back propagation*, which enables the computer to adjust its priorities in the light of successful or unsuccessful outcomes. Their proponents argue that this can provide insights into the process of language acquisition.

See also: **Augmented Transition Network, Connectionism, Model, Syntactic parsing**

Further reading: Garnham (1985: 11–15)

ASSOCIATION

An early experimental technique in psychology required subjects to look at or hear a word, then to report the word or words which first came to mind. The technique continues to provide evidence of how words are associated in the mind.

Subjects in word association tasks usually respond with a word that is connected to the stimulus by meaning rather than form. Words which rhyme with the stimulus (*clang* responses) are relatively rare. This suggests that meaning associations in the lexicon are stronger than those of phonological or graphological similarity. The meaning associations are usually based upon semantic groupings, not physical resemblance (*needle* associates with *thread* rather than with *nail*). There is also a tendency to choose a word in the same word class as the stimulus.

The three strongest types of association appear to be: co-ordination (*salt* and *pepper*), collocation (*butterfly* and *net*, *salt* and *water*) and superordination (*butterfly* and *insect*). However, co-hyponyms (*butterfly* and *moth*, *red* and *green*), synonyms (*hungry* and *starving*) and 'opposites' (*hungry* and *thirsty*) also feature.

Further evidence for the strength of certain associations comes from patients suffering from brain damage. When reading a word, they may substitute an associate: *mauve* for *purple* or *sister* for *daughter*.

See also: **Lexicon, Semantic network, Spreading activation**

Further reading: Aitchison (2003: Chap. 8)

ATTENTION₁ (SELECTIVE ATTENTION)

We possess an ability to tune in to certain sources of input and exclude others. There is a classic *'cocktail party' effect* where a listener can attend to a single person at a large party despite many other (often loud) voices in the room. Yet, when somebody the other side of the room mentions the listener's name, he/she is immediately aware of it. It seems that we tune in to a particular speaker but that we continue to monitor speech elsewhere at a low level of attention.

Early work on attention accounted for this with a 'filter' theory. We are bombarded with information from the environment (e.g. voices and sounds), but our perceptual system is said to filter out what is not relevant. There was disagreement as to whether the filter was applied:

- at the outset, limiting sensory evidence to the voice of the interlocutor;
- while the evidence was briefly stored in the mind – picking out the important voice from the others;
- after perception – matching all voices to words, but focusing only on the interlocutor's.

Further reading: Lund (2001); Styles (1997)

ATTENTION₂ (ATTENTIONAL CAPACITY)

Attention involves mental effort, with some tasks requiring more than others. However, the capacity of our **working memory** (WM) is regarded as limited; our ability to carry out two tasks simultaneously thus depends upon how much of that capacity each task demands.

An influential model (Kahneman, 1973) represents attention as using up memory capacity but makes allowance for other contributory factors:

- variations in the *working memory capacity* of each individual;

- variations in the *affective state* of the individual (tired, depressed);
- variations in the *motivation* of the individual.

Visual attention in particular is sometimes likened to a spotlight which lights up a chosen portion of the visual field. Like a spotlight, it can be highly focused or diffuse. Where a task makes heavy demands, attention is concentrated very closely on a target. Where a task demands fewer attentional resources, there seems to be a peripheral area to which partial attention is given. Thus, adjacent letters may influence a reader's ability to perform a letter identification task.

As well as influencing models of first-language reading and listening, the notion of attention plays a part in theories of second language acquisition. There, an important issue is: Do we have to *notice* (give attentional focus to) the form of a word or of a grammatical structure in order to acquire it? To what extent is our attention directed towards meaning in an L2 communicative situation and away from the form of words that a native-speaker is using?

See also: **Automaticity, Working memory**

ATTRITION

The decline of competence in a language over time, usually as the result of contact with another language. Attrition is distinguished from *language loss* as a result of **ageing**.

□ *Primary language attrition* particularly affects immigrant populations, and arises as the result of extended exposure to a second language and of circumstances in which the first language is little used. *Integrative motivation* may also be a strong factor, especially in the case of children. Attrition may be indicated by a speaker's inability to make grammaticality judgements in the native language, but is often evident in performance: in an inability to retrieve vocabulary, in a loss of native-like pronunciation, in the use of non-standard syntax or in a general lack of fluency. Attrition tends to affect production to a greater degree than reception, and may also vary between writing and speaking.

Some bilinguals show evidence of attrition as a result of employing one of their languages to a greater degree than the other. As grammatical competence in one language declines, the grammar of the other may become the benchmark for both.

However, an alternative phenomenon with some bilinguals is *code-switching*, where the two languages become reserved for specific domains (e.g. one for the home and one for the school).

□ *Second language attrition* commonly occurs when a speaker has not had occasion to use a foreign language for some time. It is difficult to research because of the difficulty of establishing the level of competence in L2 prior to the attrition; but it would appear that lexis is more readily subject to attrition than syntax. Some commentators argue that language is represented differently in the minds of native and non–native speakers. If this is the case, then L2 attrition may be different in kind from primary language attrition.

See also: **Ageing, Fossilisation**

Further reading: Seliger (1996); Hansen (2001)

AUDITORY PERCEPTION *see* **Speech perception**

AUGMENTED TRANSITION NETWORK (ATN)

A type of computer program designed by researchers in **Artificial Intelligence**, which attempts to represent the way in which an utterance is processed syntactically by a listener or reader. An ATN consists of a series of points at which accumulated evidence can lead to a 'change of state' and thus a new direction for the processing. The points occur after each complete phrase and sentence as well as after each word, thus enabling syntactic structures to be built.

The processing occurs **top-down**. At the highest level, a network seeks evidence of a complete sentence in a pattern of a Noun Phrase followed by a Verb Phrase. Control then passes to the Noun Phrase level, where a parallel network seeks evidence of a determiner followed possibly by an Adjective and then followed by a Noun. Once the Noun has been located, the outcome is sent to the sentence level and a Verb Phrase is sought.

While computer networks of this kind enable programs to process pieces of text, they are heavily dependent upon conventional sentence structures, and their top-down nature leads to many incorrect predictions and much backtracking.

See also: **Artificial Intelligence, Syntactic parsing**

AUTISM

A condition characterised by a withdrawal from linguistic interaction with others. The sufferer is often mute or uses language in a non-communicative way. The symptoms of autism appear between the ages of one and three, and are sometimes misdiagnosed as deafness. They include delayed cognitive and linguistic development and a reduced ability to react to people, events and objects. Autistic children tend to have exceptionally low IQs but they may excel in one or two isolated skills such as painting or music. The syndrome is much more common in males than in females and appears to be caused by a physical dysfunction of the brain.

It was once suggested that the child's mutism represents a deliberate withholding of language or possibly a dislike of human speech; but it may be part of a general difficulty with all forms of communication. Some children remain mute until the age of five and beyond. With others, the mutism gives way to a delayed acquisition of speech. Here, pronunciation of phonemes will generally be unimpaired, though rhythm and intonation may be flat and monotonous. Other aspects of language, including the processing of meaning, may deviate from normal patterns – perhaps partly because of an inability to make links between world knowledge and linguistic experience.

An important symptom of autism is **echolalia**, where the child meaninglessly repeats what has been said to it. It was once believed that echolalia indicated a rejection of interaction. Now, it is sometimes interpreted as evidence that the autistic child does not succeed in grasping the true function of language. Delayed echolalia, where the child repeats an earlier string of words out of context, appears sometimes to have a communicative intent.

Other symptoms are an unwillingness to meet the gaze of a speaker and difficulties with the use of pronouns. One interpretation is that autistic children find it hard to develop an awareness of the separate viewpoint of others (a **theory of mind**). Even where sufferers from autism go on to achieve a relatively normal use of language, they may experience problems with pragmatics.

See also: **Disorder, Echolalia, Modularity₁, Theory of mind**

Further reading: Baron-Cohen *et al.* (1985); Fay (1993)

AUTOMATICITY

The ease or efficiency with which knowledge can be retrieved or manipulated. A distinction can be made between *controlled* and *automatic* processes. When a task is unfamiliar, it demands conscious attention (control) and sometimes has to be performed step-by-step. Gradually, as we become more skilled at the task, the process becomes automatised, demanding less and less mental effort. The advantage in developing automatic processes is that they do not impose demands upon **working memory** capacity, and thus enable us to give attention to other tasks. Thus, adults open doors with a high degree of automaticity because they have performed the operation many times. This permits them to perform more attention-demanding tasks at the same time, such as holding a conversation.

Automatic processes are slow to set up, but, once set up, are difficult to modify or suspend because they are not immediately under our voluntary control. A good example is the **Stroop** effect. When a literate English speaker is presented with the word RED written in green and asked to name the colour of the ink, they find the task very difficult. The reason is that the response of a reader to the visual stimulus RED is so highly automatised (giving immediate access to the notion of redness) that it is hard to suppress it and to focus instead on the colour of the script.

Because automatic processing is rapid and does not demand attentional resources, it is not usually available to report. An automatic process is often a set of sub-processes which have become *composed* (combined) into a larger sequence. Once this sequence has been established, we are no longer consciously aware of the sub-sequences and unable to report on them.

The concept of automaticity is especially important in theories of reading. A skilled reader is seen as one who is capable of *decoding* a text (recognising words on the page) automatically. As this decoding operation makes few or no demands on working memory, there is ample memory capacity available for constructing a mental representation of the text and for bringing world knowledge to bear on what is read.

The degree of automaticity with which we perform a language task may vary according to the demands of the task. A conversation in a bar is likely to be highly automatic, while writing a business letter demands a degree of control.

See also: **Analysis, Expertise, Task demands, Working memory**

Further reading: Kellogg (1995: 83–9); Oakhill and Garnham (1988)

AUTONOMOUS

Descriptive of a model of language use in which each level of processing is independent of the others. For example, an autonomous model of listening assumes that the recognition of speech sounds is unaffected by knowledge of the possible words which those sounds might form. We hear distinctly that the non-word sequence DABLE begins with /d/ and this perception is not influenced *while we are processing for phonemes* by the resemblance to the actual word TABLE – though it may be at a later stage.

See also: **Modularity₂**

BABBLING

A pre-linguistic stage when infants produce sounds which resemble adult consonant-vowel (CV) syllables. Infants begin to babble at about 6–10 months; and the stage lasts for up to 9 months. Two types of babbling are observed: *reduplicated* babble, with the same CV sequence repeated (*bababa*) and *variegated* babble, with different CV sequences combined (*bamido*). Both sometimes adopt an intonation pattern which resembles adult speech.

There are conflicting views as to whether babbling contributes to **phonological development**. A *discontinuity hypothesis* claims that there is no link. Exponents point out that some infants undergo a 'silent period' between babbling and the emergence of speech and that, regardless of target language (TL), there seems to be a set order in which phonological features are acquired.

A *continuity hypothesis* maintains that babbling is a precursor to speech, enabling the infant to practise a range of potentially useful sounds, which increasingly resemble those of the TL. The CV syllables produced during later babbling are said to recur in the infant's first words; and there is said to be a strong correlation between the frequency of sounds in babbling and their frequency in the TL. That said, it should be noted that the omnipresent English sound /ð/ emerges late, as do fricatives in general.

See also: **Phonological development: production**

Further reading: Ingram (1989) Chap. 5

BASIC LEVEL

A level in a system of hyponymy which is neither too specific nor too general. It is often shown as intermediate between two other terms. For example, DOG is a basic level term which is a hyponym of ANIMAL and a superordinate of POODLE. The importance of basic level terms seems to lie in the fact that they have clearly identifiable attributes in terms of shape and behaviour; this distinguishes them from higher and lower categories.

A large percentage of a child's early words are basic level terms. This suggests that both the adult carer and the infant find such terms easier to categorise. The structure of the lexicon also seems to support the acquisition process: the word forms attached to basic level categories are often simpler than those at other levels.

See also: **Concept formation, Vocabulary acquisition**

Further reading: Clark (1993); Ungerer and Schmid (1996)

BEHAVIOURISM

A movement in psychology important in the first half of the twentieth century. It was based upon a view, prevalent from the 1920s to the 1950s, that we can only speculate about the operations of the human mind and that psychologists should therefore restrict themselves to studying external manifestations of human behaviour. Some of the proponents of behaviourism denied the existence of consciousness. It was suggested that thought was dependent upon language, and was a sub-vocal form of speech.

Behaviourism is principally a theory of learning based upon the relationship between an external *stimulus* and the individual's *response* to it through acquired behaviour. One type of learning is *classical conditioning*, where an established response becomes attached to a new stimulus. Example: Pavlov trained dogs to associate food with the ringing of a bell and they finally began to salivate when they heard the bell alone. Another is *operant conditioning*, where a response becomes established because it is rewarded or *reinforced*.

Asserting that language is simply 'verbal behaviour', Skinner (1957) put forward an account of first language acquisition based upon operant conditioning. His view was that a child acquires language through imitating adult utterances. Parents provide models of language. They also provide reinforcement through showing approval, through carrying out the child's wishes or through recognising, responding to and echoing the child's utterances. Utterances which approximate to adult language are rewarded; others are not. Grammar is said to develop in the form of sentence frames into which words or phrases can be inserted. A process of 'chaining' accounts for the way in which words are organised in sequence, with the first word in the sentence providing a stimulus for the second, the second for the third and so on. This account considerably stretches what was originally understood by the terms 'stimulus' and 'reinforcement'.

Skinner attempted to categorise child language in terms of the behavioural functions involved. He identified *echoic* utterances (= imitation); *mands*, where the child expresses a wish for something; *tacts*, where the child responds to non-verbal cues by, for example, naming something; and socially driven *intraverbal* responses which bear no syntactic relationship to the verbal stimulus that gave rise to them.

Skinner's account of language acquisition received a scathing review from the young Noam Chomsky, who asserted that adult speech is 'impoverished' and therefore does not provide a good or adequate model for imitation. Nor can imitation explain why infants produce incorrect utterances such as *I goed*. Chomsky pointed out that parents reinforce and correct very few of their children's utterances. Most importantly, he drew attention to the *generative* nature of language: suggesting that a theory of language acquisition must account for the way in which the infant acquires the capacity to produce an infinite number of grammatical utterances, most of which it cannot have heard before.

Until Chomsky's riposte, behaviourism exercised considerable influence on thinking in both pure and applied linguistics. Especially prevalent was the behaviourist view that language is a set of acquired habits. This shaped early theories of foreign language learning, which saw the process as involving the replacement of first-language habits with habits appropriate to the target language.

See also: **Connectionism, Empiricism, Nativism**

Further reading: Chomsky (1959); Greene (1975: 26–53); Owens (2001); Skinner (1957)

BILINGUALISM

In principle, the 'habitual, fluent, correct and accent-free use of two languages' (Paradis, 1986) – or of more than two languages. However, on this definition, few individuals qualify as complete bilinguals. It often happens that a bilingual is not equally competent in different aspects of the two languages: they might, for example, have a more restricted vocabulary in one than in the other or might exhibit different abilities in respect of speaking, listening, reading and writing. Furthermore, many bilinguals use their languages in ways that are *domain-specific*: one language might be used in the family and one reserved for educational contexts.

The imprecision of the term 'bilingual' is not helped by a tendency among some psycholinguists to use it when referring to foreign language learners who are relatively advanced but have certainly not achieved a competence that is native-like.

Grosjean (1982) defines bilingualism in terms of language *use* rather than language proficiency. For him, a bilingual is somebody who needs and uses two or more languages in everyday life. A majority of the world's speech communities use more than one language; and about half the world's population is believed to be bilingual in this sense. In addition, there are many bilinguals who are the offspring of mixed-language couples.

An early account of bilingualism (Weinreich, 1968) proposed three types. In *compound* bilingualism, conditions in infancy are equally favourable for both languages, and words in both are attached to one central set of real-world concepts. *Co-ordinate* bilingualism occurs when conditions in infancy favour one language over the other; the consequence is that the infant develops two independent lexical systems, though meanings overlap. *Subordinate* bilingualism occurs when the second language is acquired some time after the first, and so remains dependent upon it.

These categories have proved difficult to substantiate. However, the stage at which the two languages are acquired remains an important consideration in recent accounts, which often distinguish *simultaneous* bilingualism (both languages acquired concurrently), early *successive* or *sequential* bilingualism (both languages acquired in childhood but one preceding the other) and late bilingualism (the second language acquired after childhood).

Simultaneous bilingualism arises during 'primary language development', which commentators regard variously as occurring during the first three or the first five years of life. Exposed to two languages, infants initially *mix* vocabulary and syntax from both. In naming objects and actions, they often adopt the first word they encounter, regardless of which language it comes from; though in their morphology they may exhibit a preference for the less complex of their languages.

The *unitary language hypothesis* concludes that these infants start out with undifferentiated language systems. They begin to distinguish between the two sets of data by restricting each language to particular interlocutors, situations or pragmatic intentions. At the next stage of development, the infant distributes its vocabulary between two separate lexical systems, and becomes capable of translating words from one language to the other. However, the same syntactic rules are usually applied to both systems. In a final stage, the languages become differentiated syntactically, and mixing declines.

An alternative *separate development hypothesis* maintains that the two languages are distinguished from the start by the infant and that the phenomenon of mixing simply shows two incomplete systems operating in parallel.

Simultaneous bilingual acquisition appears to follow a very similar path to monolingual acquisition. There is no evidence that the acquisition process is delayed when more than one language is involved, though early vocabulary levels may be slightly lower in bilingual children. Nor do similarities between the two target languages appear to assist acquisition: an English-French bilingual does not develop language faster than an English-Chinese one.

In successive bilingualism, there is much greater variation between individuals. The time of acquisition of the second language (during the primary period/before puberty/in adulthood) may be a factor; while mastery of the later language may be limited to certain domains. In some cases, the acquisition of the later language is *additive*, resulting in the use of two systems in parallel. In others, the effect may be *subtractive*, with the later language replacing the first in some, many or all domains. The acquisition of a second language by an immigrant may even lead to the **attrition** of the original language if the speaker has to communicate mainly or exclusively with members of the host community.

A distinction is made between adult bilinguals who are *balanced* and those for whom one language is *dominant*. A balanced bilingual has been represented (Thiery, 1978) as somebody who is accepted as a native speaker in two linguistic communities at roughly the same social level, has learnt both languages before puberty and has made an active effort to maintain both of them. Fully balanced bilinguals are said to be rare.

Bilinguals may not always be aware of which language is their dominant one, and it has not proved easy to establish dominance. One approach has been to ask individuals which language they are conscious of having spoken first; though many recall acquiring both simultaneously. Another is to ask individuals to express a preference for one of their languages. There may be a relationship between dominance and **anxiety**, with the dominant language resorted to in times of stress or tiredness. Experimental methods to determine dominance have included rating bilinguals' language skills across languages, self-rating questionnaires, fluency tests, tests of *flexibility* (checking the ability to produce synonyms or draw upon a range of senses for a particular word), and *dominance tests* where bilinguals read aloud cognates which could be from either of their languages. Even where dominance is established, the situation may not remain constant: the relationship between languages may shift as the individual's linguistic needs and circumstances change.

Psycholinguistic research has especially considered three aspects of bilingualism:

☐ *Storage.* Are the two languages stored separately in the user's mind or together? Possible evidence for separate stores comes from the phenomenon of *code-switching* where, often prompted by a change of topic, bilinguals shift with ease between their languages. However, it has been noted that code-switching takes place almost exclusively at important syntactic boundaries (the ends of clauses, phrases, sentences) and that these boundaries are often common to both languages.

There is evidence that the two lexicons are indeed linked, at least partly. Bilinguals undertaking the **Stroop test** show delays in naming ink colours regardless of whether the stimulus word is in the language they have been asked to operate in or in their other language. Similarly, bilinguals' affective responses to words in Language A have been shown to be influenced by the existence of cognates in Language B which bear negative connotations. This suggests that the cross-linguistic links between words are primarily semantic; but contradictory evidence from priming experiments appears to support the idea that similar *forms* are stored together. In a French-medium task, French–English bilinguals recognise the word FOUR (= 'oven') more rapidly if they have been recently exposed to the English word FIVE.

☐ *Cross-linguistic influence.* Is performance in one language affected by the user's knowledge of the other? Constituents from one language are sometimes introduced into an utterance involving the other in an effect called *code-mixing*. The transfer can occur at many different linguistic levels: phonological, orthographic, morphological, semantic and phrasal, and can involve structural features such as word order.

Cross-linguistic lexical influence is seen in *borrowing*, where a word is transferred from one language to the other with its pronunciation and morphology adjusted accordingly.

☐ *Costs and benefits.* Does being bilingual have positive or negative consequences? The consequences might be linguistic, educational, cultural, affective or cognitive. In terms of linguistic development, a *balance theory* suggests that the possession of two languages makes increased demands on **working memory**, and thus leads to some decrement in proficiency in at least one of the languages. There has been little evidence to support this. An alternative view is that there is a language-independent 'common underlying proficiency' which controls operations in both languages. Early studies in bilingual contexts such as Wales led to the conclusion that bilingualism had an adverse effect on educational development; but these are now generally discredited. Recent research has tended to stress the positive outcomes of bilingualism: it appears that bilinguals may benefit from more flexible thought processes and from a heightened language awareness.

See also: **Critical period, Lexical storage**

Further reading: Bhatia and Ritchie (1996); Grosjean (1982); Hoffmann (1991); Macnamara (1969); Romaine (1995, 1996)

BIOLOGICALLY TRIGGERED BEHAVIOUR

Lenneberg (1967) pointed out parallels between language acquisition in infants and those types of human behaviour (e.g. the development of vision or the growth of teeth) which are not under our control but are part of biological development. He suggested that language shares a number of the characteristics of biologically triggered behaviour, of which the most important (Aitchison, 1998) are:

1   It emerges before it is necessary.
2   Its development does not result from a conscious intention.
3   Its development is not triggered by external events – though it may be dependent upon an appropriate environment.
4   Teaching and practice have relatively little effect.
5   Its development goes through a series of stages.
6   There may be an optimal period for the behaviour to develop.

See also: **Critical period, Nativism**

Further reading: Aitchison (1998: 66–90)

BIRDSONG

The sounds produced by birds can be categorised as *calls*, short bursts which warn of danger or keep flocks together, and *song,* which is more complex and mainly serves functions related to territorial claims or to mating.

Calls are apparently innate, and their form and function vary little between generations. However, the process of acquisition of songs seems to vary from one type of bird to another, and even seems to be subject to regional variation. The song of the skylark appears to be mainly learned, while that of the thrush appears to be innate, but subject to modification after exposure to the song of adults. Most curious of all is the song of the chaffinch. Here, the basic tune seems to be innately acquired, but the rhythm and pitch have to be learnt. If a chaffinch does not hear any adult song during the first 15 months of its life, it does not acquire the full song. It has been argued that there may be a **critical period** for this species of bird and for others like it.

There are two views as to how birdsong is learned. One is that birds are born with or develop an auditory template which only admits to long-term memory the song of their own species. The other is that birds learn a range of songs but that an innate tuning of their sensory pathways causes them to focus attention on songs produced by their own species.

See also: **Animal communication, Critical period, Species specificity**

BLINDNESS

A major issue is whether visual impairment has an impact on language acquisition. Does it lead to delays in acquisition given that the child's route to meaning is not supported by adult facial expressions, by gesture or by the ability to map words on to visible real-world objects? Does it lead to imbalances in the vocabulary that is acquired? Chomsky cited blind children as evidence that language is innate, claiming that their pattern of language development does not differ from that of a sighted child. However, research has indicated that the situation is more complex than Chomsky suggested.

At a pre-linguistic stage, adults appear to find it more difficult to engage blind children in communicative activities, because they lack conversational cues provided by the direction of the infant's gaze. The infant responds less – suggesting that it needs to focus heavily upon listening at this stage. Nevertheless, the onset of **babbling** appears to take place at about the same time as with sighted infants.

Blind infants appear to acquire a phonological system a little more slowly than is normal. They sometimes confuse phonemes which are similar in manner of articulation but visually distinct: for example, substituting /n/ for /m/. This difficulty appears to influence their early choice of words.

The first words emerge at about the same time as with sighted infants. However, there may be differences in the content of the early vocabulary. It has been suggested that the first 50 words of a blind child are likely to include fewer common nouns; and that they are more likely to be used referentially for a single object instead of generalised to a whole class of objects. Blind children generally engage less in sorting activities; this suggests that blindness may limit the capacity to form categories, with consequences for vocabulary acquisition.

At an early stage, blind children are more likely than others to engage in *echolalia*, the meaningless repetition of words and chunks of language. However, their later speech is not (as was once suggested) marked by *verbalism*, the use of words whose sense they have not grasped. Even verbs of vision appear to have approximate meanings mapped on to them (*see* = 'be aware of').

Overall, visually related terms are used less frequently than happens with sighted children. Lack of sight also seems to affect the acquisition of terms relating to space. The notion of deixis appears to be difficult for blind infants to acquire and there is usually a delay in the acquisition of personal pronouns, demonstratives and some prepositions.

The language that is acquired by an infant may partly reflect the nature of the speech that is directed at it by adult carers; this has been shown to vary somewhat when the infant is visually impaired. Adults tend to use third-person pronouns less and (strangely) spend more time labelling objects and less describing them.

In summary, the example of the blind infant does not provide the clear cut endorsement for **nativism** that was once claimed; but nor does it show conclusively that language acquisition is dependent upon input and upon the ability to map word forms on to a visible environment.

See also: **Deafness, Special circumstances**

Further reading: Landau and Gleitman (1985); Mills (1993)

BOOTSTRAPPING

A prelinguistic infant has no lexicon against which to match the sound sequences encountered in the speech signal. Furthermore, connected speech provides few cues to where word boundaries lie. It is therefore difficult to explain how the language-acquiring infant comes to identify word forms and to map them on to meanings relating to the real world. It has been suggested that the infant can only achieve this task by relying on some kind of technique which gives it a head start – just as straps can help one to pull on a pair of boots (the metaphor comes via computer science). This technique might be specific to the process of language acquisition or it might be the product of general cognition, reflecting, for example, a predisposition to impose patterns upon diverse information.

Three main types of bootstrapping have been proposed:

☐ *In prosodic bootstrapping* (Cutler and Mehler, 1993), the infant exploits rhythmic regularities in the language it is acquiring. At the phoneme level, it can distinguish a difference between *steady-state* sequences representing full vowels and *transitional* sequences representing consonants. It is thus sensitive to syllable structure. From this and from its innate sense of rhythm, the infant acquiring English is able to recognise the difference between longer stressed syllables featuring full vowels and shorter unstressed syllables featuring weak quality vowels. It may be that the infant develops a *metrical template* (Gerken, 1994) which reflects the tendency of English towards an SW (strong-weak) rhythmic unit. The template encourages the child to seek words which follow an SW pattern, and provides it with the working hypothesis that a stressed syllable in the signal is likely to mark a word onset. This accounts for the following versions of adult words:

giRAFFE	→	raffe
MONkey	→	monkey
baNAna	→	nana

It also accounts for evidence of children joining words to form an SW pattern as in: *I like-it the elephant.*

The concept of prosodic bootstrapping has been applied to larger constituents than the word. It is suggested that infants learn to recognise intonation patterns (especially the placing of the tonic accent) and the regular occurrence of pauses. These features, which are often heightened in **Child directed speech**, provide infants with cues to phrase boundaries and to the structure of typical phrases.

☐ *Syntactic bootstrapping* (Gleitman, 1990) assumes that an infant uses surface form to establish syntactic categories. The early mapping process draws upon an assumption (innate or learnt) that there is a word-class which relates to objects in the real world, one which relates to actions and one which relates to attributes. Once this is established, the infant can add less prototypical items to each class (abstract nouns, state verbs) by noticing that they share grammatical properties with words that have already been acquired: in particular, their morphology and their distribution.

It learns to associate count nouns with the frame *It's a . . .* and mass nouns with the frame *It's . . . .* Experiments with non-words (*It's a sib, It's sib*) have demonstrated that infants are capable of making this association as early as 17 months. Infants are also capable of using formal evidence to recognise that non-words like *nissing* refer to a potential action and non-words like *a niss* refer to a potential object.

Later on, infants may use syntactic structure to establish distinctions of meaning. Thus, they can distinguish the senses of the words *eat* and *feed* by their distribution: *eat* occurring in the structure Verb + Noun [edible] while *feed* occurs in the structure Verb + Noun [animate]. Among evidence cited in support of syntactic bootstrapping is the fact that blind infants manage to acquire the words *see* and *look* without difficulty. The suggestion is that they are able to do so by relating the words to the contexts in which they occur, even though they lack a concept to which to attach them.

☐ *Semantic bootstrapping* (Pinker, 1994a) hypothesises the reverse process: that infants use their world knowledge in order to recognise syntactic relationships within sentences. Assume an infant has acquired, in isolation, the nouns *rabbit* and *duck*. Presented with a sentence such as *The rabbit is chasing the duck* and evidence from a cartoon film, the infant comes to recognise that the position of the word *rabbit* in the sentence is reserved for the Agent or syntactic subject and the position of the word *duck* is reserved for the Patient or syntactic direct object. The assumptions would be confirmed if the cartoon film later showed the reverse situation and the associated sentence was *The duck is chasing the rabbit*.

As formulated by Pinker, semantic bootstrapping also incorporates the assumption that certain linguistic concepts are innate in the infant: these include the notions of noun and verb as word classes and the notions of agent and patient as roles.

Other bootstrapping theories are:

☐ *Perceptual bootstrapping* (Nusbaum and Goodman, 1994): where the infant focuses its attention on the most salient parts of the input; this might explain why early utterances do not usually contain weakly stressed function words.

☐ *'Logical bootstrapping'* (Bates and Goodman, 1999): a process whereby an infant systematically directs its attention first to physical objects (nouns), then to events and relationships between the objects (verbs and adjectives) and then to word order and syntax. This step-by-step building of meaning reflects the general pattern of vocabulary acquisition.

See also: **Lexical segmentation, Operating Principles, Phonological development, SW (strong-weak) pattern, Vocabulary acquisition**

Further reading: Cutler and Mehler (1993); Gleitman (1990); Peters (1983); Pinker (1994a)

BOTTOM-UP PROCESSING

An approach to the processing of spoken or written language which depends upon actual evidence in the speech signal or on the page. Smaller units of analysis are built into progressively larger ones. There is a contrast with **top-down processing**, the use of conceptual knowledge to inform or to reshape what is observed perceptually. The terms 'bottom-up' and 'top-down' are derived from computer science, where they refer respectively to processes that are data-driven and processes that are knowledge-driven.

Underlying the metaphors 'top' and 'bottom' is the idea that listening and reading proceed through levels of processing, with bottom-up information from the signal assembled into units of ever-increasing size. In listening, the lowest level (i.e. the smallest unit) is the phonetic feature. The listener's task might be portrayed as combining groups of features into phonemes, phonemes into syllables,

syllables into words, words into clauses and clauses into propositions. At the 'top' is the global meaning of the utterance, into which new information is integrated as it emerges.

The truth is more complex. First, it is not certain that bottom-up processing involves all the levels described. Some researchers have argued that we process speech into syllables without passing through a phonemic level; others that we construct words directly from phonetic features. Nor does bottom-up processing deal with one level at a time. There is evidence that in listening it takes place at a delay of only a quarter of a second behind the speaker – which implies that the tasks of analysing the phonetic signal, identifying words and assembling sentences must all be going on *in parallel*.

A quarter of a second is roughly the length of an English syllable – so the listener often begins the processing of a word before the speaker has finished saying it. Part of bottom-up processing therefore involves the listener forming hypotheses as to the identity of the word being uttered, which are *activated* to different degrees according to how closely they match the signal. The candidates *compete* with each other until, when the evidence is complete, one of them outstrips the rest. An important issue is the extent to which top-down evidence (from world knowledge or from knowledge of the text so far) can contribute to the activation of these word candidates.

Non-psychological accounts sometimes refer to a conflict between 'bottom-up models' of reading and 'top-down models'. This is misleading, as it implies that a choice has to be made. The issue is not to argue the case for one processing type over another, but to establish how the two interact and which one predominates in case of conflict.

The evidence is contradictory. Some commentators would say that top-down information is only used for checking bottom-up; some argue for *bottom-up priority* with contextual evidence only invoked once sufficient bottom-up evidence has become available. Those who favour a fully **interactive** model of listening or reading contend that both sources of evidence are available throughout. One argument for relying initially on bottom-up information is that bottom-up processing is more automatised than top-down, and therefore faster. Another is that multiple sources of information prevent rapid decision-making. Conversely, those who favour an interactive model argue that it is better to have all the information available at one time.

Some commentators prefer to describe the processing of the letters, sounds and words of a message as *lower-level processing* (the opposite being *higher-level*). It is also referred to as *perceptual processing* (as against *conceptual processing*).

See also: **Interactive activation, Interactive compensatory hypothesis, Modularity₂, Reading: decoding, Speech perception, Top-down processing**

BRAIN

The brain has a number of language-related functions. It controls the cognitive processing involved in producing or understanding language; the *motor* activities involved in **articulation** (the movement of tongue, lips, vocal cords etc.); and *involuntary* activities such as breathing which need to be co-ordinated with speech.

The human brain consists of two hemispheres linked by a complex web of nerve connections, the *corpus callosum*. Generalising somewhat, the left hemisphere in most individuals is associated with analytic processing and symbolisation, while the right is associated with perceptual and spatial representation. The left hemisphere is particularly implicated in language processing (see **brain lateralisation**), though the right contributes as well. The vast network of connections between the two ensures that any operation can draw upon both.

The hemispheres have a *contralateral* relationship with the rest of the body: the right side of the brain controls the left side of the body and vice versa. Signals received by the right ear have a preferential link to the left hemisphere and vice versa. However, the situation with the eye is less straightforward: information from the left visual field in both eyes is transmitted to the right hemisphere and vice versa.

The upper surface of the brain, the *cortex*, is especially associated with language processing, though the sub-cortical areas also contribute. The cortex is marked by a pattern of hills (*gyri*) and valleys (*sulci*). Some of the deeper sulci divide each hemisphere into four (see Figure B1). These are the *temporal lobe*, which runs from front to back, the *occipital* and *parietal lobes* at the back and categorised as 'posterior', and the *frontal lobe*, sometimes described as 'anterior'. The occipital lobe is associated with visual stimuli, and the temporal lobe with auditory stimuli.

A strip running centrally across the hemisphere controls much motor activity, including operations involving the articulators. Other linguistic functions are associated with some of the lower levels of the brain: the *medulla* regulates involuntary activities including breathing, and the *cerebellum* plays a major part in controlling and co-ordinating articulation.

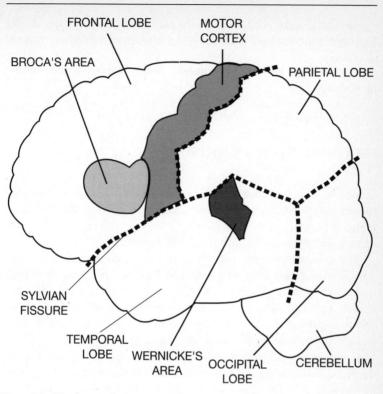

Figure B1 The human brain

The transmission of information in the brain takes place by means of nerve cells or *neurons*. The human brain contains about 100 billion of these. The power of the brain derives not so much from the activity of individual neurons, as from the multiple interconnections between them and the way in which they operate in parallel. The human cortex contains about three-quarters of the brain's neurons, and is proportionately much bigger than the cortex in other mammals.

Information is transmitted within the brain by the discharge of a chemical across a *synapse* (a gap between neurons), which causes a change in the receiving neuron. The change may involve an increase in the neuron's electrical potential (termed *excitatory*) or a decrease (termed *inhibitory*). It accumulates until it reaches a threshold, when it triggers a pulse (or *action potential*), which is transmitted along the neuron and on to others.

The transmission can potentially take place on a massive scale, so small effects can become greatly magnified. This pattern of activity is referred to as **activation** – and has provided an influential model of how words are accessed from the lexicon during listening or reading.

See also: **Brain: human vs animal, Brain lateralisation, Brain: localisation**

Further reading: Dingwall (1998); Libben (1996); Obler and Gjerlow (1999)

BRAIN: HUMAN VS ANIMAL

It may be that human beings have developed language when other species have not because the human brain operates in distinctive ways. Hence an interest in discovering how our brain differs physically from those of other creatures, including other primates.

The critical difference is not one of brain capacity: elephants and whales have larger brains than human beings, mice have a greater brain/body ratio and a number of rodents and small mammals have denser neural connections. The discussion therefore focuses on whether the human brain is different in certain of its components, in its structure and in the way it develops.

It was once surmised that a locus for an innate language faculty might be found in the left hemisphere of the human brain. It is in this hemisphere that, for most humans, functions involving syntax and lexis appear to become *lateralised*, and it was noted that the left hemisphere is often larger than the right. However, the same kind of left-hemisphere dominance has been found in several other species, including birds.

The operation of language is currently envisaged as being very widely distributed in the brain, with many different areas (including some in the right hemisphere) contributing cognitive and motor sub-skills. Attention has focused on specific areas of the human brain which are markedly larger relative to the whole organ than the equivalent areas in other primate brains.

☐ *The cortex* is proportionately much greater in human beings. This is the area that controls complex operations including making connections with stored information, analysing input and co-ordinating sophisticated muscular movements.

☐ *Human pre-frontal areas* are up to six times bigger than those of chimpanzees in relation to body size. These areas appear to be responsible for recognising similarities between objects and grouping

44

them into categories. Damage there may limit the ability to perform tasks that involve seeing things from the perspective of others.

☐ *The human cerebellum* at the base of the brain is much larger, relative to brain size, than in other species. It co-ordinates a range of highly automatic muscular movements.

☐ In human beings, a greater proportion of the *motor area* is given over to the control of mouth, tongue and jaw. Human motor areas also exercise a high degree of control over the larynx, which regulates the passage of air in breathing and speech. In other species, the operation of the larynx is mainly or entirely controlled by the lower parts of the brain, which means that it is largely involuntary. Control of the larynx enables us to co-ordinate breathing and **vocalisation** and is an important factor in the ability to produce speech.

What also appears to distinguish human beings is brain growth in infancy. The ratio of brain weight to body weight resembles that of other mammals pre-natally but, after birth, brain growth in humans greatly outstrips body growth as compared with other primates. This suggests a very different evolutionary history from other species, one which may uniquely have favoured the development of the sophisticated cognitive processes which are a condition of language.

See also: **Animal communication, Evolution of language, Vocalisation**

Further reading: Deacon (1997)

BRAIN IMAGING

Methods of obtaining images of activity in the brain. They have been used in order to determine which parts of the brain are associated with particular language tasks.

In early experiments, *electrical stimulation* of the brain (ESB) was used in order to map its operations. By applying a low-level electrical current to an exposed area of the cortex, one can temporarily disable its associated functions. In this way, experimenters traced connections between parts of the body (including the articulators) and various points along the central strip of the cortex, which controls motor activities. They also applied currents to the parts of the brain traditionally associated with language, and identified the language functions which were affected.

Today, the brain can be x-rayed in sections using a method known as *computerised axial tomography* (or *CAT scanning*); this is useful for locating lesions but only provides a representation of a single state. Other techniques have therefore been developed to show the brain in action from moment to moment.

One group of methods exploits the fact that blood flow in the brain closely reflects patterns of activity because of the need to supply oxygen to the neurons which are in operation. In *positron emission tomography* (PET), a small intake of radioactive gas or fluid renders the subject's blood radioactive. The degree of radiation within the brain (and thus the intensity of blood flow) can then be measured by gamma ray detectors. A computer picture is generated of the metabolic activity in the brain: bright colours showing the areas where it is at its most intense and darker colours those which are less active.

Even more precise images can be obtained through a technique known as *functional magnetic resonance imaging* (FMRI), which exploits the fact that neural activity results in an excess of oxygen in the blood in the brain. The oxygen level can be tracked because it results in changes in magnetic susceptibility. Researchers are thus able to monitor the changing patterns of blood flow.

An alternative technique records brain states sequentially by measuring electrical activity occurring in the brain. Electrodes are attached to the subject's scalp and indicate where a change in activity ('*evoked potential*') takes place in response to a given stimulus such as seeing or hearing a word. The most common method seeks to identify *event related potentials* (ERPs), small deviations in voltage level from the normal baseline.

See also: **Brain: localisation, Event-related potential**

Further reading: Deacon (1997); Posner and Raichle (1994)

BRAIN LATERALISATION

The view that one of the hemispheres of the brain has or develops a special responsibility for language. In most human beings, language appears to be particularly associated with the left hemisphere. Evidence comes from:

☐ *Brain damage*. When the left hemisphere is damaged by an accident, a stroke or invasive surgery, it often has a serious impact upon the victim's language.

☐ *Commisurotomy*. In this operation, the corpus callosum joining the two hemispheres was severed to reduce the effects of epilepsy. Patients who underwent the operation could name objects in their right field of vision (connecting with the left hemisphere) but not those in their left field of vision.

☐ *Wada injections* of sodium amytol were once used to de-activate one side of the brain prior to surgery, in order to ascertain which hemisphere was the dominant one for language. It was usually the left one.

☐ ***Dichotic listening***. When different messages are presented to the two ears, the right ear (the ear that links to the left hemisphere) usually overrides the left. The right ear appears to be dominant for speech generally but the left for music, rhythm and intonation.

There appears to be a partial relationship between lateralisation and handedness. Rather fewer left-handers than right-handers appear to have a dominant left hemisphere for language.

When damage occurs to the left hemisphere of the brain before the age of five, the victim's powers of speech sometimes recover completely, and language dominance appears to re-establish itself in the right hemisphere. Some researchers have concluded that the language faculty may be generally distributed at birth, and that lateralisation occurs gradually as part of maturation. The hypothesis has been linked to the notion of a **critical period**. First language acquisition, it is argued, has to take place during the period of lateralisation if complete command of L1 is to be achieved. If acquisition is delayed, the result may be the inadequate mastery observed in cases of language **deprivation**.

However, the 'plasticity' hypothesis has been challenged by evidence that a degree of left-hemisphere lateralisation exists from birth. Furthermore, recent studies have identified cases of infants who have not recovered some aspects of their linguistic competence after left-brain damage, and of adults who seem to have recovered their language by relocating it to their right hemisphere.

In addition, we now have more evidence about right-hemisphere damage. While damage to the left hemisphere affects primary language functions such as syntax and lexis, damage to the right appears to affect the processing of discourse. It also seems that, while phoneme-level processing is chiefly the prerogative of the left hemisphere, the processing of suprasegmental features, especially prosody, takes place on the right. One current view of the lateralisation issue is thus that the left hemisphere specialises in more rapid language operations, and the right in those connected to higher-level meaning processes. This division of functions makes sense when the brain has to deal with two closely associated processes such as processing phonemes (left side) and prosody (right side). It also accords with evidence from modern imaging techniques showing that language is much more widely distributed in the brain than the original lateralisation hypothesis supposed.

It may be that the human brain is more flexible than once believed, even in adulthood when the critical period is long over. In the exceptional circumstances of simultaneous translation, some professionals appear to distribute their two operating languages between the two hemispheres – usually reserving the left for the native language and the right for the second. In this way, they keep their two languages apart and manage to cope with the lack of synchronicity between the incoming auditory signal and the outgoing translation. Again, the key seems to be the need to keep two closely associated operations distinct.

It was once believed that lateralisation might be peculiar to human beings and afford an explanation of why language is unique to our species. However, an enlarged left hemisphere has been found to occur in other species, including birds. Frogs have a dominant hemisphere which appears to be associated with croaking. This suggests that, across species, the larger side of the brain has special functions related to vocalisation and the processing of rapid auditory stimuli.

See also: **Brain: localisation, Critical period, Deprivation**

Further reading: Aitchison (1998); Deacon (1997); Dingwall (1998); Obler and Gjerlow (1999); Springer and Deutsch (1997)

BRAIN: LOCALISATION

Early research suggested that there are two areas of the brain which are closely associated with language. *Broca's area* (after Paul Broca, 1824–80) lies just in front of and above the left ear. *Wernicke's area* (after Carl Wernicke, 1848–1904) is just above and behind the left ear. See Figure B1 under **Brain**. Attention was first drawn to these parts of the brain by the aphasic effects which were noted when they suffered damage. Generalising considerably, Broca's **aphasia** appeared to give rise to problems of syntax while Wernicke's aphasia resulted in problems of lexis and of comprehension. However, the effects of damage varied greatly in type and degree between patients, suggesting a more complex state of affairs. It is also, of course, dangerous to theorise about normal processing on the basis of evidence from medical cases.

Recently, **brain imaging** methods have added greatly to our knowledge:

☐ Language appears to be widely distributed throughout the brain. A critical role is played by the system of massive interconnections which enables information to be transmitted rapidly from one part to another. There is evidence that the classic language areas (Broca's and Wernicke's) are points where various language processes overlap; their vulnerability thus lies in the fact that many processes pass through them.

☐ Language appears to be organised hierarchically, with the central parts of the brain looking after more rapid analytic operations and the outer looking after slower, associative operations.

☐ There appear to be distinct language processes according to the physical form of the signal (speech vs writing); the way in which the signal is to be handled (e.g. repeating words, finding vocabulary, associating meanings); and whether production or reception is involved. Low-level listening is not as closely connected to speech as some hypothesised.

☐ There is evidence that (at least in detecting errors) there are strong links between syntax and semantics.

☐ Activities involving the form of words (e.g. mnemonic tasks) seem to activate different parts of the brain from those involving word meaning.

☐ Grammar appears to be widely distributed throughout the brain. Function words are stored and processed separately from lexical words. They seem to be processed rapidly, perhaps so as to provide a syntactic frame for the sentence. Regular past forms seem to be processed morphologically while irregular ones are processed as lexical items.

☐ Comparative studies of aphasia across languages suggest that syntactic parsing draws on different areas of the brain according to whether a language is heavily dependent upon word order (like English) or on morphology (like Italian). English speakers suffer especially as a result of damage to Broca's area; Italian as a result of damage to Wernicke's area. Hence a view that language processes map in an opportunistic way on to whichever brain functions best support them.

See also: **Aphasia, Brain imaging, Function word processing, Modularity₁, Syntactic parsing**

Further reading: Deacon (1997); Posner and Raichle (1994)

BROAD-CLASS TRANSCRIPTION

A transcription which features only the most general phonemic or phonetic cues which are taken to be present in the speech signal. A broad class transcription might characterise words in terms of the manner of articulation of their constituent phonemes and nothing more. One purpose of using a transcription of this kind is to establish how much information is necessary for a listener to uniquely identify a particular word.

See also: **Informativeness**

BUFFER

Speech needs to be pre-assembled in chunks of several words before we produce it; only in this way could we impose intonation patterns upon an utterance. It is therefore assumed that the speaker has some kind of mental buffer in which to store a blueprint of each upcoming utterance prior to articulation. The term is borrowed from the buffer in which a PC stores information ahead of printing it. Without such a resource, we would be incapable of producing connected speech as fluently as we do.

What goes into the buffer at this final stage of planning must be extremely detailed – or there may be several buffers operating in parallel. Levelt (1989) describes a *phonetic plan* which assembles the entire set of articulatory gestures which are necessary in order to produce the target words. In addition, intonation, lexical stress, word order etc. must be fully specified prior to articulation.

A further function of a speech buffer is to enable the pre-assembled sequence to be reviewed at the last possible moment before it triggers articulation. Evidence from self-correction data indicates that speakers not only monitor their utterances at the time they are producing them, but also subject them to a final check immediately before speaking.

Writers appear to need a similar storage process to that of speakers. While Dickens was penning the line *It was the best of times*, he must have had the rhetorical structure of the whole sentence already marked out, with the reprieve *it was the worst of times* already available as '*pre-text*'. There is uncertainty as to the form that written language takes when it is stored in this way. Both reading and writing appear to have a strong phonological component; it may well be that words in the writing buffer are stored in some kind of quasi-phonological form as **'inner speech'**. In this case, there may be a separate buffer dedicated to the low-level process of assembling graphemes.

See also: **Articulation, Self-monitoring, Speech production, Writing**

Further reading: Levelt (1989)

CAPACITY THEORIES

Theories based on a view that the processing of linguistic information is affected by the limitations of the human processor. The constraints on performance are usually said to derive from our limited **working memory** capacity, which determines the amount of information we can process at any given time and/or the number of processes that we can apply. If one task demands great resources of attention, it restricts the amount of working memory that is available for performing others. Thus, if a reader has to focus a great deal of attention upon decoding the words on the page, he/she has very limited resources to spare for building the words into higher-level meaning. It is advantageous for us to develop a high degree of **automaticity** in performing tasks such as decoding. Automatic processes make few demands upon working memory, leaving us with ample capacity for other operations.

See also: **Attention, Working memory**

Further reading: Gathercole and Baddeley (1993)

CATEGORICAL PERCEPTION

The identification of phonemes by reference to sharply demarcated categories which are consistent across listeners. The example usually given involves distinguishing plosives such as /b/ and /p/. For the listener, the chief difference between the sequences /ba/ and /pa/ is that, in the first, the onset of voicing for the /a/ begins very close to the 'burst' of the plosive, whereas in the second there is a short delay before voicing occurs. By manipulating this *Voice Onset Time* (VOT) using a computer, one can produce recordings where it increases in increments of 5 milliseconds. These might range from an exemplar with immediate voice onset which is clearly /ba/ to one with a 60 milliseconds VOT delay which is clearly /pa/.

Tests have shown that English listeners are consistent in the point at which they switch their interpretation from *ba* to *pa*; it is always around the 25–30 millisecond mark. Presented with two exemplars which fall within the /ba/ range (from 0 to 25 milliseconds), they find it difficult to say whether they are the same or different. They experience similar difficulty in distinguishing two exemplars within the /pa/ range with VOTs of more than 30 milliseconds. But they have no problem in distinguishing an exemplar which falls on one side of the 25 millisecond divide from one which falls on the other – even when the VOT difference between the two is quite small. Hence the conclusion that the distinction between /b/ and /p/ is dependent upon sharply delimited category boundaries. Perception along the *ba-pa* continuum is said to be *discontinuous*. (This finding is not unchallenged. Some experimenters have suggested that listeners are able to rate a stimulus as a good or bad example within a phoneme category.)

The VOT results with *ba* and *pa* have been replicated with other plosives in both initial and final position and with fricatives in final position. Similar tests have shown categorical perception in distinguishing place of articulation for plosives, fricatives, nasals and liquids. As for vowels, there is some evidence that those of short duration may be perceived categorically, but that longer ones are not. It would appear that perception along a vowel-vowel continuum is generally continuous, with one value shading into another. This is unsurprising, given the considerable acoustic diversity between realisations of the same vowel, from speaker to speaker and from context to context.

Using the *high-amplitude sucking procedure*, researchers obtained evidence of categorical perception in infants as young as 1–4 months old. The infants were shown to apply categorical distinctions in relation to both VOT and place of articulation. This provided possible evidence of some kind of innate capacity for discriminating the sounds of speech. However, it was then discovered that chinchillas apply the same kind of categorical distinctions as human beings. One conclusion is that the categorical boundaries identified in these experiments represent points in the speech range to which the mammalian ear is particularly sensitive. The implication would be that language has shaped itself to take advantage of these sensitivities.

Evidence supporting this hypothesis comes from Thai, which divides the *b-p* continuum three ways, between /b/, /p/ and /p^h/. The Thai /b/ is identifiable by an onset of voicing which occurs at least 20 milliseconds *before* the plosive 'burst' while the boundary between /p/ and /p^h/ falls around 25–30 milliseconds after it. Tests have shown that three-year-old children acquiring Thai are much more able to make the distinction between /p/ and /p^h/ than that between /b/ and /p/. They appear to be born with a sensitivity to the 25–30 millisecond boundary of other languages, but to acquire at a later stage the boundary which is specific to Thai.

The phonemic categories of an adult are narrowly related to native language: hence, for example, the difficulties of Japanese speakers in distinguishing auditorily between English /l/ and /r/, which are variants of the same sound in Japanese. Studies have attempted to establish the age at which children become so attuned to the categories appropriate to their first language that they can no longer distinguish those of other languages. The findings suggest that the ability to make certain categorical distinctions may be lost as early as 10–12 months of age.

Though categorical perception is sometimes treated as if it were absolute, there is evidence that it is subject to external influences.

☐ *Phonetic context.* The position of the category boundary between two consonants may shift according to the following vowel. The same synthesised sound may be perceived as [ʃ] when followed by [a] and as [s] when followed by [u]. A similar effect has even been recorded across word boundaries: along the /t-k/ continuum, there is a shift in favour of perceiving an untypical exemplar as a /t/ after /s/ (*Christmas t/capes*) and as a /k/ after /ʃ/ (*foolish t/capes*).

☐ *Lexical constraints.* There is some evidence (not universally accepted) that lexical knowledge may affect perceptual boundaries, with subjects more likely to accept a poor exemplar from the /g/–/k/ continuum as a /k/ if it contributes to forming an actual word (KISS) than as a /g/ if it entails a non-word (GISS).

☐ *Desensitisation.* If a listener is exposed repeatedly to the same sound, their acoustic feature detectors tire, and perceptual boundaries become shifted in a way that disfavours the sound being heard. For example, extended repetition of the syllable /ba/ desensitises a listener to the VOT features which characterise /b/, with the result that they manifest a perceptual bias in favour of /p/. This phenomenon is known as *selective adaptation*.

See also: **Phonological development, Speech perception: phoneme variation**

Further reading: Jusczyk (1997); Miller (1990); Pickett (1999: Chap. 12); Yeni-Komshian (1998: 130–6)

CHILD DIRECTED SPEECH (CDS)

A speech register used by adults when addressing infants. Also known as *motherese, parentese, caretaker talk, baby talk*.

Parents simplify their speech in consistent ways when speaking to children. For English speakers, the linguistic modifications include:

- *Phonological features*: simplification, higher pitch, emphatic stress, greater pausing, longer pauses, a slower speech rate.
- *Lexical features*: restricted vocabulary, local topics, special forms.
- *Syntactic features*: shorter utterances, less complex utterances.

In addition, CDS is characterised by less dysfluency than adult speech and much repetition and rephrasing. It may employ its own lexical variants (*beddy byes*).

Many of these modifications potentially assist the child in the **bootstrapping** process of identifying words and recognising phrase boundaries, or in making matches between words and objects in the real world. However, in the light of Chomsky's 'poverty of stimulus' argument, the major issue is whether CDS is accurate, explicit and comprehensive enough to provide the infant with the data it needs in order to acquire a language.

In fact, CDS is not as 'degenerate' as Chomsky argued. It is generally well formed syntactically, though it contains more imperatives and questions than normal conversation. While nativists are correct in asserting that adults rarely correct infants' language, a great deal of indirect teaching takes place when parents echo, revise or expand their child's utterances. Parents also support acquisition with **scaffolding**, where the adult's initiating utterance provides a syntactic and lexical framework for the infant's responses (*You want milk? You want juice? You want milk or juice?*). Furthermore, it appears that adults fine-tune their CDS as the child's understanding of language progresses.

CDS thus provides a richer source of linguistic data than was once assumed. However, it has proved difficult to establish precisely how the modifications to adult speech assist the infant. No correlation has been found between the degree of simplification in the carer's CDS and the rate at which the infant acquires language. Furthermore, CDS does not appear to be universal. In non-western societies, it may have different characteristics. There are even cultures in which the child is exposed to adult discourse but no language is specifically directed towards it.

Within a given culture, CDS is strikingly consistent across carers – suggesting either that it is transmitted as folk knowledge or that the speaker somehow taps into their own experience of language acquisition. Similarities have been traced between CDS, **foreigner talk** and some pidgins and **creoles**. One nativist view holds that, in constructing any of these forms, speakers draw upon an innate sense of what constitutes the basic properties of language. This may be a relic of the **Universal Grammar** which enabled us to acquire our first language.

See also: **Creolisation, Foreigner talk, Input, Nativism, Scaffolding**

Further reading: Gallaway and Richards (1994); Snow (1986, 1995); Valian (1996)

CHILD GRAMMAR

The notion that the grammar of a language-acquiring infant may have its own internal consistency; and that we should approach it on its own terms rather than by reference to the norms of adult grammar.

Syntactic analysis of the infant's early two-word utterances (Example *more nut, two sock* represented as 'NP → modifier + N') was found to be insufficiently informative. Researchers therefore argued for a richer interpretation using semantic criteria. It was concluded that three language functions predominated in the earliest two-word utterances:

- *nomination* (naming), using nouns and deictic terms (THIS, HERE) already used singly;
- *recurrence*, expressed by terms such as MORE, ANOTHER;
- *non-existence*, expressed by terms such as ALLGONE, NO.

Syntactic patterns in the later two-word utterances were sub-classified to show the semantic relationships involved. For example 'Modifier + Head' could be interpreted as *attributive* ('big doggie'), *possessive* ('Daddy shoe') or *recurrent* ('more up').

See also: **Syntactic development**

Further reading: Bloom (1973); Brown (1973)

CHIMP STUDIES

A number of projects have investigated whether other primates (especially chimpanzees) can acquire language if properly taught. Positive evidence would have important implications for **nativist** theories of language acquisition by humans. If chimps can be shown to recognise semantic categories like FOOD and to apply syntactic patterns (e.g. word order), then it might suggest that they too have access to the basic principles underlying language. This would lend itself to one of three interpretations:

☐ Chimps share the human language mechanism in some form, but lack a genetically transmitted trigger which sets it off as part of maturation.

☐ There is no innate mechanism peculiar to human beings: acquiring a language depends upon the input a child receives.

☐ Language maps on to established cognitive operations which human beings share with other primates.

Chimps do not have an appropriate vocal apparatus to produce the sounds of human speech. Early attempts were therefore made to teach them a modified form of the **sign language** used by the deaf. One (Washoe) mastered 130 signs in three years – a rate of acquisition much slower than that of a human infant. Washoe managed to produce sequences of two or three signs, including some original combinations; but never developed a consistent word order. Another chimp (Nim Chimpsky) managed strings of up to four signs; and produced an impressive variety of sequences. However, Nim's productions involved much repetition of the same items and, like those of Washoe, showed great inconsistency of Subject-Verb-Object word order.

More recently, researchers have trained chimps to communicate by indicating *lexigrams*, simple abstract shapes in various colours. Each shape is associated with a word such as JUICE or BANANA, but they bear no resemblance to the objects they refer to. The lexigrams appear on large keys mounted on a computer screen in the chimpanzee's cage. One chimp, Lana, learned over 100 of these symbols. Two others, Austin and Sherman, were taught only a few and were then rewarded for semantically correct combinations (EAT + BANANA rather than DRINK + BANANA). After thousands of trials, they came to recognise these combinations and (importantly) proved quick to categorise new items of food and drink when they learnt them.

One of the most successful results has been achieved with a bonobo (or pygmy chimpanzee) called Kanzi. He was originally present at the training sessions of his foster mother, Matata. When the researchers felt that he was old enough to begin learning, he showed that he already knew much of what they wanted to teach him. He mastered combinations of lexigrams without the thousands of trials that Austin and Sherman had needed. In all, he learnt about 400 symbols. More importantly, he could group them in lexical sets and showed signs of using a consistent word order. He could understand some simple spoken English, and could respond appropriately to commands such as 'Put the soap on the apple'.

Kanzi's relative success has suggested that chimp training should begin earlier. Deacon (1997) links the Kanzi findings to the **'less is more'** view of language acquisition, which suggests that at a certain point children are particularly sensitive to the symbolic nature of a system such as language precisely because they have not yet fully developed cognitively. However, it is not clear whether Kanzi can be said to have acquired a form of 'language' which resembles the human one in structure or complexity. It may be that the whole concept of chimp training is misleading because it aims to teach a form of communication that is a quintessential product of the human mind.

See also: **Animal communication, 'Less is more', Species specificity**

Further reading: Premack (1986); Premack and Premack (1983); Savage-Rumbaugh and Lewin (1994)

CHOMSKYAN THEORY

Noam Chomsky (b.1928) formulated what is currently the leading model of language, *generative* grammar. His goal was to create a set of rules to account for the creativity of language: the way in which a potentially infinite number of sentences can be generated from a finite set of words. A Chomskyan grammar offers a symbolic representation of the system which native speaker-hearers internalise in acquiring the language, a system which enables them to formulate or to understand sentences that they may never have said or heard before. The grammar is generative in that its rules serve to specify all possible sentences which are grammatically correct and to exclude from consideration all those which are not. These 'rules' are not the prescriptive rules of traditional grammar. They are more like the laws of physics, which account for disparate natural phenomena in terms of general underlying principles.

Chomksyan theory highlights the fact that language is *structure dependent*, and provides models of standard phrase types. These are taken to represent the underlying form of an utterance, its *deep structure*. In the first version of the theory, a set of *transformational rules* showed how the user might reorganise the constituents of a deep structure string to produce a *surface structure* one. For example, they showed, in stages, how a speaker derived a passive sentence from an underlying active form.

Current theory has replaced the cumbersome transformational rules with *movement rules*. These show diagrammatically how the deep structure (now *d-structure*) constituents are moved to new slots to provide a derived *s-structure* pattern. See Figure C1, which illustrates how a *wh-* question is derived from the d-structure string *Sara is reading what*.

An important feature of this revised theory, sometimes referred to as *government and binding*, is that when a constituent is moved it leaves behind a *trace* (t). This enables the listener to retrieve the original deep structure from the sentence that is heard. Studies in psycholinguistics have attempted to verify the existence and effect of such traces.

Chomskyan theory has recently taken a new direction, known as *minimalism*, which emphasises the importance of simplicity in formulating syntactic rules. One development is that much of what is traditionally represented as syntax can be explained by reference to the constraints which are imposed by lexis. Thus, if one decides to construct a sentence around the verb GIVE, the choice of verb determines the possible structure VP + NP + NP (*Elizabeth gave Philip a book*). This information is stored as part of the lexical entry for GIVE in the user's lexicon.

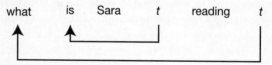

what   is   Sara   *t*   reading   *t*

Figure C1   Illustration of a movement rule

Chomskyan theory provided a boost for cognitive psychology. It moved the discussion on from the simplified accounts provided by **behaviourism**; and redirected attention to the mental processes involved in the production and understanding of language, processes which behaviourism regarded as inaccessible or non-existent. Chomsky made an important distinction between *competence*, the set of principles which enable a native speaker to generate an infinite set of grammatically acceptable sentences and *performance*, the spoken/ written language to which the system gives rise. This differs somewhat from de Saussure's distinction between *langue* and *parole*. Where de Saussure defines 'langue' in relation to the speech community which shares the language in question, Chomsky relates competence to the individual user of the language.

Chomsky argues that linguistic theory needs to be based upon competence, not performance. The goal of the linguist should be to specify the means by which the native speaker-hearer constructs grammatically correct sentences rather than to analyse what he/she actually says. Generative grammar thus assumes an *ideal* speaker-hearer, one from whose speech idiolectal, dialectal and hesitational features have been removed. It is here that linguistic approaches and psychological ones diverge, since the data upon which a psychologist traditionally works is provided by examples of human behaviour in performance.

In psycholinguistics, those who work within the Chomskyan tradition follow a theory-driven approach which seeks evidence of the psychological reality of Chomsky's constructs. However, they face a problem in attempting to tap into competence rather than relying on performance data. A solution adopted by many researchers is to ask subjects to make *grammaticality judgements*. They might, for example, be asked to decide if a sentence such as *Who did you introduce the man you got the present from to?* is grammatically acceptable.

A second complication is that Chomsky's grammar is specifically a model of language. Chomsky has much to say on the human mind; but he does not claim that phrase structure and movement rules represent the actual process taking place within the mind of the user as he/she constructs a sentence. Hence there is discussion as to whether these generative rules are **psychologically real**. Early research in **syntactic parsing** attempted to demonstrate that the complexity of a transformational rule did, indeed, influence the listener's ability to process a sentence. The hypothesis was not supported.

Chomskyan thought has had a strong impact on psycholinguistics in the area of **language acquisition**. Chomsky argues strongly for a *nativist* view. His main point relates to the 'poverty of stimulus' afforded by **child directed speech**. The language to which the infant is exposed in its early years could not possibly, he suggests, cover the whole range of possible sentences. Furthermore, it is 'degenerate' in that it constitutes performance data (complete with ungrammatical forms, hesitations, false starts etc.). How then can the infant succeed in deriving competence from it in a comparatively short time?

Chomsky concludes that we can only account for first language acquisition by assuming that a child is born with an innate knowledge of the principles of language and a predisposition to employ them in analysing the speech which it encounters. Current theory attempts to bridge the gap between the universal principles with which we are born and the specific form of the language which we finally acquire. We are said to be endowed with a **Universal Grammar** (UG) in the form of an innate awareness of the nature of language and the various forms that language adopts. UG is represented in terms of a set of *principles* common to all languages and a set of *parameters* which are adjusted to reflect the characteristics of the specific language to which the infant is exposed.

See also: **Behaviourism, Language acquisition: theories, Nativism, Principles and parameters, Syntactic parsing, Universal Grammar**

Further reading: Cook and Newson (1996); Lyons (1970); Smith (1999)

CHUNKING

Memory constraints mean that we can only deal with a limited number of pieces of information (probably around seven) at a time. The way in which we overcome this limitation is to 'chunk' or combine items into larger units.

There appear to be a large number of lexical phrases and syntactic sequences in our lexicon which are *pre-assembled* and which we produce as a single chunk with a single or composite sense (e.g., *should've* = past + obligation + unfulfilled). These sequences make a major contribution to **fluency**: they enable speakers to assemble sentences efficiently without undue pausing for planning.

Some chunked sequences are *lexicalised* (have a single meaning and the status of a dictionary entry) and some are partly lexicalised. But many are simply 'memorised' or 'institutionalised': they are stored as chunks as a result of the frequent co-occurrence of the words within them, and produced as unanalysed wholes. They may take the form of complete sentences (*Need a hand? What's for dinner?*) or they may provide frames with constituents which vary (*Sorry to keep/have kept you/them waiting*).

There is evidence that chunking plays a part in the way in which children acquire lexical, pragmatic and syntactic sequences (*whyncha* + verb = why don't you?; *wammeda* + verb = do you want me to?). Language acquisition appears to include a process whereby recurrent chunks are acquired formulaically and then gradually deconstructed into their parts. There is evidence of a similar process among second language learners acquiring their L2 in naturalistic conditions.

See also: **Fluency**

Further reading: Pawley and Syder (1983); Peters (1983); Wray (2003)

CLUTTERING

A disorder affecting **fluency**, in which the sufferer attempts to speak too quickly, resulting in distorted articulation and disrupted rhythm. Syllables may be truncated, words repeated, sounds omitted or misarticulated. It is possible that planning at the phonetic level is implicated: speech is uttered in staccato bursts, which sometimes interfere with syntax. As the utterance proceeds, the speaker may well speed up (*festination*) rather than slowing down. Cluttering sometimes occurs in conjunction with **stuttering**. One possible cause is brain damage.

See also: **Fluency, Stuttering**

Further reading: Dalton and Hardcastle (1989: Chap. 7); Myers and St Louis (1992)

COGNITION

The use or handling of knowledge; hence, (a) the faculty which permits us to think and reason and (b) the process involved in thought and reasoning. It is sometimes contrasted with *metacognition*, which can be defined as 'thinking about thinking' and involves pre-planning a cognitive process, exercising control over the process or taking steps to ensure that its results are stored long term. Metacognition involves some degree of awareness, whereas cognitive processes may not be available to report.

An important issue is whether language is part of general cognition or is a separate faculty. One argument supporting the latter (*modular*) view is the fact that all normally developing infants achieve a first language whatever their cognitive capacities in other areas.

See also: **Modularity₁**

COGNITIVE PSYCHOLOGY

The study of human mental processes and their contribution to thinking, sensation and behaviour. The discipline is often traced back to Wundt, who founded a psychology laboratory in Leipzig in 1879. Wundt's method was to ask subjects to perform a mental process, then report on the experience. This introspective approach produced inconsistent results. There was a strong reaction against it by psychologists who took an *anti-mentalist* stand, arguing that the mind was unknowable. They insisted that the only scientific source of data for psychology was human behaviour, which was observable in a way that mental processes were not. From this grew the movement known as **behaviourism**.

Another influential movement in the early twentieth century was led by the **Gestalt** group of psychologists, who investigated how the mind shapes our perceptions of the world. In particular, they examined how we perceive separate elements (e.g. dots on a page) as falling into groups and patterns.

Reaction against behaviourism came from an **information-processing** approach developed in the 1950s which aims to chart the flow of information through the mind as a particular cognitive task is performed. It underpins much current thinking in cognitive psychology. From it has developed a view of much human rational behaviour as based upon **problem-solving**; this has especially informed research into the nature of **expertise**.

A recent movement in cognitive psychology has been **connectionism**, an attempt to model in computer programs the **neural networks** which form the basis of the operations of the brain.

See also: **Behaviourism, Connectionism, Expertise, Gestalt Theory, Information processing**

COGNITIVISM

Approaches to language acquisition which view the process as closely linked to general cognition and to cognitive development. Some accounts leave open the extent to which certain aspects of language are innate; but all take the view that acquisition is primarily driven by the way in which the infant's cognitive abilities are brought to bear upon the input to which it is exposed. These cognitive abilities may reflect developing awareness of objects, spatial relations, defining characteristics etc., or they may take the form of perceptual biases which incline the child to recognise patterns in linguistic material. Among views on acquisition which can be characterised as 'cognitive' are:

☐ *An infant cannot express concepts in language unless it has previously developed them.* Example: A child cannot use language to refer to objects that are not visible unless it has grasped the idea of *object permanence*. For Piaget, language was the product of cognitive and perceptual processes. His research with children led him to conclude that there were four stages of cognitive development. They represent a gradual progression and not a sudden shift in behaviour; and the age at which a particular child goes through each varies considerably. However, they are closely linked to linguistic development.

☐ *Both language and cognition are part of a staged maturation programme, in which they operate in parallel, supporting each other.* For Vygotsky, thought exists pre-verbally. There is initially a separation between thought and language: the infant's first words are devoid of thought. During three phases, the separate roles of thought and language become established.

☐ *Innate cognitive tendencies may predispose us:*

a. *To find patterns in language data (as in data in general).* A theory of syntactic **bootstrapping** postulates that infants reach conclusions about words on the basis of their inflections and other grammatical properties: thus the child learns that the difference between *It's sib* and *It's a sib* serves to distinguish real-world entities that are mass from those that are count.

b. *To adopt certain strategies in response to language data.* Slobin (1973) concludes that infants apply a set of universal strategies or **operating principles** in order to deconstruct the input to which they are exposed. (*Pay attention to the ends of words. Pay attention to the order of words and morphemes.*) More cognitively complex features are acquired later.

c. *To apply individual learning styles to language data.* Some infants appear to break the input into words, while others acquire chunks of language in a holistic manner.

□ *The infant's limited cognitive capacity renders it more sensitive to the features of language than it might be before or later.* The **'less is more'** argument holds that it may be the very limitations of the infant's early cognitive state which enable it to identify structure in language and to recognise that language constitutes a set of inter-related symbols.

See also: **Bootstrapping, 'Less is more', Modularity₁, Operating Principles, Piagetian stages of development, Vygotskyan**

Further reading: Bates *et al.* (1995); Deacon (1997: Chap. 4); Piattelli-Palmarini (1980)

COHORT THEORY

A model (Marlsen-Wilson, 1987) of the way in which words are retrieved from the **lexicon** in listening. A listener processes an utterance at a delay of around a fifth of a second behind the speaker; this is often not enough to provide full evidence for a particular word. Cohort Theory adopts the hypothesis that the listener retrieves a set of words (a *cohort*) which match the evidence of the signal so far. Thus, on hearing the phonetic string [kæp] they would retrieve CAP, CAPITAL, CAPRICORN, CAPTURE, CAPTAIN, CAPTIVE, etc. as word candidates. If the next sounds proved to be [t] and [ɪ], the cohort would narrow to CAPTAIN, CAPTIVE and CAPTIVATE. Finally, the sound [n] would mark a uniqueness point, where only one word match, CAPTAIN, was possible. The uniqueness point of a word is not necessarily its last phoneme: for example, the word PSYCHOLOGY becomes unique at the /l/.

A major objection to the early version of Cohort Theory was that it was heavily dependent upon correct identification of word-initial phonemes. If a slip of the tongue led a speaker to produce 'shigarette' rather than *cigarette*, the appropriate cohort would not be selected. In addition, account needs to be taken of phonetic **accommodation**, which leads many words to diverge from their citation forms when they occur in connected speech. The model was therefore revised to include a principle of *closeness of fit* rather than exact match. An **activation** dimension was added: the cohort is now represented as a set of lexical items whose strength is boosted or weakened by incoming perceptual evidence until one of them achieves a match. Contextual evidence can play a role in narrowing down the cohort; but it is not taken into account until after about 150–200 milliseconds of the word; this is referred to as *bottom-up priority*.

A weakness of the model remains the fact that it assumes that a word is a discrete and easily identified unit. Many sequences that appear to constitute monosyllabic words may prove instead to be the initial syllables of polysyllabic ones, and vice versa. Using the 'captain' example, how is one to know if a match has been achieved after the word CAP or if one has to continue reducing the cohort? There may also be ambiguities of **lexical segmentation** where word candidates cross boundaries (for example, the word SISTER occurs within the sequence *insist upon*).

The 'uniqueness' concept has also been challenged. A study of the lexicon has suggested that over a third of words in normal speech are not unique by their offsets, while there is evidence that many monosyllabic words are not identified until well after their offsets.

Nevertheless, the notion of the cohort is implicitly or explicitly adopted in many accounts of auditory processing.

See also: **Lexical access, Lexical segmentation, Speech perception, Uniqueness point**

Further reading: Marslen-Wilson (1987)

COLOUR SYSTEMS

All human beings have similar perceptual systems; yet languages vary in the way in which they divide up the spectrum. This provides a test case for *linguistic determinism*. Does language simply provide a set of convenient *categories* or does it affect the way in which colours are actually perceived?

Research by Berlin and Kay (1969) suggested that *focal points* (prototypes) for particular colours are not only shared by speakers of the same language, but are also shared across languages. There was agreement on 'typical values' even where a language possessed fewer colour terms than English. This finding was supported by later research on naive subjects (English-speaking young children and speakers of Dugum Dani, which has only two basic colour terms). Focal colours were said to be perceptually more salient, more accurately remembered and more rapidly named.

A second finding by Berlin and Kay was that there were restrictions on which colours can appear in a colour system. They claimed that a two-colour system could only have white and black (effectively, light and dark); while a three-colour system added red. Next was a five colour system, adding green and yellow. The maximum system was said to be one of eleven basic colours, like the English one.

There are some problems with the data on which this second finding was based. There are also problems in simply counting the number of colour terms, when languages vary in the importance which they attach to hue, brightness and saturation. Furthermore, the maximum figure of eleven colours has been challenged: Hungarian and Russian have twelve.

See also: **Concept, Linguistic relativity**

Further reading: Berlin and Kay (1969); Palmer (1981: 71–5); Ungerer and Schmid (1996)

COMMUNICATION STRATEGY (CS)

A linguistic or paralinguistic technique used for overcoming obstacles to communication. Communication strategies are often *compensatory*, with a language user making adjustments in response to a gap in linguistic knowledge. A useful distinction can be made between the *productive* CSs used when expressing oneself in speech or writing and the *receptive* ones used to counter problems of understanding. The extent to which both types of CS are used may reflect the personality of the language user. There is likely to be much greater use by *risk-takers* with a strong impulse to communicate than by *risk-avoiders* who feel constrained by the need to achieve accuracy.

Productive CSs have particularly been studied in relation to second language acquisition, where *strategic competence* (the ability to express oneself despite limited linguistic means) is seen as an important factor in the ability to communicate. Second language users, wishing to express a concept for which they do not have adequate language, make a choice between two courses of action:

☐ *avoidance behaviour* aimed at circumventing a topic, grammatical structure or lexical item;

☐ *achievement behaviour* where a linguistic goal is maintained, but achieved by a less direct route than a native speaker might employ.

Possible types of strategy include: switching into the first language, using a more general or approximate term, paraphrasing, inventing a possible word by analogy with a word in L1 or L2 and adopting a simpler syntactic structure. Also available are paralinguistic techniques such as pointing or miming.

Research into receptive strategies has mainly been restricted to a first language context, with studies of how less-skilled young readers compensate for an incomplete understanding of a text. A central issue has been the extent to which weak decoding skills lead the reader to rely upon top-down information. Stanovich's **interactive compensatory** theory provides one possible model of strategy use which can be applied to both written and spoken modalities.

See also: **Interactive compensatory hypothesis, Strategy**

Further reading: Cohen (1998); Faerch and Kasper (1983); Kasper and Kellerman (1997)

COMPETITION

A comparison between all possible lexical matches to a signal, in order to establish which most closely fits the available evidence. Most models of **lexical access** assume that visual or auditory evidence leads us to select a set of word *candidates* between which we have to choose. In, for example, **Cohort Theory**, hearing the initial sequence [ɪksp] would lead a listener to retrieve from the lexicon a set of items which include EXPIRE, EXPECT, EXPLODE, EXPLAIN, EXPRESS etc. These would all receive **activation**; but, if the next sound proved to be [r], the activation for EXPRESS would be boosted to the point where it 'fired' – i.e. was accepted as the only possible match for the evidence available. The activation of all others would decline. That said, some allowance has to be made for lack of clarity in the signal. This might mean that the activation of EXPLODE and EXPLAIN remained high until more of the signal had been processed and it became clear that the disambiguating phoneme was indeed [r] rather than [l].

Competition between words is not simply a question of how closely they match the signal. The activation of a word is boosted if it is of high frequency. Thus, EXPECT would start off at a higher level of activation than the less frequent EXPIRE – or alternatively would require a lower level of activation in order to achieve a match. Another criterion is the number of *neighbours* a word possesses. A reader is slower to recognise a written word such as HEAD which faces competition from a number of words (*hear, heat, heap, heal*) than a word such as HEED which (on a left-to-right basis) only competes with *heel*.

In some accounts of lexical access, the cues provided by **context** boost the activation of one or more competitors. Other accounts maintain that contextual information is only used to check the appropriacy of the winning candidate. A third view is that a minimal amount of the speech signal needs to be processed before contextual cues can be brought to bear.

Studies of **lexical segmentation** in listening have extended the notion of competition to any string of phonemes in the signal. Thus the sequence *the waiter* is represented as competing with the alternative interpretation *the way to*.

See also: **Activation, Bottom–up processing, Interactive activation, Lexical access**

Further reading: Aitchison (2003: Chaps 18–19); Altmann (1997: Chap. 6)

COMPETITION MODEL

A model of the way in which syntactic processing is influenced by the nature of the language in question. The hypothesis is that speakers of different languages rely on different syntactic cues in constructing meaning. There are four possible cues: word order, world knowledge, animacy and morphology. The *cue strengths* (the degree to which a listener is influenced by each of these criteria) reflect the nature of the listener's language – in particular, how rigid its word order is. Thus, in processing an utterance in Italian such as:

La matita	guarda	il cane
[the pencil	looks at	the dog]

English speakers are said to be very dependent upon word order, while Italian speakers place greater reliance on morphology and animacy.

In acquiring a second language, cue strengths from L1 appear to be transferred. Thus, English learners of Japanese employ rigid word-order cues based on the standard Subject-Object-Verb pattern of the target language, and fail to recognise that it is more flexible than

English. The competition between L1 and L2 values leads second-language learners firstly to apply the values of L1 and then to fall back on semantic (world knowledge) criteria. Part of the process of acquiring a second language is said to be a gradual adjustment to the cue strengths appropriate to that language.

Further reading: Bates and MacWhinney (1982); Gass and Selinker (1994: 139–44)

COMPONENTIAL ANALYSIS

An attempt to reduce the core concepts associated with words to a small set of components of meaning.

An influential paper (Katz and Fodor, 1963) argued that core meanings can be broken into a finite set of components (HUMAN, ADULT etc.). These components were to be determined on a binary basis (+ or −HUMAN). The meaning of a word would be specified by using features that were *necessary* (TAIL could be omitted in a description of a tiger) and *sufficient* in number to uniquely identify the referent (it is not enough to say that a tiger is a cat). There were many problems with this approach. It takes no account of affective or connotational meaning. The number of components which need to be specified varies from word to word; and the more precisely the components are worded (*bachelor* = 'not available for marriage and not married yet'), the less useful they are as part of a general system.

CONCEPT

The core (decontextualised) meaning of a word; the set of entities or events in the real world which a word is understood to refer to. The notion has impinged upon psycholinguistics in several ways:

☐ Issues raised by *linguistic determinism*. If our perception of the real world is indeed shaped by the language we speak, then it should be possible to provide evidence that conceptual categories vary markedly from language to language.

☐ The question of how concepts are represented in the mind. How can we recognise an animal as a tiger if it does not possess the full characteristics of the animal – if it has lost its teeth or its tawny colour? The situation is complicated by the fact that some concepts have *vague boundaries*: it is difficult, for example, to say where a RIVER ends or where a MOUNTAIN becomes a VALLEY.

☐ The process of **concept formation** in which initial conceptual categories developed by infants are gradually adjusted to resemble those of adults.

See also: **Colour systems, Concept formation, Linguistic relativity**

Further reading: Ungerer and Schmid (1996)

CONCEPT FORMATION

The way in which an infant adjusts the range of senses attached to a word until it resembles the range of an adult.

An infant's early nouns are used in two ways: *context-bound*, applied to a single referent, and *context-free*, applied to a class of items. Strikingly, most words are generalised to more than one referent within about a month of acquisition. Once acquired, words appear to be categorised into lexical sets: this is seen in occasional substitutions, such as the word SPOON being used for a fork.

From early on, an infant seems to recognise three types of conceptual category: concrete objects, actions and relationships. In initially mapping a word form on to a meaning, it appears to adopt without question a number of assumptions, which may reflect innate tendencies. These constraints include:

● the *whole object assumption*: that the term DOG refers to a whole animal rather than the tail or the teeth;
● the *taxonomic assumption*: that labels refer to categories of objects rather than to the temporary co-occurrence of two features (i.e. a dog under a tree or a dog lying down);
● the *mutual exclusivity assumption*: that there is only one label per category of objects;
● the *type assumption*: that a word refers to a class of objects or events rather than a single one (DOG does not just refer to the family pet).

To these, Clark (1993) adds the principles of *conventionality* (the assumption that there is a standard adult form to which a sense is attached) and *contrast* (the fact that every difference in form marks a difference in meaning). In addition, there is an assumption shared between infant and caretaker that the first words provided are *basic level* terms (thus, DOG will be introduced before ANIMAL or

POODLE). Basic level terms are those which are most clearly distinguishable in terms of their characterising features. The important consideration for the infant is that, in acquiring such terms, it is applying roughly the same level of detail in establishing each of its early concepts. It appears initially to apply a *no-overlap assumption* which leads it occasionally to reject formulations involving higher-level terms such as *A dog is an animal*. In time, it comes to accord priority to the words acquired first: it assumes that the term DOG refers to a basic class of objects in a way that the later-acquired ANIMAL and POODLE do not.

It appears that the formation of early noun categories is very much guided by the shape of the objects (the *shape bias*); but that other characteristics (including how human beings relate to the objects) play a part. The *functional core hypothesis* emphasises the role played by interaction with an object (a *brush* acquires brushness through being used).

An infant's early conceptual categories are markedly different from those of an adult, since they lack the complete set of characterising features. The infant may make wrong assumptions about what it is that qualifies an object or action for inclusion. Infants *over-extend* adult categories in some ways (for example, classifying an ostrich as a duck) but *under-extend* them in others (denying that Donald Duck is a duck).

Over-extensions of concepts take three main forms: *categorical* where two categories are combined (DADA = both parents), *analogous* where a single defining characteristic is adopted (BALL = all round objects; COMB = centipede) and *predicative* where an object is related to an action (DOOR = to open, COOKIE = plate). In some cases, these over-extensions simply reflect gaps in the infant's vocabulary.

Vygotsky gives an example of a *chain complex* (or *associative complex*) which illustrates how a child might over-extend a category by a process of loose association. The child acquired QUAH (= quack) for a duck on a pond, then extended it to a cup of milk (liquid like the pond), to a coin with an eagle on it (a bird like the duck) and to a teddy bear's eye (round like the coin).

Over a period of time, the infant gradually reshapes its conceptual categories to correspond to those of adults. One of the longer-term developments is a move from reliance upon perceptual and functional characteristics (UNCLE as a giver of presents) to *defining* ones (UNCLE as sibling of parent).

One approach to concept formation has proposed that infants establish a central reference point for a word in the form of a **prototype**; this is based either upon the first exemplar of a word which they meet or upon the referent most frequently used by adults. The infant then extends the word to other entities which appear to share a 'goodness of fit' with the prototype. An alternative account is provided by a *multiple-trace model*, which assumes that each encounter with an exemplar of a conceptual category leaves a memory trace. The overlapping experiences (of, say, a variety of types of dog) gradually enable the infant to recognise features which are common to all of them and thus to form criteria for allocating further exemplars to the category.

See also: **Basic level, Mapping, Prototype Theory, Vocabulary acquisition**

Further reading: Bowerman and Levinson (2001); Clark (1993); Golinkoff *et al.* (1999); Neisser (1987); Owens (2001)

CONFUSABILITY

The likelihood that, in a neutral context, a native speaker of a language will interpret a particular phoneme as another. Confusability varies somewhat according to the position of the phoneme in the sequence and to level of external noise; but some phonemes have been shown to be highly confusable. English speakers often interpret word-initial [p] as [k] and [θ] as [f], even in conditions where there is no noise.

When English speech is put through a low-pass **filter**, eliminating higher frequencies in the signal, the consonants of the language appear to fall into certain groups within which confusion occurs and between which it does not often occur:

[ptk] [bdg] [fθsʃ] [vðzʒ] [mn]

A research method in which subjects are asked to detect mispronunciations in a read–aloud text has added to our knowledge of which phonemic contrasts are most salient. It seems that the distinction between voiced and voiceless consonants is detected most readily for stops (70 per cent of mispronunciations detected) followed by affricates (64 per cent) and fricatives (38 per cent). The low score for fricatives may be perceptual (they contain relatively weak acoustic cues) or a matter of conditioning (they do not feature in a large number of voiced-voiceless contrasts in English). The same method suggested that subjects are accurate in detecting mispronunciations which involve place (80–90 per cent); and that (for some consonants), mispronunciations are more readily detected in word-initial position than in word-final. The latter finding suggests strongly that listeners pay special heed to the opening sounds of a word, as the **Cohort** model assumes.

See also: **Intelligibility**

Further reading: Clark and Yallop (1990: 309–22); Miller and Nicely (1955)

CONNECTIONISM

A design and set of working assumptions which characterise a group of models of language processing. Connectionist models are often designed for computer implementation. They are constructed in a way that resembles the configuration of the human brain, where information is transmitted via massively interconnected *neural networks*. The belief is not that one necessarily replicates the operations of the brain by taking it as a model. It is (a) that a model which resembles the brain potentially provides a more plausible account than one that does not; and (b) that by using this kind of architecture we may gain incidental insights into at least some of the brain's functions.

Like the brain, connectionist models consist of a large number of simple processing units with multiple connections linking them. **Activation** flows along the connections, just as electrical impulses transmit information through neurons in the brain. The ease with which activation spreads from one unit to another is determined by the *strength* of the connections along which it travels. The stronger the connection to a unit, the more readily that unit becomes activated. A connection's strength depends upon how frequently it is used. Thus, over time, connections to a frequent word will become strong, ensuring that the word is activated more rapidly than other less common ones.

One of the earliest connectionist models was the IAC (Interactive Activation and Competition) model (McClelland and Rumelhardt, 1981), which explored written word recognition. The architecture of the IAC contains a number of aspects which characterise later connectionist models. It consists of units at three different levels, corresponding to letter features (curves, vertical lines, oblique lines, etc.), whole letters and whole words. Figure C2 shows a simplified version. An important characteristic of all connectionist models is that the various levels of operation are regarded as being active simultaneously (*in parallel*).

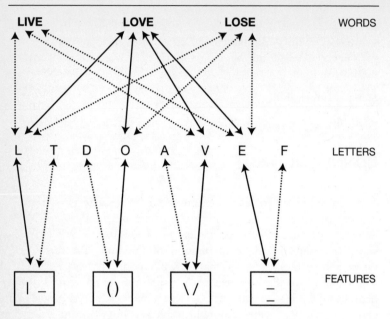

Figure C2 Simplified three-level connectionist model of reading

Note: Dotted lines indicate weak activation. Note the interactive nature of the model, with knowledge of the word LOVE influencing recognition of the letters as well as vice versa. Within-level inhibitory links (e.g. evidence for LOVE reducing the activation of LIVE, are not shown.

Each unit is connected to all the units in the levels above and below it. These connections can be *facilitatory* (or *excitatory*), meaning that they enhance the level of activation in the unit to which they lead. Or they can be *inhibitory*, in which case they reduce the level of activation. The connection between a curve at feature level and the letter G at letter level would be facilitatory; but the connection between the curve and the letter F would be inhibitory since the curve provides evidence against the presence of an F.

In the IAC model, there are also inhibitory connections between units at the same level. As evidence accumulates for the presence of G, its activation increases and at the same time that of (say) V is reduced. Not all connectionist models include these within-level connections.

The operation of a connectionist model of word recognition is assumed to take place over time, with the activation of some candidate words building up gradually while that of others declines. As configured on computer, processing takes place in cycles, which correspond to the passage of time. After each cycle, the activation level of each unit is updated. In time, one unit outstrips all the others at that level, permitting recognition to occur; the system is then said to have achieved equilibrium.

Some connectionist models, including the IAC, permit activation to flow in a *top-down* direction: i.e. not just from letters up to words, but also from words down to letters. Suppose that evidence has built up at word level for the unit WORK. Activation then flows back down to letter level, where it facilitates the recognition of the final letter K but inhibits the letter F since there is no such word as WORF. Models which permit this kind of two-way flow of activation are described as *highly interactive*.

The connectionist concept has been widely applied. Just as the IAC simulates written word recognition, so a later model, **TRACE** (McClelland and Elman, 1986), simulates spoken word recognition. Connectionist principles also underlie standard accounts of **lexical storage**, in which connections link a particular concept to its characteristics (TOMATO is linked to ROUND, to RED and to SOFT), as well as to associated concepts including co-hyponyms and superordinates (LETTUCE and SALAD). As ever, the connections between units vary in strength. Thus, the connection between TOMATO and SALAD is stronger than the connection between TOMATO and FRUIT.

A strength of the connectionist approach is that, besides modelling processes such as word recognition, it can also model learning. In a computer simulation, each connection receives a number or *weight* to indicate its relative strength. At the outset, these can be set at 0; but, as connections are used, their weights are adjusted by means of a complex formula. If a connection is not used, its weight declines to a negative value, indicating an inhibitory relationship.

The effectiveness of this learning process has been increased by a feedback mechanism known as *back propagation* which provides the program with a kind of memory. It compares what a connectionist network outputs from a particular stimulus with what it should output (given the input SING, it might compare its output of the past tense form *singed* with the correct form *sang*). By dint of many repeated presentations of the input, some connections within the network become strengthened while others become weakened. In this way, the network can gradually be 'trained' to produce correct responses through a process of *error reduction*.

Using back propagation, a connectionist program has managed to simulate the acquisition of a set of regular and irregular English Past Simple verb forms. It succeeded in discriminating between cases where an *-ed* inflection was appropriate (WALK – WALKED) and those where a new form had to be learnt (WRITE – WROTE). It also, in the process, manifested the kind of **U-shaped development** observed both in first and second language acquisition, where a speaker acquires a correct irregular form, then later replaces it with a regular form that has been over-generalised (*writed*). Simulations such as this are sometimes cited in support of an **empiricist** view of language acquisition. They suggest that linguistic patterns can be identified through exposure to multiple examples, with no need to presuppose a genetically transmitted mechanism which drives the acquisition process.

However, some caution is needed: the program only acquired a small subset of verb forms and did so after a large number of passes. It was also dedicated to a single learning operation, whereas a child has to acquire meaning as well as form and encounters a verb in many more forms (*writing, written*) than simply the past. In addition, current connectionist programs are dependent upon the operator inputting precise lexical or phonemic information; this cannot be said to resemble the connected nature and considerable variation of natural speech.

A feature of the early connectionist models was that each operating unit was deemed to represent a word. Thus, there was a unit for WRITE and another for WROTE, to which it was connected. Current theory questions whether words are explicitly represented in this way. Instead, the evidence for (say) WROTE may take the form of a state in which several abstract units reach a particular level of activation. The cues which characterise WROTE are thus *distributed* over a number of units. This more recent type of connectionist architecture is referred to as **parallel distributed processing** or PDP.

See also: **Interactive activation, Parallel distributed processing**

Further reading: Ellis and Humphreys (1999); Elman *et al.* (1996: Chap. 2)

CONTEXT

A term sometimes used loosely to cover any of:

- *Immediate situation*: knowledge of speaker/writer; analogy with a similar linguistic exchange.
- *Meaning representation* built up from the text so far.
- *Topic*: world knowledge in the form of pre-established **schemas**.

- *Co-text*: a group of words which provides syntactic or semantic evidence for the words which occur next.

Contextual information appears to be used by readers in two different ways. Weaker readers use it to compensate for inadequate decoding skills, while stronger ones use it to enrich their interpretation of the text.

See also: **Context effects, Interactive compensatory hypothesis, Reading: bottom-up vs top-down**

CONTEXT EFFECTS

Ways in which contextual information may (a) influence the interpretation of a word or an utterance or (b) speed up lexical access.

The use of contextual cues demands attentional resources. It should be distinguished from the phenomenon of **spreading activation**, which is highly automatic and not normally subject to our control. However, the two are sometimes difficult to distinguish. Suppose recognition of the word SPOON is speeded up when it occurs in the utterance: *He laid the table with a knife, fork and spoon*. To what extent is this effect due to the table-laying context and to what extent is it due to the spread of activation from the forms KNIFE and FORK?

There is considerable disagreement as to how contextual information influences the construction of meaning. Possible views include:

- *Bottom-up driven*. Perceptual information is primary; contextual information is used to check and enrich it.
- *Top-down driven*. Context biases interpretation ahead of perception.
- *Interactive*. Contextual information interacts with perceptual information at all stages of processing.
- '*Bottom-up priority*'. A minimal amount of perceptual data is processed before contextual influences can apply.
- *Ambiguity resolution*. Contextual data is only used in cases of ambiguity.

The timing of context effects is especially a matter of debate in relation to **lexical access**. Most accounts assume that, when a listener hears part of a word, he/she forms a list of potential matches. Does context operate to limit the number of word candidates that are chosen? Does it (by increasing or reducing **activation**) influence the choice of the successful candidate? Or is it simply used to check the appropriacy of the candidate that has been chosen?

A connected issue is whether and how context plays a role in resolving **ambiguity**. Does it simplify the process by enabling the listener or reader to select a single appropriate sense for a polysemous or homonymous word? Or does the listener/reader automatically access all possible senses before using context to determine which is the correct one? A much-cited finding (Swinney, 1979) suggested that the latter is the case. Subjects were presented with sentences containing ambiguous words. (Example: *The man was not surprised when he found several bugs in the corner of his room.*) Even where there was a highly specific context (*several spiders, roaches and other bugs*), they showed signs of having retrieved both possible senses (BUG = spy gadget, BUG = insect). The same finding has been reported with homonyms which come from different word classes: i.e. where the context provides syntactic as well as semantic cues. Thus, the word [wiːk] speeds the recognition of both MONTH and STRONG, even when it occurs in a sentence where it is clearly a noun.

Further evidence is based on the eye movements of readers. The presence of an ambiguous word in a text increases gaze duration. Two factors contribute:

a. whether the two senses of the word are balanced in terms of frequency or whether one is *dominant* (more frequent);
b. whether disambiguating contextual information occurs in advance of the word.

Recent findings indicate that:

- Only the dominant sense is retrieved when a context indicates the dominant one.
- Both senses of a word are retrieved when a context indicates the subordinate one.

However, the possibility remains that all senses are retrieved – but foregrounded to different degrees depending upon their frequency and contextual appropriacy.

See also: **Interactive activation, Lexical access, Listening: higher-level processes, Reading: bottom-up vs top-down, Reading: higher-level processes, Speech perception: autonomous vs interactive, Top-down processing**

Further reading: Brown and Yule (1983); Reeves *et al.* (1998: 202–8); Simpson (1994)

CONTROLLED *see* **Automaticity**

CREOLISATION

The emergence of a creole language even though the children of pidgin-speakers have only been exposed to pidgin forms. Creoles are much more sophisticated than pidgins and have many of the features of a fully fledged language (structure-dependency, complex sentences, articles, consistent word order). The question therefore arises of how the child acquires the creole forms.

One conclusion might be that infants are more sensitive than adults to the standard language outside the family. However, creoles also differ significantly and systematically from both the ambient language and the first language of the pidgin-speaking parents. Furthermore, similarities have been demonstrated between creoles which have developed independently in different parts of the world. It has therefore been suggested that creolisation affords important evidence that infants possess an innate **Universal Grammar**, in the form of a language bioprogram. The hypothesis is that, even when normal linguistic input is not available, the bioprogram ensures that infants shape what they hear to fit certain patterns which characterise all languages. This is sometimes referred to as the **nativisation hypothesis**.

The bioprogram theory has been challenged in terms of both the evidence and the interpretation put upon it. However, support comes from studies of deaf infants who have not been taught sign language, but have nevertheless developed their own gestural language, *homesign*. Homesign bears interesting resemblances to the language of hearing children, both in its semantic content and in the ages at which utterances of different lengths emerge.

See also: **Critical period, Nativisation hypothesis, Nativism, Sign language, Universal Grammar**

Further reading: Bickerton (1990)

CRITICAL PERIOD

A period early in life during which a human being is uniquely endowed with the capacity to acquire a first language. Also applied to second language acquisition. Some commentators prefer the term *sensitive period*, arguing that language can be acquired outside the period, even if less completely.

Lenneberg (1967) concluded from studies of **brain lateralisation** that there was a period up to puberty during which the configuration of the brain was flexible. If there were damage to the left hemisphere during this period, the language faculty could relocate itself on the right. A parallel was traced between the timing of lateralisation and evidence from language **deprivation**. Children deprived of language go on to develop full linguistic competence if they are brought into society before the age of about eight or nine; those who are rescued at a later stage may develop an extensive vocabulary but often manifest an incomplete system of syntax. Hence a conclusion that lateralisation was closely associated with the acquisition of a first language and that, if acquisition were to be fully successful, it had to occur during the period of flexibility.

In fact, the evidence is not as clear as was once suggested. Not all children who suffer left-hemisphere damage develop a right-hemisphere dominance for language; while adults with left-hemisphere damage may sometimes do so. There is evidence shortly after birth that a degree of lateralisation has taken place, and the process may be complete by five years old. Importantly, **brain imaging** technology has shown us that language is much more widely distributed in the brain than was once thought.

The deprivation evidence is also open to challenge. There is considerable variation in the way deprived children develop, and no evidence of a sharply defined point when language is no longer achievable. Account must also be taken of the background of the cases studied and the extent to which early trauma may have affected the ability to acquire language and to relate to others.

If there is indeed a sensitive period, there are other possible explanations besides the purely neurological one:

☐ An innate **Universal Grammar** may be available to the infant for only a limited period; or it may be suppressed by the development of adult cognitive capacities more suitable for 'problem-solving' but less apt for the acquisition of language.

☐ Maturation may provide for a stage when a successfully internalised set of grammar rules becomes separated from the evidence which gave rise to it.

☐ Modified input (**child directed speech**) is less likely to be addressed to older children than to infants.

☐ The **'less is more'** hypothesis suggests that, precisely because an infant is not fully developed cognitively, its limited attention span enables it to focus on discrete aspects of the input.

The notion of a critical period has been extended to second language acquisition and is sometimes cited in support of an early start for foreign language learning. The evidence is complex and mixed. A distinction has to be made between the rate at which a second language is acquired and the final level of competence that is achieved. Contributory factors to be taken into account include: age at which acquisition begins (*age of arrival* in the case of immigrant learners), length of exposure, type of input (naturalistic, immersion, classroom) and type of motivation.

The acquisition of a second language can be regarded as the acquisition of a range of skills and information types (phonology, lexis, syntax). Different domains may be differently affected by the age at which acquisition begins. Generalising considerably, it would appear that there may be a critical period (up to the age of eight or nine) for the acquisition of a native or near-native accent. Some evidence suggests that adults initially acquire syntax faster than younger learners; but that adolescents score best, both short term and long term, on a wide range of tasks. Early starting age naturally results in longer exposure. To the extent that these factors can be separated, an early start seems to lead to greater accuracy and long exposure to greater communicative competence.

The question remains of why many adults find it difficult to acquire a second language. Explanations include the loss of the universal grammar which triggers first language acquisition; cognitive development which results in a more analytic approach to the language-learning task; intervention of the first language in the process; the loss of perceptual sensitivity with the development of **categorical perception**; the fact that the adult has a fully developed personality expressible through the medium of L1; and again, the hypothesis that the cognitive limitations of the child make it more sensitive to individual features of linguistic input.

See also: **Brain lateralisation, Deprivation, 'Less is more', Universal Grammar**

Further reading: Aitchison (1998); Birdsong (1999); Singleton (1989); Skuse (1993)

CUE TRADING

A process of weighing the evidence provided by one acoustic cue against the evidence provided by another. A phonetic contrast in natural speech is usually signalled by several acoustic properties of the speech signal; what is important is the strength of each cue *relative to the others*. For example, both pitch level and duration can serve to mark stress in English. If the pitch level of a given syllable is neutral (at the middle of a speaker's range) then a listener automatically increases the importance attached to duration as a marker of stress.

With consonant recognition, cue trading does not simply involve features associated with the articulation of the phoneme itself. Important *co-articulatory* cues to a consonant's identity are provided by the preceding or following vowel, and features such as *Voice Onset Time* also contribute to the judgement that is made. The consequence of this is that a set of articulatory gestures associated with a particular consonant in one vowel context may be associated with a different consonant in another vowel context. To give an example, the acoustic features that indicate the presence of /s/ in [su] are similar to those that indicate the presence of /ʃ/ in [ʃa]. Listeners' judgements are influenced by the following vowel, resulting in a shift in the perceptual 'boundary' where /ʃ/ becomes perceived as /s/. In some cases, the same synthesised sounds are perceived as [ʃ] when followed by [a] and as [s] when followed by [u].

A further source of evidence is the **articulation rate** of the speaker. It seems that listeners are sensitive to the rate at which syllables are being uttered and adjust their perceptions accordingly. For example, exposed to a continuum of synthesised sounds which progress from [b] + vowel to [w] + vowel, listeners incline increasingly to a /b/ interpretation as the length of the vowel increases. Vowel length is an indicator of speed of articulation.

Trading relations between cues have been shown to vary according to whether a signal is processed as speech or not; this has been cited as evidence that there is a special **speech mode** which is distinct from other forms of auditory perception.

See also: **Acoustic cue, Speech perception: phoneme variation**

Further reading: Pickett (1999)

DEAF PARENT

When a hearing child has deaf parents, the contribution of parental speech to language acquisition is necessarily restricted. This affords a test case for nativist theories. If a child can achieve language normally despite limited input, it suggests that innate processes must play a part.

Many such children do display normal acquisition, though some (possibly around 20 per cent) show signs of delayed or unusual development. What assists early acquisition appears to be oral communication with the principal carer in the form of the limited *telegraphic speech* which many deaf adults rely on – always provided the utterances observe the usual Subject-Verb-Object pattern and relate to local context. This affords sufficient information for a two year old to establish the basic syntactic-semantic foundations of language. The first syntactic forms which infants produce replicate those of their parents, though the productions of the infant quickly outstrip those of the parents in terms of syntactic complexity.

External factors play an important part. To ensure normal acquisition, the child appears to need a minimum of about 5–10 hours' contact each week with hearing adults, plus exposure to radio or television. However, there is no close correlation between time spent in the company of hearers and the rate and success of linguistic development. The existence of siblings does not necessarily enhance acquisition; and some children continue to manifest linguistic problems after spending long periods with hearing peers at school.

It is remarkable that, exposed to two different forms of adult language, the child appears to avoid the simplified syntax of the deaf parents and to adopt the syntactic models provided by hearing adults outside the immediate family. If simplifications occur, they are those of all L1-acquiring infants rather than those of the profoundly deaf. Even two-year-old children appear capable of making a distinction between the type of speech they use for their parents (more signs, extended pitch patterns, shorter utterances) and the type they use with other speakers. All this would suggest to a nativist that the child is following some predetermined programme.

Against this, the intelligibility of the principal carer often appears to play an important part in determining how great a child's language difficulties are. Certain areas of speech and language are more affected than others. Delays in phonological development are not infrequent, and the speech of some children of deaf parents may appear 'deaf-like'.

However, the order in which the features of language are acquired seems to follow very much the same path as that recorded of infants in more normal circumstances. Furthermore, the children of deaf parents rarely show any signs of delay or impairment in pragmatic knowledge or in their ability to interact with others.

See also: **Deafness, Sign language**

Further reading: Schiff-Myers (1993)

DEAFNESS

Hearing loss differs widely between affected individuals, and is classified as mild, moderate, severe or profound.

Human conversation typically takes place within a frequency range of 250 to 8000 Hz and at an intensity of around 60 decibels. Deaf listeners suffer from a restriction in the frequency range and/or a reduction in the perceived loudness of the signal. Hearing aids can increase loudness but cannot restore gaps in the frequency band. Profoundly deaf listeners appear to compensate by making use of *time/ intensity cues*. They can perceive changes in the intensity of the signal; the duration of the changes provides a rough indication of voiced/ voiceless contrasts and enables stops and fricatives to be distinguished.

A major issue is the extent to which prelinguistic deafness affects language acquisition. There is evidence of delayed acquisition – infants may reach the 50-word vocabulary threshold around ten months later than their hearing peers. But whether the acquisition route deviates from that of a hearing infant is less clear.

Because of their slower acquisition, it was thought that deaf children might provide evidence as to whether there is a **critical period** for developing a full mastery of a first language. However, only a very weak association has been found between the age at which a child is diagnosed as deaf and the level of language (speech or sign) which is later achieved. Stronger factors appear to be the degree of hearing impairment and the quality of the input which the child receives. **Child directed speech** is often impoverished when a child is deaf, with shorter and fewer exchanges and the adult speaker exercising a high degree of control.

The effect of deafness upon **phonological development** has also been studied. At the **babbling** stage, the consonant repertoire of deaf infants appears to be smaller and intonation flatter. Visual cues may play a part, favouring the early emergence of labial sounds. However, the speech of deaf infants contains phonological irregularities similar to those in the speech of hearing infants – the major difference being that they occur at a later chronological age. Delay rather than deviance thus appears to be the pattern.

Lexical development differs from that of a hearing infant in that labelling plays a less important part; early nouns are fewer in number. This may reflect the carer's difficulty in holding and directing the attention of a deaf child. However, the lexical associations which are ultimately built up appear to be similar to those of all language users.

So far as syntax is concerned, deaf infants who achieve speech tend to rely on shorter utterances and to adhere more closely to the standard Subject-Verb-Object word order. Sometimes their speech is *telegraphic*, with function words and inflections omitted. Even adults sometimes experience problems in making grammaticality judgements and in interpreting passive and negative structures. It would appear that they cope with the unreliability of the signal by relying upon a strategy that is semantic rather than syntactic and that assumes a standard agent–action–patient word order.

Because profoundly deaf children do not have a strong basis of spoken language, they often encounter literacy problems. They are slow in developing reading skills. An obvious explanation is that deaf readers cannot make use of *grapheme-phoneme rules* to break unfamiliar words into their constituent sounds. However, there is evidence that many deaf readers do achieve a kind of phonological code which enables them to associate words by their rimes and to distinguish homographs.

Typically, the writing of a deaf child uses a limited range of sentence structures and a grammar system which frequently omits inflections, auxiliary verbs and articles. However, spelling is often accurate, suggesting an ability to handle visual vocabulary as whole words.

See also: **Blindness, Sign language**

Further reading: Gallaway and Woll (1994); Mogford (1993b); Strong (1988)

DELAY VS DEVIANCE

An important issue in discussion of language impairment is whether a condition such as deafness causes language acquisition to be *delayed* relative to infants who are unaffected by the condition. A second issue is whether the acquisition process deviates from that observed in more typical conditions. *Deviance* (an unfortunate but widely used term) can take the form of a different **order of acquisition** for particular features of language or the emergence of non-standard forms and concepts in the acquirer's language. Comparisons are not usually made with infants of the same chronological age of the subjects studied, but with those at the same stage of linguistic development.

Further reading: Bishop and Mogford (1993)

DEMENTIA

Progressive cognitive dysfunction due to deterioration of **brain** tissue. A major problem lies in determining whether the resulting language impairment is linguistic (reflecting damage to the stored systems of grammar and lexis) or cognitive (reflecting damage to areas such as memory, attention and problem-solving which facilitate the use of the grammar and the lexicon).

A second problem lies in distinguishing the effects of dementia from the normal effects of **ageing**. Some commentators suggest that dementia represents a heightening of the impact of ageing, seen, for example, in difficulties in retrieving words. However, an elderly speaker can often locate a 'lost' word if given a cue to its initial sound, whereas dementia sufferers cannot. Dementia sufferers frequently resort to coining a new word when a known one cannot be retrieved.

The way in which dementia impacts upon language depends greatly upon the area of the brain which is affected. Some forms of dementia such as Alzheimer's disease affect the *cortex* while others (including many cases of Parkinson's disease) affect the *subcortical* areas.

☐ *Subcortical dementia* leads to a general slowing of activity, which may result in problems of articulation. Speech tends to be affected more noticeably than the language system as a whole, though the ability to retrieve words may be impaired. Similarly, writing may be affected at the level of execution: typical symptoms are small letters and irregular spacing between words. Subcortical dementia is sometimes interpreted in terms of damage to the capacity to control and focus attention: hence problems with manipulating information such as the attachment of inflections in writing.

☐ When *cortical dementia* begins relatively young, there is a higher probability of extensive language impairment than when the onset occurs at a more advanced age. Some of the effects resemble those of

aphasia, especially Wernicke's aphasia; this is unsurprising, given that the syndrome affects similar areas of the brain.

Sufferers from cortical dementia retain some of the more highly automatised linguistic skills until quite late in the condition. Their phonology is spared, and they usually remain capable of reading aloud. Their utterances show some degree of syntactic structure, including correct word order; and they may be able to correct grammatical errors. Well-established formulaic utterances are especially well preserved, though they may not be used appropriately.

However, their conversation is marked by a lack of cohesion and multiple changes of topic. Lexical retrieval is severely affected: whereas aphasics can often provide clues to a word which they cannot locate (e.g. initial letter, number of syllables), cortical dementia sufferers cannot. Despite this, the semantic relations which support **spreading activation** (the links between DOCTOR and *nurse, patient, hospital*) appear to be relatively robust. This suggests that the semantic system is at least partly intact; and that the speaker's difficulties lie in accessing it.

There has been interest in the way in which dementia affects bilinguals. The language acquired first is more likely to be spared than one acquired later. There is also evidence that some bilinguals become less adept at switching between their languages, and use the wrong one in certain circumstances.

See also: **Ageing**

Further reading: Hamilton (1994); Maxim and Bryan (1994); Obler and Gjerlow (1999: Chap. 8)

DEPRIVATION

Lack of access to linguistic input in the early years of life – especially in the period up to puberty, which is sometimes said to be a **critical period** for language acquisition. Deprivation arises when a child is abandoned or is confined in some way which separates them from language. These unfortunate cases enable researchers to explore (a) the extent to which language is innate and develops regardless of adult input; and (b) the hypothesis that it cannot be fully acquired once a particular period of maturation is over.

A well-known instance of a *feral child* is Victor, the 'Wild Boy of Aveyron', found living wild in the French countryside in 1800. Victor's case was documented by a French doctor, Itard, who attempted to train the boy for human society but recorded very limited linguistic progress. Victor achieved the notion that nouns are used for classes of objects rather than single items and acquired a number of verbs and adjectives, but his syntax remained rudimentary.

There have been a number of more recent cases of *attic children*. The best documented is that of Genie (USA) who was isolated in a small room from 20 months until 13 years 7 months with no exposure to speech. After she was rescued, she quickly learnt to distinguish speech from other sounds and to recognise recurrent words. She began to speak, though her pronunciation remained idiosyncratic and at times she fell back upon a sign system. She seems, like a normal infant, to have gone through a two-word and a three-word stage, but extended over a much longer period than usual. She acquired a relatively wide vocabulary but her syntactic development remained incomplete. She used few function words and, though some inflectional morphology emerged, it later disappeared. Her use of articles, pronouns, demonstratives and auxiliary verbs was extremely limited. By contrast, her cognitive development was rapid: she progressed by two years of mental age for every year of the study, suggesting a dissociation between general cognition and language.

Other cases include:

□ *Isabelle* (USA), the child of a deaf mute, rescued from a darkened room at the age of six-and-a-half. A week after rescue, she began to vocalise; her speech acquisition then went through the normal developmental stages but extremely rapidly. Within two years, she had a vocabulary of 2000 words and her language aptitude was comparable to that of other children of her age.

□ *the 'Koluchova twins'* (Czechoslovakia), rescued from isolation at seven years three months but with a mental age of around three. In a children's home and later a foster family, they made great cognitive advances and developed above average linguistic skills.

□ *Louise and Mary* (UK), rescued and put into care at the ages of three years six months and two years four months respectively. Neither had begun to develop language or social behaviour. Louise went on to achieve normal linguistic competence; but Mary continued to show signs of autism, possibly inherited.

These cases provide tenuous evidence for a *sensitive period* during which infants are particularly receptive to language. After this period, it seems, vocabulary is acquired but a full syntactic system may not develop.

Important factors seem to be the age at which a child is rescued; the extent to which, on rescue, they show signs of responding to speech; and the opportunity they are given to develop language and cognition through play. Their later linguistic development is strongly assisted by the opportunity to develop normal social and familial relationships.

However, caution has to be exercised in reaching hard-and-fast conclusions. These cases of deprivation do not demonstrate a clear cut-off point at puberty; and later language development seems to vary considerably. More importantly, children who are deprived of language are deprived of affection as well. The trauma of their early experiences may well affect their ability to acquire language. Additionally, some may originally have been neglected by adults because they showed early signs of mental handicap or autism.

See also: **Autism, Critical period, Specific language impairment**

Further reading: Curtiss (1977); Foster-Cohen (1999: 123–9); Skuse (1993)

DEPTH OF PROCESSING

A theory that information is more likely to be retained if it is processed in a meaningful way. **Rehearsal** of a piece of information in short-term memory is said to strengthen its representation in long-term memory; but only if the rehearsal involves manipulating the information or paying heed to its meaning. Subjects were asked to perform three different types of operation on sets of words: a shallow one (*Is it in capitals?*), an intermediate one (*Does it rhyme with X?*) and a deep one involving meaning rather than form (*Does it fit into this sentence?*). Recall of the words in the third condition was much better than in the other two. The finding has been applied to second language vocabulary learning.

See also: **Rehearsal**

Further reading: Craik and Lockhart (1972)

DERIVATIONAL THEORY OF COMPLEXITY

Early **Chomskyan theory** was based upon a set of *transformational rules* which derived surface structure sentences from their underlying deep structure forms. Thus the following sentences:

a.   *The old woman was warned by Joe.*
b.   *The old woman wasn't warned by Joe.*

were both regarded as derived from *Joe warned the old woman*.

Early psycholinguistic research adopted an assumption (the *correspondence hypothesis*) that Chomsky's transformational grammar was psychologically real and represented the exact processes employed by a language user. The user was thought to assemble a sentence in deep structure, then take it through a series of transformations. Hence the derivational theory of complexity (DTC), which hypothesised that the more transformations there were, the more difficult it would be for a listener or reader to process a sentence.

Initial research demonstrated that subjects were faster to match a jumbled sentence to its negative form (one transformation) than to its negative passive form (two transformations). However, the experiment suffered from flaws of design – not least, the greater length of the more complex sentences; and later trials turned up sentences where processing time and number of supposed transformations did not correlate. It also emerged that passive transformations only delayed the matching task in the case of *reversible passives* such as *The boy was chased by the girl* and not in the case of irreversible ones such as *The flowers were watered by the girl*. This suggested that semantic as well as syntactic factors were involved in the matching task. Finally, the DTC theory was based on the assumption that readers wait until the end of a sentence before decoding it, which we now know is not the case.

See also: **Syntactic parsing**

Further reading: Aitchison (1998)

DESIGN FEATURES

A set of characteristics which specify the nature of speech. Hockett (1963) produced the first list of such features; his aim was to provide a principled means of contrasting speech with animal communication systems. The following design features are the most cited:

a.   *Vocal-auditory channel* – speaking and listening.
b.   *Interchangeability* – a transmitter and a receiver.
c.   *Complete feedback* – the ability to self monitor when speaking.

d. *Specialisation* – speech production as an end in itself, not part of a biological function.
e. *Semanticity* – linguistic signs associated with specific meanings.
f. *Arbitrariness* – no necessary connection between the form of the signal and what it signifies.
g. *Discreteness* – distinctive units of sound (phoneme) and meaning (word).
h. *Displacement* – the possibility of referring beyond the 'here and now'.
i. *Openness* – similar to Chomsky's notion of the infinite creativity of language.
j. *Cultural transmission* – language being acquired in a social setting.
k. *Duality of patterning* – sounds combined into words; words into syntactic patterns.

To these, modern commentators might add:

l. *Structure-dependency* – language as a set of hierarchically structured phrases.

Other minor but distinctive design features are said to be:

m. *Prevarication* – the ability to lie.
n. *Reflectiveness* – the ability to analyse thoughts.
o. *Learnability* – the possibility of learning others' codes.
p. *Spontaneous usage* – production that is unrehearsed.
q. *Turn taking* – sequential production and reception.

See also: **Animal communication**

Further reading: Aitchison (1998)

DEVIANCE *see* **Delay vs deviance**

DICHOTIC LISTENING

An experimental method where different messages are played into the left ear and the right. A linguistic signal in the right ear (linked to the left hemisphere of the brain) usually overrides that in the left. Findings from this task suggest that the right ear is dominant for most aspects of speech but the left for music, rhythm (including prosody) and the tones which distinguish words in languages such as Thai or Mandarin. This provides evidence that speech is processed differently from other types of auditory stimuli.

DISORDER

In psycholinguistics, a divergence from the normal processes of speech and comprehension which is due to cognitive or affective factors. Elsewhere, the term also covers problems of speech production and reception which are physiological in origin.

Language disorders can be categorised in the following ways:

☐ *Acquired vs developmental*. An acquired disorder is an impairment which occurs after a first language has been fully established. It may derive from brain damage (particularly to the left hemisphere) caused by illness, accident or surgery. It can also be part of general cognitive deterioration as the result of **dementia**.

A developmental disorder is an impairment which manifests itself during the acquisition of a first language. It might derive from processing problems, as with **dyslexia** and **dysgraphia**; or it might have affective causes, as in cases of stammering. The term also covers the effects upon language of the learning difficulties associated with **autism**, **Down's Syndrome** or **Williams Syndrome**; and cases of delayed language acquisition known as **specific language impairment** (SLI). In principle, a developmental disorder has three possible effects: it can delay the normal process of language acquisition, it can change the order in which elements are acquired or it can result in language which deviates from what has been observed in studies of normal development. A major issue for researchers has been the attempt to establish whether a disorder results in **delay** or **deviance**.

The distinction between acquired and developmental disorders is sometimes marked by the use of different terms: the prefix *dys-* (= impaired) indicates a developmental condition and the prefix *a-* (= without) an acquired one. Thus, *aphasia* = acquired dysphasia; *alexia* = acquired dyslexia; *agraphia* = acquired dysgraphia.

☐ *Organic vs functional*. In an organic disorder, there is a clear neurological or physiological cause. In a functional one, there are problems of psychological processing.

☐ *Reception vs production.* Language disorders affect reception, production or both. With aphasia in particular, the condition may be mainly restricted to *receptive aphasia* or to *expressive aphasia*.

☐ *Performance vs system.* In productive disorders, a distinction is sometimes made between *speech disorders* affecting phonology and *language disorders* involving the lexicon and the system of syntax. However, a more appropriate distinction is between disorders which affect performance at phonetic and graphetic level and disorders which affect the underlying system (phonological, graphological, semantic or syntactic).

The major topics of research fall into three areas:

☐ *Problems of fluency.* For some speakers, these problems are largely psychological, as in cases of **stuttering**. Other speakers have difficulty because of physiological problems involving malformation or mis-operation of the *articulators* (mouth, tongue, jaws, palate etc.). Cases such as these might appear to lie outside the scope of psycholinguistics; however, they raise questions about the nature of language and of language acquisition. Provided hearing and intelligence are not affected, it seems that the inability to speak does not prevent the development of language comprehension and inner speech.

☐ *Problems of written language.* A distinction is made between **dyslexia** (reading difficulty) and **dysgraphia** (writing difficulty), though many subjects manifest both. The degree of impairment varies between individuals, as do specific symptoms. Some dyslexics appear to suffer from a phonological deficit – they have problems in guessing the spellings of non-words. Others show signs of a 'whole word' deficit and cannot recall the spellings of unusual words.

☐ *The relationship between language and cognition.* Most human beings grow up to achieve full competence in their native tongue, regardless of wide variations in their intelligence and environment. This has suggested to some commentators that language develops independently of general cognition. Some of the evidence from language acquired in **'special circumstances'** appears to contradict this hypothesis, while some appears to support it. Thus, studies of Down's Syndrome and autism seem to demonstrate links between cognitive development and language. However, the reverse is suggested by evidence from two other conditions, specific language impairment and Williams Syndrome.

One difficulty in researching language disorders, both developmental and acquired, is the extent to which they vary from one sufferer to another. It has been suggested that some disorders may not be unitary conditions, but may represent combinations of impairments which are present to different degrees in different sufferers.

See also: **Ageing, Aphasia, Autism, Cluttering, Dementia, Down's Syndrome, Dysgraphia, Dyslexia, Savant, Specific language impairment, Stuttering, Williams Syndrome**

Further reading: Bishop (1997); Chiat (2000); Crystal and Varley (1999); Harris and Coltheart (1986)

DOWN'S SYNDROME

Studies of Down's Syndrome suggest a connection between cognitive impairment and failure to acquire full linguistic competence. Down's sufferers show limitations of attention, short-term memory and perceptual discrimination; they also have difficulty with symbolic representation of any kind. All of this appears to affect language performance, though there is great variation between individuals. Phonological development is slow. Only a limited vocabulary is acquired, and utterances usually remain short and 'telegraphic' (lacking function words and inflections). There has been much discussion as to whether language development in Down's sufferers is different in kind from that of unaffected children or simply delayed. The issue is hard to resolve because of the wide differences in individual performance, and because a delay in one area of language (say, a limited vocabulary) might well affect the course of another (say, length of utterance).

See also: **Autism, Modularity₁, Savant, Williams Syndrome**

Further reading: Crystal and Varley (1999)

DUAL ROUTE

The hypothesis that the reader of an alphabetic language has two ways of matching the form of a word on the page to a mental representation. The first (the *lexical route*) seeks a match for the word as a whole; the second (the *sub-lexical route*) interprets the letters phonologically, by means of **grapheme–phoneme correspondence** (GPC) rules. In normal reading, the lexical route is faster and more efficient; but it is argued that readers need the sub-lexical route when encountering a word which they have not seen before in written form, an unusual proper noun, a neologism, a non-word etc.

The dual-route model faces problems in situations where a sequence of letters permits of more than one interpretation. The model assumes that the sub-lexical route offers access to standard GPC rules, while the lexical route handles 'exception' words. On this analysis, a reader would take the same time to identify GOPE as a non-word as to identify HEAF. However, **neighbourhood** effects are found to apply. Words like GOPE with only 'friends' (HOPE, ROPE) are identified faster than those like HEAF with 'enemies' (LEAF vs DEAF). One solution to this is found in **analogy** theory which suggests that words are interpreted phonologically by analogy with others, perhaps mainly on the basis of their **rime**. Another is to assume that the sub-lexical route contains information on all possible interpretations of a particular letter or digraph (-EA- being recognised as potentially both /iː/ and /e/); hence the slower reaction time.

The strongest evidence supporting a dual route model comes from studies of acquired **dyslexia**. One type, *surface dyslexia*, seems to involve impairment of the lexical route but permits use of the sub-lexical. Subjects thus regularise irregular words. A second type, *phonological dyslexia*, seems to involve an intact lexical route but an impaired sub-lexical one. The subjects can pronounce familiar words, both regular and irregular, but are incapable of suggesting pronunciations for non-words.

The extent to which the sub-lexical route is employed may vary from language to language. A relatively *opaque* orthography like the English one may involve greater dependence upon the lexical route than the *transparent* orthography of Spanish. However, there is some evidence from Spanish dyslexics of semantic exchanges (when a word like APE is read as *monkey*); this suggests that both whole-word and phonological routes are employed.

See also: **Grapheme-phoneme correspondence rules, Reading: decoding**

Further reading: Balota (1994); Harris and Coltheart (1986)

DUPLEX PERCEPTION

A phenomenon that occurs when the phonetic features of a synthetic stimulus are split into two and part is presented to each ear.

Experimenters have found that part of the third (highest frequency) **formant** is critical to the distinction between /da/ and /ga/. When this section is excised, the remainder (or 'base') is heard by the listener as intermediate between the two syllables. If the base is played to one ear and the distinctive section of the third formant to the other, subjects report hearing the whole syllable (/da/ or /ga/) in the first ear and a non-speech chirp in the second. It seems that the speech-perception mechanism groups acoustic elements together even when they are derived from different sources.

There is interest in duplex perception because it violates a principle which states that an acoustic category cannot be assigned to more than one sound source. This provides support for a view that there is a special **speech mode**: i.e. that speech and non-speech sounds are processed differently.

DYSARTHRIA

A type of disorder (neurological or physiological) which affects the **articulation** of speech.

DYSGRAPHIA: ACQUIRED

The loss or partial loss of the ability to write as the result of illness, accident or brain surgery. It is often associated with **dyslexia**, though it is possible for reading to be impaired without writing and vice versa.

Impairments involving the physical act of writing are termed *peripheral dysgraphias*. A patient may not be able to retrieve the letters that are needed, whether for the spelling of words or of non-words, but may be able to write letters perfectly. The reverse syndrome occurs where a patient is capable of a correct grapheme match but cannot form the letters.

There are three main types of *central dysgraphia* which are similar to the categories of central dyslexia. Some of the underlying causes may be similar.

☐ In *surface dysgraphia*, once-familiar spellings cannot be retrieved but the patient makes an attempt to recall them on the basis of phonological information. Irregular spellings thus become regularised: *biscuit* → *BISKET.* Sometimes patients show awareness

that a spelling is irregular, but misallocate letters: *yacht* → *YHAGT.*
The condition may show impairment of the lexical (whole word)
system.

☐ In *phonological dysgraphia*, patients can spell familiar words correctly
but are unable to devise spellings for dictated non-words. The
condition appears to show impairment of the sound-spelling
connection.

☐ In *deep dysgraphia*, there are semantic errors like those of deep
dyslexia, e.g. a patient wants to write *chair* but writes *TABLE.* Patients
are better at writing concrete than abstract words. Typically, they are
unable to write dictated non-words. The condition appears to show
impairment of form-meaning associations; but a deep dysgraphic need
not be a deep dyslexic.

See also: **Disorder, Dyslexia: acquired**

Further reading: Caplan (1992); Ellis (1993); Harris and Coltheart (1986)

DYSGRAPHIA: DEVELOPMENTAL

Delayed acquisition of writing skills and/or the development of
writing which deviates markedly from what is generally observed in
children. Dysgraphia is often associated with dyslexia, and there may
be parallels in the symptoms presented. *Surface dyslexics* often have
severe problems with irregular spellings. *Phonological dyslexics* can learn
to spell on a whole-word basis, though they may insert incorrect
letters or produce letters in the wrong order. They cannot spell non-
words or new words, just as they cannot read them. The handwriting
of both types of dyslexic is usually poor.

   It has been suggested that normal writing acquisition in English
proceeds through three stages: imitative, phonological and orthographic. Dysgraphia may emerge at the phonological stage. Here, one
possible explanation is that the child is unable to segment the speech
signal into phonemes; another is that it is unable to match phonemes
to graphemes. Either way, the child fails to develop an adequate
grapho-phonological system, and thus cannot guess the spellings of
words from their spoken forms. Alternatively, dysgraphia may emerge
at the orthographic stage, when a child fails to move on from
phonological spellings to irregular whole-word ones.

In addition to the symptoms described, there may be problems of *peripheral dysgraphia* involving the formation of letters. A classic example is the substitution of *b* for *p*. These indications may reflect difficulty in analysing letter shapes visually, in storing letter shapes in the mind or in linking the execution of a letter to its stored representation.

See also: **Disorder, Dyslexia: developmental**

Further reading: Ellis (1993); Harris and Coltheart (1986)

DYSLEXIA: ACQUIRED

The loss or partial loss of the ability to read as the result of illness, accident or brain surgery. Acquired dyslexia is conventionally divided into *peripheral dyslexias*, where there is impairment of the system which permits visual analysis, and *central dyslexias*, where the processing of the signal is affected.

The peripheral dyslexias are:

☐ *Attentional dyslexia,* where the reader is distracted by adjoining words (or sometimes adjoining letters). *GLOVE* and *SPADE* seen together might produce the response *glade*. There is apparent damage to the reader's attentional filter, so that they are no longer able to focus on one piece of visual evidence at a time.

☐ *Neglect dyslexia,* involving a failure to attend to the onsets of words: a reader might interpret *GROSS* as *cross*.

☐ *Letter-by-letter reading,* where words are decoded letter by letter but the letters are given their alphabetic names: *BED* = *Bee-Eee-Dee*.

The central dyslexias are:

☐ *Surface dyslexia,* where patients can read words with regular spellings but regularise those with irregular. One view is that they suffer from impairment of the lexical (whole word) route but continue to use the sub-lexical (letter-by-letter) one.

☐ *Phonological dyslexia,* where patients can pronounce familiar words, both regular and irregular, but are incapable of suggesting pronunciations for non-words. This suggests an intact lexical route but an impaired sub-lexical one.

☐ *Deep dyslexia,* where there is disruption not just to the processing of form but also to the processing of meaning. Like phonological dyslexics, deep dyslexics find non-words impossible to read aloud. But they also make semantic errors where the word produced is different in form from the target but similar in meaning (APE read as *monkey,* ARTIST read as *picture).* They substitute function words (HIS read as *in)* and suffixes (BUILDER read as *building).* They also have a greater success rate with concrete than with abstract nouns. This condition may provide valuable information about the distribution of information in the lexicon. On the other hand, it may represent a loss of reading processes from the left hemisphere and their transfer to the right, which is less adapted to language processing.

☐ *Non-semantic reading,* where the processing of meaning seems to be affected but not that of form. A patient can read aloud words and non-words but has difficulty in attaching meanings to them.

See also: **Aphasia, Disorder, Dysgraphia: acquired, Dyslexia: developmental**

Further reading: Caplan (1996); Ellis (1993); Harley (2001); Harris and Coltheart (1986)

DYSLEXIA: DEVELOPMENTAL

Delayed acquisition of reading skills and/or the adoption of reading processes which deviate markedly from those that are generally observed in children.

The first stage of learning to read, based purely on sight-reading, does not appear to be critical. In the second, children use parts of words to form matches (often inaccurate) with known written forms. There is evidence that some dyslexics may not achieve this kind of analytic processing. At the third stage, phonics begins to play a part: the child establishes a set of **grapheme-phoneme correspondence rules** which enable it to deconstruct written words into sounds. Many dyslexics appear to experience problems at this point, which result in delay or deviance in their reading. An important indication is whether, at the age of about 8, the child is able to transcribe non-words. Reading difficulties of this type are characterised as *phonological dyslexia.*

The final stage, especially important for orthographies like English which are not transparent, involves the ability to achieve whole-word matches, and possibly the associated ability to trace analogies between word rimes (LEAD (n.) with HEAD; LEAD (v.) with BEAD). Here, dyslexics may experience problems with spellings that permit of two interpretations (e.g. PINT/MINT) and with homophones such as SAIL/SALE. This type is sometimes termed *surface dyslexia*.

Developmental dyslexia varies enormously between individuals. Some show strong signs of a phonological impairment, some of a surface impairment; but most cases represent a combination of both. Clear cases of the semantic errors which characterise *acquired deep dyslexia* are not common.

One research approach is to compare the performance of dyslexic children with that of children of a similar reading age. Dyslexics tend to perform less well on phonological tasks, naming tasks and tasks involving working memory.

Another method is to treat reading as a set of sub-skills and to analyse a child's performance in terms of which sub-skills form part of its reading repertoire and which are absent. There have also been attempts to trace connections between dyslexia and other cognitive processes related to language. Links are sought with poor higher-level comprehension and short phonological and visual memory. Some phonological dyslexics may have problems with the rapid processing of speech sounds; it has been suggested that this may lead to difficulty in sequencing the sounds they hear.

There may be a genetic factor in developmental dyslexia. The children of parents with reading problems are more likely to experience problems themselves; and there are recorded cases of similar types of dyslexia in twins but not in other family members. Word-level problems (SAIL/SALE) do not appear to be inherited, whereas difficulties with phonological processing (e.g. the ability to read non-words) may be.

Recent neurological evidence supports a view that developmental dyslexia may be partly attributable to differences in brain configuration. In non-dyslexics, an area of the brain known as the *planum temporale* tends to be larger in the left (language-associated) hemisphere than the right. However, in many dyslexics the two appear to be the same size. There have also been suggestions that some dyslexics manifest a larger right-hemisphere, indicating a bias towards higher-level language processing rather than decoding. Dyslexia appears to be more common in left-handers, who sometimes manifest an unusual right brain *lateralisation* for language.

See also: **Disorder, Dysgraphia: developmental, Dyslexia: acquired**

Further reading: Ellis (1993); Harris and Coltheart (1986); Miles (1993)

DYSPHASIA

Delayed acquisition of speech and/or the manifestation of speech which deviates markedly from generally observed patterns. For developmental dysphasia, see **specific language impairment**; for acquired dysphasia, see **aphasia**.

ECHOLALIA

Repeating an utterance immediately after it has occurred, without understanding and sometimes with the intonation pattern preserved. A common feature of early language acquisition and of **autism**.

EFFECT

The impact of a given factor upon a psychological process. For example, if subjects are asked to recall words from a list, there will usually be **position effects**, where words are remembered better when they occur at the beginning of the list and at the end. A number of important **lexical effects** feature in studies of vocabulary retrieval.

ELABORATION

Interpreting incoming information in terms of knowledge of the world. This is part of the process of building a **mental representation** in comprehension and has been shown to support recall of the information. Many more subjects recalled the adjective *fat* when it occurred with a relevant elaboration, *The fat man read the sign warning about thin ice*, than when it occurred with an irrelevant one, *The fat man read the sign that was two feet high*.

See also: **Mental representation**

Further reading: Stein and Bransford (1979)

EMBEDDED PROCESSES MODEL

A model of **working memory** (Cowan, 1999: 62–6) which treats it as an integral part of **long-term memory** (LTM). It envisages a vast LTM containing permanently stored information, of which a small part may, at any given moment, be *activated*. Within this area, a smaller part forms the current *focus of attention*. Stored information needs to be activated before it can be focused on.

In this model, activation is limited by *time*, and decays after a short period. The ability to focus attention on part of the activated material is limited by *capacity*: there are restrictions on how much information can be focused on at any one time.

See also: **Activation, Attention, Working memory**

EMPIRICISM

A view that all knowledge is acquired through experience. In a language-acquisition context, a view that an infant acquires language chiefly through exposure to the speech of those about it.

The origin of knowledge has been a recurrent topic in philosophy. Plato enunciated a view (*Plato's problem*) that a child could not possibly, in the short time available to it, acquire the range of knowledge that an adult commands. The issue was the cause of much debate in the eighteenth century. Continental philosophers such as Descartes and Kant adopted a *nativist* view that some knowledge must be present at birth; whereas British philosophers, such as Locke, Hume and Mill, took the empiricist or *rationalist* view that knowledge is acquired through the action of the mind upon the environment.

Empiricist approaches to language acquisition maintain that the speech to which the child is exposed (**child directed speech** plus ambient adult speech) provides linguistic information of sufficient quality and quantity to support acquisition. An assumption of this kind underlies:

- **behaviourism**: a view of language as a set of habits acquired when the child imitates the carer and is rewarded;
- **connectionism**: a view that the infant receives sufficient evidence to support a learning process in which connections are established between certain words and certain concepts and are strengthened by further exposure;
- **social-interactionism**: the view that language is the outcome of

the child's need to relate socially to those about it and/or the child's need to achieve certain pragmatic functions.

See also: **Behaviourism, Connectionism, Functionalism, Social-interactionism**

EVENT-RELATED POTENTIAL (ERP)

A small change in the level of electrical activity in the brain, in response to a stimulus such as hearing or seeing a word. The electrical activity is monitored by means of electrodes attached to the scalp and the change is identified against a baseline level of activity.

The peaks of an ERP are characterised in terms of their polarity (positive or negative voltage) and in terms of how many milliseconds intervene between stimulus and effect. Especially studied has been the N400, a negative peak which occurs 400 milliseconds after the subject reaches a semantically anomalous point in a text (example: *The cats won't bake the food that Mary leaves them*). It is entirely distinct from the P600, a positive peak 600 milliseconds after a syntactic anomaly (example: *The cats won't eating the food that Mary leaves them*). Where a sentence contains both semantic and syntactic anomalies, both ERPs are observed. The finding has suggested to researchers that semantic and syntactic processing are independent of each other.

See also: **Brain imaging**

EVOLUTION OF LANGUAGE

Attempts to date the emergence of language have linked it to various types of archaeological find: evidence of abrupt technological change which suggests the ability to transmit information by speech; evidence of cultural artefacts which show a degree of societal interaction; or evidence of human remains which show physiological features indicative of an ability to produce speech.

There are three distinct views of how language evolved:

☐ *Social*. Language arose through increased socialisation in early settled communities and the need for a communication system to support hunting and farming. Variations on this theme can be found in two recent social-psychological theories. The '*gossip*' view suggests that language developed in response to the need to extend grooming behaviour to settled groups of up to 150 people. The '*Machiavellian intelligence*' view holds that language became an evolutionary necessity because it enabled human beings to manipulate others within and outside their communities.

□ *Physiological.* The human articulators appear to be specially adapted to language; it is argued that language could not pre-date their emergence in their present form. There have been studies of the flexibility of the human tongue, jaw and soft palate and of the complex muscular co-ordination involved in using them for speech. An important factor is the low larynx of the adult human, which permits the production of the common vowel sounds [iː], [uː] and [ɑː], and allows nasalisation to become optional. This contrasts with a high larynx just below the nasal passage in other primates, new-born infants and Neanderthals. The low larynx comes at some cost since it exposes the human being to the danger of food entering the air passage; it thus seems more likely to be the outcome of linguistic evolution than an adaptive response to normal survival needs.

□ *Neurological.* A lay view holds that human beings are able to master the complexities of language because they have developed a higher intelligence or a larger brain. The 'intelligence' argument would indicate the likelihood of 'simple' languages spoken by less intelligent species; yet none has been found. The 'brain size' argument is factually incorrect. It has therefore been suggested that what marks out human beings is not brain size or density of connections, but the fact that, during childhood, increases in body size slow down whereas increases in brain size do not. *Neoteny*, the extended childhood of the human, supports not only brain growth but the development of human cognition and human language.

The question remains of whether certain parts of the brain have evolved in a way that has enabled the invention of language and possibly its genetic transmission. Attempts to locate a physical centre for language have not been successful. The left hemisphere is believed to control many of the basic processes associated with speech, and is usually larger than the right. But similar large left hemispheres have also been found in birds.

Language evolution poses a problem for the *nativist* idea of a genetically transmitted mechanism which equips an infant to learn language. Nativist accounts tend to focus upon *ontogeny* (acquisition by the individual) rather than *phylogeny* (the transmission of the gene between generations) – begging the question of how humans came to evolve this language-specific device in the first place. Some nativists (including Chomsky) argue that the coincidence of a number of social and evolutionary factors led to a sudden (or *catastrophic*) emergence of the genetically transmitted language component. Other commentators suggest that language emerged as a by-product of other fully fledged cognitive processes: this is termed the '*spandrel*' view, after an analogy with architectural splendours which arise incidentally.

An alternative account has language developing gradually over a period of time. However, for the brain to shape itself to language over hundreds of generations, the underlying forms of the language would have to remain constant. As the history of English shows, a language changes enormously over only 1000 years (or 30 generations).

Hence a further theory that language evolved to take advantage of the nature of human cognition rather than vice versa. Evidence is found in the way language appears to exploit perceptual biases in human faculties. **Colour systems** across languages take advantage of universal visual focal points, while **categorical perception** appears to map on to fine acoustic distinctions to which the mammalian ear is particularly sensitive.

Language, it is said, has been shaped over many generations into a system which reflects the way human thought is structured. Supporters of this view generally reject the notion of a self-contained language faculty. They represent language as opportunistic – taking advantage of generalised operations of the brain. This kind of cognitive development may have been supported by a process of *co-evolution*. As language has evolved, so, in conjunction with it but more slowly, have the organs associated with speech and the synaptic connections within the human brain which transmit linguistic information.

Yet another approach (Donald, 1991) proposes that the current human mind retains layers of earlier and more primitive uses of language and of cognition. They are said to remain in evidence in the stages which the infant goes through in acquiring a language.

See also: **Animal communication, Species specificity**

Further reading: Aitchison (1996); Deacon (1997); Hurford *et al.* (1998); Lieberman (1998)

EXEMPLAR MODELS (also INSTANCE MODELS)

Models which assume that language is stored in the mind in the form not of rules or prototypes but of sets of examples. The examples constitute a record of the speaker's many encounters with a particular syntactic structure, item of vocabulary or phonological feature. From them, the speaker can extrapolate certain central tendencies or shared features; but they can also make allowance for a range of variants.

Exemplar models assume that human beings possess a vast memory capacity for linguistic data, which enables hundreds of individual tokens of a particular linguistic feature to be stored and recalled. This remains a large assumption, but proponents argue that it is the only way of accounting satisfactorily for our capacity to deal with individual variation in language. As evidence, they cite our ability not only to recall the content of a message but also to recognise the voice of the speaker if we hear it again. Exemplar models can account for problematic phenomena such as the recognition of vowels within vowel space, the **phonological representation** of words, speaker **normalisation** and the storage of local exceptions alongside global syntactic principles.

The theory provides for the storage of meaning as well as form. For example, Hintzman's *multiple-trace model* (1986) attempts to account for the way in which we form lexical categories. It postulates that every time a child encounters an exemplar of a word such as DOG, the exemplar leaves a trace. From the accumulating set of traces, the child is able to identify certain central characteristics shared by all members of the category – but also to accept that certain deviations from these core values still form part of its experience of the concept DOG.

Sometimes cited in support of exemplar models is the finding that high-frequency irregular syntactic forms tend to resist change over time while low-frequency ones are subject to regularisation. The argument goes that it is not possible for a user to gauge the frequency of a form unless individual tokens of it are stored.

Exemplar models accord well with connectionist approaches, and with the belief (see **learning theory**) that a first language can be acquired through multiple trial-and-error encounters.

See also: **Connectionism**

Further reading: Bybee (2001: Chaps 1–2); Harley (2001: 288–93)

EXPERT SYSTEMS

Computer programs which simulate human problem-solving, reasoning and decision-making processes within a particular domain (e.g. they aim to represent the expertise of a doctor or a chess player). The knowledge of the system is often represented in the form of *production rules*, which specify how to respond to a particular stimulus.

EXPERTISE

The achievement of a high level of automaticity and accuracy in solving a problem. A current view has it that the development of expertise in general areas such as driving a car, opening a door or reading is no different from the development of expertise in specialised domains such as playing chess or computer programming. Theories of expertise have been applied to the acquisition of linguistic skills such as reading and writing as well as to second language learning. Especially cited in this connection have been Anderson's **ACT** models.

There are said to be three stages in the development of expertise:

☐ a *cognitive stage,* where information is acquired, usually as *declarative knowledge* (knowledge *that*). The information may take the form of a set of sub-goals. Carried out in sequence, they enable a larger goal to be achieved. The information may need to be committed to memory; and the process can be supported by **rehearsal** (including verbal rehearsal of the individual stages). Examples: Somebody using a new phone number might repeat it aloud; a child learning to write might say the letters as it forms them. At this stage, the target process is highly **controlled**, and makes considerable demands upon **working memory** capacity.

☐ an *associative stage,* where errors are detected and eliminated and the overall process is simplified. Declarative knowledge gradually becomes *proceduralised*: i.e. rule-based knowledge develops into a procedure for carrying out the operation (knowledge *how*). This happens as stages in the process are omitted or combined and connections between the stages become strengthened by practice. Example: the phone user *chunks* digits into sequences of three or four; the child writes a letter with one sweep of the pen. The procedure which develops is faster and more automatic than working through the steps in the declarative routine; though declarative knowledge may still remain available.

☐ an *autonomous stage,* where the procedures become increasingly automatic, demanding less working memory capacity. At this stage, the learner no longer needs to verbalise the process; indeed, the original declarative information may no longer be reportable. Alternatively, it may be retained to support the procedure in case of failure. Example: the phone number user dials the number without thinking about the individual digits; the child employs a set of automatic wrist and finger movements for each letter.

Emergent experts learn to recognise familiar sub-sequences of steps which recur in different contexts. Example: young readers learn to notice analogous spellings. Through using their skill, they develop a range of procedures which enables them to deal rapidly with almost any problem that arises. Many of these problems would require a conscious effort at solution by a *novice*. Experts also learn to *self-monitor*: they become capable of judging their success or failure in a particular activity and of taking remedial action if necessary (e.g. young readers learn to judge the extent to which they have achieved understanding).

The basic principle is thus that expertise involves automatic processing, with the result that the expert expends less cognitive effort than the novice and achieves goals more quickly. It has been suggested that there may be an exception to this in writing, where (at least in higher-level processes) greater skill seems to require greater cognitive effort in terms of conscious planning and revision.

Studies of many types of skill acquisition have shown that performance (especially performance speed) improves as a direct function of practice. If a particular skill ceases to be employed, expertise may decay; however, the beneficial effects of earlier practice will survive to some extent.

The effects of practice have been demonstrated through **brain imaging**. Subjects were asked to produce a verb associated with a noun (example HAMMER → HIT), and activation was observed in several parts of the brain, suggesting a distributed process involving attentional resources. However, after 15 minutes of practice, much of this activation disappeared as automatic processes took over.

See also: **ACT, Automaticity, Chunking, Knowledge, Problem-solving, Working memory**

Further reading: Anderson (1990); Posner and Raichle (1994)

EYE-MIND HYPOTHESIS

The view that, in reading, the interpretation of each word encountered is immediate and takes place while the word is being *fixated*. There is thus minimal delay between fixation and cognitive processing. The hypothesis is supported by evidence of **eye movements**, showing that (for example) infrequent words are fixated for longer than frequent ones.

EYE MOVEMENTS

The way in which the eyes cross the page during reading. Reading involves a series of rapid shifts along the line of print or writing (known as *saccades*), followed by periods when the eye rests upon a point in the text. A saccade typically lasts from 20 to 30 milliseconds while a *fixation* can last from 150 to 500 milliseconds and sometimes longer. Saccades cover no more than about 7–9 characters in reading English – fewer in logographic writing systems and alphabetic systems like Arabic which do not represent vowels. This means that almost every word is fixated. Indeed, processing a long word may sometimes involve two fixations. It is therefore useful to distinguish the duration of the *first fixation* of a word from the overall *gaze duration* of the word (all fixations).

It was once believed that reading efficiency improved if saccades were extended; however, modern methods of tracking eye movements have suggested that good readers do not use fewer fixations than poor ones. What marks out less-skilled reading (and reading in the early stages of acquiring a second language) is a much higher level of *regression*, where the reader makes a backwards saccade to check information or understanding. For an average reader, regressions only account for about 10–15 per cent of saccades.

In a skilled reader, forward saccades are mainly driven by lower-level processes (i.e. the eye moves on as soon as the currently fixated word is decoded) while regressive saccades usually indicate higher-level processing (checking comprehension, integrating incoming information, making anaphoric links). Evidence does not support the much-aired theory that a skilled reader is able to guess ahead and thus substantially reduce the amount of decoding that is necessary. A highly constraining context only leads to a reduction of about 10 per cent in fixation duration.

The reading process varies considerably from text to text. A reader adjusts length of saccade and duration of fixation to reflect the propositional density of the text, the text genre and the type of reading being undertaken. Other factors which determine how long a fixation lasts include the length, frequency and potential ambiguity of the word that is being fixated. Words at the beginning of a line tend to be fixated for longer than words that occur later. Fixation time and amount of regression increase markedly when there is a need to perform an *antecedent search* (e.g. where there is a pronoun which refers back). There is also an increase in fixation time at clause boundaries, presumably reflecting the need to construct a syntactic representation (see **wrap up effects**).

A fixation usually falls on the early part of a word and encompasses a *perceptual span* of about 31 characters or 15 to either side of the fixation point. Focus is sharpest in the centre of the visual field, the *fovea*, which provides the fine detail which enables the fixated word to be decoded. However, it appears that characters beyond the foveal area, and especially to the right of it, are also processed at a low level of attention, providing a representation which may involve little more than letter shape and sequence and possibly the length of the next word. This *parafoveal preview* enables the reader to anticipate certain general features of the next fixation. The effect seems to be to speed up processing – hence the longer fixation times when a new line of text is begun and no pre-processing is possible. Parafoveal preview supports *word skipping* when a short, frequent or highly predictable word lies ahead, and warns of the need for a longer saccade when a long word is in the offing. (Major source: Rayner and Pollatsek, 1989.)

See also: **Reading: decoding**

Further reading: Just and Carpenter (1987: Chap. 2); Rayner and Pollatsek (1989: Chap. 4)

FAMILY RESEMBLANCE

An analogy used by Wittgenstein (1958: 66) in discussing the word GAME whose range includes chess, football, gambling and Hide and Seek. Languages group real–world phenomena into lexical categories according to certain traits which they have in common; any given member of the category is likely to share some of the traits of another member but not necessarily all.

See also: **Prototype Theory**

FIELD DEPENDENCY

A theory which accounts for apparent differences in the way in which individuals perceive visual (and, by extension, auditory) material. In a *field-dependent* (FD) mode, perception is dominated by the way in which a visual field is organised overall; individual parts of the field are seen as 'fused'. In a *field-independent* (FI) mode, the parts are perceived distinctly from the overall shape. Parallels to this distinction have been found in language acquisition. Some infants appear to adopt a field-independent *analytic* approach, building their utterances word by word; while others adopt a more field-dependent *holistic* approach, producing chunks of language. In second language acquisition, attempts have been made to distinguish the performance of FI-inclined learners from that of FD-inclined. Responses have been measured to different types of test and types of instruction; degree of interaction with native speakers has also been compared. The results have been inconclusive.

FIGURATIVE LANGUAGE

The main issue is how a listener or reader recognises a statement as figurative rather than literal and processes it accordingly. In principle, the process of identifying figurative language can operate lexically in terms of *selection restrictions* or semantically in terms of failure to conform to a real-world state-of-affairs. Thus, *The letter-box disliked the postman* could be rejected as a factual statement either because the verb LIKE requires an animate subject or because real-world experience tells us that letter-boxes do not have feelings.

However, this type of analysis does not entirely explain:

a. How to distinguish a literal comparison such as *Copper is like tin*, from a figurative simile such as *Sermons are like sleeping pills*.
b. How to recognise the metaphorical intention of a sentence such as *No man is an island*, when the sentence is also literally true.

There are three major solutions:

□ *Incoherence models,* where the listener/reader is assumed to derive a literal interpretation of a sentence, assess its likelihood, then opt for a non-literal meaning if a literal one seems improbable. Against this view, studies of reading have shown no difference in the time taken to process literal and metaphorical interpretations of sentences – provided the supporting context is sufficiently clear. Research has also shown that readers are slower to reject a sentence as literally false when it has a potential metaphorical interpretation than when it has none. The conclusion is that they are unable to block out a metaphorical interpretation, even when they are required simply to make a truth value judgement.

☐ *Comparison models,* where the reader or listener balances the attributes of two items. One way of distinguishing the sentences in a. is that the literal one is reversible but the figurative one is not. The reason is that there is a *salience imbalance* in the second sentence which makes the attributes of SERMONS in subject position less important than that of SLEEPING PILLS in complement position.

☐ *Interaction models,* in which the *vehicle* of the metaphor illuminates the *topic,* which then illuminates the vehicle. Thus, in *Man is a wolf,* *wolf* serves to point up the animal nature of MAN, while *man* serves to anthropomorphise WOLF.

An unresolved issue in these approaches is the way in which comprehenders decide which attributes form the basis of the figurative relationship. The attributes selected may be multiple, and not expressible in a single literal word, as with *Mary's been a rock.* Or they may involve considerable selectivity similar to that involved in **instantiation**. The sentence *His face was a tomato.* potentially draws upon softness, roundness and redness; without a context, the processor has to favour the attribute most likely to be employed in a metaphorical situation. (Major source: Cacciari and Glucksberg, 1994.)

See also: **Instantiation, Metaphor**

Further reading: Cacciari and Glucksberg (1994)

FILTER$_1$

A mechanism which enables the listener to focus **attention** upon one part of the input. Different models disagree on whether the filtering process occurs early, with the system only capable of processing a single stimulus at a time; or later, with the filter choosing between competing information after it has been processed.

FILTER$_2$

A means of altering the frequency range of a recorded speech signal before it is converted into sound by a headphone or loudspeaker. A *high-pass filter* suppresses frequency components above a certain frequency level; while a *low-pass filter* suppresses those below a certain frequency. A *band-pass filter* conserves frequency components between two frequency levels but erases them above and below.

FLUENCY

The ability to speak a first or foreign language at a natural rate, with appropriate prosody and without disruptive hesitation patterns. The impression of fluency derives partly from predictably placed planning pauses and from a lack of pausing within syntactic or intonational units. Fluency is partly achieved by composing recurrent sequences into *memorised chunks* which can be produced ready-formed, thus reducing the burden of planning utterances. Foreign language learners who have been resident in target-language environments give an impression of increased fluency which derives from reduced pausing and greater average *length of run* (number of syllables between each pause). Their rate of articulation does not increase markedly, however.

See also: **Accuracy, Chunking, Pausing, Speaking rate**

Further reading: Levelt (1989); Pawley and Syder (1983); Towell and Hawkins (1994: Chap. 12)

FOCUS (also FOREGROUNDING)

An account of the way in which some items of information in a text are easier to retrieve or recall than others. For example, readers appear to accord different levels of attention to main characters in a novel than to subsidiary ones. The set of currently focused items appears to be revised when an episode in a narrative comes to an end. Characters specifically associated with the episode become defocused, and references to them are more difficult to resolve.

A distinction can also be made between items in *explicit focus*, which have been mentioned in a text and foregrounded by the reader, and items in *implicit focus*, which may not have been specifically mentioned but are 'givens' associated with those that have been. If a house is in explicit focus, its constituent parts (rooms, walls, roof) are in implicit focus. This explains how readers make bridging **inferences** which link sentences such as: *I looked around the house. The kitchen was very spacious.*

Focus is an important concept in accounting for anaphor resolution, especially in listening. A reader can, if necessary, look back at an earlier part of the text to resolve a problematic anaphor (*she, it, the incident I mentioned earlier*). That option is not open to a listener. Accurate listening appears to be heavily dependent upon the extent to which an individual carries forward a set of items and concepts which are foregrounded in the current discourse.

See also: **Inference, Meaning construction**

FOREIGNER TALK

A register sometimes employed by native speakers when addressing non-native ones. The term relates to linguistic features of the register; while *foreigner discourse* (FD) includes wider characteristics such as the types of interaction between native and non-native speakers.

In English, foreigner talk (FT) is characterised phonologically by:

- slower speech rate;
- greater pausing;
- greater segmentation of words;
- increased stress marking;
- more careful articulation;
- reduced assimilation.

Lexis is usually simplified, relying on high-frequency items and avoiding idiom and slang. Syntax uses a limited range of basic structures and sometimes omits functors and inflections. There is a preference for transparent forms (e.g. full rather than contracted forms), for shorter utterances and for co-ordination rather than subordination. The standard SVO word order is adhered to quite strictly, though there may be some fronting of the current topic of conversation.

FT is also characterised by a low level of information per sentence and by a high level of **redundancy**, including repetition and rephrasing. It may employ syntactic forms which are incorrect (*you no like?*).

Attempts have been made to establish which features of FT most assist understanding. It has been suggested that slower delivery has more impact upon understanding than does linguistic modification. Repetition and rephrasing are particularly effective.

Foreigner talk appears to exist in most cultures. It is of special interest to psycholinguists because it is relatively consistent across individual speakers of a given language. It is employed by children, even at a relatively young age; and it has many features in common with **child directed speech** (CDS) and with pidgin languages. Hence a theory that human beings may possess universal simplification strategies as part of their linguistic competence. Alternatively, CDS and FT may show residual traces of the **Universal Grammar** which enabled us to acquire our first language. Or it may be that we regress to our own experience of learning our first language and thus identify the features which were most salient to us at the time.

Opposed to these hypotheses are interactional accounts, which suggest that FT and FD chiefly arise from the way in which a speaker accommodates to the language of their interlocutor. There is certainly evidence of **accommodation** at word and phrase level, with native-speakers echoing incorrect forms used by non-natives. In addition, the extent to which FT deviates from normal adult speech is partly determined by the speaker's assessment of the level of linguistic knowledge of the non-native listener (NNL), the speaker's previous experience of such interactions and the extent to which the speaker empathises with the NNL. Recent work in FD has particularly concerned itself with the *negotiation of meaning* that takes place when interlocutors do not share the same native language; and with the kinds of *repair strategy* that are employed when communication breaks down.

See also: **Child Directed Speech, Input**

Further reading: Ellis (1985); Wesche (1994)

FORMANT

A concentration of acoustic energy within a narrow frequency band in the speech signal. The vocal tract acts as a resonator: it responds to the vibration of air from the lungs at particular frequencies, depending upon its current shape. This creates bands of intensity in the sound that is produced, which show up as dark bars on a *spectrogram*.

Three of these formants, numbered by frequency as F_1 (the lowest), F_2 and F_3, are sufficient to distinguish a vowel. For a pure '*steady-state*' vowel, they appear on a spectrogram as parallel horizontal bars. A front vowel is indicated by a wide gap between F_1 and F_2 while a back vowel is indicated by a narrow one.

Consonants are distinguished by a *formant transition* from the obstruction used to form the consonant to the steady position which marks the succeeding vowel. There is usually sufficient information in F_2 to distinguish the consonant. However, a problem for research into speech perception is that the F_2 formant transition of a given consonant varies considerably according to the vowel that follows. (See Figure F1.)

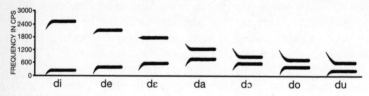

Figure F1   Simplified spectrographic pattern of the sequences [d] + vowel, showing marked differences in the second (upper) formant of [d]

See also: **Speech perception: phoneme variation**

Further reading: Ball and Rahilly (1999); Denes and Pinson (1993); Pickett (1999)

FORMULAIC

Descriptive of a string of words which is produced as an unanalysed chunk. Some commentators use the term principally for sequences which have a phatic or pragmatic function (*Know what I mean?*, *How do you do?*). Others extend it to all strings that are produced already assembled (*must have done*) or have been acquired by first and second language learners as if they were single lexical items.

See also: **Analysis, Chunking**

FOSSILISATION

Persistence by a second language learner in producing an incorrect syntactic form despite continuing exposure to correct forms. Or a state in which the overall linguistic and communicative competence of a language learner reaches a *learning plateau* and fails to progress – sometimes because the learner is no longer motivated, sometimes because he/she is conscious of having achieved an acceptable level of comprehensibility.

FREQUENCY₁ (FREQUENCY OF OCCURRENCE)

How regularly a lexical item occurs throughout a whole corpus or within a given spoken or written text. It is sometimes necessary to specify whether one is referring to the frequency of a word form (e.g. RIGHT in both its senses) or that of a lexical item.

Frequency effects are well attested in **lexical access**. There is a close correlation between the frequency of a word in connected speech and how quickly it is recognised. Frequency thus plays an important part in models of lexical access which involve **competition** between words. More frequent words are represented as more easily activated.

See also: **Lexical effect, Neighbourhood, Probability**

FREQUENCY₂

The number of complete cycles achieved by a sound wave in a second. If a plucked violin string vibrates 400 times a second, the frequency of the sound it emits is measured as 400 cycles per second or 400 Hertz (Hz). If the string is tightened, it will vibrate more rapidly, and its frequency will increase. The result is that the *pitch* of the sound (its frequency as perceived by a listener) will also rise. However, there is not a simple relationship between pitch and frequency: the ear does not judge a sound of 1000 Hz to be twice as high as one of 500 Hz.

The range of frequencies handled by the human ear goes from about 250 to 10,000 Hz. Most human conversation occupies a range of between 250 and 8000 Hz. But the *frequency band* may be narrowed in certain forms of speech transmission (e.g. the telephone), with the result that some of the cues to a particular phoneme may be missing. Especially affected is /s/.

Speech has a *fundamental frequency* which derives from the tension and speed of vibration of the vocal folds. Other cycles of the sound wave are multiples of this base value. Fundamental frequency or F_0 is an important measure in that it serves as a base value for listeners, enabling them to detect pitch movements, which, in English, might mark sentence stress or intonation. Average F_0 values vary from voice to voice. Male speakers often have thicker vocal folds than female, so a typical F_0 for a man is lower (between 100 and 160 Hz) than that for a woman (200 Hz and above).

See also: **Formant, Intelligibility, Speech signal**

Further reading: Ball and Rahilly (1999); Denes and Pinson (1993); Gimson (1994); Pickett (1999)

FUNCTION WORD PROCESSING

There is evidence that function words are processed differently from those bearing lexical meaning, which leads some commentators to conclude that the two sets of items may be stored separately.

There are many examples of **Slips of the Tongue** where content words exchange places but function words are correctly positioned (*rules of word formation* → *words of rule formation*). This suggests that semantic and syntactic assembly are two distinct processes. Further evidence comes from studies of patients who have suffered damage to *Broca's area* in the brain. Their lexicon remains relatively intact, but access to grammar (word order, inflection and function words) is often impaired. This may be because the ability to assemble syntactic structure has been affected; or it may be that the patient's attentional capacity has diminished so that they restrict themselves to the words which are most semantically and phonologically salient, namely the lexical items. Some patients manage to retrieve function words if they are given time to do so.

A third possibility is that these aphasics have lost access to the set of 'closed class' items, but not to the general lexicon. This would suggest that the two categories are stored separately and accessed differently. Early support for the 'double storage' view came from a study which suggested that, while the recognition of lexical words is affected by their frequency, that of function words is not. The conclusion was that there was a separate 'frequency free' processing route for functors. The finding has since been challenged, and more recent results suggest that, even if it holds for reading, it does not apply in listening.

However, recent evidence from **brain imaging** appears to confirm that function words are stored and processed separately. They seem to be more localised than lexical words and thus more available for rapid processing. It is also suggestive that language-acquiring infants produce function words relatively late, despite their high frequency. This may indicate that a different retrieval process needs to be established.

Processing a lexical word involves two operations: matching a string of sounds against a mental store of spoken words and accessing meaning. By contrast, processing a function word need only involve the first. Some models of speech recognition assume that strong syllables in the speech stream trigger full lexical access (form and meaning) while weak syllables are simply *pattern-matched* against a separate 'closed class' store. In this way, the listener exploits an association in English between weak stress and function words.

Further findings in this area have been produced by studies of **verbatim recall** which show that content words are remembered more accurately than functors. This may indicate that it is functors which feed first into the construction of a **mental representation**, and are thus more quickly lost to recall. Or it may suggest that function words are processed at a lower level of attention: they are less **informative** because they are more frequent. A recent suggestion has been that we do not store language input in verbatim form at all. If we have to report a speaker's exact words, we do so by identifying words in our lexicon which have been recently activated. This is possible with lexical words but not with functors, which have not been subject to the same activation process.

See also: **Aphasia, Lexical access, Lexical segmentation, Lexical storage, Verbatim recall**

Further reading: Caplan (1992: 329–50); Cutler (1989); Grosjean and Gee (1987); Potter and Lombardi (1990); Shillcock and Bard (1993)

FUNCTIONAL LOAD

The importance of a phoneme within a language's phonological system, as measured by the number of minimal pair oppositions in which it appears. For example, /ð/ is extremely frequent in English, but has a small functional load because it serves to distinguish very few minimal pairs (the exception is its function in *that*, where it marks a contrast with other fricative-initial items such as *sat*, *fat* and *vat*). There is some evidence that the sounds which appear in an infant's early phonological system are those with the greatest functional load. However, this may be because languages tend to assign the highest functional loads to sounds which are easiest to form and thus easiest to acquire.

See also: **Informativeness**

FUNCTIONALISM

A semantic approach to syntax associated with M.A.K. Halliday. Applied to language acquisition, it foregrounds the part played by the child's wish or need to communicate pragmatically. The theory resembles other **social-interactionist** accounts by placing importance on the interaction, both verbal and gestural, between carer and child and on the 'exchange of meanings' to which it gives rise. Much of the evidence supporting the theory draws upon Halliday's observations of the early language of his son, Nigel.

When an infant is between 9 and 15 months, it shows signs of constructing *proto-words* from its babble. It reserves certain sounds or sequences of sounds for particular purposes: examples would be a child consistently using [nã] when it wanted something and [ɳɳ] for a taste it enjoyed.

The child's early words are said to represent four general functions:

- *instrumental* ('I want')
- *interactional* ('me and you')
- *regulatory* ('Do as I tell you')
- *personal* ('Here I am')

To these, the child later adds three more:

- *imaginative* ('Let's pretend')
- *informative* ('I have something to tell you')
- *heuristic* ('Tell me why')

In a second phase, there is a gradual increase in the range of meanings which the child learns to express within these functional areas, even if the forms used are not those of adult language. This coincides with what other commentators term the *vocabulary explosion*; Halliday argues that it is a semantic and syntactic explosion as well. The personal and heuristic functions are said to merge into a single *mathetic* function (involving 'learning' through language), while the other five merge into a rudimentary *pragmatic* system (involving 'doing' through language).

See also: **Social-interactionism**

Further reading: Cattell (2000: Chap. 8); Halliday (1975)

FUZZY BOUNDARY

The absence of a sharp demarcation between one lexical concept and another. Originally, the term was applied to **family resemblance** concepts such as GAME, where items within the class have different characterising traits, and no two bear exactly the same characteristics. It was later found that even a simple concept such as CUP has a fuzzy boundary in that there is no clear 'cut-off' point at which observers unanimously agree that the shape of a vessel is not that of a cup but that of a bowl or vase. Fuzzy boundaries are also affected by visual context; thus an object whose shape is between a cup and a bowl is more likely to be described as a bowl when it contains potato than when it contains coffee.

See also: **Prototype Theory**

Further reading: Aitchison (2003); Labov (1973)

GARDEN PATH SENTENCES

Sentences which temporarily mislead the reader or listener when they are being processed *on-line* (word by word). The initial part of the sentence is ambiguous and permits of at least two possible endings. One of them is strongly indicated by semantic probability: *The lawyer questioned . . .* (*the witness* is more likely than *by the police confessed*); or by syntactic frequency: *The old man . . .* (*retired* is more likely than *the boats*).

Interest lies in establishing:

☐ Whether readers are strongly biased towards the more predictable outcome (raising the question of whether, during processing, they carry multiple possible interpretations of a sentence or prefer a single one).
☐ The impact upon the reader of encountering an unpredictable resolution.
☐ Whether listeners use phonetic and prosodic cues to anticipate the correct syntactic structure before the disambiguation point.

See also: **Ambiguity: syntactic, Prosody, Syntactic parsing**

Further reading: Aitchison (1998)

GATING

A research method (Grosjean, 1980) which involves presenting subjects with ever-increasing slices of recorded text. A sentence is usually divided into regular time-slices of 20–50 milliseconds, which are termed *gates*. After hearing the first, subjects report what they think they have heard. They then hear the first gate again followed by the second (i.e. the first 100 milliseconds of the text) and again report what they hear. This continues to the end of the sentence. Gating experiments have demonstrated that on average a word can be recognised within about a third of a second of its onset. In some cases, that is before the word is complete. The finding would appear to support the notion of a **uniqueness point** as embodied in **Cohort Theory**: i.e. a point during the utterance of a word where no other item fits the evidence and the word is therefore recognised before it is complete. However, gating has also shown that many short words (especially function words) are not recognised until up to three words after they have been heard. Furthermore, subjects often do not report recognising longer words until some time after their uniqueness points.

Experimenters sometimes ask subjects to record confidence ratings for the words they report. They make a distinction between an *isolation point* (how much input is needed before a target word is first mentioned), a *recognition point*, where a confidence level of 80 per cent is reported and (sometimes) a *total acceptance point* where confidence reaches 100 per cent.

While gating has proved a useful research tool, it involves multiple hearings of parts of the utterance and decision-making which occurs after the stimulus. Some commentators have therefore questioned the extent to which it really taps in to **on-line processes**.

See also: **Uniqueness point**

Further reading: Grosjean (1996)

GESTALT THEORY

The Gestalt group of psychologists (early twentieth century) investigated how the mind shapes our perceptions of the world. In particular, they examined how we perceive separate elements (e.g. dots on a page) as falling into groups and patterns when set against a neutral background. They proposed four principles of perceptual organisation: *proximity, similarity, continuation* (forms that continue a straight line rather than going off at a tangent) and *closure* (a preference for complete and unbroken shapes). Gestalt Theory has relevance to letter and word recognition in reading and to the way in which infants impose conceptual categories upon the world around them.

GIVEN/NEW

A distinction between information in an utterance which is treated as already established and information which is introduced for the first time. It provides a rationale for intonation patterns where the tonic accent falls upon new information (*The 17th of June was my BIRTHday*).

There is a preference in many languages for sentence structures which present 'given' information early and 'new' information late. This may reflect the way in which language has evolved so as to support the processing of spoken sentences as they unfold in real time. The listener is given a breathing space in which to construct a preliminary syntactic and semantic interpretation before having to confront a new proposition.

See also: **Syntactic parsing**

Further reading: Brown and Yule (1983)

GOODNESS OF FIT

A categorisation based upon the best available match rather than an exact one. The term is particularly used in **Prototype Theory**, which proposes that the ease with which real-world objects are associated with a lexical category (BIRD, FURNITURE, FRUIT) is determined by the closeness of their match to a central prototype and/or by how many of the characterising features of the category they possess.

The term is also used in theories of phonological representation. The intelligibility of the speech signal is often reduced by, for example, external noise, **Slips of the Tongue** or the unfamiliarity of the speaker's voice. The only way we can explain our ability to match strings of sounds to words in our lexicon is to assume a **probabilistic** system of matching which does not demand a precise match but accepts the best-fitting one.

See also: **Phonological representation, Prototype Theory**

GRAPHEME-PHONEME CORRESPONDENCE (GPC) RULES

Rules which specify the relationship between a written letter and the phoneme which it conventionally represents. In a *dual route* model of reading, a *lexical route* permits the reader to match known words on a 'whole word' basis; but a second (*sub-lexical*) route is also available which draws upon the reader's knowledge of GPC rules. The two routes appear to operate in parallel and the ability to apply GPC rules rapidly has been shown to be a characteristic of a skilled reader. The particular advantage of the sub-lexical route is that it enables the reader to process unknown words. The latter might be words never encountered in visual form, new coinages or proper nouns.

GPC rules have a more limited value with an *opaque* alphabetic system like that of English than with a more transparent one like that of Spanish. Indeed, if the rules were applied on the strict basis of one letter-one sound, up to 50 per cent of English words would be characterised as 'irregular'. In an opaque system, GPC rules are therefore often taken to extend to clusters of letters (including digraphs such as SH- or -EA-). Alternatively, they are regarded as operating in conjunction with *analogy* effects which permit parallels to be drawn between, for example, RIGHT, FIGHT and MIGHT.

A connectionist view suggests that we interpret written words by means of a set of *distributed* representations based upon three-letter clusters: so an interpretation of the sequence HEAT would be the outcome of activation produced by the phoneme values for -HE, HEA, EAT and AT-. Simulations of this process, however, have been restricted to four-letter words.

See also: **Dual route, Reading: decoding, Reading: development**

Further reading: Goswami and Bryant (1990); Oakhill and Garnham (1988); Rayner and Pollatsek (1989)

GRAPHOTACTIC RULES

A specification of which letters can co-occur in the **orthography** of a particular alphabetic language and which cannot. Thus, the sequences GN and PH are graphotactically acceptable in English, but the sequences GV and PW are not. An implicit knowledge of graphotactic rules appears to play a part in reading, assisting in the processing of letter order within words.

HARD-WIRED

Describes an aspect of human cognition which is linked to an innate component of the brain rather than deriving from a learning process. The term comes from computer terminology, which contrasts the hard-wired physical contents of a computer with the software programs that are installed into it.

HEARING

The sensation of sound reaching the ear, and the process of converting it into neural impulses which can be analysed into the component features of speech.

Sound waves are first processed by the *peripheral auditory system*. After reaching the *pinna* (the visible part of the ear), they are channelled into the *ear canal*, which acts as a resonator, amplifying the waves which pass along it. It can provide resonance for a range of frequencies from 500 Hz to 4000 Hz, but is especially sensitive to those between 3000 Hz and 4000 Hz. It is thus well fitted for transmitting the most important information in a speech signal.

The sound reaches the *eardrum*, and sets in vibration three small bones behind it known as the *ossicles*. This has the effect of producing a focus of acoustic energy which is much greater than that at the ear drum. The sound waves pass into the *inner ear* as variations in pressure, and produce movement along the *basilar membrane*. This in turn causes movement in a set of highly sensitive hair cells which rest on the membrane; and the movement is converted into neural impulses by the *auditory nerve*. The nerve consists of a bank of around 28,000 receptor neurons, each finely tuned to a particular frequency.

The brain then decodes the impulses. However, it is not easy for researchers to determine which pieces of the encoded information actually contribute to the identification of a particular speech sound.

See also: **Deafness**

Further reading: Ball and Rahilly (1999: Chaps 10–11)

HIGHER-LEVEL PROCESSING

Language processing which involves the building of a *meaning representation*, and may involve the use of contextual information such as world knowledge.

See also: **Level of representation, Listening: higher-level processes, Meaning construction, Reading: higher-level processes, Top-down processing**

HYPOTHESIS TESTING

A theory that human cognition is constructed in a way that favours the active testing of hypotheses about the defining features of a concept. It explains how natural term concepts such as BIRD are established by identifying their defining features on a trial-and-error basis; and it explains the continuous process of checking and **restructuring** which is said to underlie first and second language acquisition. If feedback is positive, the hypothesis is retained; if negative, it is rejected or revised. This is referred to as the *win-stay lose-shift* assumption.

See also: **Problem-solving**

I-LANGUAGE

Internalised language. According to Chomsky, traditional approaches to grammar focus on *E-language* (externalised language). They base their conclusions on samples of language that have been 'understood independently of the properties of the mind' (1986: 20). By contrast, studies of I-language treat language as a product of the human mind and ask what type of knowledge it is that enables the individual language user to construct grammatically correct sentences.

See also: **Chomskyan theory**

IMAGEABILITY

The extent to which it is possible to visualise the entity to which a word (especially a noun) refers. Imageable words are said to be easier to learn and recall, whether in a first or a second language; abstract words are slower to be acquired.

IMMEDIACY OF INTERPRETATION

The view that a reader attempts to interpret each word in a text immediately it is encountered rather than using a 'wait-and-see' strategy. An associated **eye-mind hypothesis** asserts that this interpretation takes place at the moment the reader's eye fixates the word. There is thus minimal delay between what is fixated and what becomes available for cognitive processing. Evidence supporting this position indicates that the time taken to identify a word is strongly influenced by the characteristics of the word such as its length, but not by those of the preceding word. There are two benefits to immediate interpretation: it reduces memory load and it enables the reader to detect misperceptions at the time they occur.

See also: **Eye-mind hypothesis, On-line process**

Further reading: Just and Carpenter (1987: Chap. 2)

IMPLICIT LEARNING

The acquisition of information without an awareness on the learner's part that learning has occurred; the reverse of *explicit learning*. Not to be confused with **incidental learning**, where information or skills are acquired which were not part of the original learning intention or task.

It has been argued that implicit learning may play a part in second language acquisition. Experiments have been conducted with *artificial grammars* consisting of strings of letters whose order and co-occurrence is determined by specific rules. After extended exposure to these letter strings, subjects have proved capable, at a level higher than chance, of distinguishing strings which are 'grammatical' (permissible) from those which are not. However, this result may be attributable to an 'analogy' effect, where subjects learn to recognise certain recurrent patterns rather than necessarily accessing the rules which underlie them. Questions have also been raised as to whether the acquisition of a 'grammar' of this kind can be said to model the acquisition of normal grammatical rules. The grammar can be said to possess 'phrase structure' but it is not meaningful or contextualised in the way that natural language data is; nor is there any speaker-listener interaction to support acquisition.

See also: **Incidental learning**

Further reading: Ellis (1994)

INCIDENTAL LEARNING

The acquisition of information or skills which are not part of the original learning intention or task; the reverse of *intentional* learning. Particularly applied to the way in which a child or foreign language learner might acquire new items of vocabulary without deliberate intention, while in the process of reading or listening for global meaning. Evidence supporting incidental learning of this kind includes the acquisition by adult readers of large numbers of words of 'nadsat', the artificial language of *A Clockwork Orange* (Burgess, 1962). However, there is much contradictory evidence. More studies are needed which specifically contrast incidental acquisition of vocabulary with intentional, and which examine whether vocabulary learnt in this way persists over time. Questions have also been raised as to whether some level of peripheral attention is present in incidental learning, so that it is not entirely attention-free.

See also: **Implicit learning**

Further reading: Paribakht and Wesche (1997)

INDETERMINACY

The storage of information that is recognisably incomplete. Sometimes the information in a text is not sufficient for readers to form a complete **mental model**. In these cases, they might choose one model from among several possibilities; or they might content themselves with an indeterminate model, one that is less than complete but is sufficient for their purposes. Other reasons for storing an indeterminate mental model are:

☐ where a text is informationally or linguistically complex and makes excessive attentional demands;
☐ where there are gaps in the reader's linguistic understanding of the text (perhaps because it contains unknown vocabulary);

☐ where a reading task only requires the reader to process the text at a relatively shallow level. A classic example is when subjects give the response *Two* to the question: *How many animals of each kind did Moses lead into the ark?*

See also: **Meaning construction, Mental model**

INDUCTIVE LEARNING

A type of learning in which the learner is encouraged to extrapolate a generalisation from a set of internally consistent data. In foreign language teaching, the teacher might present the learner with a set of contexts from which they can draw conclusions as to the circumstances in which a particular language form is generally used, without necessarily having recourse to a formally expressed 'rule'.

INFERENCE

The process of adding information which is not linguistically present in a text. This is often because a speaker/writer has recognised that certain details and logical connections do not need to be specifically expressed because the recipient will co-operate in supplying them. Several types of inference have been identified:

☐ *Logical inference*. If a speaker uses the word BACHELOR, it *entails* that the person referred to is male.

☐ *Bridging inference* (also termed *necessary, backward* or *integrative* inference). To achieve a full understanding of:

a. *Bill had been murdered. The knife lay by the body.*

it is necessary to infer that *the body* refers to Bill, that *the knife* was the weapon and that Bill was murdered by stabbing. Only in this way can the reader impose *coherence* upon the text. The need to make a bridging inference is often signalled by the introduction of a new entity marked for definiteness as if it were **'given'**. Thus, in a above, the article *the* marks out both body and knife as understood in relation to the text that has preceded them. In many cases, the 'given' may be a component of the meaning of an earlier word (perhaps a *meronym*).

b. *He went into the room. The windows were open.*

(Given the word ROOM, the presence of *windows* is taken for granted.) Bridging inferences demand extra attentional capacity and therefore slow down processing. It takes longer to process *the beer* in context c than in d.

c.   *We checked the picnic supplies. The beer was warm.*
d.   *We got some beer out of the trunk. The beer was warm.*

☐ *Elaborative inference* (also termed *forward* or *predictive* inference). The reader uses this type of inference to enrich an interpretation, but it is not essential to understanding and can readily be reversed if later information indicates it is incorrect. Cancellation does not cause disruption to the representation of the text that has been constructed. The distinction between necessary and elaborative inferences is not always a clear one.

Bridging inferences are stored as part of an ongoing **mental representation**. Listeners often fail to distinguish what they have inferred from what they have heard. Many subjects, presented with the sentence:

e.   *He slipped on a wet spot and dropped the delicate glass pitcher on the floor,*

later recalled being told that the pitcher broke. However, there is disagreement as to the extent to which bridging inferences are integrated. A *constructivist view* holds that all bridging inferences are added to propositional information from the text, whereas a *minimalist view* argues that only a minimal number is stored in this way.

Elaborative inferences differ from bridging ones in that they do not appear to form part of the mental representation. It has been suggested that, while bridging inferences are made on-line during text processing, elaborative inferences may not be made until later, during recall.

Some apparent elaborative inferences may represent no more than the effects of the automatic process of **spreading activation**, in which a recent encounter with a word speeds up the recognition of associated ones. The word SHOVEL turned out to be a good cue for recalling the sentence:

f.   *The grocer dug a hole with a pitchfork*

because of its association with the verb DIG.

See also: **Given/new, Mental model, Mental representation, Schema theory**

Further reading: Brown and Yule (1983); Oakhill and Garnham (1988); Singer (1990, 1994)

INFORMATION PROCESSING

An approach developed by Donald Broadbent in the 1950s which aims to chart the flow of information through the mind as a particular cognitive task is performed. Underlying the approach is a view that the information is acted upon stage by stage and progressively reshaped. There is a fixed sequence to the mental operations involved, which can be represented in flow-chart form.

This approach to analysing cognition has influenced psychological descriptions of the language skills, which are seen to involve passing linguistic information through various **levels of representation** (e.g. sound, syllable, word, syntactic structure), at each of which it is combined and reclassified.

The information-processing approach also underlies the influential *three-store model* of human memory. This represents information from an external stimulus being passed in turn through: a sensory store, a short-term store and (potentially) a long-term store.

See also: **Levels of representation**

INFORMATION THEORY *see* **Informativeness**

INFORMATIVENESS

The notion that, within a system of language, certain features may have greater *information value* than others. A feature's information value lies in the extent to which it serves to distinguish between units of language (e.g. to distinguish one word from another). On this analysis, the vowel [ə] is not very informative in connected English speech because it is very frequent, whereas the vowel [ʊ] is informative because it is comparatively rare.

Noise, accent or speaker error often prevent a listener from perceiving all the phonological cues that are present in the signal. This raises the question of how much information is necessary for a word to be recognised. Surprisingly, even if the only cue to a word's identity is its stress pattern, the listener can still produce an *equivalence class* (a group of words matching the available information) which is much smaller than the English lexicon as a whole – probably between 15 per cent and 19 per cent of the total. Several studies have used lexical statistics to examine how the *candidate search space* (the size of a group of possible word matches) reduces as more and more phonological information is available. Knowing the number of phonemes in an item reduces the search space to 5 per cent of the English lexicon. Adding in information as to whether the phonemes in question are vowels or consonants reduces it to about 1 per cent.

With a **broad-class** phonetic transcription which represents only manner of articulation, the largest group of possible word matches was calculated at about 1 per cent of an English lexicon of 20,000 words and the average group size at around 2. It was also claimed that about 32 per cent of items could be identified uniquely. However, this result was challenged on the grounds that average class size is skewed by a few very small or very large groups and that the frequency of the items needs to be considered. A formula was therefore proposed which enables the calculation of an *expected class size* (ECS) weighted for frequency. With the 20,000-word lexicon, ECS was 34 and uniquely identifiable words represented only 6 per cent.

An alternative way of approaching this kind of analysis (and one more in line with information theory) is in terms of how much information is needed in order to narrow the class size down to one – i.e. how much information is needed to identify every word in the lexicon. Measuring the *percentage of information extracted* (PIE) gives very different results from measuring ECS. To give an example, the ECS for a broad transcription of the items in an English dictionary was calculated at 31.1 (0.25 per cent) – suggesting that 99.75 per cent of the original lexicon could be eliminated as not matching the information given. However, a PIE calculation indicated that the information available in the broad-class transcription represented only 79.8 per cent of what would be needed if every single word were to be uniquely identified.

See also: **Probabilistic, Underspecification**

Further reading: Altmann (1990)

INNER SPEECH (also INTERNAL SPEECH, INNER VOICE)

The impression of a 'voice in the head' while one is reading or writing. In discussing the impact of phonology upon reading, it is important to distinguish two types of *speech code*: the post-lexical inner voice, which encodes into phonological form the words that the reader has just read; and the pre-lexical *phonological route*, which, in an alphabetic system, enables the reader to work out the pronunciation of unfamiliar words.

Readers whose languages do not employ an alphabetic system still appear to employ an inner voice. Chinese readers sometimes confuse words which are phonologically similar as well as words which are similar in shape, suggesting that, during reading, logogram characters are encoded phonologically.

Inner speech should be distinguished from **subvocalisation** – evidence of activity in the speech tract while reading or writing is taking place. Subvocalisation may well assist the 'voice in the head' but it is not essential to it, since occupying the articulators by uttering nonsense noises during reading does not seem to impede inner speech.

Three important issues have been discussed:

☐ *Does inner speech contribute to adult reading or is it a relic of the way in which children acquire reading skills by reference to the spoken word?* Adult silent readers read tongue twister sentences more slowly than sentences which are easier to pronounce. They also take longer to process sentences composed of words which rhyme but vary in spelling; and they make more errors in interpreting sentences which are homophonically misspelt (*tie the not*) than those which are anomalous (*I am kill*). These findings suggest that phonological coding does indeed contribute to the reading skill and affects speed of processing.

☐ *How does inner speech contribute to reading?* Early experiments suppressed inner speech, so as to see how reading was affected. They asked readers to engage in *concurrent articulation*, repeating meaningless spoken words while reading. This had a small slowing effect on the readers' ability to judge whether two words on the page were similar in form (LEMON/DEMON) and similar in meaning (MOURN/GRIEVE). It interfered much more with their ability to decide whether two words rhymed (HEARD/BEARD); and importantly, much more when they were required to process meaning at sentence level. From this, it was concluded that the inner voice does not support the process of matching words on the page to representations in the mind; but that its principal role is to support **working memory**. Working memory favours the storage of information in phonological form. By encoding a reading text phonologically, one ensures that it can be stored for longer and is thus available for higher-level comprehension processes.

□ *What form does inner speech take?* Silent reading (average: around 300 words a minute) is much faster than reading aloud (average: around 150–200 wpm). However, the 'voice in the head' appears to follow closely behind the reader's eye. So inner speech cannot involve an exact replication of the articulatory processes of spoken language. It may be that certain sounds are shortened or that certain words are omitted – or it may be that inner speech involves a code which is speech-like but much more condensed. When readers attempt to analyse what the inner voice says, they receive the impression that it encodes in full everything they have read. However, in focusing full attention upon inner speech, they may have resorted to a slower, more *controlled* and less efficient process than is involved in normal silent reading.

See also: **Dual route, Phonological representation, Reading: decoding, Rehearsal, Subvocalisation**

Further reading: Just and Carpenter (1987); Perfetti (1985); Rayner and Pollatsek (1989: Chap. 6)

INPUT

The language to which a listener or reader is exposed: a term used especially in relation to first and second language acquisition.

Input in first language acquisition is referred to as **child directed speech** (CDS), *motherese*, *caretaker talk* or *baby talk*. Controversy attaches to whether it is rich, accurate and comprehensive enough for the child to develop full linguistic competence from it; or whether the data it provides is 'impoverished'. In the latter case, we have to assume the existence of an innate mechanism, specific to language, which assists the process of acquisition.

Speech to non-native speakers sometimes takes the form of a simplified register known as **foreigner talk**, which shares many phonological and syntactic characteristics of CDS but is more likely than CDS to use structures which are syntactically deviant (*You no like?*). There has been debate as to whether a certain level of attention is necessary in order for second language acquisition to occur. A distinction has been made between simply encountering a new linguistic structure in the input and '*noticing*' that the structure is different from the form which the learner might employ in the same circumstances.

See also: **Child Directed Speech, Foreigner talk, Intake, Nativism**

Further reading: Ellis (1994: 243–91); Gallaway and Richards (1994)

INSTANTIATION

The selection of attributes of an object or action which are specific to the immediate context.

In principle, **lexical access** makes available to us all the attributes of a particular word. In practice, we foreground those features of meaning which are most germane to the context in which the item is encountered. Compare the different attributes of TOMATO which are foregrounded in each of the following.

The tomato was ripe (redness)
I trod on a tomato and squashed it (softness)
The tomato rolled across the floor (roundness)

The effects of instantiation can be demonstrated with *recall cues*. After encountering the sentence *The fish attacked the swimmer*, subjects were more able to recall the exact wording if they were given SHARK as a cue than if they were given FISH. Similarly, BASKET was found to be a better recall cue for *The container held the apples*; but BOTTLE for *The container held the cola*.

An alternative view would suggest that these results derive from the listener or reader constructing a **mental model** on the basis of an *elaborative inference* which goes beyond the linguistic evidence in the text.

See also: **Inference, Mental model, Mental representation**

Further reading: Garnham (1985: 162–5)

INTAKE

The proportion of the propositional information in the **input** that a listener or reader comprehends and retains. In a second language situation, the term is sometimes used more narrowly to refer to the proportion of the linguistic and pragmatic content of the input that the listener/reader processes as potential learning material.

See also: **Input**

INTELLIGIBILITY

Many factors affect the intelligibility of a speech signal. They include:

☐ *Intensity,* perceived by the listener as *loudness.*

☐ *Background noise.* For successful communication, the average speech level should exceed the noise level by 6 decibels (the *S/N ratio* should be + 6Db). Below this, the listener becomes increasingly reliant upon contextual cues.

☐ *Restrictions in the frequency band.* Telephone lines, for example, limit the range of frequencies transmitted to a band from 0 to 3000 Hz, removing many of the acoustic cues which indicate the sound [s]. Research has shown that no particular frequency band is essential to intelligibility. Conversation remains intelligible if a *low-pass filter* suppresses frequency components above 1800 Hz or if a *high-pass filter* suppresses components below that level. Because the speech signal contains a great deal of **redundancy**, a narrow frequency band of between 1000 and 2000 Hz (excised from the signal by a *band-pass filter*) can achieve 90 per cent intelligibility.

Other factors contributing to intelligibility relate to the individual speaker. They include the fundamental frequency of the speaker's voice and the pitch range used; how precisely and how fast the speaker articulates; the frequency and length of pausing; and how familiar the listener is with the speaker's accent.

See also: **Speech signal**

Further reading: Denes and Pinson (1993); Pickett (1999)

INTERACTIONAL VIEW (of reading and listening)

The notion that the receptive skills demand active engagement. The listener/reader is seen as interacting with the speaker/writer and *remaking the message* which has been formulated. The message as understood may well be different in substance from what was intended by its originator. The listener/reader is free to impose upon it their own:

- sense of what is or is not relevant and what is or is not important;
- interpretation of what the speaker/writer intended;
- world knowledge, which may differ from that of the speaker/ writer.

They may also narrowly interpret what they hear or read in terms of their own interests. One study showed that a politically neutral recording was interpreted as right or left wing according to the listener's personal beliefs.

For the above reasons, it has been argued that we should not refer to a 'correct' interpretation in testing language comprehension, but simply an 'adequate' one.

Further reading: Brown (1995: Chap. 1)

INTERACTIVE ACTIVATION

A model of language processing which assumes that all **levels of representation** freely influence each other. This might mean, for example, that a listener's perception of a distorted sound at the beginning of the sequence *eel would be influenced at the time of processing by knowledge of the word WHEEL or by a context such as 'He changed the *eel on the car'. An interactive account contrasts with **modular** accounts which suggest that the sequence *eel must first be processed phonologically; only then can information from other levels be brought in to disambiguate it.

Interactive activation models thus present the processing of a spoken or written word as subject simultaneously to both **bottom-up** (data driven) and **top-down** (context driven) influences. Their proponents argue that this makes all sources of information immediately available to the listener or reader, enabling an informed choice to be made as to the identity of the word. Their opponents argue that a model of this kind overloads the processor with information, making a decision more difficult.

The various cues are said to assist recognition by supplying **activation** to a particular letter or word. Thus, evidence of WHI on the page would provide strong bottom-up activation for the words WHICH and WHITE but only weak activation for partial matches like WHO or WRITE. If top-down information suggested that a question word was needed, WHICH would receive further activation. The activation of a letter or word can be increased by a positive (*facilitatory*) connection or reduced by a negative (*inhibitory*) one. When one particular word is supported by overwhelming evidence, it 'fires', i.e. becomes accepted as the correct match.

A distinction can be made between interactive models which incorporate *between-levels* activity and those which also feature *within-levels* activity. In a within-levels model, activation supporting the word WHICH has an inhibitory effect on other likely words – reducing the activation of competitors such as WHITE, WRITE etc. Similarly, at letter level, any increase in the activation of H would reduce the activation of R.

Although the term 'interactive activation' is now used generically for this type of account of listening or reading, it was originally used for a specific **connectionist** model of visual word recognition (McClelland and Rumelhardt, 1981). This model operates on three levels: feature, letter and word, with excitatory and inhibitory connections between elements at all levels. Recognition of the word WORD is supported, bottom-up, by evidence from features (oblique strokes, circle etc.) and letters; but it is also supported, top-down, by the existence of WORD in the lexicon. In this way, the model accounts neatly for *word superiority effects*, where letters prove easier to detect when they occur in actual words than when they occur in non-words or even when they occur alone.

Similar interactive models (**TRACE**, Shortlist etc.) have been designed to account for auditory perception.

See also: **Activation, Bottom-up processing, Modularity$_2$, Top-down processing**

Further reading: Carroll (1999: 97–9); Whitney (1998: 187–9)

INTERACTIVE COMPENSATORY HYPOTHESIS

A theory that in reading there is a trade-off between the quality of the information achieved by *decoding* and the extent to which the reader needs to make compensatory use of contextual information. Thus, a weak reader who is a bad decoder is more heavily reliant upon contextual information because he/she has need of it in order to compensate for words which have not been recognised. If a text is *degraded* (through small print or bad handwriting), then even a skilled reader may rely upon top-down information to fill gaps in the message.

The interactive compensatory hypothesis has been extended to the situation of the foreign language reader. Here, the premise is that those with a more elementary knowledge of the syntax and vocabulary of the target language will rely more heavily upon the compensatory use of context.

See also: **Context, Reading: decoding**

Further reading: Stanovich (1980)

INTERFACE VIEW

A view that explicit knowledge of the grammar of a foreign language can feed in to performance in that language. Also associated with the view that instruction can positively affect progress in learning a language. Contrasted with a *non-interface* view that it is implicit knowledge alone (gained through naturalistic encounters) which drives L2 development.

INTONATION

A melodic pattern created by varying the prominence of parts of the speech signal. In English, it is usually achieved by movements in the pitch of a speaker's voice, but changes in duration, loudness and tempo may also contribute. Intonation appears to be a language universal: even tone languages show some intonational marking. Its importance is indicated by the fact that infants appear able to distinguish the intonational characteristics of their mother's language as early as 4 days old. Intonation is one of the last features to be lost in cases of **dementia**, and one of the most difficult to adjust when acquiring a second language.

In psycholinguistics, intonation is often discussed under the more general term of **prosody**, which includes consideration of features such as pausing, speech rate etc. It is useful to distinguish it from **lexical stress**, which is invariable and the property of an individual lexical item. While lexical stress is conceptualised as forming part of a **lexical entry**, it is less clear how intonation is stored in the mind and how basic intonation patterns are recognised.

The basic unit of intonation is the *intonational phrase* (IP) (also termed *intonation group, tone group* etc.), which may or may not coincide with a syntactic unit such as a clause. Each IP centres upon a *nucleus*, which bears a *primary* or *tonic accent*. Researchers have studied the prosodic cues that signal to a listener where one IP ends and another begins. They include:

- *pausing*, while the speaker plans the next IP;
- *a lengthening of the final syllable* of an IP;
- a *speeding up* of speech (*anacrusis*) at the beginning of a new IP;
- *resetting the pitch* at the start of a new IP;
- *a lack of assimilation* between adjacent words that cross an IP boundary.

However, IP boundaries often prove difficult to locate precisely in natural (as against read-aloud) speech.

Intonation fulfils a number of important functions in speech processing. Some are relatively systematic. IP boundaries may coincide with *syntactic boundaries*; pitch movement provides cues to *sentence mode* (e.g. declarative vs question); and tempo provides cues to completeness and thus willingness to hand over the conversational *turn*. Other functions represent the moment-to-moment decisions of the speaker. The placing of the tonic accent provides *information focus* and (assisted by heightened pitch movement) can indicate contrast and emphasis. Pitch and overall intonation pattern can provide *affective* (emotional) signals.

The multiplicity of intonation patterns causes difficulties for accounts of the perception of intonation – and particularly of the way in which patterns are stored in the mind and recognised. The systematic functions above would suggest that the listener possesses templates for certain prototypical *tunes*, against which the signal can be matched. However, the functions that reflect moment-to-moment decisions demonstrate the considerable freedom which the speaker can exercise in diverging from standard patterns. One solution is supplied by an **exemplar** account, where the mind records each intonation pattern that is encountered and recognises consistencies that are shared by some but not all.

Evidence of the acquisition of intonation by infants suggests that certain prototypical patterns may form the basis on which an adult system is built. During the **babbling** period before their first words, infants appear (as early as 8 months) to imitate adult pitch patterns. The onset of true intonation occurs during their 'one-word' period, when they show recognition of the difference between rising and falling tones, often reserving a rise for requests and a fall for deixis. At the two-word stage, the child begins to use tonic accent to distinguish utterances: with, for example, *DADdy garden* marking possession and *daddy GARden* marking location. In its third year, a child begins to shift the nucleus to take account of **'given/new'** distinctions. Information focus then becomes increasingly common with three- and four-word utterances.

See also: **Given/new, Lexical stress, Phonological representation, Prosody, Speech production**

Further reading: Brown (1990); Brown and Yule (1983); Cruttenden (1986); Laver (1994); Levelt (1989)

KNOWLEDGE

Linguistic knowledge takes the form of a number of dichotomies:

☐ *Declarative/procedural.* Declarative knowledge (knowledge *that*) is explicit and can be expressed verbally. It contrasts with procedural knowledge (knowledge *how*) which determines our ability to handle highly automatic routines such as retrieving words or constructing sentences in our first language. Declarative knowledge involves *control*: it demands attentional resources and is therefore costly in terms of **working memory** capacity.

Declarative knowledge can be transformed into procedural knowledge through practice. This leads (a) to separate steps becoming combined and (b) to ever-increasing automaticity. The declarative/ procedural distinction has been used in accounts of second language acquisition to describe the way in which some learners move from rule-based information to the relatively automatic generation of utterances.

☐ *Implicit/explicit.* Implicit linguistic knowledge manifests itself in performance but the possessor is unable to express it verbally. In second language acquisition, a system of phonology or syntax acquired in a *naturalistic* (i.e. non-instructional) environment might be stored by means of a mapping between a particular form and a particular context, with no explicit rule attached. Similarly, **inductive** teaching might present the learner with a typical set of circumstances in which a structure is to be used, without expressing these conditions of use in the form of a rule. In these cases, inferencing is necessary on the part of the user in order to turn implicit knowledge into explicit.

The implicit/explicit distinction is also important in research into first language processes. Certain traditional psycholinguistic tasks draw upon explicit knowledge: requiring subjects, for example, to memorise lists of words, and thus store explicit information. Today psycholinguists increasingly prefer to use *indirect* or *incidental* tasks. They might, for example, demonstrate that a reader reads a word more quickly as a result of having been exposed to it recently, even though the reader cannot specifically recall having seen the word.

☐ *Categorical/probabilistic.* Some linguistic knowledge is categorical in form, enabling the possessor to classify material on an 'all or none' basis. An example is the way in which a sharp and consistent boundary is maintained between a set of phonetic exemplars which are perceived as representing one consonant and a set perceived as representing a contrasted one. Other types of linguistic knowledge are **probabilistic** and operate on the basis of 'best fit'. This might permit us to recognise lexical items that have been subject to assimilation (e.g. *ten* pronounced [tem] in the sequence *ten pounds*).

☐ *Formulaic/analysed.* Many infants first acquire and produce whole **chunks** of language in a formulaic way, without being able to analyse them into their constituents. Conversely, a minority appear to acquire speech *analytically* (word by word). They then have to assemble the words into chunks which are integrated phonologically and can be stored as pre-assembled lexical units. Second language learners in a 'naturalistic' context are more likely to acquire language formulaically, while those learning in a classroom setting acquire language in a more analysed form.

See also: **ACT, Analysis, Categorical perception, Implicit learning, Incidental learning, Probabilistic**

Further reading: Kellogg (1995: Chap. 6)

L1

First or native language as distinct from L2, a second or foreign language.

LANGUAGE ACQUISITION DEVICE (LAD)

Term formerly used by Chomsky (1965) for a hypothesised innate mechanism in the brain of an infant which triggers and supports the process of acquiring a first language. Now replaced by the notion of an innate **Universal Grammar** which specifies features common to all languages.

LANGUAGE ACQUISITION: RESEARCH METHODS

Much language acquisition research is longitudinal. Three general approaches can be found:

☐ *Theory-driven.* The researcher adopts a theoretical framework; then seeks support for it in their data. This approach is particularly favoured by those who subscribe to **Chomskyan theory**, and who seek (for example) to trace evidence of infants setting *parameters* in the direction of the target language. The children might be asked to make *grammaticality judgements*, indicating whether they regard a sentence as grammatically acceptable or not.

☐ *Observational,* analysing the data without prior assumptions. Diary studies have proved informative – though their disadvantage is that they do not preserve a record of the actual speech event. Video and cassette recordings have been widely used. They are obtained during regular meetings between researcher and infant; or by use of a timer.

☐ *Experimental.* It is obviously difficult to engage very young subjects in experimental tasks. Two types of method have proved useful:

● *the high amplitude sucking procedure.* An infant's sucking on a teat settles down to a regular rhythm if there is little in the environment to distract the child – but speeds up markedly if something novel engages its attention. This phenomenon can be used to establish the extent to which infants discriminate between similar linguistic features, a change of sucking rate showing that they have identified a sound or rhythm that differs from an earlier one.

- *the operant headturn procedure*, in which an infant is trained to turn its head when it encounters a novel stimulus. An independent observer notes when the infant moves its head through at least 30°, and this is taken to show that the infant has noticed a change in the signal. A variant is the *Headturn Preference Procedure*, where different stimuli are played from different sides (e.g. an utterance in the ambient language on the left followed by an utterance in another language on the right). The infant's headturns are monitored as an indication of which stimuli it finds more interesting.

For older infants, 'listen and repeat' tasks have been used to investigate areas such as phonological memory and lexical segmentation. In addition, many experimenters (especially those researching morphology acquisition) have used simple picture-based tests. The researcher might, for example, show the infant a picture of an object and name it *a wug*; then show the infant a picture of two and ask for a response.

Language acquisition researchers have the benefit of a rich archive in the *Child Language Data Exchange System* (CHILDES) database collected by Brian MacWhinney and Catherine Snow, which brings together data from nearly a hundred research projects in a variety of languages.

Further reading: Foster (1990: Chap. 6); Jusczyk (1997: Appendix)

LANGUAGE ACQUISITION: STAGES

All infants pass through the same stages in the acquisition of a first language; but they progress at different rates. So, while a child's age in years and months is often cited (as two figures separated by a semicolon), it is not a reliable indicator of development. Many accounts record development in terms of the phonological or linguistic content of the child's productions. The following stages are universal, the first two being *prelinguistic*:

☐ *Cooing* (about 0;3). Gurgling moves on to vocalisation involving sounds which resemble vowels. The infant responds vocally to human speech.

☐ *Babbling* (from 0;6). The infant produces consonant-vowel (CV) sequences which may resemble those of the target language. The child's later productions become imitative: there is often a phase of

echolalia from about 0;8, when the child imitates adult intonation patterns with some degree of accuracy.

☐ *One-word stage* (from 1;0). Sometimes termed *holophrastic speech*. The first words appear at about 1;0, and by 1;6 the child may have a vocabulary of around 50 words, usually nouns. The child recognises the referential function of words, using them to name objects.

☐ *Two-word stage* (1;6 onwards). Sometimes described as *telegraphic speech* because of the absence of most function words. The two-word combinations exhibit a set of primitive semantic relationships (constituting a **child grammar**) of which the earliest are usually naming (*this*), recurrence (*more*) and non-existence (*no*). At about the same time, the **vocabulary spurt** begins, with an increase of about six to ten words a day in the child's repertoire.

☐ *Multi-word stage* (2;6 onwards). The child uses strings of three or more words, often based upon established two-word patterns. Adult syntactic patterns gradually become more prevalent.

Instead of age, a more precise way of calibrating the development of an infant is by **mean length of utterance** (MLU): a figure based on the average number of morphemes in the infant's productions. This is said to be a reliable marker of development until the age of about 4;0. Using MLU, early researchers proposed six stages of development (Table L1).

Those who take a Piagetian perspective have attempted to relate progress in language to the cognitive developments of the *sensorimotor period* (age 0–2) and the *pre-operational period* (2–7). These include *object permanence*, the formation of categories and an understanding of causality and displacement. The argument is that the child cannot

Table L1 Six stages of first language acquisition (Brown, 1973)

Stage	MLU	Approx. age	Characteristics
I	1.0–2.0	1;0–2;2	Holophrastic speech
			Telegraphic speech
II	2.0–2.5	2;3–2;6	Inflections added
III	2.5–3.0	2;7–2;10	Full sentences
IV	3.0–3.75	2;11–3;4	Embedded sentences
V	3.75–4.5	3;5–3;10	Co-ordination
V+	4.5+	3;11+	

understand linguistic forms representing such notions until the notions themselves have been acquired. Vygotsky's developmental stages also provide a loose framework for language development. Vygotsky identified a first stage when thought and language (a child's first words) are unrelated; a second stage of *egocentric speech* when the child expresses its thoughts aloud; and a third when egocentric speech becomes internalised.

Yet another account of the stages of acquisition represents them in terms of the pragmatic functions which the child commands rather than surface features of syntax (see **functionalism**).

In any of these accounts, some caution has to be exercised in accepting productions as evidence of development. Receptive recognition of form and understanding of meaning may occur well before an item appears in production. Conversely, the production of a form might predate 'acquisition': it might, for example, result from mimicry without understanding.

See also: **Functionalism, Phonological development: production, Piagetian stages of development, Syntactic development, Vocabulary acquisition, Vygotskyan**

LANGUAGE ACQUISITION: THEORIES

A number of theoretical positions can be identified:

☐ Language is a set of habits, with associations formed between words and the real-world states/objects which they refer to. See **behaviourism**.

☐ Language is acquired through extended exposure to adult speech and a desire to make sense of the environment. See **empiricism**.

☐ There is an innate language faculty, which is (a) fully developed at birth; or (b) programmed into the *maturation* process. See **nativism**.

☐ A general cognitive predisposition equips infants to trace patterns in the miscellaneous language which they encounter. See **cognitivism**.

☐ The cognitive limitations of the infant equip it for cracking the language code. See **'less is more'**.

☐ Language is acquired through the infant's desire to interact with its carers. See **social–interactionism**.

The original behaviourist view is much out of favour, but the recent emergence of **connectionism** has raised again the possibility that language is acquired by a process of association and without the need of cognitive pattern-recognition skills.

LANGUAGE UNIVERSALS

Universally shared patterns of meaning which shape all languages (contrary to the notion of **linguistic relativity**). Language universals are associated with the nativist argument in language acquisition and the notion of a **Universal Grammar** that is part of our genetic makeup. However, they are not incompatible with a **cognitivist** approach, which would view languages of all types as products of the human mind and thus similar in certain features. They could also be viewed as deriving from the way the real world is structured, from similar basic needs across different societies or from a common origin for all languages.

There are two ways of establishing language universals. One, in the Chomskyan tradition, seeks to analyse a single language in depth by constructing a set of rules, then to establish the extent to which those rules can be said to apply elsewhere. The second approach takes the form of *typological* studies which compare a range of different languages. Greenberg (1966) examined word order and morphology in 30 languages, and identified 45 universals. He found that most languages adopt one of three word orders: by frequency, they are SOV (Subject-Object-Verb), SVO and VSO. Other patterns (VOS and OVS) are rare – suggesting a universal reluctance to place the object before the subject. This may tell us something about the needs of the listener when undertaking **syntactic parsing** of a sentence.

The word order adopted by a language seems to determine other important syntactic features. Thus languages with a VO order tend to use *prepositions* and to place prepositional phrases and adverbs of manner *after* the verb, while those with an OV order tend to use *postpositions* and to place postpositional phrases and adverbs of manner *before* the verb. 'If X then Y' findings of this kind are sometimes termed *implicational universals*.

See also: **Linguistic relativity, Universal Grammar**

147

LATENCY (also REACTION TIME)

The time taken to respond to a stimulus. For example, when subjects are asked to shadow (repeat) what a speaker says, they are able to do so at a latency of about 200 milliseconds.

LEARNING STYLE

An approach to learning determined by the personality or the cognitive bias of the learner. In studies of language acquisition, learning style is taken as evidence of the part played by individual factors.

For Nelson (1973), most infants adopt a *referential* style in acquiring vocabulary. Their first 50 words include a high proportion of nouns and appear to reflect a strategy of naming entities. Referential infants are said to respond well to contacts with adults and to build up their language in a 'bottom-up' way which is reliant upon single words. Vocabulary increase during the first year of life is usually rapid.

By contrast, the first 50 words of a minority of infants, classified as *expressive* learners, contain more verb-like forms. This group tends to produce a larger proportion of unanalysed strings of words, which they later break into their constituents. They tend to interact more with other children than with adults.

The single word/multiple word distinction is made by other commentators, who note that some children show evidence of an *analytical* style, acquiring words and then building them into larger units, while others manifest a *holistic* or **Gestalt** style, acquiring **chunks** of language which they later deconstruct into words.

A similar distinction may apply to second language learners, though here an important factor is whether the learner is learning through instruction or naturalistically. Second language learners have also been characterised as *risk-takers* anxious to achieve communication, and *risk-avoiders* who are reluctant to engage in conversation unless they are sure that their language is accurate. A further distinction recognises that some language learners learn best by **inductive** methods (generalising from examples) while others learn best *deductively* (applying rules to situations of use).

Further reading: Foster (1990); Peters (1983)

LEARNING THEORY

A theory that extensive exposure to linguistic input is sufficient to enable an infant to recognise recurrent syntactic forms and patterns. The theory effectively treats language as no different from other forms of learned behaviour. It is supported by evidence from computer modelling, where a system of feedback ensures that a connection which produces a correct outcome is strengthened and a connection which leads to a wrong outcome is weakened. In this way, computer programs have been 'trained' to produce correct Past Simple forms.

See also: **Behaviourism, Connectionism, Empiricism, Parallel distributed processing**

LEFT-TO-RIGHT PROCESSING

The parsing of a grammatical structure on a word-by-word basis. One of the insights provided by Chomsky is that languages are *hierarchical*, consisting of phrases embedded within phrases. Chomsky criticises the limitations of a *finite-state* (or linear) grammar, suggesting that syntax cannot be adequately analysed word by word because to do so is to overlook the dependencies which underlie it. This poses problems for accounts of psychological processing, since it is clear from eye movement data that readers do indeed process texts linearly. The case is even clearer with listeners who have been shown to process constituents of the speech signal **on-line** – about 200 milliseconds behind the speaker. There is thus a tension between the hierarchical syntactic pattern that is ultimately extracted from the signal, and the linear means by which it is assembled.

See also: **Syntactic parsing**

'LESS IS MORE'

A view that infants are assisted in their acquisition of language by their cognitive limitations.

Nativists argue that it is difficult to understand how infants can acquire language without some kind of innate learning mechanism since they are easily distracted, have great difficulty with tasks that require conscious memorisation, and have very limited working memory. However, a lack of focus at local level may enable infants to achieve larger insights into the symbolic function of language. It may actually be an advantage in terms of language acquisition that they notice only the most general syntactic patterns and only manage to hold a few words of an utterance in short-term memory. These very limitations may assist them in recognising the large-scale logic of language without being distracted by confusing details. The theory has been supported by computer modelling which simulates the partial attention which infants bring to bear on language.

Further reading: Deacon (1997: Chap. 4); Newport (1990)

LEVEL OF REPRESENTATION

A view of language processing originating in **information processing** theory, which assumes that comprehension involves a series of stages at which information from a spoken or written stimulus is progressively reshaped into larger and larger units. Thus (in principle), what is perceived as a cluster of features at phonetic level is converted into phonemes at phonological level, and then reclassified as, respectively, syllables, words, syntactic structures and finally propositional information. A similar assumption underlies models of speaking, which proceed in the opposite direction. A speaker first represents a concept abstractly, then syntactically and/or lexically, then phonologically, then phonetically and finally in the form of instructions to the articulators.

Questions have been raised about the validity of some of the postulated levels. For example, because there is so much variation in the speech signal, some commentators have suggested that the listener proceeds directly from phonetic features to syllables or half-syllables without a phonological level. In speaking, the syntactic level may precede the lexical, providing slots into which words can be fitted. Or it may follow it, since lexical choice often predetermines the syntactic structure that is to be used (choosing GIVE entails adopting one or two patterns: GIVE + NP (noun phrase) + NP or GIVE + NP + to + NP). Or syntax and lexis may operate at the same level.

A major controversy concerns the extent to which any given level is *encapsulated*. Does a level apply its own criteria independently of the rest of the system, and then hand on the outcome of its processing to the next level? Or can information be transmitted between levels? The advantage of the first (**autonomous**) solution is that it leads to straightforward choices made on a single set of criteria and thus (its proponents say) faster processing. The advantage of the second (**interactive**) solution is that it enables all the evidence to be considered at once.

See also: **Bottom-up processing, Context, Interactive activation, Modularity$_2$, Top-down processing**

LEXICAL ACCESS

The retrieval of a **lexical entry** from the lexicon, containing stored information about a word's form and its meaning.

Serial models of lexical access assume that we work through lexical entries in turn until we find a match for a word that we are hearing or reading. It is well established that frequent words are identified more quickly than infrequent ones. These models therefore propose that words are stored not just by similarity of form but also in order of frequency: words beginning with /kær/ would be accessed in the order CARRY – CARROT – CARRIAGE – CARRIER – CARRION. This is the approach favoured, for example, by Forster's (1979) **search model**.

Serial access makes few demands on the processor, but is slow in terms of time. The original assumption was that the human mind operated like early computers, which were restricted to serial operations. An alternative view is that words are accessed *in parallel*. A search might retrieve a large number of similar words and compare them simultaneously with the word on the page or in the speech signal. These words are sometimes referred to as *candidates*, and, in many parallel models are seen as *competing* with each other to be the one that is selected.

Competition between words is often represented in terms of **activation**. Prompted by a particular string of letters or sounds, we access a number of possible word matches. They are activated to different degrees – with the more likely ones (those that are most frequent and those that form the closest match to what is in the input) receiving more activation than the others. Activation level can change as the language user reads or hears more of the word – so some candidate words may have their activation boosted by late-arriving information while others may have their activation depressed.

A major issue for lexical access concerns the extent of the information that is used in order to achieve recognition. Is it solely perceptual information from the speech signal or page – or is other information brought to bear that is based on world knowledge or syntactic expectations? An **autonomous** view has it that information sources are kept separate in the interests of clear and rapid decision making; and that initial access is triggered on the basis of perceptual cues alone. Contextual and other information may become available at a later stage to check the outcome or to resolve ambiguity. An **interactive** view has it that all sources of information are available at the outset. In this case, context and syntax as well as the form of the input contribute to the activation of a particular candidate. A compromise adopted by **Cohort Theory** is that there is '*bottom-up priority*' in spoken word recognition, with a word's first 200 milliseconds or first syllable opening up a set of candidates on the basis of form. Activation is then modified in response to **top-down** contextual and syntactic considerations.

It is clear that **context** must be invoked at some point in order to deal with ambiguities created by homonyms or words that are polysemous (possessing multiple related senses). A much-quoted finding by Swinney (1979) suggests that all possible senses are automatically accessed before context is invoked to determine the appropriate one. Subjects briefly activated both senses of a word such as BUG despite a disambiguating context. There is evidence that the same may even happen with a form such as [wiːk] whose two senses are from different word classes.

An alternative view, supported by evidence, suggests that a great deal may depend upon the relative frequency of a word's senses. If a sentence context favours the *dominant* sense, then that is likely to be the single meaning that is retrieved. If it favours a subordinate sense, all the senses are likely to be retrieved.

The effects of context on lexical access are distinct from the effects of **spreading activation**, where, after encountering the word FLOOR, a listener or reader is quicker than normal to identify associated words such as CEILING, DOOR or ROOM. This is a highly **automatic** effect which operates entirely at lexical level and reflects the way in which items are stored in the mental lexicon.

Discussion of lexical access tends to focus on word recognition by listeners and readers. But writers and speakers also need to retrieve words. Evidence from **Slips of the Tongue** and from **aphasia** indicates that they make use of both sense and form. If a speaker needs a word for a particular vegetable, they select candidates from a group of words associated by the concept 'vegetable'. But they may also have a *retrieval cue* to the word's form indicating that it begins with the stressed syllable /ˈkæ/. This might lead them at the same time to access a second group of words linked by their initial syllable. The double search would narrow the choice to CARROT and CABBAGE.

See also: **Activation, Autonomous, Cohort Theory, Context, Interactive activation, Lexical recognition, Lexical storage, Logogen, Modularity₂, Search model, TRACE**

Further reading: Aitchison (2003); Forster (1990); Garnham (1985: Chap. 3); Reeves *et al.* (1998)

LEXICAL EFFECT

The effect of a characteristic of a particular lexical item upon the ease with which it is retrieved from the lexicon. Evidence supports the following:

- *A frequency effect*, with frequent words recognised more rapidly than infrequent.
- *A degradation effect*, with words that are clearly presented recognised more rapidly than those which are not.
- *A word/non-word effect*, with non-words rejected more quickly if they cannot form a possible English word (LGAJ) than if they follow the rules of English orthography (FEMP). The closer their resemblance to an actual word, the harder they are to reject.
- *A word superiority effect*, with letters identified more quickly in a word than in a string of other letters or even a string of XXXs. This suggests that part of the process of recognising whole words involves taking note of their constituent letters. However, there is also a pseudo-word superiority effect, where a letter is detected faster in a non-word that resembles an actual word (MAVE) than in one that does not (RVIH).
- *A neighbourhood effect*, with a written word such as FEED processed more quickly because all analogous words (WEED, SEED etc.) bear the same pronunciation. The processing of a written word such as HEAD is said to be constrained by a conflict between two possible pronunciations for its rime (DEAD etc. vs BEAD etc.). The effect has particularly been evidenced in different reaction times to non-words (GEAD vs GEED).
- *A length effect*, with longer words taking more time to process. This suggests that reading operates at the level of letter recognition as well as whole-word recognition.
- *An imageability effect*, where words that are easy to visualise are more readily recalled than those (e.g. abstract words) that are not.

See also: **Lexical access, Neighbourhood, Priming effect**

Further reading: Garnham (1985: 42–6)

LEXICAL ENTRY

The information that is stored in the mind concerning a particular lexical item. Levelt (1989) represents a lexical entry as consisting of two parts, one related to form and one (the *lemma*) related to meaning and use.

□ *'Form' includes:*

a. *Mental representations* of the item which enable it to be identified when it is encountered. There must be a **phonological representation** against which a spoken stimulus can be matched, and an *orthographic representation* for decoding the item when it occurs in written form. We can assume that the two are closely connected and linked to the same unit of meaning. However, both phonological and orthographic representations have to allow for variation – the fact that a speaker may have any one of a number of accents or that a written text may appear in any one of a number of different typefaces.

b. Information on the *morphology* of the item – both inflectional (providing a plural for a noun or a past tense form for a verb) and derivational (indicating the component parts of a word such as UN-HAPPI-NESS). This is a contentious area. Evidence suggests that inflected items may be assembled from their parts: WALKS and WALKED would be constructed from WALK. However, the evidence on derivational structure is not so clear.

□ The *lemma* of an entry includes:

a. Information on the *syntactic* structures in which the item features. This reflects current approaches to grammar which view vocabulary and grammar as closely linked. The lexical entry needs to contain information on word class to enable the word to be used in generating sentences. It also needs to include information on the types of syntactic structure that are associated with the word. Thus, the entry for GIVE might include GIVE + NP (noun phrase) + NP and GIVE + NP + to + NP, indicating that, once we choose to construct a sentence around the verb GIVE, we commit ourselves to using one of two sentence patterns: *give Mary a present* or *give a present to Mary.* The entry contains additional semantic information about what fits into each of the NP slots. It might tell us that, in the GIVE + NP + NP pattern, the first NP has to be a recipient (probably animate) and the second NP has to be a gift (probably inanimate).

b. A range of senses for the word. The issue of word meaning is complicated by the fact that many words do not refer to single objects in the real world, but represent a whole class of objects or actions. There are two important issues here, so far as lexical storage is concerned. Firstly, the area of meaning covered by any given word is heavily influenced by the existence of other words alongside it. We can only fully understand how to use the word HAPPY if we recognise the existence of alternatives such as CONTENT or PLEASED or DELIGHTED, which limit the semantic boundaries within which HAPPY operates. There must be very close links between lexical entries that fall within a particular area of meaning; only in this way are we able to select exactly the item we need and rule out others. Secondly, the area of meaning that we associate with a word is heavily dependent upon the way in which we categorise the world around us. A major area of research in psycholinguistics attempts to establish the nature of the *categories* that we form, and how they become established in the process of acquiring our first language.

Note that 'lexical access' refers to items which carry lexical meaning. The position of function words is not entirely clear.

See also: **Lexical access, Lexical storage, Morphology: storage, Word primitive**

Further reading: Aitchison (2003); Levelt (1989)

LEXICAL RECOGNITION

The point at which a one-to-one match is achieved between a word encountered in speech or writing and a word in the mind.

Models of lexical access such as **Cohort Theory** assume that spoken words are processed by the listener **on–line**. A number of possible matches are activated on the basis of early evidence (perhaps the first syllable of a word) and the set is gradually reduced as more and more of the word is heard. Finally, a **uniqueness point** is reached when only one candidate matches the information in the input. However, the concept of a uniqueness point assumes that the listener identifies each phoneme in the signal with a high degree of accuracy. It has therefore been suggested that a *recognition point* may occur a short while after the point at which a unique match is possible. This would allow the listener to interpret the signal *probabilistically* if an exact match was not achieved.

See also: **Cohort Theory, Gating, Lexical access, Uniqueness point**

Further reading: Grosjean (1985)

LEXICAL RETRIEVAL *see* **Lexical access**

LEXICAL SEGMENTATION

The division of connected speech into words, assisted by cues which indicate where word boundaries lie.

Pausing in connected speech is very variable, but occurs on a rough average about once every 12 syllables. A chunk of speech thus contains several words, with no gaps between them. In principle, some word boundaries are marked by *allophonic* cues (lengthening, aspiration etc.); but such cues are often not present in informal speech. Furthermore, **accommodation** (assimilation, elision etc.) may vary the form of a word at precisely the point where the listener needs information most – namely, at the boundary between it and the word that follows.

A number of solutions to the segmentation problem have been proposed:

□ *A linear solution*. The listener identifies a word and the end-point of that word marks the beginning of the next. Unfortunately for this view, many words are not unique by their end (*few* might be the beginning of *future*), while many others have words embedded in them (*catalogue*) and others still can be segmented two ways (*a sister/assist her*).

□ *A phonological solution*. There is evidence that listeners make use of *phonotactic* cues. For example, the sequence /mgl/ does not occur in any English word, so there must be a boundary between /m/ and /gl/. However, cues of this type are relatively infrequent.

□ *A 'unit of segmentation' solution*. Evidence suggests that French listeners segment the speech signal syllable by syllable. However, the syllable is not such a reliable unit in English. There is a marked difference in length and salience between weak and strong syllables (compare the two syllables in PROCEED) and some syllables have ambiguous boundaries (the /m/ in LEMON seems to belong both to *lem-* and to *-mon*).

☐ *A time-based solution.* Computer models of speech recognition (see **TRACE**) process the message in *time-slices*. However, this involves a very complex procedure for matching the phonemes within each time-slice against all possible words, and for relating them to the phonemes in previous slices.

☐ *A rhythmic solution.* The most convincing solution for the segmentation of English exploits the fact that the majority of content words in running English speech begin with a strong syllable. Cutler and Norris propose a *Metrical Segmentation Strategy* whereby a listener works on the assumption that each strong syllable initiates a new word. An initial weak syllable is assumed to be a weakly stressed function word; other weak syllables are attached to preceding strong ones as a first segmentation hypothesis. This account of English segmentation is supported by evidence from language acquisition. Infants from an early age exercise a preference for the strong–weak rhythmic alternation which characterises English speech.

Computer modelling and numerous on-line experiments have demonstrated the validity of this theory. Note that it defines the strong syllable as one with full vowel quality rather than one that bears stress; the argument is that this enables the listener to make a simple binary judgement (full vowel vs weak vowel) whereas judgement of stress is relative.

There has been considerable cross-linguistic research into lexical segmentation. The working assumption was that languages which are loosely termed '*stress-based*' (German, Dutch) might lend themselves to a metrical strategy like that of English, while those characterised as '*syllable-based*' (Spanish, Italian) gave rise to a syllabic strategy like the French one. However, the research findings with European languages have been contradictory. Where strong evidence has emerged is of a third strategy specific to Japanese listeners and based upon the *mora*, a sub-syllabic unit characteristic of Japanese. Segmentation research has also been extended to language features not specifically metrical: it has been suggested that Finnish listeners employ a combination of stress and *vowel harmony*, reflecting the unique characteristics of their language.

The question has also been raised of whether a listener can acquire a segmentation strategy specific to a second language and distinct from their native language routine. There is some evidence to suggest that, in these circumstances, they attempt to apply a native strategy or revert to a more generalised one.

The point should be made that lexical segmentation is not an issue for all listeners. It has been estimated that about half of the world's languages feature fixed **lexical stress** which occurs exclusively on the first or last syllable of a word. This enables stress to be used *demarcatively* as a signal of word boundary location.

See also: **Bootstrapping, Phonotactic rules, SW (strong-weak) pattern, Unit of perception**

Further reading: Cutler (1990, 1996); Cutler and Mehler (1993); Grosjean and Gee (1987)

LEXICAL STORAGE

The way in which lexical items are organised in the **lexicon** so as to ensure rapid access.

Most current models assume that words are linked in a complex network which reflects semantic relationships such as partial synonymy, antonymy and hyponymy. Similar links enable us to make collocational associations; these may be established as a consequence of repeated co-occurrence (*heavy + smoker, highly + emotional*) or of semantic association (*fish + chips*). It seems probable that a whole sequence like *fish* and *chips* is stored as a single **chunk**.

Lexical items are similarly associated by form. This has obvious benefits for understanding language; but evidence from **Slips of the Tongue** (SOT) indicates that it also assists in language production. A word substituted in error frequently has formal resemblances to the target word (*average* for *avarice*). The SOT evidence suggests that important criteria for characterising word forms are:

- number of syllables: *sleep → speak*; *obsolete → absolute*
- location of stress: *unanimously → anonymously*; *comprehensive → contraceptive*
- initial syllable: *syllables → cylinders*; *Protestant → prostitute*
- final syllable or **rime**: *decimal → dismal*; *Alsatian → salvation*

The last two constitute what is sometimes termed the *bathtub effect*, with the first and last syllable of a word more robust and more likely to be retained in a Slip of the Tongue (*antidote → anecdote*). The analogy is to the head and knees of somebody in a small bath.

A simple view of lexical storage might suggest that words are in some way stored 'together' according to semantic and to formal criteria. This would assume an extremely large store with much replication. For example, the word CABBAGE would be stored with POTATO and PEA in a subset of vegetables; in a set of thousands of disyllabic words which bear initial stress; in other relatively large sets of words beginning with /kæ/ and CA; and in rather smaller sets ending in /ɪdʒ/ and -AGE. One solution is to assume that reception and production are separate processes, the former accessing words grouped by meaning (with cross-checks to form) and the latter accessing words grouped by form (with cross-checks to meaning).

However, a *network* model offers a more convincing account. Influenced by **connectionist** theory, such a model assumes that words are not stored together in sets but are linked by connections of varying strengths. Thus, there are strong semantic links between CABBAGE and POTATO and strong formal links between CABBAGE and CARRIAGE. Strong links might also be the consequence of regular co-occurrence – associating CABBAGE with (for example) CHINESE or RED. These links are strengthened as more and more examples are encountered of the two words used in conjunction.

Importantly, network models incorporate the principle of **spreading activation**. It is well documented that hearing or seeing a word such as DOCTOR will *prime* (speed up recognition of) associated words such as NURSE, PATIENT or HOSPITAL. This effect is represented in the form of **activation** – best envisaged as a kind of current which diminishes in strength as it travels further from the initial word. Thus, DOCTOR primes NURSE, but is unlikely to prime PLUMBER, even though the term is also a job.

An interesting finding in priming has been that concrete words do not appear to prime closely associated abstract words; and vice versa. This has suggested to some commentators that there may be separate lexical stores for the two types.

The notion of words as linked by a network of forms and meanings is an important one when considering language acquisition. Learning a new lexical item is not just a matter of mastering the form of the item and associating it with a sense or range of senses. The item also has to be linked to the whole network of previously learned words. If a child learns the word TERRIFIED, it has to (a) form a connection with HORRIFIED and TERRIER which are similar in form; (b) form a connection with AFRAID and SCARED which are similar (but distinct) in meaning.

Psycholinguistic research into second-language vocabulary acquisition and into the vocabulary of bilinguals has especially concerned itself with the question of whether the individual operates with a single unified store or two parallel ones. If the former is the case, words in L1 might be linked to those in L2 by shared meaning or by similarity of form. There is some evidence of formal links. With native Spanish speakers studying in the USA, the word RED in an English language task was shown to prime the word RED in a Spanish language task, even though in Spanish the word means 'net'. The same effect did not obtain between English FROG and Spanish *rana*.

See also: **Lexical access, Lexical entry, Semantic network**

Further reading: Aitchison (2003)

LEXICAL STRESS

A phonological feature of many languages, where one syllable of a word carries greater prominence than the others. Lexical stress does not vary, and is assumed to be part of a word's lexical entry. In English, lexical stress is marked acoustically by duration, loudness and/or pitch movement; and only falls on syllables with full quality vowels. In addition to the syllable bearing primary stress, others in a word may bear *secondary* stress – as in the third syllable of *SUperMARket*.

Stress appears to play an important part in the way speech is processed. There is evidence that listeners accord a higher level of attention to stressed syllables in English than to unstressed. This may be because stressed syllables are more *prominent*, especially in a noisy environment. They are also more *reliable*. They contain full quality vowels, and their phonemic segments, vowels and consonants alike, are less subject to reductions in duration. In addition, they are more *informative*. One way of representing imprecision in speech is to transcribe a corpus using a simplified system with only six phoneme categories. When researchers did this, they discovered that the number of words that were indistinguishable increased enormously if information relating to stress was not included.

One suggestion is that stressed syllables may provide the trigger for **lexical access**. POSS would form the **access code** for the word *imPOSSible* and TER for *alTERnative*. In this case, lexical access would not operate on strictly left-to-right principles, since access might be delayed until a stressed syllable was reached.

Listeners closely associate English weak syllables with functors. Indeed, it may be that unstressed syllables are not submitted to the lexicon at all, but are simply subjected to a *pattern-matching* process on the assumption that they constitute function words and have no lexical meaning.

A majority of the world's languages (perhaps around 70 per cent) have lexical stress that consistently falls on the same syllable of a word. Where it always falls on the first or last syllable, it can be regarded as *demarcative*, enabling the listener to determine where word boundaries fall. About 50 per cent of languages appear to fit this profile.

Although English does not, stress patterns still seem to assist listeners to locate word boundaries. Subjects have proved quite accurate in dividing up pieces of '*reiterant speech*' (utterances whose prosody is retained but whose syllables are replaced throughout by a sequence such as /mɑː/). This may be because the majority of content words in English consist of a stressed monosyllable or have a stressed first syllable.

A difficulty in assessing the contribution of stress to speech processing is that stress is relative. A syllable that bears primary stress is more prominent *in relation to the syllables around it*. On this argument, some commentators have concluded that vowel quality is a better discriminator of syllable types since quality lends itself to clear and rapid binary distinctions (+ or − weak vowel).

See also: **Lexical segmentation, SW (strong-weak) pattern**

Further reading: Laver (1994)

LEXICON (also MENTAL LEXICON)

The system of vocabulary which is stored in the mind in the form of a **lexical entry** for each item.

LINGUISTIC RELATIVITY

A theory of the relationship between speech and thought associated with Edward Sapir and Benjamin Whorf, and sometimes termed the *Sapir–Whorf Hypothesis*. The term is often used to cover two distinct theories:

- *linguistic relativity*: a view that each language has categories and distinctions which are unique to it;

- *linguistic determinism*: a view that the way in which we perceive and categorise the world is shaped by the language we speak.

The Hypothesis arose from anthropological work among speakers of Polynesian, North American Indian and Eskimo languages. The researchers adopted the questionable assumption that concepts not represented in the languages they studied were absent from the world view of the people who spoke them.

Today's view is that all human beings have access to basic concepts, but that languages differ in whether they *codify* (give form to) a particular concept or not. Thus, English codifies many more types of walking than most languages (WALK, STROLL, AMBLE, LOITER, WANDER, SCURRY, MARCH etc.); but speakers of other languages are still capable of recognising the concepts involved.

A major test for linguistic determinism was found in the fact that languages divide up the colour spectrum differently. If it could be shown that we do not all perceive the spectrum in the same way, it would suggest that our perception of the real world is indeed shaped by the way in which our language classifies and subcategorises it. In fact, research suggests that *focal points* (prototypes) for particular colours are not only shared by speakers of the same language, but are also shared across languages. There is agreement on 'typical values' for colours even where a language possesses fewer colour terms than English.

Directly opposed to linguistic relativity is a widely held view that **language universals** underlie the way in which languages encode reality. Some commentators would see these universals as deriving from the similar life experiences that human beings share across cultures. Others might attribute them to the fact that all human beings possess similar cognitive faculties and thus similar ways of viewing the world and organising information.

See also: **Colour systems, Concept, Language universals**

Further reading: Berlin and Kay (1969); Palmer (1981); Ungerer and Schmid (1996)

LISTENING *see* Cohort Theory, Lexical segmentation, Listening: higher-level processes, Normalisation, Speech perception, Speech signal, Unit of perception

LISTENING: HIGHER-LEVEL PROCESSES

The processing of spoken input at a *conceptual* level as distinct from a *perceptual* one. This entails:

□ *Constructing abstract meaning* from the linguistic material in an utterance.

□ *Employing contextual knowledge* to enrich understanding and to supplement what is stated by the speaker. Here, the listener draws upon:

- background knowledge, including world knowledge and knowledge of the speaker;
- previous experience of this type of speech event, of the level of attention that has to be accorded and the type of response that the listener is required to give;
- information gained in the course of the speech event.

□ *Integrating incoming information* into a *meaning representation* of the speech event so far. The process entails an ability to identify main ideas, to determine the relative importance of others and to establish relationships between ideas. Incoming information has to be related to what has gone before, so as to ensure that it is consistent and relevant.

□ *Monitoring comprehension* by checking the viability of the current interpretation.

As described so far, these higher-level processes are not dissimilar to those employed in reading. However, there are important differences between the two processes in that reading is potentially *recursive*: the reader can back-track to check understanding. By contrast, the listening signal is transitory. In addition, the time course of the reading process is under the control of the reader. In the listening process, the rate at which the signal is transmitted and processed is controlled not by the listener but by the speaker.

These factors have an important bearing on the way a listener builds meaning. Listeners have to carry information forward in their minds, without evidence against which to check it. Because of limitations of **working memory**, they only retain the actual words used by a speaker for a relatively short period of time. There is evidence of a **wrap up** process after each clause, in which the speaker's words are turned into abstract propositional information and can no longer be quoted.

However, while the clause is being uttered, the listener can, if necessary, **rehearse** the actual form of words used (recycle them in the mind in a phonological code) in order to retain them. The purpose is not to assist the listener in identifying words, since word recognition has been shown to take place **on–line**, as the words are being heard. It is to support the processing of any clauses and sentences that are syntactically complex or ambiguous. The phonological component of working memory plays an important role in this process. The amount that can be processed in **phonological working memory** appears to vary between individuals, and may determine how well a listener retains what is heard.

At the beginning of a piece of discourse, the listener sets up a set of expectations as to what will be said. As the utterance proceeds, the listener confirms, modifies or adds to this **schema** to build an ongoing meaning representation. Critical to higher-level listening processes is an element of **self-monitoring** where the listener evaluates their current interpretation. Evidence suggests that less–skilled listeners experience comprehension problems because they fail to self-monitor or because they make reduced use of monitoring strategies.

Alongside the developing meaning representation, the listener must also carry forward an awareness of the topic(s) currently being foreground by the speaker. This is necessary in order to achieve **anaphor resolution**. Anaphora (the use of referring words such as *she*, *it*, *this*) is generally less precise in speech than in writing and the listener cannot, like the reader, look back in order to identify what an anaphor is referring to.

The listener's meaning representation may not necessarily accord closely with the message intended by the speaker. While an assessment of the speaker's intentions is an important factor in shaping the representation, listeners do not passively 'receive' a message but actively *remake* it – taking from the utterance what they themselves deem to be relevant or important. They may even reinterpret what is said to fit their own viewpoint.

Listening is often thus less precise than reading, with the listener more inclined to accept areas of ambiguity or to process for gist rather than detail. However, in some ways the auditory signal is more informative than the visual one. The listener can rely upon features such as pausing, intonation and relative speech rate (see **prosody**) to support syntactic parsing and even to disambiguate sentences that would in print be ambiguous.

See also: **Inference, Interactional view, Meaning construction,**

Prosody, Reading: higher-level processes, Schema theory, Speech perception: autonomous vs interactive, Verbatim recall

Further reading: Brown (1995); Warren (1999)

LOGOGEN

A mechanism which collects evidence of the presence of a word in spoken or written input. An early **activation** model of **lexical access** (Morton, 1969) is based upon a system of thousands of logogens, each responsible for a single word in the user's lexicon. As evidence for a particular word accumulates, the activation of its logogen increases. Each logogen has a 'threshold'. When it reaches the threshold, it 'fires' and the word is treated as identified. At this point, the listener/reader is able to access the *cognitive system* for information about the word, including its meaning. (Note that this implies that meaning is not accessed until after recognition.) The speaker/writer is able to transmit the word to a *response buffer*, where it is stored, ready to be uttered.

Once a logogen has fired, its activation level only endures for about a second before decaying. However, it does not return to its original value for some considerable time. In this way, the model accounts for *repetition priming effects*, where a word is recognised more readily if it has been heard recently. Furthermore, each time a logogen reaches its threshold, the threshold is lowered a little: thus accounting for *frequency effects*, where words of high frequency are recognised more rapidly than infrequent ones.

See also: **Activation, Lexical access**

Further reading: Harris and Coltheart (1986)

LONG-TERM MEMORY (LTM)

A store for permanent information, including world knowledge, the **lexicon** and general linguistic competence. In many accounts, LTM is distinguished from a **sensory memory** store of very brief duration, and from a limited-capacity **working memory** (WM) which holds currently relevant information and handles cognitive operations. LTM supplies information to WM when it is required and receives information from WM that is destined for long-term storage.

An item of information (e.g. a phone number or a name that we want to remember) can be consolidated and transferred from WM to LTM by **rehearsal** – by repeating it silently in our minds. Similarly, the more often we retrieve a particular item of information from LTM, the easier it becomes to access it and the less likely it is to be lost. Information that is rarely retrieved may decay, as in language **attrition**. Some accounts suggest that this is due to the loss of *retrieval cues* linked to the information sought.

LTM would appear to involve multiple memory systems, each with different functions. A distinction is made between two particular types of knowledge: *declarative knowledge* (knowledge *that*) and *procedural knowledge* (knowledge *how*). The first constitutes the facts we know about the world, and the events we recall; the second enables us to perform activities, many of which are automatic. Declarative knowledge is usually explicit and capable of being expressed verbally; it includes the kinds of grammar rule that a linguist might formulate. By contrast, procedural knowledge is implicit; it includes the ability to process language without necessarily being able to put into words the rules that are being applied.

In a classic account of how **expertise** is acquired, information is received into LTM in declarative form and gradually becomes *proceduralised* as WM makes more and more use of it. A novice first draws on declarative knowledge in the form of a series of steps to which conscious attention (*control*) has to be given. In time, some of these steps become combined (*composed*), and the process becomes more and more automatic until it comes to form procedural knowledge.

Two types of declarative memory are generally recognised:

- *episodic memory* stores events; it is specific in terms of time and place;
- *semantic memory* stores generalised world knowledge.

The second may develop from the first. Imagine that a child stores in episodic memory a set of encounters with real-world entities that adults label DOG. From these experiences, it can extrapolate a set of common features (or possibly a **prototype**); it thus forms a category in semantic memory which serves to identify the whole class of dogs. An alternative, *exemplar-based* view would minimise the role of semantic memory and suggest that we identify examples of a category like DOG by relating them to many previous encounters with entities that have received this label, all of them stored episodically as individual events.

Semantic memory in LTM is sometimes represented as schematic in form. A **schema** is a set of interrelated features associated with an entity or concept. For example, the schema for PENGUIN might include: black and white – Antarctic – ice floe – fish – paperback publisher. Schematic information strongly influences the way in which we process incoming information, and is sometimes critical to the understanding of a text.

The ease with which a memory is retrieved from LTM is determined by how strongly *encoded* it is and by how precise are the available cues. Effective remembering may depend upon activating the same cues at retrieval as were originally encoded with the memory (the *encoding specificity* hypothesis). When subjects are asked to memorise the second words of some two-word compounds (e.g. STRAWBERRY JAM), the first word (STRAWBERRY) provides a powerful cue in later recall. However, the same does not occur if a different cue such as TRAFFIC is used.

See also: **Memory, Schema theory, Working memory**

Further reading: Cohen *et al.* (1993); Kellogg (1995: Chaps 4–6)

LOWER-LEVEL PROCESSING

Processing of data which is present in the speech signal or on the page. In reading, often referred to as *decoding*. Contrasted with **higher-level processing** which involves the use of contextual information such as world knowledge and the building of a *meaning representation*.

See also: **Bottom-up processing, Level of representation**

MAPPING (FORM-MEANING)

The process of establishing a connection between the form of a word or inflection and the meaning that it represents. Mapping by an adult language user is highly automatic, as shown by the **Stroop test**, in which subjects are asked to name the colour of the ink in which a colour word such as GREEN is written. They find it difficult if the ink is (say) blue, because they have to override a highly automatised link between GREEN and the colour it represents.

An important issue is how an infant manages to establish word-meaning links in acquiring its native language. If an adult points to a medium-sized animal and says '*dog*', a child could in theory assume that the word refers to a subordinate kind (= POODLE), a superordinate kind (= PET), an individual (= FIDO), a quality (= BROWN) or part of the whole (= TAIL). In mapping the word DOG on to a sub-class of animals, the child appears to make a number of (possibly innate) assumptions about words and the way they are used. The following constraints have been identified:

- *The whole object assumption.* Assume that the word relates to the whole rather than the part.
- *The taxonomic assumption.* Assume that the word refers to a class of objects or actions rather than a chance association (*dog* does not mean an animal with a bone in its mouth).
- *The mutual exclusivity assumption.* Assume that there is one label per concept. So, if a child does not have the word *dog* in its vocabulary, it will apply it to the whole object. If it already knows *dog* and hears *tail*, it will apply it to part of the object.

In its early form-meaning mappings, the child appears to make two further assumptions. There is the expectation that the first words encountered will be at **basic level** (referring to DOG rather than ANIMAL or POODLE). There is also an assumption of equal detail: having acquired the concept DOG, the child assumes that the label *cat* will be at the same level of specificity.

Clark (1993) identifies two larger-scale assumptions:

- *Conventionality*: that language is a system which links words and meanings in a consistent way.
- *Contrast*: that distinct forms represent distinct meanings. This principle leads infants to reject apparent synonyms. Preference is given to an established word; and a new one is treated as filling a lexical gap (which may involve narrowing the range covered by the earlier word).

The principle of contrast becomes more difficult to apply as the child's vocabulary expands and it encounters instances where there is not a one-to-one mapping between form and concept. Lexically, homonymy presents the infant with the challenge of having to map multiple meanings on to a single form (*right* = 'correct' vs *right* = 'not left'). But there is no evidence that infants avoid homophones such as TAIL/TALE, and they appear to accept readily that a single word form may fall into two different word classes (A NAME, TO NAME).

Children need minimal exposure to a new word form (sometimes just a single occurrence) before they assign some kind of meaning to it.

This phenomenon, referred to as *rapid mapping*, appears to help them to consolidate the form in their memory. The meaning first assigned may not coincide exactly with the adult one, though it often overlaps with it. Instances of **over-extension** or under-extension of the adult meaning are frequent. The initial hypothesis about the **concept** represented by a word is continually revised as new examples of the word form are encountered. If the word is polysemous, new variants of the core meaning are added.

Besides lexical items, the child also has to learn to attach significance to inflections. There is evidence that inflections are acquired more easily when mapping is one-to-one. Two-year-old infants growing up bilingual in Hungarian and Serbo-Croatian could produce accurate inflections to express location in Hungarian; but expressed the concept erratically in Serbo-Croatian (Slobin, 1973). The difference was attributed to the fact that there is a single suffix for each type of location in Hungarian, whereas Serbo-Croatian uses a mixture of prepositions and less sharply differentiated inflections.

See also: **Bootstrapping, Concept formation, Over-extension, Vocabulary acquisition**

Further reading: Bloom (2001); Bowerman and Levinson (2001); Clark (1993: Chaps 3–5); Markman (1990, 1994); Markman and Hutchinson (1984); Slobin (1982)

MARKEDNESS

The extent to which a particular linguistic form can be regarded as untypical, by comparison with others. Markedness theory states that, in a pair of minimally contrasted forms, one is likely to be more striking ('marked') than the other. Consider the sentences *I can* (/kən/) *swim* and *I CAN* (/kæn/) *swim*; the second is 'marked' because it is less usual and is emphatic.

The concept of markedness can be applied to phonology, morphology, lexis, syntax and word order. However, very mixed criteria (frequency, lack of inflection, regularity, neutral meaning etc.) are applied in determining whether one form is more primary than another.

Markedness applies within a single language, but it has also been suggested that certain features are 'unmarked' universally. They can be identified because they are less complex than other possible forms or because they are found to occur in most of the world's languages.

Awareness of unmarked forms is said to form part of an innate **Universal Grammar** (UG) which supports first language acquisition. An individual's language competence is represented as consisting of an unmarked *core grammar*, which forms part of UG and a *periphery* which contains exceptions to the rules, which have resulting from anachronisms, idioms etc. We are innately endowed with the core grammar but acquire the periphery through contact with the native language.

Chomskyan accounts make a further distinction (within the core grammar) between universal *principles* which apply to all languages and *parameters* which have to be set in relation to the language being acquired. An example of the latter is the *Pro-drop Parameter*, which has to be set either (a) to license the omission of a pronoun in Spanish (*Vivan aquí*) or (b) to enforce an obligatory pronoun in English (*They live here*). An important issue here is whether parameters are neutral at the outset or set at a 'default' (i.e. unmarked) value. Observational evidence suggests that pronoun omission is the unmarked setting: infants often miss out subject pronouns in the early stages of producing English.

The view that certain forms are universally unmarked has been used to account for the way in which language learners transfer certain features of their native language into a foreign language and not others. Eckman's (1977) *Markedness Differential Hypothesis* suggests that transfer is most likely to affect areas of the target language which are not just different from the native language but are relatively more marked. Thus, English speakers appear to have little difficulty in omitting pronouns when they learn a 'Pro-drop' language such as Spanish; but Spanish speakers sometimes have trouble adding the compulsory pronoun in English. This again suggests that the Pro-drop situation may be the unmarked one. (But see also **principles and parameters**).

See also: **Language universals, Universal Grammar**

Further reading: Archibald (1996: 512–20); Cook and Newson (1996)

MASKING

Intervention which makes a written or spoken word less easy to perceive. Masking is used experimentally to determine which cues in the signal are used by the reader or listener and what level of masking prevents recognition.

☐ *Visual masking.* Evidence from visual masking supports the view that readers process a word at many different levels – feature, letter and whole word. Briefly shown a word on a screen, subjects find it more difficult to report what the word is if it is immediately followed by another stimulus.

- In *brightness masking*, the subject is presented with a bright screen immediately after the word. If the brightness mask follows the word very rapidly, it interferes with recognition to such a degree that the word becomes indistinguishable from its background. Subjects report seeing a word for a reasonable length of time, but claim that it was not sharply enough defined. Brightness masking is said to block processing by interfering with the detection of features (the shapes that make up each letter).

- In *pattern masking*, the target word is followed immediately by a stimulus that conflicts with it. The stimulus might be a *feature mask*, a random assortment of lines and curves like those in actual letters. The newly introduced features interfere with those just detected in the target word and with the process of assembling them into letters. The result, again, is a reduced ability to identify the word. This time, subjects report seeing a sharply defined word, but not for long enough to recognise it. In another type of pattern mask, the interfering stimulus is an actual word. These *word masks* appear to interfere with processing at both letter and word level.

☐ *Auditory masking.* Experimenters use auditory masking to measure the amount by which the audibility of one sound is reduced by the presence of another (the '*masker*'). With *simultaneous masking*, the audibility of a signal is most strongly affected when the added sound has frequency components which are similar to the target one. This is taken as evidence of how selective the ear is in distinguishing frequencies. The decibel level of the masker is also an important factor: the effect on audibility relates closely to the ratio between signal and masker. Simultaneous masking thus has practical applications: showing, for example, what level of machinery noise prevents spoken communication between workers in a factory.

Audibility can also be affected by *forward masking*, where added sounds immediately precede the stimulus, and *backward masking*, where they follow it. The degree of forward masking is determined by the duration of the masker and how closely it precedes the target; here, increases in decibel level do not have a proportionate effect on audibility. Forward masking may possibly be caused by a reduction in the sensitivity of the ear following the masker or by the hearer retaining the masker signal after it has finished.

See also: **Intelligibility, Noise, Reading: decoding**

Further reading: Harris and Coltheart (1986: 153–9)

McGURK EFFECT

The impact of visual evidence (lip movements) on the sounds a listener reports hearing. Video recordings are made of a speaker saying two syllables which differ markedly in lip movements: for example [ba] and [da]. A range of synthesised sounds which advance in slow degrees from [ba] to [da] is then substituted for the soundtrack. When presented with a marginal example of [da], subjects are more likely to interpret it as [ba] if that is what the lips of the speaker are signalling. It thus seems that listeners make use of lip movements as cues when certain phonemes are not clearly articulated. The effect may be restricted to certain consonants such as bilabials and those which involve lip-rounding. Other phonemes are clearly not so visually distinctive.

MEAN LENGTH OF UTTERANCE (MLU)

The average number of morphemes produced per utterance. Irregular past forms are treated as single morphemes as are *gonna* and *wanna*. MLU is used to measure an infant's syntactic development. It is a more reliable measure than age, due to great variations in the rate at which infants acquire language.

See also: **Syntactic development**

MEANING CONSTRUCTION

Current theory rejects the idea that readers and listeners are passive and represents them as actively engaged in a task of meaning construction. An *'effort after meaning'* impels them to impose an interpretation even on an obscure text, and to keep updating it as new information comes in. They do not 'receive' the message encoded by a speaker/writer; they have to reconstruct it from the material of the utterance.

Central to meaning construction is the distinction between: (a) the words on the page or in the ear; (b) the *propositional* information that a text contains (loosely, its literal meaning); and (c) the enriched and selective interpretation which a reader or listener takes away. In processing a text, a comprehender performs a number of operations.

At sentence level, they:

- extract *propositional information*;
- make any necessary *inferences*;
- enrich the interpretation by applying *world knowledge*;
- integrate the new information into their *mental representation* of the text so far;
- *monitor their comprehension* in case of misunderstanding.

At discourse level, they also have to:

- recognise the *hierarchical structure* of the text;
- recognise *patterns of logic* which link the parts of the text;
- determine which parts of the text are important to the speaker/ writer or relevant to their own purposes.

A number of accounts of discourse comprehension attempt to describe the way in which text information is built into an overall meaning representation:

☐ The *early Kintsch and Van Dijk models* (Van Dijk and Kintsch, 1983) feature higher-level units of meaning, termed *macro-propositions*, which are achieved through the reader making judgements about which items of information are central to the text. Meaning construction operates in three stages. There is a *surface level* which takes the form of the actual words used in the text. There is a *text-base level* at which propositional information is established on a sentence-by-sentence basis. Finally, there is a *situational level* which brings in external knowledge; it is at this stage that propositional information is transformed into macro-propositions. Kintsch *et al.* attempted to support this theory experimentally by constructing texts based upon sets of propositions, which they categorised at several levels according to how critical they were deemed to be to the development of the text. They recorded that the more important propositions were more likely to be recalled.

☐ The two-step *Construction-Integration model* (Kintsch, 1988) updates the earlier theories, relying more heavily on **'bottom-up'** information from the text. At the *construction stage*, meanings are activated in the form of a loose network of associations. At the *integration stage*, a boost is given to information which is contextually relevant, so that a coherent text base can be created. Textual cues lead readers to give added weight to some sections: they might, for example, pay more heed to the opening sentence of a paragraph.

☐ The theory of *mental models* (Johnson–Laird, 1983) also postulates two stages: one at which propositional information is available and one at which an enriched interpretation is achieved through the listener/reader making inferences and bringing world knowledge to bear. A mental model is the representation of a text which they hold at any given moment. Whenever the latest proposition appears to make no reference to entities in the current model, the listener/reader initiates a new model. Similarly, two models are combined when the proposition seems to refer to entities that feature in both. Throughout, propositions are tested to ensure that their truth conforms to the truth of the model as a whole.

☐ The *Memory Focus Model* (Sanford and Garrod, 1981) has developed from work on **anaphor resolution**. At any given moment, a reader has a model of a text, in which there is an *explicit focus* upon the elements of the text that are currently foregrounded and an *implicit focus* upon other information being carried forward. The processing of a text is *selective* and can be shallow or deep. In some circumstances, top-down notions of the purpose of the text may override information at local level. Hence the *Moses illusion*: asked the anomalous question *How many animals of each kind did Moses put in the Ark?*, many subjects answer 'Two'.

☐ The *Structure Building Framework* (Gernsbacher, 1990) also provides a model of how readers build a coherent representation of a text. Here, the first stage of comprehension consists of laying a foundation, which is why reading times are longer for the first word of a sentence or the first sentence of a paragraph. The reader maps incoming information on to a current information substructure if it coheres with what is there. If it does not, the reader employs a *shifting process* which involves creating a new information substructure. Less-skilled comprehenders are said to shift too often because they do not make the appropriate connections. As a result, they build meaning representations at a very local level and fail to construct more global ones.

See also: **Focus, Mental model, Proposition, Schema theory, Story grammar**

Further reading: Garnham (1985: 152–82); Gernsbacher and Foertsch (1999); Kintsch (1994: 729–36); Stevenson (1993: Chap. 5).

MEANING POSTULATE

A device in formal semantics which aims to capture relations between the meanings of words by representing their *arguments*. An example for BUY and SELL is:

> *for any x, y, z: (x SELLS y to z if and only if z BUYS y from x)*

Two words are defined as synonymous if they have identical meaning postulates, a single word form as homonymous if more than one set of postulates is associated with it. Meaning postulates are said to be stored in long-term memory and retrieved in order to deal with issues of synonymy, ambiguity or entailment. The weakness of the postulates view is that it accounts for within-language relations but not for relations between language and the real world.

MEMORY

Early research into memory led to a *multi-store model* consisting of: sensory memory, short-term memory and long-term memory. The flow of information between these different stores is often represented as controlled by a *central executive*.

☐ *Sensory memory* is of extremely short duration, enabling the language user to retain a brief verbatim impression of the actual sound of speech (*echoic memory*) or the distribution of words on the page (*iconic memory*).

☐ *Short-term memory* (STM) holds a limited number of items for current processing. They might be items extracted from an incoming signal or items retrieved from the permanent store of long-term memory. Current theories of STM view it not simply as a store but as actively engaged in cognitive operations; hence a preference for the term **working memory**.

☐ *Long-term memory* (LTM) has unlimited capacity. It can be of extremely long duration, though the information it contains is reinforced by being used. LTM is said to contain knowledge of two types: *declarative knowledge* which gives us access to facts (knowledge *that*) and *procedural knowledge* which enables us to perform processes (knowledge *how*).

When subjects are asked to recall written or spoken lists of words, there is a *primacy effect*, with the first words on the list recalled better than those in the middle. This is associated with successful storage in LTM, subjects having had more opportunity to *rehearse* these earlier words in their minds. There is also a *recency* effect, with higher recall of the most recent words. This is attributed to subjects being able to retrieve words that are still available in STM. Patients suffering from a certain type of amnesia manifest the recency effect but not the primacy effect. This finding supports the theory that there are two separate components of memory, since it appears to reflect an inability to transfer words from one store (STM) to another (LTM).

However, other researchers have produced contradictory findings, and one body of opinion now favours a unitary memory store. In support of this view, there is evidence that the *code* in STM (the form in which information is stored) resembles more closely that of LTM than was originally supposed. An **embedded processes model** of memory suggests that STM as a whole is simply the currently activated part of LTM.

See also: **Long-term memory, Sensory memory, Short-term memory, Working memory**

Further reading: Baddeley (1982, 1997); Cohen (1989); Cohen *et al.* (1993); Henderson (1999)

MENTAL MODEL

A higher-level **mental representation** of the state of affairs conveyed by a text. It includes propositional ('core') meaning plus additional information contributed by the reader/listener and based upon inference and world knowledge. A model is continuously updated as more information from the text is integrated into it. The terms *situational model* and *referential representation* are used for very similar concepts.

The process of constructing a mental model is *elaborative* (adding inferences to achieve coherence), *integrative* (adding and relating incoming information) and *selective* (reducing stored information to what is essential/relevant). At the selective stage, the reader's goal may be important. Readers who are told to read a text about a house as if they were burglars will construct a different mental model from those who read it as potential purchasers.

Evidence confirms that readers/listeners form representations that are more detailed than purely propositional ones. A short while after reading or hearing a sentence, they may be unable to distinguish information which the text contains from information which they themselves have added by way of inference.

However, there is some disagreement as to the extent and nature of the inferences that a reader/listener adds. Those who take a *constructivist view* believe that the mental representation includes all inferences that are made; while those who take a *minimalist view* assert that only a limited number of necessary inferences are added in to the model. There is some evidence to suggest that *bridging inferences* are stored as part of an ongoing mental model, whereas *elaborative inferences* may not be. See **inference**.

In some situations, the mental model that is constructed is *indeterminate*. We might choose the most likely model from among several possibilities; or we might satisfy ourselves with a model that is less than complete but is sufficient for our purposes. It has been suggested that, in cases of **indeterminacy**, we may not construct a model at all, but rely on a representation that incorporates some of the wording of the text. However, there are also clearly instances when we satisfy ourselves with an incomplete mental model because of the complexity of the information we have to process – or because a given task only demands that we process the text at a relatively shallow level.

See also: **Inference, Meaning construction, Proposition, Schema theory, Story grammar**

Further reading: Garnham (1985: Chap. 7); Johnson-Laird (1983: 243–50, 370–87)

MENTAL REPRESENTATION

A non-verbal construct which forms a reader's/listener's understanding of a text and which is constantly updated as more information is processed. Sometimes referred to as a **mental model**, without necessarily implying a full commitment to Johnson-Laird's (1983) detailed theory of meaning. The terms *situational model* (Kintsch and Van Dijk) and *referential representation* (Just and Carpenter) are also used.

METACOGNITION

The ability to think about thinking. It involves being aware of mental processes, monitoring them and controlling them. Metacognition is regarded as an important part of **expertise** since it enables problem solving and strategy selection.

METAPHOR

Research has considered how we recognise that a statement is metaphorical rather than literal. A traditional view envisages three stages: forming a literal interpretation of the utterance; relating that interpretation to the immediate context and to world knowledge; then seeking a non-literal interpretation. The second stage has been related to Grice's (1975) maxim of quality: 'Do not say anything which you know to be false'. If the utterance is false in literal terms, then a metaphorical meaning must be intended.

Against the three-stage view, there is evidence that subjects take longer to reject as 'false' a statement that is potentially metaphorical (*Some desks are junkyards*) than one which is not (*Some desks are roads*). This suggests that they cannot resist the metaphorical association, and raises questions about whether the second stage actually occurs. Some commentators claim that clearly contextualised metaphors do not take longer to understand than comparable literal statements, and argue for a single-stage process, with literal and metaphorical statements processed in the same way.

One theory traces parallels between metaphorical and class-inclusion statements. The statement *My dog is an animal* relates an example to a category whose characteristics we understand. The statement *Rambo is an animal* can thus be processed in a similar way. Like many class-inclusion statements, metaphors appear to be highly context-dependent. In these examples, different attributes of *time bomb* are foregrounded (or **instantiated**) depending on the context:

a. *Cigarettes are time bombs.*   b. *Human beings are time bombs.*

See also: **Figurative language**

Further reading: Cacciari and Glucksberg (1994); Stevenson (1993: 148–55)

MIGRATION

A research method (Kolinsky, 1992) for investigating the units that are used in speech perception. Pairs of non-words are designed, where the first part of one word and the second part of the other form an actual word. An example is /kɔʒu/ and /bitɔ̃/ which, recombined, form the French words *bijou* and *coton*. The non-word pairs are presented *dichotically* to the listener – one to the left ear and one to the right. If the listener reports the illusion of hearing an actual word, it indicates that they have employed a representation unit lower than the word (in the example given, the syllable) at some point in the perceptual process.

See also: **Dichotic listening**

MODALITY

The form in which a piece of language is produced – whether speech (*spoken modality*) or writing (*visual modality*).

MODEL

A theoretical step-by-step account of a psychological process, sometimes represented in diagrammatic or flowchart form. Many psycholinguistic models draw conclusions about human processing by analogy with the operations of computers. The different components of a model and their interconnections are described as the model's *architecture*.

The stages of the process might take the form of a *heuristic*: a rule-of-thumb **problem-solving** procedure which can usually (but not always) be relied upon to achieve a desired outcome. Or they might be presented as an *algorithm*, a failsafe step-by-step problem-solving procedure which is certain to achieve the desired outcome but may be slower than a heuristic.

Today, some models (notably **connectionist** ones) also mirror the way in which the brain transmits information by electrical impulses across multiple neural connections.

MODULARITY₁

The hypothesis that language is a separate faculty, supported by general cognition but not dependent upon it. It is especially associated with the **nativist** view that language is genetically transmitted.

Arguments in favour of modularity include the fact nearly every infant manages to achieve full linguistic competence, regardless of variations in intelligence and in ability to perform other cognitive functions. There are also forms of impairment where language and general intelligence seem dissociated:

- In **specific language impairment**, sufferers show signs of normal cognitive development but their language remains incomplete in certain important features (particularly inflections and function words).
- Williams Syndrome presents the opposite symptoms. Sufferers show signs of cognitive impairment, including low IQs. However, language is spared; indeed Williams sufferers are often extremely communicative and their vocabulary and speaking skills may be above normal at early ages.
- A remarkable case has been identified of a **savant** named Christopher who was diagnosed as brain-damaged and has to live in care but who is able to translate into and out of sixteen languages.

However, contrary evidence comes from other forms of impairment such as **Down's Syndrome**, where both language and mental capacity are impaired. Likewise, **autism** presents symptoms of cognitive and social impairment which affect all forms of communication.

Incompatible with the modularity hypothesis is the view of some neuroscientists that language maps on to operations of the brain which originally served other cognitive functions. Evidence from brain imaging is cited which shows that language operations are widely distributed throughout the brain. An explanation given for the Williams symptoms is that certain parts of the brain are affected but that those which subserve language are spared. There is also an evolutionary argument which suggests that it is more likely that language adapted to the brain than that the brain adapted to language.

See also: **Brain: localisation, Evolution of language, Nativism**

Further reading: Bishop (1997); Crain and Lillo-Martin (1999: 61–70); Pinker (1994b)

MODULARITY$_2$ (also AUTONOMY)

A view that each level of language processing operates independently of the others.

In an *autonomous* model, each level achieves an output, which it then passes on to the level above. This enables the processor to accurately interpret a sequence such as /kɑ:dn/ at phoneme level without suffering bias from the fact that the sequence closely resembles the word GARDEN. The latter consideration only comes into play when the output of phoneme processing reaches word level. The advantage of having information *encapsulated* in this way is that the processor can focus on one set of criteria at a time.

An alternative view regards language processing as **interactive**. At the very least, this implies that information from a particular level can influence processing at the level immediately above or below: thus, in the example just given, there would be an interaction between the phonemic evidence and the knowledge from word level of the existence of GARDEN.

In a *highly interactive* model, all levels of processing influence all others in both a **bottom-up** and a **top-down** way. Thus, our recognition of the word GARDEN might be influenced by the preceding context: *My neighbour's planting flowers in his-*. The advantage of this kind of model is that all sources of information can be considered at once in order to resolve ambiguities. The disadvantage is that decisions become much more complex and thus, in principle, make heavier demands on **working memory**.

Often cited in favour of modularity is evidence (Swinney, 1979) that both meanings of a homophonous word become activated, even when the preceding context indicates which is the appropriate one. This suggests that the lexical stage has to be completed before the listener/reader is able to consider evidence at a higher (contextual) level.

Discussion of modularity is much influenced by Fodor (1983). He views the mind as composed of a set of central systems which handle generalised operations such as attention or memory. These are supplied with information by *input systems* which process sensory information and language. The input systems are modular and each has specific functions. Fodor characterises the systems as:

- *Domain specific.* Input via the ears is processed as simple auditory input in the case of music or the noise of traffic, but is recoded phonologically by the speech module if it takes the form of speech.

- *Mandatory.* We cannot help hearing an utterance as an example of speech.
- *Fast.* The processes are highly automatic.
- *Informationally encapsulated.* A module receives information from other modules and passes it on, but its immediate operation is not affected by information contained elsewhere. So, while engaged in processing a spoken word we cannot use context to identify the word more quickly (this does not preclude the use of contextual information at a later, **post-perceptual** stage).
- *Localised.* Input systems are part of the *hard-wiring* of the brain; there is a fixed neural architecture for each.

See also: **Interactive activation**

Further reading: Fodor (1983); Wingfield and Titone (1998: 253–7)

MORPHOLOGY: ACQUISITION

A child's early utterances lack a system of inflections; the child tends to adopt a single form for all contexts – either the root or the most frequent inflected form. One theory in the Chomskyan tradition (Radford, 1990) suggests that the grammar with which an infant is born lacks a morphological component, which develops later as part of *maturation*.

The speed with which inflections are acquired appears to be partly determined by whether there is a single form for each function. For example, infants growing up bilingual in Hungarian and Serbo-Croatian produce inflections of location earlier in Hungarian, which has a different suffix for each type of location in a way that Serbo-Croatian does not.

Some commentators have suggested that *perceptual saliency* may also be a factor in the acquisition of inflections. English inflections are of low perceptibility compared with (say) those of Italian – one possible explanation of why the use of inflections is much less affected in the speech of Italians with **specific language impairment** than it is with English sufferers.

Early research suggested that basic English inflections appear in the infant's productions in a fixed **order of acquisition**. However, it is difficult to say precisely when a form has been 'acquired'. Indeed, a suggestion has been made that many regular verb forms may first be acquired by an infant as separate items (WALKED, WAITED, FOLLOWED) before an inflectional rule ('add -*ed*') is later inferred.

Semantic notions also appear to support the development of morphological knowledge. Early use of the *-ing* inflection in English seems to be associated with extended events: it often appears first with durative verbs such as WAIT. Similarly, the *-ed* inflection is associated with momentaneous events, and often appears first with verbs like DROP.

See also: **Mapping, Order of acquisition, Syntactic development**

Further reading: Derwing and Baker (1986); Owens (2001); Peters (1995)

MORPHOLOGY: STORAGE

Research has focused on how inflectional and derivational morphemes are stored and accessed, and on what constitutes a **word primitive**, the smallest unit of meaning stored in the lexicon. Three views are possible:

☐ Each lexical item is stored in the lexicon as an individual entry. There are thus entries for HAPPY, UNHAPPY and HAPPINESS and for WALKED as well as WALK. However, there are close links between related items.

☐ There are separate entries for productive bound morphemes: affixes like UN- and -NESS have entries alongside actual words such as HAPPY.

☐ Inflected forms are stored under their root. In order to retrieve UNHAPPY, one has to access HAPPY.

Evidence from **Slips of the Tongue** and from **aphasia** strongly suggests that inflected forms are constructed during the planning of speech: i.e. that we access WALK and then attach -ED to it at a later stage. Any other solution would appear to be wasteful in terms of what is stored in the lexicon. However, certain items may possibly be stored as wholes because they are usually encountered in an inflected form (EYES, HAPPENED).

The situation for derived forms is less clear-cut. In forming UNHAPPY from HAPPY, the language effectively creates a new unit of meaning. Furthermore, the connection between HAPPY and UNHAPPY is not fixed by a rule like that between WALK and WALKED. There would have to be strong links between HAPPY and the prefix UN- to avoid misassembled forms such as DISHAPPY or INHAPPY.

The 'separate storage' account entails considerable complications for the reader or listener. In order to access the meaning of a word like UNHAPPY, a reader would have to ignore the prefix UN- and focus on the word's root. Listeners would have to identify the prefix and store it in memory until the root had been heard. Since listening takes place in real-time, they would need to operate on the assumption that all sequences such as /ɪn/ or /rɪ/ or /dɪs/ were prefixes. This would mean that they ended up stripping off pseudo-prefixes such as *re-* in *return* or *dis-* in *display*, which would then have to be restored in order to identify the target word. There is some evidence that this is what happens: readers are said to be slower to recognise words with pseudo-prefixes, perhaps because they lead to erroneous *prefix-stripping*.

But the process is not an efficient one – and the existence of large numbers of pseudo-prefixes in certain languages raises serious questions about the validity of the prefix-stripping account. It has been calculated that up to 80 per cent of words in English beginning with strings that appear to be prefixes are in fact pseudo-prefixed. One compromise solution is that lexical access of derived forms does not depend critically upon decomposition but that decomposition *can* occur.

It should be noted that the same complication does not arise with suffixes. Here, stripping is not necessary, since the root has already been identified by the listener before the suffix is reached. It is interesting to note that, across languages, suffixation is much more frequent than prefixation; this may be because suffixes cause fewer problems of processing.

Despite the above complications, an investigation by Marslen-Wilson *et al.* (1994) appears to provide new evidence for separate storage of affixes. It made use of the **priming** task, which indicates how closely words (in this case, spoken words) are associated with each other. The results suggested two-way links between affixed forms and their roots. But whereas a prefixed form appears to give a boost to other forms bearing the same prefix, there is no such effect with suffixed forms. The explanation offered is that hearing a prefix or pseudo-prefix activates a whole group of associated words; but that no **competition** between the words takes place until the root is reached, so all the words remain highly activated. The researchers suggest that their results support a decomposition model in which potential affixes are clustered around a root (UN- and -NESS attached to the head word HAPPY).

See also: **Access code, Lexical entry, Word primitive**

Further reading: Aitchison (2003: Chap. 11); McQueen and Cutler (1998); Marslen-Wilson (1999); Stemberger (1998); Taft (1981)

NATIVISATION HYPOTHESIS

A theory that, when linguistic input is not available or not accessible, children fall back on an innate biological capacity for language and construct a language for themselves following universal norms. Evidence to support this theory comes from **creolisation** and from *homesign*, a gestural language constructed independently by deaf infants who have not been taught Sign. When sufficient linguistic data is available, a process of *denativisation* occurs, with the learner adjusting their original innate grammar in accordance with the ambient language.

See also: **Creolisation**

NATIVISM

The view that language is genetically transmitted, and that children are born with an innate language faculty.

A conflict between two views of the origin of knowledge (including linguistic knowledge) goes back over two thousand years. Plato expressed the view (*Plato's problem*) that a child could not possibly, in the short time available to it, acquire the range of knowledge that an adult displays. Nativist arguments were eclipsed in the mid-twentieth-century heyday of **behaviourism**, when language was viewed as a habit acquired through a process of stimulus, reinforcement and reward. But they resurfaced powerfully with Chomsky's critique of behaviourist doctrine in his 1959 review of B.F. Skinner's *Verbal Behavior*. Chomsky concluded that language acquisition was only explicable if one postulated the existence of a faculty, present from birth, which supported it. The neurologist Lenneberg also argued in favour of nativism on the grounds that language shows features similar to other types of behaviour which are *biologically triggered*. This suggested to him that it was controlled by some innate mechanism.

In the Chomskyan tradition, a number of standard arguments are invoked against the empiricist view that language is acquired entirely through exposure to adult speech:

a. *Timescale.* In the space of only five years, the child acquires a vocabulary of about 5000 words and the ability to produce a range of well-formed utterances, some of which it may never have heard before.

b. *Lack of correlation between intelligence and language acquisition.* All children achieve mastery of their first language regardless of variations in intelligence and in their ability to perform other cognitive operations.

c.1 *Input: 'Poverty of stimulus'.* Chomsky (1965) described as 'degenerate' the adult speech from which the child supposedly acquires language. It contains all the features of natural connected speech (hesitations etc.) – including errors of grammar. It exemplifies only a limited range of the possible sentences of the language. The child is exposed to a range of speakers, with different voices, intonation patterns and accents. Finally, the input provides examples of language *performance* when the child's goal is to develop *competence*. How is the child to build the latter solely on random evidence of the former?

c.2 *Input: linearity.* An empiricist view assumes that the child induces the rules of grammar by generalising from specific utterances. But *Gold's theorem* (1967) calculated that this process cannot account for the way in which the child acquires the concept of *structure-dependency* (the recognition that language is composed of sets of phrases which are organised into a hierarchy). It cannot account for anything more than a *finite-state* (word-by-word) grammar.

c.3 *Input: negative evidence.* Infants are said to require negative evidence (evidence of sentences which are not acceptable) to show them which syntactic patterns are not permissible; this is self-evidently not available in the input they receive. Example: An infant exposed to Italian has evidence that utterances occur 'with subject pronoun' and (more frequently) 'without subject pronoun'. An infant exposed to English encounters many examples of the 'with subject pronoun' condition, but never any of the negative rule that 'without subject pronoun' is not permissible in English.

c.4 *Input: carer correction.* Carers tend to correct facts rather than syntax (though they are more likely to repeat grammatically correct sentences). Any attempts to correct syntax and phonology produce little immediate effect.

d. *Order of acquisition.* Within a given language (and even across languages), there is evidence that children acquire certain syntactic features in a set order. The child also produces language for which there is no evidence in the input: for example, incorrect Past

Simple forms such as *goed* or *seed*. This cannot come from adult examples; it indicates that the child is in the process of building up a system of language for itself.

Nativist accounts of language acquisition vary widely: not least, in how they represent what it is that is genetically transmitted. Chomsky originally (1965) hypothesised that infants are born with a **Language acquisition device** (LAD), a mechanism which enabled them to trace patterns in the impoverished data with which they were presented. In his later work, the LAD is replaced with the concept of a **Universal Grammar** (UG), alerting the child to those features which are common to most or all of the world's languages and enabling it to recognise them in the speech it hears. UG consists of a set of **principles** which specify the essential nature of language: they include structure-dependency and the presence of words. It also includes a set of *parameters*, linguistic features which can be set according to the language that the child is acquiring.

Pinker (1994b) takes a more radical nativist view, asserting that we are innately endowed with *mentalese*, an internal language of thought. First language acquisition involves translating this language into strings of words specific to the language being acquired. Mentalese is abstract but closely parallels speech. The mapping between mentalese and speech is assisted by Universal Grammar which, in Pinker's account, includes specific linguistic information such as the existence of nouns and verbs and the categories of subject and object.

There are differing accounts of the status of Universal Grammar at the time the child is born. *Continuity theory* asserts that UG is **hard-wired** in the child, with all its features present from birth. They cannot all be applied at once, however, because the development of one piece of linguistic knowledge may be dependent upon another having been established and/or upon the child's cognitive development. Thus, the concept of Subject + Verb + Object cannot be achieved until after the child has recognised the word as an independent unit and developed the memory capacity to retain a three-word utterance.

By contrast, *maturational theory* suggests that the acquisition of syntactic concepts is biologically programmed in the child, just as the growth of teeth or the development of vision is programmed.

While the nativist view still commands widespread support, alternatives have increasingly come under consideration. This is partly because research into **child directed speech** has shown that it is not as degenerate as Chomsky assumed. It is partly because the

Chomskyan view of language as infinitely productive has been questioned in the light of evidence that pre-assembled formulaic **chunks** play an important role in many utterances. It is also because **connectionist** computer models have demonstrated that learning can indeed take place by dint of tracing patterns across multiple examples of linguistic features and adjusting the system to take account of errors.

A further problem for nativist accounts is the need to explain the concept of a genetically transmitted universal grammar in terms of *phylogeny* (the development of the language faculty in the species) as well as *ontogeny* (the development of the faculty in the individual). Chomsky has tended to favour the view that language appeared as the result of a mutation or accident. Other nativists have suggested that the brain gradually evolved to include a language component. However, brain evolution is very slow, whereas language change is rapid. This has suggested to non-nativists that perhaps it was language that evolved to fit the functions of the brain rather than vice versa.

See also: **Child Directed Speech, Chomskyan theory, Cognitivism, Empiricism, 'Less is more', Modularity₁, Principles and parameters, Social-interactionism, Universal Grammar**

Further reading: Pinker (1994b); Smith (1999: Chaps 1, 3)

NEIGHBOURHOOD

The neighbourhood of a word is the set of all the words in the **lexicon** which are minimally different from it. The term is usually applied to written forms but has also been used in theories of spoken word recognition. In theory, a neighbourhood includes words that are different by one letter, regardless of the position of the letter: on this analysis, REAP, BEAD, REED and ROAD are neighbours of READ. However, the term is often restricted to words which differ in their initial letter, initial digraph (TH-, SH-) or initial consonant cluster (PL-, BR-). For READ, it would include LEAD, BEAD, HEAD, DEAD etc. Within a neighbourhood, there are *friends*: words which share the same **rime** as well as the same spelling (the verb LEAD, BEAD). There are also *enemies*: words with the same spelling but a different rime (HEAD, BREAD, DEAD, the noun LEAD).

The neighbourhood concept serves to identify words which are in **competition** with each other by virtue of similarity of form. The sight of the word *read* on the page activates not only READ but also neighbours which form close matches to the target.

There is evidence that the time it takes to recognise a given word is affected by the size of its neighbourhood and the number of friends and enemies it possesses. Thus, recognition of a word like READ will be slowed by the existence of friends such as BEAD and particularly by the existence of enemies such as DEAD, HEAD, BREAD etc. By contrast, words like FEET or SIDE are recognised rapidly because they have few friends and no enemies.

The situation is complicated by the need to take account of the possible effects of **frequency**. A word such as HAVE has no friends and a number of enemies (CAVE, WAVE, RAVE, SAVE etc.) but happens to be a very frequent item. Some accounts therefore represent neighbourhood effects in terms of the frequency of the target word in relation to the accumulated frequencies of its neighbours. There is some disagreement between experimenters who have found that delayed recognition correlates with *neighbourhood density* (number of neighbours) and others who suggest that it correlates with total *neighbourhood frequency*.

In the *Neighbourhood Activation Model*, the speed with which a word is matched to a form on the page is determined by the probability that it, rather than its neighbours, is the correct choice. A formula has been devised to calculate this *neighbourhood probability*: the frequency of a given word is divided by the sum of frequencies of the entire neighbourhood.

It has been demonstrated that a sequence like GOPE (friendly neighbours in HOPE, ROPE) is identified as a non-word more rapidly than a sequence like HEAF (conflicting neighbours in LEAF, DEAF). This challenges the idea that reading non-words involves simply applying rules based on standard sound-spelling relationships. One solution is to assume that these rules include all possible interpretations of a particular letter or *digraph* (-EA- being recognised as potentially both /iː/ and /e/). Another approach, sometimes represented as an alternative to a neighbourhood account, is **analogy** theory, which suggests that words are interpreted phonologically by analogy with others, perhaps mainly on the basis of their rime.

See also: **Analogy model, Competition, Rime**

Further reading: Harley (2001: 182–8); Luce *et al.* (1990)

NEURAL NETWORK

The basis of a **connectionist** model of language processing: a set of massively interconnected nodes which resemble neurons in the brain. The power of such a network derives not from the nodes themselves but from the connections that link them. Energy (or **activation**) spreads around the system in a way that is constrained by the strengths of the connections between the nodes. The connections are strengthened by frequent use.

The term 'neural network' is sometimes used as a synonym for a connectionist or **parallel distributed processing** model.

See also: **Connectionism, Parallel distributed processing**

NEUROLINGUISTICS

The study of how the brain stores and transmits language. Important areas of research include where language is localised in the brain, which parts of the brain are active during different linguistic processes and the effects of brain damage or disease on language.

NOISE

Non-speech sounds which potentially reduce the intelligibility of speech. The term is also sometimes used for factors (e.g. ink blots) which reduce the legibility of written text and even for factors such as individual voice quality which are not essential to speech processing.

The intelligibility of a speech signal depends upon the ratio between the level of speech and the level of noise; this is termed the *S/N ratio*. For normal understanding, there should be an S/N ratio of +6 decibels (i.e. the average speech level should exceed the average noise level by 6 decibels). Where speech and noise are at equal levels, only about 50 per cent of words are recognised. However, even with negative S/N ratios, speech may remain partly intelligible – especially if the listener is familiar with the topic or if the sources of speech and noise are widely separated. An important factor is also whether the noise is continuous or intermittent: continuous noise has a far more powerful effect in masking speech.

In order to test the capacity of the human ear or the ways in which we process a *degraded* speech signal, experimenters sometimes add *white noise* to speech. White noise is a constant hiss like an extended fricative or like radio static. It is *aperiodic*: its average loudness remains constant over the entire range of audible frequencies.

See also: **Intelligibility**

NORMALISATION

Applying a standard interpretation to material which contains non-standard features. Especially used for the way in which a listener matches highly variable speech input to a set of phoneme values.

The assumption is often made that **phonological representation** consists of 'core' or prototypical phoneme values stored in memory. The question then arises of how one is able to identify phonemes in connected speech when they often diverge enormously from this core value. And how is one to edit out the many features in the speech signal (some individual to the talker) which do not contribute in any way to the task of phoneme identification, and may even obscure it?

It is assumed that listeners edit (*normalise*) the material in the speech signal in order to achieve a 'best match' with the standard phoneme values stored in their minds. In the process of editing, irrelevant features are suppressed. These might include features that are:

- *specific to the talker*: characteristics of the talker's voice, the talker's accent or the talker's individual speaking style;
- *specific to the environment*, e.g. hiss on a recording;
- *specific to the phonological context* in which a phoneme appears.

Such features were initially assumed to interfere with the matching task and were treated as **'noise'**. However, if they were completely deleted from the record, then they could not be transferred to long-term memory. This cannot be what happens since we succeed extremely well in recalling the characteristics of individual voices. It was therefore suggested that the phonetic information in the input is processed separately and at a different level of attention from the *indexical* information relating to voice type and quality.

Recent research has raised questions about this view of normalisation. There is now considerable evidence that phonetic information and indexical information are more closely linked in the listening process than was supposed: for example, words are identified more quickly if they are heard in a known voice. It appears that the indexical features of a talker's voice are encoded in memory together with the linguistic message.

Some commentators have questioned the long-held assumption that we match widely variant input to a set of standard values. They suggest that phonological representation is much more detailed, taking the form of *multiple traces* of all the encounters we have had with a particular phoneme. We are thus able to match the input directly to a previously encountered variant of a phoneme, without recourse to a normalisation process that involves editing what we hear. Among the details stored may be representations of an individual talker's accent and of their personal speech characteristics.

Even if one accepts this view, there still remain ways in which a listener needs to accommodate to a talker. The term 'normalisation' is also used for a process whereby a listener adjusts their analysis of a speech signal in order to take account of characteristics of the voice of the speaker, including accent, loudness, speech rate and intonation patterns. The most obvious example is when meeting somebody whose voice or whose accent is unfamiliar. The pitch of the speech signal appears to provide information about the size and shape of the speaker's vowel tract – information which influences a listener's interpretation of the sounds they hear.

Similarly, listeners make fine judgements based upon an assessment of the rate at which a talker is speaking. Experiments in which slow speech is inserted into a more rapid utterance have shown that **articulation rate** contributes importantly to phoneme identification. Judgements of this type cannot be based upon a talker's average speech rate, but must be revised from moment to moment during a conversation.

See also: **Phonological representation, Speech perception: phoneme variation**

Further reading: Johnson and Mullenix (1997)

ON-LINE PROCESS

A process that analyses a signal as it is being received (in *real time*). The term is often used to describe listening, since it has been shown that listeners begin to process what they hear about 200–250 milliseconds after a speaker has uttered it, rather than waiting until a major constituent such as a phrase or sentences is complete.

ON-LINE TASK

An experimental task that taps into a process at precisely the moment it is occurring. The task is designed so that it does not include effects which are due to memory or, for example, to decisions which interpret what a subject has perceived.

See also: **Post-perceptual**

OPERATING PRINCIPLES

A set of strategies used by an infant which enable it to analyse the utterances it encounters and to formulate its own utterances. Evidence of such strategies has been drawn from a number of languages.

The notion of operating principles (Slobin, 1970, 1985) accounts for the speed and apparent ease with which infants acquire language, but avoids the standard **nativist** assumption that infants are pre-programmed with strong linguistic constraints which form part of a **Universal Grammar**. Slobin's operating principles include:

- Pay attention to the ends of words.
- Words can be modified phonologically.
- Pay attention to the order of morphemes and words.
- Avoid interrupting or rearranging units.
- Underlying semantic relations should be clearly marked.
- Avoid exceptions.
- The use of grammatical markers is meaningful and systematic.

Certain strategies are prioritised: for example, the child concentrates first on mapping speech on to objects and events. A more recent set of operating criteria (Table O1) extends the notion that acquisition occurs through prioritising certain features.

See also: **Bootstrapping**

Further reading: Aitchison (1998: 154–9); Taylor and Taylor (1990)

Table O1 Operating principles based on prioritisation (adapted from Taylor and Taylor, 1990)

Priority given to...	before...
simple and short	complex and long
gross distinctions	fine distinctions
perceptually salient real-world items (in terms of size, colour)	less salient items
personal	non-personal
here and now	displaced in space and time
concrete	abstract
frequent, familiar	infrequent, unfamiliar
regular forms	irregular forms
isolated units of language	interconnected units of language
whole units (e.g. chunks)	constituent parts

ORDER OF ACQUISITION

A fixed order in which an infant acquires the syntactic, morphological or phonological features of its target language. If a *natural order* of this kind exists, it might provide evidence in support of the **nativist** notion that human beings are innately endowed with a **Universal Grammar** which determines the way in which their first language is acquired.

Early evidence from so-called *morpheme studies* suggested that certain inflections of English were indeed acquired in a fixed order. The age and rate at which they were acquired by the infant might vary; but the order remained relatively constant. The first inflection acquired (between 19 and 28 months) is usually *-ing* as in *Mommy driving*. It is followed by the *-s* plural at 27 to 33 months. Next come the possessive and the irregular Past Simple. The features selected for these studies included function words as well as inflections. Some of the functors (e.g. prepositions) were semantically quite transparent and shown to be acquired early; others (e.g. the articles) were more complex and delayed.

The results were not as conclusive as is sometimes suggested: they showed a considerable time overlap between certain features. In addition, there are a number of serious problems with this kind of study – not least the difficulty of establishing at what point a child can be treated as having 'acquired' a particular form. The usual yardstick is

90 per cent accuracy of use, but this ignores the fact that the child might have mastered the form receptively long before producing it. Furthermore, many inflections first occur attached to a limited set of words – suggesting that these particular items may have been acquired as a single unit. A further problem in determining 'acquisition' is that, after apparently mastering a form, the child may show signs of **U-shaped development** where the correct form is replaced by an erroneous one. Finally, considerations of meaning as well as form may be involved: *-ing* tends to appear first on durative verbs (e.g. *driving*) and *-ed* on verbs of rapid action (*dropped*). This suggests that these forms are first acquired as unanalysed vocabulary items.

Later research has considered semantic as well as formal criteria. It suggested that deixis (*this, that, here, there*) emerges early, though infants have difficulty in adjusting to the viewpoint of their co-locutor. There seems to be considerable variation in the age at which definite and indefinite articles are used consistently, though the distinction between common and proper nouns (*That's Dax* vs *That's a dax*) is grasped quite quickly. It has been noted that subject pronouns are often absent from early utterances. *I* and *it* tend to appear before *you*, singular forms before plural and masculine before feminine.

If there is indeed a consistent order of acquisition for certain inflections and syntactic features, the reasons may lie within the language being acquired rather than in the projections of a universal grammar. It appears that the frequency with which an item occurs in adult speech does not correlate with the speed at which an infant acquires it. Instead, cross-lingual studies have suggested that the order of acquisition may reflect the relative difficulty of a feature within a particular language. Thus the plural is acquired quite early in English but later in Arabic (which has a dual form as well as a plural and distinguishes gender). Similarly, gender emerges early in English, where it is related to natural gender and chiefly affects the *he/she* contrast; but much later in Fulani, a West African language which is remarkable for having 12 genders.

Variations may also reflect the relative importance of a feature. Children acquiring highly inflected languages (Russian, Hungarian) show an early sensitivity to inflections. There is evidence of rapid and accurate mastery of inflections among children acquiring Greenlandic Eskimo, Japanese, Turkish and German. Similarly, in languages where word order is important, children seem to recognise the importance of order very early.

Variation in order of acquisition between languages is neatly accounted for in **Chomskyan theory** by suggesting that the infant has to set certain *parameters* in relation to the language it is acquiring (for example, it has to determine whether the language licenses the omission of subject pronouns or not). Order of acquisition thus reflects the relative difficulty of setting different parameters.

One theory in the Chomskyan tradition (Radford, 1990) suggests that infants start out with an innate grammar that is based upon a reduced system, lacking inflections, determiners and complementiser phrases (*I know that he is innocent*). The order in which features of language are acquired is determined by the gradual development of these tree branches within the child's grammar.

See also: **Language acquisition: stages, Syntactic development**

Further reading: Aitchison (1998: Chap. 4); Fletcher and Garman (1986: 307–447); Foster-Cohen (1999: Chaps 6–7); Slobin (1982)

ORTHOGRAPHIC CODING

The ability to recognise written words purely by their form. It is tested by asking subjects to determine which of two potentially homophonous forms is an actual word (e.g. RAIN vs RANE). By contrast, phonological coding is tested by asking subjects to read aloud nonwords. Evidence from monozygotic (same egg) twins suggests that phonological coding ability is heritable whereas orthographic coding ability is not.

ORTHOGRAPHY

The spelling system of a language. It is important to distinguish between a language's orthography, its **writing system** (employing letters, syllables or whole-word characters) and its *script* (the character shapes it uses as in 'Arabic script', 'Greek script').

Alphabetic orthographies vary considerably. Some, such as Arabic, represent consonants but do not always display vowels. Orthographies can also be characterised according to how close the match is between *graphemes* (units of writing) and phonemes. Spanish, for example, provides an example of a *transparent* orthography, with a one-to-one relationship between written forms and sounds. All its words can be interpreted using consistent **grapheme–phoneme correspondence** (GPC) rules. English provides an example of an *opaque* orthography, because it contains a mixture of:

- words that can be spelt using GPC rules (e.g. *clinic, practising*);
- words with the weak vowel /ə/ represented by any one of the five vowels;
- words that can be spelt by analogy with other words (e.g. *light, rough*);
- words that are unique in their spellings (e.g. *yacht, buoy*) and thus demand the kind of whole-word processing by an English writer that we find in a *logographic* system like Chinese.

Children acquiring transparent orthographies such as Spanish make faster initial progress than those acquiring opaque ones such as English. There are even different patterns of **dyslexia**, with readers of transparent orthographies manifesting problems of speed while English dyslexics have problems of both speed and accuracy. Despite this, adult Spanish readers appear to employ whole-word processing as well as GPC rules. This finding accords with an **interactive** model of reading, in which information is processed at several levels simultaneously (feature, letter, letter order, word).

See also: **Grapheme-phoneme correspondence rule, Graphotactic rules, Writing system**

Further reading: Coulmas (1989); Harris and Coltheart (1986); Rayner and Pollatsek (1989: Chap. 2)

OVER-EXTENSION

In language acquisition, the use of a lexical item to refer to a wider range of entities than is normal in adult usage. For example, the word DUCK might be extended to many more types of bird than the adult concept would admit. Over-extension can involve up to a third of an infant's early words and is common up to the age of about 2 years 6 months. The child's reasons for including items within a concept often seem to be based upon similarities of shape; but size, texture, sound and movement are also important defining features. Other over-extensions reflect similarity of function or association with the same event (NAP to refer to a blanket).

Some over-extensions involve a whole series of loosely linked common features called by Vygotsky a *chain complex*. An infant was found to apply the term QUAH (= 'quack') to a duck on a pond, then extend it to any liquid including milk in a bottle, to a coin with an eagle on it and from that to all round coin-like objects.

Several reasons have been suggested for over-extension. The child may simply have unformed impressions of the world and thus be unable to recognise similarities between items. Or it may be using an approximate word for a concept for which it does not yet have a term. Or it may be actively engaged in forming concepts: imposing patterns upon its experience and learning by trial and error which items are classed together. One version of this last view suggests that the child is trying to assemble a range of exemplars in order to form a **prototype** for a particular concept.

The opposite phenomenon, *under-extension*, also occurs, but rather less frequently. It may be the result of a word being acquired in a way that is too dependent upon context. A child might apply WHITE to snow but not to a blank page or DEEP to a swimming pool but not to a puddle.

See also: **Concept formation, Mapping, Over-generalisation**

Further reading: Aitchison (2003: Chap. 16); Clark (2001); Kuczaj (1999); Neisser (1987)

OVER-GENERALISATION (also OVER-REGULARISATION)

In language acquisition, wider use of a grammatical feature or concept than adult norms permit. One example is over-generalisation of inflections. Children recognise the use of *-ed* to mark past tense but extend it to all past forms including those that should be irregular. This often happens after the child has already mastered the correct irregular form. In a process known as **U-shaped development**, the child abandons accurate forms such as *went* and *brought* and adopts *goed* and *bringed*. Examples such as these provide important evidence that children do not simply parrot the words of adults but are actively engaged in a process of rule formulation and adjustment.

One account, the *rule-and-memory model*, represents the phenomenon in terms of a tension between a desire to apply a general rule and a memory for specific exceptions. Gradually, through exposure to multiple examples, memory comes to prevail over the rule in the case of irregular forms. An alternative, **connectionist** view would be that verb forms are represented by means of a set of mental connections rather than by the child forming rules. Since there are strong connections between many verb roots and past tense forms in *-ed*, competition determines that there is a phase in development when this is the dominant (because most statistically probable) form. Computer programs have modelled precisely this learning process.

The child may also over-generalise standard sentence patterns in its repertoire. It seems that the child learns to recognise syntactic patterns by associating them with prototypical verbs: GIVE, for example, as an exemplar of the pattern Verb + Noun Phrase + Noun Phrase (*gave + Mary + a present*). Other verbs are then tried out with the pattern, sometimes mistakenly. Researchers are interested in how the child seems to avoid over-generalisation in some instances, apparently recognising that these verbs are inappropriate for a given pattern.

One type of over-generalisation that has been much studied involves a double auxiliary, as in *Why did you did scare me?* or a double tense marking as in *What did you brought?* It is explained in terms of the child having imperfectly acquired the *movement rules* which in Chomskyan theory permit the formation of inverted questions, negatives etc.

See also: **Over-extension**

Further reading: Aitchison (1998: 125–34); Marcus (1996); Tomasello and Brooks (1999)

OVER-REGULARISATION ERRORS

Errors made by dyslexics suffering from *surface dyslexia*, when they read aloud words with irregular or infrequent sound–spelling relationships. They might interpret STEAK as /stiːk/ because the digraph -EA- more commonly represents /iː/ than /eɪ/.

PARALINGUISTIC FEATURES₁

Variations in tone and quality of voice which do not form part of a surprasegmental phonological system. Examples are pitch span, tempo, loudness, voice setting ('breathy', 'creaky' etc.), precision of articulation and pausing.

PARALINGUISTIC FEATURES₂

Features such as facial expression, gesture and gaze which contribute to communication but are not specifically linguistic. There is interest in establishing the extent to which, in conversation, these features support or supplement information in the signal. Also relevant is the extent to which they form such an intrinsic part of speaking that a speaker continues to employ them even when (say) talking on a mobile phone.

Certain of these features, such as laughter, are universal; but some (for example, nodding the head in affirmation) are culturally determined.

Some specialists in communication studies reserve the term 'paralinguistic' for hesitation markers, involuntary sounds (yawning and laughing) and pausing. They use the term '*kinesic*' for movements of the face and body, while factors such as the physical distance between interlocutors are referred to as '*standing features*'.

PARALLEL DISTRIBUTED PROCESSING (PDP)

A description of the architecture of one type of **connectionist** model of language processing; the term is sometimes used as a synonym for 'connectionism'.

Simulating the neural structure of the brain, connectionist models feature a large number of highly interconnected nodes or *units*. The power of the models lies not in the units themselves but in the connections between them. These connections increase or reduce the **activation** that runs between the units and may be strengthened or weakened as the result of experience.

Early connectionist models embodied an assumption that each unit represented a single piece of information. A typical *facilitatory* connection might be one between a unit which represented WRITE and one which represented WROTE. Later thinking modified this assumption, suggesting that a form such as WRITE or WROTE might not have a unit specifically dedicated to it but might be identified more abstractly, on the basis of a pattern of activation among a set of sub-units. In a PDP model, the representation of a word form is thus *distributed* across a number of units rather than being located in a single one.

See also: **Connectionism, Parallel processing**

Further reading: Whitney (1998: 105–8)

PARALLEL PROCESSING

A model of language production and perception where the user operates at several different **levels of representation** (sounds, words, semantics, syntax) at the same time.

It is easy to assume that processing is *serial*, with a listener, for example, first assembling phonemes into a word, then accessing the word's meaning and then fitting the word into a developing syntactic structure. However, current evidence suggests that the listener begins to process the message about 0.2 seconds (roughly the length of a syllable) after the speaker starts speaking. This would seem to favour a system in which all levels of processing are operative simultaneously (*in parallel*). Similar evidence for reading suggests that a written word is also processed at several different levels at the same time: letter features (lines and curves), letters, order of letters, whole word.

Many parallel processing models are **interactive**. Each level of processing communicates with those above and below it to produce evidence which supports or rules out a particular interpretation. However, parallel processing is not necessarily incompatible with a **modular** system. In such a system, each level has to complete its processing operation before passing on the outcome to the level above; but this does not exclude the possibility of all levels being active simultaneously.

The distinction between serial and parallel processing is relevant to models of **lexical access**. Serial models of access (e.g. Forster's *search model*) assume that we work through **lexical entries** in turn until we find a match for a word in the stimulus. In parallel models such as Morton's **logogen** system, potential word matches are represented as being in competition with each other: evidence builds up for and against each candidate until a correct match is made.

See also: **Lexical access, Search model**

Further reading: Forster (1990); Jackendoff (1987: Chap. 6)

PARAPHASIA

A type of error resulting from **aphasia** and involving the substitution, transposition or addition of a unit of language. In *phonemic paraphasia*, a word might be substituted which bears a phonological resemblance to the target word, while in *semantic paraphasia*, the substituted word might be linked to the target by meaning.

PATTERN RECOGNITION (also PATTERN MATCHING)

The establishment of a one-to-one match between, on the one hand, a set of features drawn from a stimulus and held temporarily in a sensory store; and, on the other, a stored representation in the mind. Pattern recognition enables us to identify familiar patterns (e.g. letter shapes) with a high degree of **automaticity**, and to impose patterns upon unfamiliar forms (as when users of the Latin alphabet are exposed over time to signage in the Greek or Russian ones).

Approaches to pattern recognition offer different accounts of how a pattern is stored in long-term memory. They include:

☐ *Template matching theories:* where the pattern is matched with an exact counterpart in long-term memory. This would appear to entail storing all possible variants of the pattern – a very inefficient solution since, in order to recognise (say) the letter E, one would have to store it not only in all possible fonts but also in all possible sizes. The solution is to assume a two-stage process, where a stimulus is *normalised*, with non-essential features edited out, before being matched to the template.

☐ *Feature analysis theories:* where the pattern is broken into constituent parts; and is identified as a combination of those features. For example, a small number of distinctive features (lines, curves etc.) would allow us to identify all the letters of the alphabet. There is evidence that the visual cortex in mammals is so organised as to detect the presence of simple features within a complex pattern.

☐ *Prototype theories:* where the pattern is compared on a 'best fit' basis with an idealised example of the pattern in long-term memory.

See also: **Normalisation, Phonological representation, Prototype Theory**

Further reading: Anderson (1990: Chap. 3); Kellogg (1995: Chap. 2); Lund (2001: Chap. 5)

PAUSING

The length and frequency of pausing in speech varies greatly from speaker to speaker and from situation to situation. A distinction is made between a speaker's **speaking rate** (in syllables per second), which includes pauses, and their **articulation rate**, which does not. Comparisons between the two show that much of the difference between what is perceived as 'normal' speech and 'fast' speech is due not to faster articulation but to reduced pausing.

There are a number of positions in which pauses potentially occur; they include: the end of an intonational phrase, the end of a syntactic constituent and immediately after a major content word. Systematic pausing of this kind performs several functions:

- marking syntactic boundaries;
- allowing the speaker time to forward plan;
- providing semantic focus (a pause after an important word);
- marking a word or phrase rhetorically (a pause before it);
- indicating the speaker's willingness to hand over the speech turn to an interlocutor.

The first two are closely connected. For the speaker, it is efficient to construct forward planning around syntactic or phonological units (the two may not always coincide). For the listener, this carries the benefit that syntactic boundaries are often marked.

Planning is vital to the speech process and pausing is necessary in order to remove what is in the speech **buffer** (i.e. the words we are currently producing) and to replace it with a new chunk of speech for the next part of the utterance. When experimenters have forced speakers to suppress pausing, it has resulted in confused and sometimes incoherent discourse.

It is useful to distinguish pausing as described above from *hesitation*. Whereas a *juncture pause* occurs at the end of a syntactic or phonological unit, a *hesitation pause* will often occur *within* such a unit, reflecting inadequate forward planning or difficulty in retrieving a lexical item from the lexicon. Rather confusingly, the term *filled pause* is used for a particular type of hesitation, where the speaker inserts fillers such as '*you know*', '*er*', '*well*'.

Hesitation pauses may be part of a speaker's speech style. They may reflect the state of mind of the speaker, who might be tired or ill or not concentrating very well. They may reflect the speaker's problems of **lexical access** when a target word is infrequent or complex in form or when a speech event such as a lecture demands precise terminology. Evidence suggests that listeners discriminate between the two types of pause: they pay heed to juncture pauses but accord a low level of attention to hesitation pauses.

See also: **Fluency, Planning, Prosody**

Further reading: Laver (1994: Chap. 17)

PERCEPTION

The operation of analysing a stimulus. Particularly applied to **bottom-up** processes, where the language user is decoding information that is physically present on the page or in the speech signal. Decoding in reading is often referred to as *visual perception* and decoding in listening as *auditory perception*.

An important distinction is made between perception and *sensation*, the unanalysed experience of sound reaching one's ear or visual patterns reaching one's eye.

See also: **Attention, Reading: decoding, Sensation, Speech perception**

PERCEPTUAL MAGNET EFFECT

The inability to distinguish between a prototypical example of a vowel and a variant. Listeners find it hard to differentiate a variant of the English sound /iː/ from a variant they have previously identified as a **'prototype'** (or extremely good exemplar) of the same sound. But they succeed in distinguishing the variant from a non-prototype which, measured acoustically, is equally distant. The prototype is envisaged as 'attracting' similar sounds to itself as a magnet attracts iron. The effect is to distort the *perceptual space* around the prototype so that variants appear to be closer to it than they really are.

The perceptual magnet effect has been demonstrated in infants as young as 6 months old; but the effect seems to demand some linguistic exposure and is not manifested by animals.

PHONOLOGICAL AWARENESS

The extent to which a pre-literate individual is capable of recognising the individual phonemes which constitute a spoken word. The ability to divide a word into its constituent phonemes cannot be taken for granted, especially since phonemes in natural speech vary greatly. Adult Portuguese illiterates have proved weak at tasks which involve analysing the phonemic structure of words (though they performed better at classifying syllables and rimes). This suggests that awareness of the phoneme as a unit may not pre-date learning to read, and indeed may be the product of literacy.

Some commentators argue for a reciprocal relationship. There is evidence that the ability to combine separate phonemes into syllables is a predictor of progress in early reading. On the other hand, progress in early reading seems to pave the way for the ability to delete an initial or final sound from a word rather than vice versa.

See also: **Reading: decoding**

Further reading: Goswami and Bryant (1990); Perfetti (1985, 1999)

PHONOLOGICAL BIAS TECHNIQUE

A technique that involves *habituating* a subject to a particular pattern of word-initial phonemes. Asked to read aloud the sequence BALL DOZE – BASH DOOR – BEAN DECK – BELL DARK – DARN BORE, there is about a 30 per cent likelihood that a subject will interpret the last item as BARN DOOR. However, a *lexical bias effect* means that the likelihood of an error drops to only 10 per cent if it gives rise to a non-word (DART BOARD rendered as BART DOARD). This result suggests that in assembling speech we develop parallel speech plans. Here, one specific to lexis and one specific to phonology are seen to be in competition.

PHONOLOGICAL DEVELOPMENT: PERCEPTION

There are several views on the extent to which a newly born infant is attuned to speech. An *articulatory learning theory* suggests that an infant has no perceptual capacity at birth and that the phonological system is entirely acquired through exposure to input. An *attunement theory* has it that the infant is born with the capacity to perceive certain fundamental sounds, which enables it to identify some of those which feature in the target language (TL). A strong nativist view (a *universal theory*) holds that the infant is endowed with the capacity to distinguish the speech sounds of all human languages but later loses it for sounds which are not relevant to the TL. Finally, a *maturational* nativist view envisages a biologically determined programme for both perception and production.

Not enough is known about the precise relationship between perception and production in phonological development. It may be that problems in distinguishing certain sounds influence the order in which phonemes are acquired. For example, in English /f/ and /r/ appear late, and one possible explanation is that they are easily confused with /θ/ and /w/. The cause does not lie in the infant's hearing, which is fully developed at this point; rather, its brain may not yet be able to process these distinctions.

An insight into the relation between perception and production is provided by the *fis phenomenon*. Assume that a child pronounces the adult word FISH as [fɪs]. If an adult imitates the child's pronunciation, the child can recognise that it is wrong but cannot put it right. This does not necessarily show that the child has a precise representation in its mind of the adult form; but it does show that it has a representation that is distinct from the form that it produces. Hence a suggestion that the infant might possess two distinct lexicons: one for perception and one for production. In its current form, this theory assumes that there is actually a single lexicon (containing elements of word meaning) but that it has separate *phonological registers* for input and output.

Many studies have shown that the development of auditory perception begins much earlier than might be supposed. Important research areas include:

□ *Categorical perception*. Experimenters have demonstrated that infants as young as four months distinguish stops by means of sharply defined boundaries and can also distinguish vowels and liquids. However, the infants do not appear to recognise category boundaries for fricatives. This finding may be significant, as, across languages, fricatives tend to emerge late.

□ *Critical period*. The issue here is whether there is a **critical period** during which infants are particularly sensitive to the phonology of their target language. It appears that infants can distinguish between sounds which are not contrastive in the language they are acquiring, whereas most adults cannot. Initial evidence suggested that infants lost the ability to make these distinctions as early as nine months. However, later findings have indicated that children of four years old can still make certain '*robust*' non-native distinctions, and that adults remain capable of distinguishing sounds which are entirely absent in the native language (e.g. for English-speakers, different Xhosa clicks). Discriminatory ability may thus be lost to different degrees, reflecting the extent to which L2 phonemes are distinct from those in the first language.

Jusczyk's *WRAPSA model* offers an account based upon focus of attention rather than complete loss of discriminatory ability. It suggests that we continue to perceive all the contrasts in the signal but that certain features are given special 'weighting'. Our perception of sounds does not change but the way we distribute our **attention** is determined by the language we acquire.

□ *Phoneme awareness.* Children find it difficult to distinguish *minimal pairs* (MEND / SEND, ROAD / WROTE) before about two years six months. This suggests that early words are represented holistically rather than in terms of the phonemes that constitute them. It is unclear exactly when the child develops an awareness of phonemes. One view is that we only come to recognise phonemic segments as a result of learning to read alphabetically. Another theory is that perception vocabulary remains holistic for a while but that production vocabulary is specified in terms of phonemes and/or the articulatory gestures associated with them.

□ *Rhythm.* Infants appear to pick up the rhythm patterns of their mother's speech even while in the womb. The child then may exploit rhythmic properties of the speech signal in order to locate word boundaries in connected speech. English-acquiring infants develop an awareness of the **SW (strong-weak) pattern** which characterises much of the English lexicon and may use it as the basis for identifying potential words.

□ *Syllable.* It may also be that a unit of phonological processing is available to the infant, the best candidate being the syllable. Infants display sensitivity to syllable structure at a very early age – probably as a result of noticing the *steady-state* sequences in the speech stream which correspond to the vowels at the centre of each syllable.

□ *Normalisation.* The adult voices to which the infant is exposed vary greatly in pitch, speech rate, accent etc. Studies have tested the infant's capacity to compensate for these features when extracting phonological information. Once a given phoneme distinction has been achieved, infants show that they are able to sustain it even when the phonemes are uttered by different voices. Infants also appear capable of making the distinction between /bɑ/ and /wɑ/ which, for adults, depends upon assessing the speech rate of the talker.

See also: **Bootstrapping, Categorical perception, Critical period**

Further reading: Goodman and Nusbaum (1994); Ingram (1989: 83–115,

179–219); Jusczyk (1997); Morgan and Demuth (1996); Tomasello and Bates (2001: 1–56)

PHONOLOGICAL DEVELOPMENT: PRODUCTION

The acquisition by an infant of the phonological system of its first language, as evidenced in signs of use.

An infant's first productions are purely *reflexive*, consisting of wailing, laughter, gurgling etc. in response to immediate sensations. Its first speech-like productions take the form of **babbling**, which begins at between six and ten months and is characterised by a limited range of sounds resembling adult consonant-vowel (CV) syllables. There is disagreement as to whether babbling is unrelated to later phonological development or whether it is a precursor of speech. At a later stage, babbling adopts intonation contours which seem to mimic those of adults. Intonation thus appears to be acquired independently of phoneme development.

The question has been raised of whether there is a *universal order* of phoneme acquisition. It is difficult to determine when a particular phoneme has been 'acquired': it may be used accurately in certain contexts but not in others. Furthermore, the ability to recognise a phoneme may precede its emergence in production by quite a long period. That said, findings suggest that, whatever the ambient language, infants do indeed acquire certain sounds early on: namely, nasal consonants, labials, stops and back vowels. Some commentators have concluded that such forms must be innate; however, the phenomenon could equally be due to early limitations on the child's perceptual system or to the child employing the easiest articulatory gestures first. Some evidence for innateness comes from the fact that sounds which are universally infrequent (such as English /æ/) tend to emerge late.

An alternative suggestion is that the order in which phonemes are acquired may reflect their frequency in the input to which the child is exposed. However, the evidence is unclear, and it is noteworthy that the omnipresent /ð/ in English emerges late.

Children develop systematic ways of reducing adult words to forms which match their production capacities. They might consistently voice unvoiced sounds (*paper* = [beːbəː]) or replace fricatives by stops (*see* = [tiː]). A common feature is the simplification of consonant clusters (train = [ten]). Analogy seems to play a part, with sets of similar words showing similar pronunciation features. But there are often anomalies, termed *idioms*: single words which continue to be pronounced wrongly when the rest of a set has been acquired phonologically. There are also *chain shifts* (if *truck* is pronounced *duck*, it may cause *duck* to become *guck*).

See also: **Phonological development: perception**

Further reading: Fletcher and Garman (1986: Part II); Fletcher and MacWhinney (1995: Chaps 10–12); Ingram (1989, 1999); Menn and Stoel-Gammon (1995)

PHONOLOGICAL REPRESENTATION

A mental representation of the individual phonemes of a language or of the phonological forms of its words, which enables the language user to recognise and to produce them.

There is a lay assumption that the sounds of a language are recognised by a simple process of matching them on a one-to-one basis with some kind of *template* in the mind. This cannot be the case, due to the high variability of phonemes in the speech signal. *Co-articulation* causes the form of any phoneme to vary considerably according to the phonemes which precede and follow it. It has also proved impossible to slice the signal into neat phonemic segments since acoustic features representing one phoneme blend into those representing the next. There is enormous variation between speakers in terms of pitch of voice, speech rate and accent. There is also great variation within the speech of a single speaker reflecting their emotional state and the genre of speech event. To this, one can add features such as *assimilation*, where the speaker modifies phonemes in the interests of ease of articulation.

Broadly, there are three ways of approaching the issue of phonological representation. One can assume an intermediate level of analysis (solution a below), one can adapt one's view of how the knowledge is stored (solutions a, b, d and e below) or one can adapt one's view of how the user processes the information in the signal (solution c):

a.   *Unit of representation*. Representation may be at a higher or lower level than the phoneme: for example, at the level of the syllable or the acoustic feature. The analysis of the signal would then involve an intermediate process of dividing it into these units.

The case for a syllabic representation is that phoneme values within the syllable remain relatively constant, thus countering the co-articulation problem. It has been calculated that for French a finite set of 6000 syllables could represent the entire repertoire of the language. Demi-syllables would be even more efficient, requiring perhaps 2000 forms.

An alternative suggestion is that words in the lexicon might be represented in terms of smaller units than the phoneme, i.e. as combinations of acoustic features (+ voiced, + nasal etc.). This has much in common with the feature theories which have been put forward to explain other aspects of **pattern recognition**.

b. *Prototype solutions.* The mind stores an idealised version of each phoneme of the language (or of the phonological form of each lexical item). Evidence in the input can then be matched to the representation on a relative 'goodness of fit' basis rather than a categorical one. The prototype might consist of a core value, with a range of tolerances around it. These tolerances would incorporate systematic deviations from the prototype which exposure to variants (e.g. local accents) has taught the listener to recognise.

c. *Normalisation.* The listener edits out or adapts any information in the signal which does not serve to identify phonemes. Allowance is made for systematic variation caused by co-articulation and assimilation. Normalisation has especially been invoked to explain how the listener succeeds in recognising the same phonemes spoken by a variety of speakers. In its strong form, the theory postulates that phonological information is strictly separated from *indexical* information (relating to the characteristics of the speaker's voice). This view has been challenged by recent evidence suggesting that the two are more closely interlinked than was supposed.

d. *Under-specification.* An under-specified phonological representation contains only information that is critical to the identification of a lexical item. This means that absent features (e.g. 'not nasal') are not recorded; it also means that features which can be predicted by rule (e.g. the nasalisation of a vowel before [n]) are omitted. An under-specified representation reduces the chances that a match will fail because of extraneous details in the speech signal.

e. *Exemplar theories.* Recent evidence has suggested that our capacity for storing information relating to individual events may be far greater than supposed. Applied to phonology, this means that the representation of a particular phoneme or lexical item may be composed of multiple traces of earlier encounters with that phoneme or item. When we hear a regional accent, we tap in to stored exemplars of items spoken in that accent; when we hear a voice operating at a certain pitch or speech rate, we can relate it to earlier stored experiences of similar voices. An exemplar approach is not necessarily incompatible with theory b: it may be that the language user also builds up a set of core values based upon the multiple traces that he/she has stored.

See also: **Exemplar models, Normalisation, Pattern recognition, Prototype Theory, Underspecification, Unit of perception**

Further reading: Bybee (2001: Chaps 1–2); Fitzpatrick and Wheeldon (2000)

PHONOLOGICAL WORKING MEMORY

The component of **working memory** (WM) which stores and recycles input in phonological form. How well a listener retains what is heard appears to be partly determined by the capacity of their phonological WM, as does their success or failure at learning a foreign language. In a child, it may affect vocabulary development and success as a reader.

Baddeley's model of working memory has a *phonological loop* which stores input in phonological form. The loop also permits *articulatory rehearsal*, a process of subvocal repetition which extends the life of stored information, ensures its transfer to long-term memory and recodes written input into a more durable phonological form.

In this model, there are thus three ways in which phonological WM might be impaired. There might be a deficit in how much an individual is able to store; there might be a rapid decay of information held in the store; or there might be a deficit in how much an individual is able to rehearse.

Phonological WM capacity is traditionally measured by *Auditory Short-Term Memory* (ASTM) tests in which a subject is asked to recall sets of digits, words or non-words. The sets increase by a digit a time until recall begins to fail; this gives a measure of the subject's *digit* or *word span*. Some experimenters question the validity of this approach on the grounds that long-term lexical knowledge may be involved. They prefer a *non-word repetition* task, in which subjects repeat non-words containing an increasing number of syllables. Others employ a *reading span* test, in which subjects read sets of sentences ranging in number from two to seven and are asked to recall the last word of each. However, reading span measures involve the processing as well as the storage of linguistic material, and thus involve other components of WM.

Phonological working memory may influence achievement in a number of areas:

☐ *Vocabulary acquisition.* In children under six, a close relationship has been found between non-word repetition scores and level of vocabulary – suggesting that phonological WM contributes to a child's ability to commit the spoken form of a new word to long-term memory. Children with better memories appear to acquire longer-lasting and more sharply defined phonological traces. This factor seems less important as the children get older, reflecting the influence of reading and the increased possibility of making word-form analogies as the vocabulary base gets larger.

☐ *Reading ability.* Measures of phonological WM correlate with reading ability. Poor reading skills appear to be associated with an inability to acquire the phonological forms of new words. It may be that the weak reader finds it harder to relate written forms to phonological ones by means of the rehearsal mechanism.

☐ *Language learning.* Studies of primary school children and of adults have found a strong correlation between repetition scores and achievement in learning a foreign language.

☐ **Speech buffer.** It has been suggested that phonological WM might be involved in language production as well as perception. In particular, it might contribute to the **buffer** in which speech output is held before it is uttered. However, patients with impaired phonological memory do not seem to suffer corresponding deficits in spontaneous speech production.

See also: **Reading: decoding, Reading span, Working memory**

Further reading: Gathercole and Baddeley (1993: Chap. 3)

PHONOTACTIC RULES

A specification of which phonemes can occur together within a syllable and of the sequence and the position in which they can occur. For example, the sequence /str/ is phototactically *legal* in word-initial position in English, whereas the sequence /gn/ is not.

There is evidence that infants acquire sensitivity to the phonotactic regularities of the language they are acquiring at a very early age, and it has been suggested that phonotactics may assist them in **boot-strapping**. Phonotactic constraints on position may also form one of the means by which adults manage to recognise word boundaries in connected speech. It has been estimated that, of 7000 consonant sequences which potentially occur across word boundaries in English, only 20 per cent also occur within a word. Furthermore, 80 per cent of cross-boundary sequences only permit of one division: thus, the sequence /mgl/ can only be parsed as /m#gl/.

PIAGETIAN STAGES OF DEVELOPMENT

For the child psychologist Jean Piaget (1896–1980) language was both a social and a cognitive phenomenon. It was not an independent **modular** faculty but part of general cognitive and perceptual processing. Language acquisition was thus dependent upon cognitive development. The child's level of language was determined by whether it had acquired certain fundamental concepts and by the complexity of the processing operations of which it was capable.

Piaget suggested that cognitive development fell into four phases. They constitute a gradual progression in which previous stages are revisited cyclically. The age at which a particular child goes through each stage varies considerably. Each stage has implications for linguistic development.

1. *Sensori-motor (0–2 years)*. The child achieves recognition of *object permanence* (the fact that an object still exists even when it is not in view). This is a prerequisite to the formation of concepts (including lexical concepts). It may be a dawning awareness of object permanence which first leads the child to name things and gives rise to the **'vocabulary spurt'** at around 18 months. The first relational words ('NO' 'UP' 'MORE' 'GONE') also reflect object permanence, with those indicating presence emerging before those ('ALL GONE') relating to absence.

   The child's language has its origins in simple signals (a bottle signifies eating) and then in *indexical relationships* (a carer with a coat on signifies going out). Early words are employed for *symbolic reference* (DOGGIE referring to one specific dog that is present) but later acquire *symbolic sense* ('doggie' referring to the class of dogs). The child's productions may show an awareness of *means–ends* (the word MILK gets the child a drink) and limited spatial awareness.

2. *Pre-operational (2–6 years).* The child's behaviour reflects *egocentric thought*: it is unable to identify with the views of others. The child's language progresses through **echolalia** (repeating others' utterances) to *monologues* (speaking aloud what would normally be private thoughts). It may engage in *collective monologues* with other children, in which participants appear to be taking turns, but express their own ideas without responding to those of others.

3. *Concrete operational (7–11 years).* The child's vocabulary shows signs of organisation into hierarchical categories. It develops the concept of *conservation* (the recognition that size or quantity is not dependent upon the container) and shows signs of *decentration*, the ability to consider multiple aspects of a physical problem. It learns to receive and respond to outside ideas.

4. *Formal operational (11–15 years).* The adolescent becomes capable of abstract reasoning. It learns to construct its own argument structures, can represent hypothetical situations and engages mentally and verbally in problem-solving.

See also: **Vygotskyan**

Further reading: Boden (1979); McShane (1991); Piattelli-Palmarini (1980)

PIDGIN

A lingua franca which develops when speakers of mutually unintelligible languages are in contact with each other. It may be a simplified version of the dominant language of the area. A pidgin is rudimentary in terms of syntax. There are no complex sentences; function words are omitted; inflections are absent; there may be verbless sentences; and word order is variable. The vocabulary is limited, with some lexical items imported from native languages or specially coined.

See also: **Creolisation**

PIVOT GRAMMAR

An attempt (Braine, 1963) to trace a consistent pattern in an infant's early two-word utterances. It was suggested that at this stage the child employed two sets of words. 'Pivot words' were used in a fixed position in the utterance, with some reserved for initial position and some for final. The other ('open') set of words was used more flexibly. Three typical patterns were noted: initial pivot + open; open + final pivot; open + open. However, the finding proved not to be universal.

See also: **Syntactic development**

PLANNING: SPEECH

Although speech appears to be spontaneous, it requires a planning process in which the components (clauses, words, phonemes) are assembled. Critical to the process are pauses in the flow of speech, which enable a speaker to construct a new chunk of language. When experimenters force speakers to suppress pausing, it results in confused and sometimes incoherent discourse.

In some types of monologue, researchers have demonstrated a pattern where hesitant phases of speech (marked by frequent and longer pausing) alternate with more fluent ones. The hesitant phases have been interpreted in terms of the speaker elaborating goals and retrieving information while the shorter and less frequent pauses of the fluent phases appear to allow the speaker to finalise the form of words. Eye contact is maintained during about 50 per cent of the fluent phase but 20 per cent of the hesitant phase.

Evidence for a unit of planning has been sought in pausing, in speech errors, in intonation patterns and in the gestures which accompany speech. Pauses tend to come at or near clause boundaries, suggesting that the clause is a major unit of planning. This is supported by evidence from **Slips of the Tongue**, in which most word misplacements take place within a single clause.

Speech planning can be conceived as taking place at a number of levels. In Levelt's (1989) model, ideas are first shaped through *conceptualisation*. This involves two stages. *Macroplanning* breaks the communicative goal into a series of subgoals and retrieves the information necessary to realise these goals. *Microplanning* involves attaching the right propositional structure to each of these chunks of information, and taking account of where the focus of information is to lie. The outcome of the conceptualising process is an abstract *preverbal message*.

This is followed by a stage termed *formulation*, which first constructs the message in abstract terms, setting up a syntactic framework, and tagging the framework for inflections and rhythm. The plan is then given concrete phonemic and syllabic form. Phonetic planning prepares the message for articulation by specifying the relative length of each syllable and incorporating co-articulation; and prosodic planning allocates intonation and determines speech rate. The outcome of these operations is an *articulatory plan*, stored in the form of a set of instructions to the articulators (jaw, tongue, vocal cords etc.).

See also: **Buffer, Speech production**

Further reading: Levelt (1989: Chaps 8–10)

PLANNING: WRITING

The term 'planning' tends to be used more narrowly in discussion of writing than it is with speaking. It especially refers to the stage at which the writer generates ideas, organises them and sets goals. The outcome of planning is a set of cues stored in memory in the form of mental images, abstract ideas, key words or partly formed sentences. But models of writing are cyclical, with the writer able to return to the planning stage to reorganise ideas and revise goals.

See also: **Writing**

POSITION EFFECTS (also SERIAL POSITION EFFECTS)

The ability to recall certain words according to where they occur in a list. A *primacy effect* favours words at the beginning of the list; the theory is that the listener has time to consolidate these words by rehearsing them; as a result, they are successfully transferred to long-term memory. A *recency effect* favours words at the end of the list. This is ascribed to the listener being able to retrieve the words from short-term memory, where they are still held.

The difference between the two effects is demonstrated by asking subjects to perform an *interference task* (such as counting or doing simple calculations) before the list is recalled. In these circumstances, the primacy effect is sustained, but the recency effect disappears. This suggests that the words which feature in the recency effect are vulnerable to being dislodged by new incoming short-term information.

The recency effect is more marked for spoken words than it is for written. This accords with a hypothesis that both types of word are held in **working memory** in some kind of phonological code. Written words are subject to a recoding process, whereas spoken words are encoded as they stand and are easier to retrieve.

See also: **Memory, Working memory**

POST-PERCEPTUAL

Many experimental methods in psycholinguistics are designed to tap in to perceptual processes **online**: at the very moment they are occurring. However, some methods demand that the subject makes some kind of conscious decision in relation to the perceived material. The decision is regarded as a secondary stage in the process, and the data derived from it as representative of a state of affairs immediately after perception rather than during it.

See also: **On-line process, On-line task**

PREDICATE

In traditional grammar, the second (Verb Phrase) division of a standard sentence: e.g. *cut the cake* in *Rachel cut the cake*. In semantic theory, it is the part of the sentence which *predicates*, i.e. which comments on a state of affairs or attributes a property to something. This represents the central idea of the sentence, the reason for producing it at all. The predicate is often but not always a verb. Examples:

Wasps frighten Paul.   Predicate: *frighten*
Paul is afraid of wasps. Predicate: *afraid of*
Brenda is in the bath.   Predicate: *in the bath*

Current views of grammar hold that, in selecting a predicate, a language user determines possible syntactic structures. Selecting the predicate GIVE obliges one to construct a sentence on the lines GIVE + Noun Phrase + Noun Phrase (*give the dog a bone*) or GIVE + Noun Phrase + to + Noun Phrase (*give a bone to the dog*).

The entities that the predicate tells us about are referred to as its *arguments*. Thus, the sentence *Maggie gave the dog a bone* has three arguments: *Maggie*, *dog* and *bone*. Sentences are sometimes represented in terms of their underlying abstract *predicate/argument structure*, using a format in which the predicate appears first followed by the arguments in brackets: *GIVE (Maggie, dog, bone)*.

PREDICTABILITY

It is sometimes claimed that many words in speech and writing are predictable from the words that precede them or from context. They can thus be processed at a reduced level of attention since the reader/listener only needs to confirm an expectation. However, evidence from studies of reading suggests that only about 40 per cent of function words and 10 per cent of content words can be predicted in this way. Similarly, evidence from eye tracking shows only a small reduction in eye fixations when the context makes a word predictable. Current views represent the reader/listener's priority as being to integrate new information into an ongoing meaning representation rather than to think ahead.

PRIMING EFFECT

An increase in the speed with which a word is recognised, which results from having recently seen or heard a word that is closely associated with it. Shown the word DOCTOR, a subject recognises words such as NURSE or PATIENT more rapidly than usual – always provided they are presented soon afterwards. DOCTOR is referred to as the *prime* and PATIENT as the *target*. The sight of the word DOCTOR is said to *prime* PATIENT.

Exposure to the prime is represented as *activating* (or bringing into prominence) a range of associated words. These words then become easier to identify because they are already foregrounded in the mind. The process, known as **spreading activation**, is highly **automatic** and not subject to conscious control. Most priming effects are relatively short-lived, and *decay* quite quickly, thus ensuring that too many lexical items are not activated simultaneously.

Priming effects have given rise to a research method which measures *Reaction Time* (how long it takes to recognise a word) in order to establish which words are most closely associated with a given prime. The experiments often involve a *lexical decision task*, where the subject is asked to press a button when he/she sees an actual word rather than a non-word. A comparison is then made between Reaction Times for targets which are associated with the prime and those for targets which are not.

Experiments often make use of *cross-modal priming*, where the prime is a spoken stimulus and the target is a visual stimulus on a computer screen. The logic for this is that it enables experimenters to tap into an abstract mental representation of the word which is independent of **modality**.

Several types of priming can be distinguished:

☐ *Repetition priming* involves repeating a recently-encountered word. This effect is surprisingly long lived: priming effects have been reported after a delay of several hours. The effects are stronger for low-frequency words than for more common ones, a phenomenon known as *frequency attentuation*. Repetition priming provides evidence of the way a reader traces patterns of coherence in a text by means of recurrent words.

☐ *Form-based priming* involves words which are orthographically similar. It has proved difficult to demonstrate that, for example, SPRING primes STRING. One explanation is that the two words are in competition with each other to form a match with what is in the stimulus, and thus reduce (*inhibit*) each other's activation.

☐ *Semantic priming* involves words which are semantically related. Strong effects have been recorded with words that fall into the same lexical set (CHAIR–TABLE), antonyms (HOT–COLD), words which share functional properties (BROOM–FLOOR) and superordinate-hyponym pairs (BIRD–ROBIN). However, the strength of the effect may depend on the strength of the association: the co-hyponyms CAT and DOG are strongly associated but the similar co-hyponyms PIG and HORSE are not.

See also: **Context effects, Research methods, Spreading activation**

Further reading: Harley (2001: 145–50)

PRINCIPLES AND PARAMETERS

A nativist theory of first language acquisition which reflects the current thinking of Noam Chomsky.

Chomsky takes the view that infants are born with an innate **Universal Grammar** (UG). This consists of a set of universal principles which characterise all (or nearly all) languages and a set of parameters, features which differentiate languages, usually on binary lines. A simple example of a parameter is the distinction between *pro-drop* languages which permit the omission of a subject pronoun and languages where the subject pronoun is obligatory (cf.: Italian *capisco* and English *I understand*). *Parameter setting* is often represented on a + or − basis (e.g. + or − Pro-drop).

A child is thus innately endowed with knowledge about language in general which gives it a head start in cracking the code of speech. However, it is also endowed with a set of choices which have to be made in relation to the language to which it is exposed.

Examples of innate principles are:

- *Structure dependency*: the structure of all languages consists of hierarchically organised phrases.
- *the Projection Principle*: syntactic structure is determined by entries in the lexicon (the choice of the verb GIVE entails the use of a particular syntactic pattern).
- *the Subjacency Principle*: any constituent of a sentence that is moved (for example, to form a question or negative) can only cross one major boundary (a *bounding node*). Where such a major boundary falls is, however, determined by a language-specific parameter.
- *Binding Principles*: unlike most pronouns, an *anaphor* (the term is used here for reflexives such as HIMSELF and reciprocals such as EACH OTHER) can only refer to an antecedent within the same sentence.

Examples of parameters set in response to the ambient language are:

- *the Null Subject (or Pro-drop) Parameter*: whether the language does/ does not oblige the speaker to express a pronoun subject.
- *the Head Parameter*: whether the *head* (major constituent) falls at the beginning or at the end of a standard phrase.
- *Bounding Parameters*: restrictions on the way in which constituents can be moved (for example, in forming negatives and interrogatives).
- *the Adjacency Parameter*: in effect, whether a transitive verb has to be followed immediately by its direct object or not. Compare English *I like music a lot* with French *J'aime beaucoup la musique*.
- *the Branching Parameter*: whether the hierarchical structure of a sentence as shown in a *tree diagram* branches towards the left or

towards the right. There are marked differences between *right-branching* languages like English which standardly place the direct object after the verb and *left-branching* ones like Japanese where the object occurs before the verb.

A further parameter in which there has been much interest concerns *preposition stranding*. English accepts both *pied-piping* (*About what were you talking?*) and *stranding* (*What were you talking about?*). However, there are some quite complex restrictions on stranding, and native speakers disagree about the acceptability of sentences such as *What meeting did she phone after?* There are wide variations between languages as to whether they permit stranding or not.

Many attempts have been made to test the Principles and Parameters hypothesis empirically. A problem here lies in the fact that UG relates to an individual's competence and not to their performance. An established procedure is therefore to ask subjects to make *grammaticality judgements*, i.e. to indicate whether for them, as users of the language, a sentence is grammatically acceptable or not. This method has been used to trace similarities between native speakers of a given language, to compare responses across languages whose parameters are said to be different and to compare the judgements made by monolinguals with those made by bilinguals or learners of a second language.

Attention has focused on the process of parameter setting. One issue is whether both parameters are neutral at the outset or whether one is the default or *unmarked* one. Some observational evidence suggests that infants acquiring their first language start off with an unmarked setting which has to be reset if it is not appropriate. For example, English-acquiring infants often omit pronoun subjects in their early productions, suggesting 'pro-drop' as a default setting. However, the 'pro-drop' example illustrates the dangers of using empirical data from language acquisition to support conclusions about UG. The data relates to the infants' productions (i.e. to their performance); it is by no means clear to what extent this reflects the underlying competence which they have derived from inherited UG. The absence of a subject pronoun may reflect a cognitive inability to process more than two words rather than any preferential parameter setting.

Parameter setting also has important implications for research into second language acquisition. When a learner acquires a language whose settings are different from those of their L1, they have to reset established parameters. There is interest in whether some parameters are more difficult to reset than others. Is it easier to move from a marked to an unmarked setting (thus reverting to the situation afforded in infancy by UG)? Or is it easier to move from an unmarked to a marked?

See also: **Chomskyan theory, Markedness, Universal Grammar**

Further reading: Cook and Newson (1996); Crain and Lillo-Martin (1999); O'Grady (1997: Chap. 13); Radford (1990)

PROBABILISTIC

Applying a criterion which identifies a word on the basis of *best fit* to a mental representation, rather than relying upon the match to be exact in all details. The probabilistic element might be part of the process of perceiving the word, so that attention is only focused on major identifying features. Or it might take the form of a **prototype** in the mind, to which the word in speech or writing is not expected to correspond 100 per cent.

PROBABILITY

The likelihood of a linguistic item being present.

☐ *Lexical probability*. In many theories of **lexical access**, multiple *candidates* (possible matches) are activated once part of a word has been heard. For example, an initial syllable /fə/ might activate FORBID, FORGET, FERMENT, FORSAKE. The candidates are activated to different degrees, depending upon their frequency: FORGET is a strong candidate, FORSAKE a weaker one. Part of the process of word recognition thus involves an assessment by the listener of the probability that one particular item is present rather than any other. This can be represented in the formula: $f / \Sigma f$ where f is the frequency of a particular candidate and Σf is the sum of frequencies of all candidates.

☐ *Syntactic probability*. A knowledge of syntactic structure often enables the listener or reader to guess the word-class of an upcoming item. For example, if the reader sees THE, the likelihood is that the next item will either be an adjective or a noun. If THE is followed by OLD, there is an even greater likelihood that a noun will follow. Once the Noun Phrase is complete (THE OLD MAN) there is then a likelihood that the next item will be a verb. The extent to which currently available syntactic structure enables one to predict future constituents is known as *transitional probability*. The term can also refer to the collocationally determined predictability of a specific word: for example, one can say that FOR has a high transitional probability after the verb WAIT.

Many engineering solutions in **Artificial Intelligence** which simulate the parsing of text involve no semantic component but are based upon a corpus analysis which indicates how probable each lexical item is in the target genre and what syntactic patterns and word-class sequences are most prevalent. This enables the program to predict what will come next, with increasing degrees of success as a sentence proceeds.

PROBLEM-SOLVING

An area of theory which attempts to model *directed thinking* (thinking which is goal-oriented and rational), often with a view to computer simulation. In cognitive psychology and **Artificial Intelligence**, the term 'problem' has a wide interpretation – referring to a desired state of knowledge towards which behaviour is directed. It thus potentially includes language production and comprehension. Many of the ideas in this field are influenced by studies of **expertise** (especially that of chess players) and by an early AI computer program, the *General Problem Solver* (GPS), which modelled rational thought.

There are two important factors in the problem-solving process. The first is a *representation* of the critical features of a task. Representation includes an *initial state*, a *goal state* and possible paths to achieving the goal. A set of *operators* based on world knowledge determine which paths are permissible and likely to achieve the goal. Together, the states and operators constitute what is known as the *problem space*.

The second important component is *search*. Much enquiry in this area has focused on the strategies adopted by individuals in searching a problem space. They tend to adopt two main approaches. An *algorithm* is a systematic procedure which gives a guaranteed solution. However, it entails evaluating all possible paths that might lead to the goal state, and is thus potentially very time-consuming. By contrast, a *heuristic* is a set of general guidelines which steer the search process so that a complete search is not necessary. Heuristics do not guarantee a solution but they enable the problem solver to economise on effort. Individual differences in problem-solving are partly attributable to differences in the ability to select and apply appropriate heuristics.

One way of formalising the knowledge that underlies problem-solving is in terms of *production systems*. These are sets of rules ('*productions*') for solving a problem, often expressed in an IF/THEN form. They are used to represent *procedural knowledge* (e.g. in Anderson's **ACT** models of expertise) and have also been used in accounts of syntactic parsing:

IF   *You see a Determiner*
THEN   *Expect the phrase to end in a Noun*
            Anticipate a Modifier between Determiner and Noun

Problem-solving theory has implications for other areas of language acquisition and use. For example, it can model the way in which listeners resolve ambiguity in the signal or can provide a framework for analysing the **strategies** employed by second language learners.

See also: **Model**

Further reading: Robertson (2001)

PROCESSING

The analysis, classification and interpretation of a stimulus. In psycholinguistics, particularly used for the cognitive operations underlying (a) the four language skills (speaking, listening, reading, writing); (b) the retrieval of lexical items; and (c) the construction of *meaning representations*. The term sometimes refers more narrowly to the receptive process of listening and reading.

Current models of processing owe much to early **information-processing** theory, which represented cognitive behaviour in terms of mental states and of processes that modify the states in clearly defined stages. One development was a view of language processing as involving the transmission of linguistic data through a series of **levels of representation** (feature, phoneme/letter, word, syntactic unit), at each of which it was reshaped.

Early models of processing tended, like early computers, to be *serial*: a particular operation (e.g. forming sounds into a word) had to be complete before the next began. However, most current models assume that processing is *parallel*, with different levels of representation active simultaneously.

See also: **Bottom-up processing, Interactive activation, Level of representation, Modularity₂, Parallel processing, Top-down processing**

Further reading: Jackendoff (1987: Chap. 6)

PROPOSITION

An abstract representation of a single unit of meaning: a mental record of the core meaning of the sentence without any of the interpretative and associative factors which the reader/listener might bring to bear upon it. Using a notation system derived from philosophical logic, propositions are often represented in the form of a *predicate* (generally a verb) followed by its *arguments*. The sentence *The dog bit a passer-by* would be represented as 'BITE (dog, passer-by)'.

When a reader or listener derives linguistic information from a text, they do not retain it verbatim but convert it into conceptual form. A working assumption is made that this form consists of minimal units of meaning, linked together in a network. The sentence *The man in the corner coughed* might be regarded as containing two linked propositions: THE MAN WAS IN THE CORNER and THE MAN COUGHED. This assumption has been put to the test in experiments in which subjects are asked to identify words from recently seen sentences. Recall is faster when two words from the same sentence occur next to each other in a list; but it is faster still when the two adjacent words are drawn from within the same proposition.

Not all propositions in a text contribute equally to the message. A measure of a proposition's relative importance is taken to be the extent to which it is recalled by readers. This typically ranges from 80 per cent for the most critical to around 30 per cent for those taken to be peripheral. Text structure is thus regarded by some as a hierarchy of propositions: a set of prominent *macro-propositions*, beneath which (like sub-headings in a table of contents) are grouped *micro-propositions* of diminishing degrees of importance.

Allowance for individual interpretation is made in an important distinction between a proposition and a **mental model**. A mental model draws upon propositional meaning, but to it is added additional material which the reader brings to bear in the form of **inferences** from the text and *world knowledge*.

See also: **Meaning construction, Mental model**

PROPOSITIONAL NETWORK

A representation of sentence meaning derived from AI research, which displays relationships in terms of nodes and links in a way similar to that used to represent **semantic networks**. The design is partly modelled on the pattern of neural connections in the brain.

In one format, a **predicate** (central concept) is shown in an oval representing a node. Branching out from it are *links* in the form of arrows representing the constituents of the proposition. The links bear labels which reflect the semantic relationships involved. Networks for connected propositions branch out from other nodes, demonstrating how they are related.

The diagram below shows a representation of the sentence *This is the house that Jack built*.

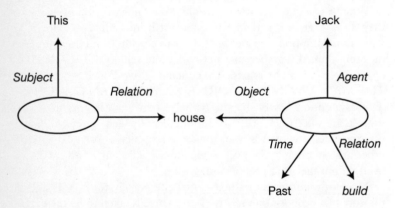

Figure P1   A propositional network representation of the sentence 'This is the house that Jack built'

See also: **Proposition**

PROSODY

Variations in the pitch, loudness, tempo and rhythm of speech. Prosody includes stress, pausing, speech rate and intonation (though not features like voice setting, which are classed as **paralinguistic$_1$**).

In most human beings, prosody appears to be processed by the right side of the brain while lower-level phonetic features are handled by the left. Research has demonstrated a left ear (hence, right hemisphere) advantage for the intonation of English, whether it marks sentence type or attitude.

Prosody has been shown to fulfil a number of important functions for the listener.

☐ *Prosody marks the boundaries of Intonational Phrases (IPs), which often coincide with syntactic boundaries.* This function is studied by asking listeners to respond to sentences which are ambiguous at some point in their utterance. The ambiguity may lie in the location of a syntactic boundary.

Before she washes, her hair is cut. / Before she washes her hair, it is cut.

Or it may derive from **garden path** situations, where probability indicates an ending different from the one that occurs.

The rescuers discovered the plane . . . had crashed (vs 'in the jungle')
The lawyer questioned . . . by the police confessed (vs 'the witness carefully')

In both cases, listeners have been shown to make use of prosodic cues (especially duration and changes of tempo) in order to *parse* the ongoing sentence syntactically and to arrive at a single correct interpretation before disambiguation occurs. However, many of the studies reported have made use of somewhat unnatural scripted sentences, read aloud on to tape. More research is needed using natural conversational speech. A further point is that, in natural speech, IP boundaries do not always coincide with syntactic ones. Here, research has shown that, when prosody conflicts with syntax, it is usually the prosodic cues that are heeded.

☐ *Pitch movement provides cues to sentence mode.* In many of the world's languages, declarative sentences are loosely associated with a pitch fall, and in around 70 per cent of languages, requests, tentativeness and certain question types are associated with a pitch rise.

☐ *Prosody provides cues to completeness.* Features such as syllable lengthening, a slowing of speech rate or a marked final fall indicate to the listener that the speaker is willing to hand over the conversational turn. By contrast, an unfinished IP contour or an increase in speech rate indicate the wish to keep the turn. A new topic is often marked by a more rapid speech rate, which slows down as the topic becomes exhausted.

☐ *Tonic accent provides information focus.* The placing of the tonic accent serves to highlight 'new' information introduced by the speaker. A study of naturalistic speech (Brown and Yule, 1983: 166) indicated that 87 per cent of new information was marked by phonological prominence (primary or secondary stress) while 98 per cent of 'given' information was unmarked. Note that the location of tonic accent does not correspond categorically to a '**given/new**' distinction, but reflects the speaker's moment-to-moment assessment of the listener's informational needs.

☐ *Tonic accent and heightened pitch movement indicate contrast and emphasis.* Here, speaker decisions reflect an assessment of immediate discourse demands.

☐ *Prosody provides affective signals.* Research into the relationship between speaker attitude and prosodic patterns has failed to find a systematic correlation between a given intonation contour and an emotion expressed by a speaker or attributed by a listener. Affective marking seems very variable; the impression adduced by a listener may well result from a bundle of features present in the signal rather than a single distinctive tune.

It is difficult to explain how a listener's understanding of prosodic cues is acquired and stored. The first four functions above are to some extent systematic, and could perhaps be accounted for by the hypothesis that we have a set of typical prosodic patterns stored in our minds. However, the last two functions are very much the product of a local decision by the speaker, and introduce a degree of variability into speech.

A related issue is how and when prosody contributes to the process of **planning** speech. Levelt's (1989) model of speaking includes a *Prosody Generator*; but it draws upon three different sources of information: the surface syntactic structure of the projected utterance, information at lexical level relating to word stress and a 'meaning' component reflecting the speaker's intentions in terms of fore-grounded topics and attitude. These relate to different stages of planning, and Levelt therefore argues that intonation is likely to be added incrementally into a speech plan. He takes the view that most features of prosody do not require a great deal of lookahead, and that a final form may only be determined at a late stage, immediately before articulation. Even features such as the relative duration and loudness of syllables might be finalised at this point.

See also: **'Given/new'**, **Intonation**, **Lexical segmentation**, **Lexical stress**

Further reading: Warren (1999)

PROTOTYPE THEORY

A theory that linguistic representation in the mind (particularly the representation of lexical **concepts**) takes the form of idealised or highly typical examples to which entities in the real world can be compared for 'goodness of fit'.

Prototype Theory evolved as a way of dealing with the problem of how we form and apply lexical categories. The American psychologist Eleanor Rosch devised a set of categories (FURNITURE, FRUIT, VEGETABLE, BIRD etc.) and asked subjects to rate around 50 examples of each according to how good an example of the category they felt them to be. The results were strikingly consistent, especially for items rated as good examples. Rosch formed the conclusion that we allocate real-world entities to categories by comparing them to a central exemplar, one which possesses all of the features associated with the category (for BIRD, robin, for VEHICLE, car). The closer an entity is to this prototype, the more confident we are about including it in the category.

There are a number of problems with Prototype Theory:

☐ Rosch's findings may have simply reflected *frequency* – with subjects choosing the most common examples of a category.

☐ It was assumed that prototypes were chosen because they possessed a *bundle of features* which were characteristic of the category as a whole. However, this certainly did not apply to VEGETABLES. The prototypical vegetable was a pea but a carrot (different in size, shape, colour) was rated highly.

☐ Prototypes may be *culturally determined*. When the Rosch experiment was repeated with subjects of Latin American origin, using Spanish words, very different results were obtained. This raises the question of whether prototypes are to some extent determined by native language, local culture or physical environment.

☐ Later experimenters asked subjects to *rate odd and even numbers for typicality* and found that they were prepared to do so, despite the fact that the task was patently nonsensical. Thus, 2 was rated as a 'prototypical' even number and 806 as a not very typical one. It was therefore argued that we need to distinguish between a *conceptual core* ('an even number is divisible by two') and an *identification function* (how easy it is to recognise a real-world example as a member of a category). This accords with research which suggests that infants begin by classifying the real world in terms of *characteristic features* (an UNCLE is somebody who gives presents) and only later recognise *defining features* (an UNCLE is a parent's brother).

Rosch's findings were based upon a limited set of categories. It is possible to demonstrate a prototype effect for categories of concrete noun, but is not so easy to do so for other parts of speech. Nevertheless, Prototype Theory has proved influential and has been extended to other domains. For example, one suggested solution to the problem of **phonological representation** is that we store in our minds a prototype of each phoneme, an idealised form against which can be matched the many variants that we encounter in connected speech.

Research into how infants form conceptual categories like DOG has suggested that they may establish central points of reference in the form of prototypes. A provisional prototype might be based upon the first exemplar of a word which they encounter or upon the exemplar most referred to by adults. The infant then applies the word to other entities which appear to share a 'goodness of fit' with the prototype.

An alternative to Prototype Theory is provided by recent **exemplar models**. These suggest that, instead of classifying real-world entities in relation to a single best example, we store multiple traces of all the exemplars that we have met.

See also: **Concept formation, Fuzzy boundary, Pattern recognition**

Further reading: Aitchison (2003: Chap. 5); Harley (2001: 288–91); Keil (1987)

PSYCHOLOGICALLY REAL

Accurately representing how the human mind stores and processes information. A model such as Chomsky's can describe how a language operates; but that is not the same thing as claiming that it reflects how the mind performs when constructing or understanding an utterance. To give another example, phonologists recognise the phoneme as a unit in their description of language; but it is by no means certain that the phoneme is a category used by the mind when processing language.

Further reading: Smith (1999: Chap. 3)

RAPID SERIAL VISUAL PRESENTATION (RSVP)

A technique used in reading research. The subject reads a text on a screen, which is presented one word at a time or in groups of up to three words. The presentations are rapid, each lasting between 50 and 250 milliseconds.

Experiments using RSVP have suggested that, if the need for **eye movement** across the page is removed, reading speeds of up to 1200 words a minute are possible. However, comprehension declines sharply with longer texts, and it appears difficult to sustain this level of reading speed for long. Besides the effects of speed, RSVP does not permit *regression* which, in normal reading, plays an important role in building a meaning representation. RSVP also differs from the natural reading process in that it does not allow access to the *parafoveal* evidence on the fringes of the perceptual span of a reader, which enables him/her to anticipate upcoming words.

READING ALOUD

Experimental work on reading sometimes requires subjects to read aloud, so as to provide a record of the process. In an approach known as *miscue analysis*, the reader's mistakes are analysed both quantitatively and qualitatively. One aim is to establish to what extent erroneous words are similar in form to the target and to what extent they are similar in meaning. Advocates of a *whole word* approach to reading sometimes claim that miscue analysis evidence shows a high preponderance of semantic errors; from this, they conclude that form does not play an important part in skilled reading. However, it is difficult to determine whether these errors are errors of identification, of interpretation or of memory. Furthermore, other researchers have produced conflicting results which suggest that reading aloud errors are relatively rare and that the majority involve substitutions of orthographically similar but semantically inappropriate words.

Results from miscue analysis should be treated with caution, as reading aloud is only about half as fast as silent reading and may not share the same processes. Studies have been made of the *eye-voice span*, the time that elapses between fixating a word on the page and reading it aloud. The average span is about two words – which indicates that reading aloud cannot provide insights into the actual **on-line process** of reading. Most semantic reading aloud errors must occur well after word meaning has been accessed.

The eye-voice span seems to be determined by the constraints of **working memory**, which would become overburdened if the eye moved too far ahead. However, this again entails modifying the normal reading process. Reading aloud relies on delaying techniques such as shorter *saccades* (eye movements), and *fixations* where the eye lingers longer than normal.

Further reading: Gough and Wren (1999); Rayner and Pollatsek (1989: 180–1)

READING: BOTTOM-UP VS TOP-DOWN

Goodman (1967) put forward what is sometimes termed a '*top-down*' approach to reading, describing it as a 'psycholinguistic guessing game'. He suggested that skilled reading was marked by the reader's ability to use contextual information in order to anticipate the words which came next. This enabled the good reader to reduce his/her dependence upon decoding symbols on the page. Word recognition could take place more rapidly and the skilled reader could even skip words that were highly predictable. Frank Smith (1971) took a similar view, arguing that skilled readers exploit **redundancy** in a text. He claimed that the speed of skilled reading showed that the reader could not attend to every single letter; instead, they must make use of syntactic and semantic information to increase their efficiency. He even argued that, on this basis, it was futile to teach decoding skills to children; one should simply encourage them to 'make sense' of texts.

The 'top-down' view does not accord with current theory about the memory processes involved in reading. Decoding is conceived as being highly **automatic**, which means that it makes small demands upon working memory. By contrast, word or content prediction of the kind postulated by Goodman is under the control of the reader, and would thus be far more demanding (and slower and less efficient) than the process which it supposedly replaces. In addition, much of a reader's working memory appears to be committed to the difficult tasks of *integrating* incoming information into the mental representation of the text that has been constructed so far and of *monitoring* for failures of understanding. These are much more pressing demands upon limited resources than the need to predict what comes next.

Goodman's theory has been influential, but there is no body of evidence that supports it. Proponents of the theory claim that results from *miscue analysis* show that a large proportion of reading aloud errors are influenced by context; but this finding has been challenged. Considerable evidence suggests that skilled readers do not anticipate words as Goodman suggested:

☐ Eye movement data shows only a small decrease in fixation time when a word is predictable from the context. The conclusion is that there is no point in compromising the efficiency of the highly automatic process of eye movement by incorporating a more conscious (and therefore slower) context-driven process.

☐ Readers show no evidence of making explicit forward guesses. Indeed, with a text that is authentic and not specially written, they are extremely inaccurate when asked to predict forthcoming words.

☐ Poor readers have been shown to be more sensitive to context than good.

☐ Only about 40 per cent of function words and 10 per cent of content words can be predicted from context.

The most widely accepted view is that it is efficient decoding which makes for skilled reading. Perfetti's *verbal efficiency theory* (or *bottle-neck hypothesis*) suggests that the processes of decoding and comprehension compete for limited space in **working memory**. Where decoding is slow, it results in smaller amounts of information being made available at any time, and therefore a focus upon local rather than global meaning relations. Where it is not automatic, it demands extra working memory capacity, leaving less for other processes. In addition, the contents of working memory decay rapidly – so information derived from a slow decoding process may be lost before it can be analysed.

There is evidence that training in rapid decoding does not improve the comprehension of weak L1 readers. What they appear to need is accurate and automatic decoding – not a higher reading speed alone. However, inaccurate decoding produces the same outcome as slow decoding. If a weak reader has to keep regressing to check word recognition, the result is to slow down the supply of data and hence to encourage a focus on small-scale rather than larger-scale patterns of meaning.

Investigating the 'top-down' hypothesis, Stanovich reviewed 22 studies of reading and found no evidence that good readers used context to support word recognition as Goodman had suggested. There was evidence that skilled readers do make greater use of context (mental model of the text so far, world knowledge, text **schemas**) but it is in order to enrich meaning. Stanovich argued that context is used in two distinct ways:

- to construct global meaning and to **self-monitor**;
- to compensate for inadequate decoding skills.

The first is more characteristic of the skilled reader and the second of the unskilled. Stanovich's **interactive compensatory hypothesis** expands on the second function. It envisages a trade-off between message quality and the extent to which top-down information is relied upon to support decoding. If a reader has poor decoding skills, then they may fall back on top-down information. However, if a text is *degraded*, then even a skilled reader may have recourse to top-down information to compensate for gaps in the message.

See also: **Bottom-up processing, Eye movements, Reading: decoding, Reading speed, Top-down processing**

Further reading: Gough and Wren (1999); Oakhill and Garnham (1988); Perfetti (1985: Chaps 6–7); Rayner and Pollatsek (1989); Stanovich (1980)

READING: DECODING

The *perceptual* process of identifying the letters and words in a text. Decoding is regarded as a distinct process from **lexical access**, since we can process the form of an unfamiliar word (even attributing a possible pronunciation) without knowing its meaning.

The process of decoding is highly **automatic** in a skilled reader. This means that it makes few demands upon **working memory**, leaving capacity spare for higher-level processes such as constructing a *meaning representation*. It also means that our recognition of written words is so little subject to our control that we find it difficult to suppress the process in order to perform a task such as the **Stroop test**.

Decoding must be linked to a phonological representation of the words that are being read. It is this which enables us to map unfamiliar strings of letters on to words that we know in speech; to assign pronunciations to words that we have never heard (e.g. technical terms or Proper Nouns); and to read rhyming poetry, puns etc.

We need to distinguish two types of phonological operation:

- *Pre-lexical*, in the form of letter-to-sound mappings which enable us to work out the pronunciation of unfamiliar words.
- *Post-lexical*, in the form of the **inner speech** which readers sometimes report hearing in their heads. This seems to be a means of retaining word-level information in working memory. The advantage of storing information phonologically is that it does not interfere with the ongoing visual process of reading. However, it must be stored in an abbreviated form. Speaking is much slower than silent reading, so we cannot store words exactly as we say them.

A **dual route** model of decoding suggests that we process written words in two ways. A *lexical route* enables us to match whole words while a *sub-lexical route* permits us to identify words by means of **grapheme-phoneme correspondence (GPC) rules** which specify the relationships between spelling and sound. Though the sub-lexical route is slower, it permits us to attribute a pronunciation to unfamiliar words.

An alternative **interactive** account of decoding represents the reader as processing a text simultaneously at several different levels of representation: taking account of letter features (curves, vertical lines etc.), letters, letter sequences and whole words. Evidence feeds up from one level to another, and also feeds down. Thus, when the letters WOR are identified at letter level and the order $_1$W $_2$O $_3$R is recorded at word sequence level, words such as WORK, WORD, WORM are *activated* at lexical level. But there is also a 'downwards' flow of information, with the reader's lexical knowledge confirming that there are indeed words in the lexicon beginning with WOR, so that the evidence from letter recognition is to be trusted. Lexical knowledge also tells us that the word is more likely to be WORD or WORK than the less frequent WORM.

A very different view, espoused by proponents of *whole word* teaching methods, holds that efficient decoding is heavily dependent upon rapid word shape recognition. Experimental evidence does not support this hypothesis. Both children and adults have little difficulty in identifying words presented in unfamiliar zigzag or vertical forms, and text presented in *AlTeRnAtInG cAsE* only delays word recognition by about 10 per cent. Furthermore, **eye movement** studies show that longer words cause longer fixations – which should not occur if words are being processed as wholes. These findings suggest that sub-word units do indeed play a part in decoding. When words are confused in reading, it may not be because they resemble each other in overall shape but simply because they contain letters which resemble each other.

Sometimes cited in support of the 'whole word' view is a finding that subjects identify target letters more quickly when they occur later in a word. One would expect the opposite if words were processed letter by letter from left to right. However, the interactive model neatly accounts for this effect by suggesting that lexical knowledge of the existence of a word becomes available as more and more of the word is seen, and assists the process of decoding.

A reader processes highly frequent letter strings such as -ATION more quickly than others; this may mean that there is a level of representation for unanalysed *chunks*. The gradual recognition of chunked sequences is an experience reported by many who have spent time in a country with a different alphabetic system from their own.

Technology allows us to *track* a reader's eye movements across the page; this has provided valuable insights into the decoding process. It has also dispelled a number of myths. It appears that skilled readers do not, as once supposed, make longer eye sweeps (*saccades*) than less skilled. Nor do skilled readers skip important words. The majority of content words (about 80 per cent) are fixated by all readers, though readers seem to have the ability to distinguish and by-pass function words, of which they only fixate about 40 per cent. What distinguishes a skilled reader from an unskilled is the degree of *back-tracking* that occurs. In a reader with good decoding skills, only about 10 per cent of saccades are regressive, and these often occur because a word is unexpected in its context rather than because it has been inaccurately processed.

See also: **Eye movements, Reading aloud, Reading: bottom-up vs top-down, Reading: skilled**

Further reading: Oakhill and Beard (1999); Oakhill and Garnham (1988); Rayner and Pollatsek (1989)

READING DEVELOPMENT

The early stages of reading require the learner to form a set of connections between the written forms of language and already-acquired spoken forms. The child also has to recognise the extent to which the written word is a different *modality* from the spoken. Spoken language often takes the form of short exchanges between two or more interlocutors who can provide feedback and clarification. The pre-literate child has to adapt to an entirely new pragmatic environment, and to accept a situation where information can only be checked by reference to the text.

An important factor is the relationship between the child's *sight vocabulary* and its oral vocabulary. Once basic decoding skills have been established, the child goes through a stage where its reading ability catches up on its ability to understand speech. There then comes a cross-over point after which much information gained through reading becomes easier to process than the same information gained through listening; and many new words are acquired first in the visual modality rather than the spoken.

Two main approaches are employed in the teaching of reading: the analytic *phonics* method, in which the learner is taught the relationship between letters and sounds, and the holistic *whole word* (or '*look and say*') method, where a match is made between complete written and spoken word forms.

Phonics would appear to tap into the child's existing knowledge of the spoken language. But pre-literate infants may well not possess **phonological awareness**, the ability to recognise the words of a language as composed of discrete sounds. In addition, there are obvious problems with phonics in relation to an *opaque* spelling system such as the English one. These include the lack of a one-to-one relationship between letters and sounds (compare A in ABOUT, HAT, HATE), the use of digraphs (SH- as in SHARP) and the existence of irregular words (YACHT).

The whole word method is said to be more motivating, enabling children to identify words in text at once. However, it does not equip learners to use a *sub-lexical route* in order to work out the pronunciation of an unfamiliar word from its spelling. This skill potentially plays a major part in the expansion of a child's sight vocabulary once it starts reading independently. In support of the whole word technique, it has been claimed that skilled readers do not decode letters but identify words by their shapes. Evidence has not supported this. A currently influential **interactive** model of reading suggests that words are processed simultaneously at many different levels (letter feature, letter, letter order, word). This entails a need for phonic as well as whole word skills.

There are a number of other approaches to reading instruction. A compromise between phonics and whole word approaches makes use of *analogy*: when the word MIGHT is taught, children are reminded of its *neighbours*, words like LIGHT and RIGHT with a similar **rime**. There is evidence that rime plays a part in the decoding of words by adult readers; and that it is a strategy employed by child readers as young as six.

The traditional *alphabetic approach* requires learners to master the names of the letters. There is no evidence that knowledge of letter names contributes to better early reading, although it may give support to letter shape recognition.

Various regularised alphabets have been devised for the teaching of reading, including some that employ colour coding of letters or diacritical marking. In Britain, the *initial teaching alphabet* (i.t.a.) enjoyed a vogue in the 1960s and 1970s. Evidence suggested that, after a year of reading, children who learnt with i.t.a. were better at word recognition though not at comprehension; however, this advantage seemed to be lost when they transferred to the standard alphabet.

Finally, a *story approach* asserts that it is not necessary to train children to read: they should instead be exposed to motivating material which is read aloud to them by an adult until such time as they feel able to read it themselves. The approach is based upon the notion that reading is a guessing game and that skilled adult readers make use of contextual information to relieve themselves of the necessity of decoding words. The theory is not supported by evidence, and the current consensus is that decoding skills have to be taught.

One model of reading development portrays novice readers as proceeding through four phases:

☐ *Phase 1: sight vocabulary.* The child acquires a small set of words by being taught them by carers or by hearing a spoken word frequently associated with a label or sign. The child can still recognise these words when they are written in different scripts or cases. This *direct procedure* appears to involve recognising words as sequences of letters rather than as wholes.

☐ *Phase 2: discrimination net.* The child assumes that every word form it encounters corresponds to a word from its limited reading vocabulary. It therefore makes highly approximate matches. It draws on minimal similarities such as length (TELEVISION read as 'children') or the presence of a particular letter (LIKE read as 'black' because it contains a *k*).

☐ *Phase 3: phonological recoding.* At this stage, the child becomes capable of reading non-words. It begins to match unknown words with words that it knows in spoken form but has not yet learnt in writing. This suggests that sound-spelling rules are being acquired by the child, possibly supported by analogy.

☐ *Phase 4: orthographic.* Sound-spelling rules do not serve to distinguish homophones such as WHERE and WEAR or to identify unique spellings such as YACHT. The importance of phonological recoding declines between six and ten years old; stronger readers lead the way in adopting orthographic form as the dominant representation.

Some researchers challenge this sequence, asserting that visual access develops first and remains the dominant mode at nine years old, with only the better readers possessing developed phonological encoding skills at that stage.

An alternative approach measures development in terms of the extent to which the young reader relies upon sentence context to decode a word. A child's first reading errors often fit the context but bear little formal resemblance to the target word. At a second stage, children become more aware of the importance of accurate decoding and stop reading when they reach words whose form they do not know. At a third stage (after about the first year of reading), the child's errors come to reflect the influence of both context and form.

Alongside decoding, children have to acquire higher-level reading skills.

☐ *Syntax.* Speech contains cues to syntactic boundaries in the form of intonation, pausing etc.; these are absent from reading. There is evidence that some young readers with adequate decoding skills read word by word and fail to recognise hierarchical syntactic patterns in text.

☐ *Inference.* Children appear to be capable of applying inferences to text quite early on. They nevertheless perform better with texts where information is explicit rather than those where it is implicit, and make fewer inferences than adults.

☐ *Relevance.* Sensitivity to what is important in a text develops gradually with experience of reading. In recall tasks, early readers are more likely to mention important points than peripheral ones; but they have difficulty in identifying main ideas or grouping sentences according to topic.

☐ *Text structure*. An awareness of logical structure seems to pre-date reading: young children are sensitive to the structure of stories, and disruptions of conventional order make stories difficult for them to follow.

☐ *Comprehension monitoring*. Younger readers often fail to check their representation of what a text says to ensure that it is consistent. They are less likely to notice internal inconsistencies in a text than problems arising from difficult vocabulary. This may be partly because the effort involved in lower-level processing places relatively heavy demands upon memory.

See also: **Phonological awareness, Reading: decoding, Reading: skilled**

Further reading: Goswami and Bryant (1990); Harris and Coltheart (1986: Chap. 4); Oakhill and Beard (1999); Oakhill and Garnham (1988: Chap. 4)

READING: HIGHER-LEVEL PROCESSES

The processing of visual material at a *conceptual* level as distinct from a *perceptual* level. Higher-level reading processes entail:

☐ *Constructing abstract meaning from linguistic material that has been decoded*. This provides a mental record of the core meaning of the sentence without any of the interpretative and associative detail which the reader then brings to bear.

☐ *Drawing inferences* which supply links that the writer has taken for granted.

☐ *Employing external knowledge to support and enrich understanding*. This external knowledge takes the form of **schemas** in long-term memory which group all that an individual knows about or associates with a particular concept. It is useful to distinguish two types:

- World knowledge, including encyclopaedic knowledge and previous knowledge of the writer. This helps the reader to construct a *content schema* for the text.
- Previous experience of the type of text and of the type of reading that the text requires. A *formal schema* of this kind helps the reader to recognise how information is likely to be distributed and how they should engage with the speaker or writer.

☐ *Integrating incoming information into the mental representation of the text so far.* Incoming information has to be related to what has gone before, so as to ensure that it contributes to the developing representation of the text in a way that is consistent, meaningful and relevant. This process entails an ability to identify main ideas, to relate them to previous ideas and to impose a hierarchical structure on the information in the text.

☐ *Monitoring comprehension* by checking how viable the current interpretation is.

See also: **Inference, Listening: higher-level processes, Reading development, Reading: skilled, Schema theory**

Further reading: Oakhill and Garnham (1988); Yuill and Oakhill (1992)

READING: SKILLED

Some have argued that reading problems mainly reflect linguistic limitations (for example, a limited sight vocabulary); others that they chiefly derive from *decoding* limitations at word level. However, instruction in these areas does not necessarily improve overall comprehension. This suggests that the perceptual and conceptual processes involved in reading are distinct. The view is reinforced by evidence that many weak readers are weak listeners – indicating that there may be a general comprehension process which applies in both modalities. However, it may be that the pattern of deficit varies from reader to reader, with some experiencing lower-level problems, some higher-level and some both.

The following are often characteristics of unskilled reading:

☐ *An inability to decode words as automatically as a skilled reader.* This can impact on the reading process in several ways. Less skilled readers might back-track too much in order to check words. The supply of words to **working memory** might be too slow, so that some traces decay before they can be constructed into higher-level structures. Processing that is not **automatic** enough might take up extra working memory resources, leaving less capacity for building meaning. Or, aware of the effort which decoding costs them, an unskilled reader might rely more heavily upon context than upon perceptual information.

☐ *Weak syntactic parsing.* Poor comprehenders tend to read word by word rather than assembling the text into higher-level syntactic structures. This may be because in reading they lack the cues provided in speech by pausing, intonation etc.

☐ *Less inference.* Unskilled readers make fewer of the inferences which are necessary in order to form connections between ideas in a text and to restore what a writer may have left unsaid. This seems to reflect a different style of processing rather than a more limited memory for verbatim text. Similarly, unskilled readers make much less use of **instantiation**, a process whereby the interpretation of a word is restricted by the context in which it appears.

☐ *Poor integration.* Unskilled readers are less capable of integrating incoming ideas into the existing representation of a text and of perceiving which are main ideas and which are subsidiary. One theory, Gernsbacher's *Structure Building Framework*, suggests that readers proceed by building informational substructures around a particular topic and shifting to a new substructure when information comes in that appears to be unrelated to the current one. Less skilled comprehenders fail to perceive connections and shift too often, creating too many low-level substructures. A similar view is that weak integration skills reflect difficulties in retaining information in working memory. There is evidence that poor readers find it difficult to associate a referent with a pronoun, a process termed **anaphor resolution**. This difficulty increases the further from the pronoun the referent occurs.

☐ *Inadequate self-monitoring.* There is also evidence that poor readers fail to monitor their understanding of a text to see if it contains inconsistencies. Asked what is wrong with an anomalous text, skilled readers manage to locate the inconsistency, whereas unskilled readers tend to place the blame at word level, mentioning difficult vocabulary. As with anaphor resolution, weak readers' inability to detect inconsistencies has been shown to increase with memory load. Thus, where an anomaly is resolved quite soon after it occurs, their comprehension differs little from that of skilled readers; but it is markedly worse when the resolving information is further away.

A feature of many accounts of reading skill is the part played by **working memory** (WM). It is necessary for a reader to hold words in the mind while imposing a syntactic pattern on them and to hold propositions in the mind in order to add new information to an ongoing representation of the text. Some children with reading problems have been found to have a more limited WM capacity, as measured by a *digit span* technique. However, it seems likely that any deficit lies in their ability to use their WM to encode information rather than in limitations upon how much they are able to store.

Poor readers often show an inability to recall recent parts of a text. One explanation for this is that they have to give extra effort to decoding words, which limits their memory capacity for more complex operations. Another is that information in their WM decays more rapidly than is usual; or that there are limitations on how much the individual is able to turn over (**rehearse**) in WM at any one time.

See also: **Phonological working memory, Reading: bottom–up vs top–down, Reading: decoding, Reading: higher–level processes, Reading span, Reading speed**

Further reading: Gathercole and Baddeley (1993); Just and Carpenter (1987); Oakhill and Garnham (1988); Perfetti (1985); Yuill and Oakhill (1992)

READING SPAN

A measure derived from a test (Daneman and Carpenter, 1980) in which subjects are asked to read a set of unrelated sentences and to recall the last word of each. The size of the set is gradually increased from two to seven sentences, and the largest set for which the subject provides accurate responses is taken as a measure of their reading span. The advantage of this test is that, unlike *Auditory Short-Term Memory* tests, it replicates the processing and storage that occurs in normal reading. The rationale is that better readers process the sentences more efficiently and thus have more working memory capacity available for remembering the words. In an early administration of the test, results from college students ranged from 2 to 5.5 and were found to correlate highly with reading ability.

READING SPEED

The chief characteristics of 'speed reading' are longer *saccades* (eye sweeps), fewer eye *fixations* and shorter fixation times, with attention focused on longer words.

Commercial speed reading courses often equate fast reading with skilled reading. However, evidence suggests that what is critical to decoding is not so much speed as accuracy and a high level of **automaticity**. If a weak reader is slow, it is often because their inadequate decoding skills lead them to back-track repeatedly to check words about which they are unsure.

Average reading speed in one's first language is around 250–300 words per minute. With training, readers can certainly increase this speed. However, very high speeds cannot be sustained for long or with adequate understanding of the text. As speed increases, comprehension quickly begins to suffer.

A better conceptualisation of a skilled reader is that he/she has the ability to adapt reading speed according to whether the task in hand demands *deep* or *shallow* reading. Reading speed may also be dependent upon the reader's familiarity with the topic of the text.

RECURSIVENESS

An important difference between reading and listening is that reading is *recursive*: the reader can go back and consult the text in order to check understanding, while the listener cannot (except in the case of a recorded signal).

REDUNDANCY

Where the presence of a linguistic or phonetic feature does not play a necessary part in identifying a unit of language, it is said to be redundant. There is redundancy at all levels of language; indeed, language as a phenomenon is often described as highly redundant. For example, several acoustic-phonetic cues serve to distinguish the sound /p/ from the sound /b/. If we can show that a listener largely relies on differences of *Voice Onset Time*, the other cues can be regarded as redundant. Likewise, in a sentence such as *The passengers are embarking*, both *passengers* and *are* are marked for plural number. Strictly speaking, it is only necessary to mark one in order to convey the relevant information.

Redundancy assists the listener or reader in processing the signal accurately, especially in conditions of **noise** where there is a high level of interference or where a text is *degraded*. It similarly assists those who have impaired vision or hearing.

It has been suggested that redundancy gives language a degree of predictability, enabling the listener or reader to anticipate what words will come next. However, it is by no means clear that this occurs as part of normal processing. It seems more likely that redundancy is used to check on what is being heard or read rather than to anticipate what is to come.

See also: **Noise, Underspecification**

REHEARSAL

The recycling of material in the mind, with a view to retaining it longer. There are two types. *Maintenance rehearsal* involves refreshing information within working memory so as to keep it available for use. *Elaborative rehearsal* involves consolidating this information with a view to transferring it to long-term memory.

The two types of rehearsal are responsible for **position effects** in word recall tasks. In the *primacy effect*, words from the beginning of a list are recalled better because they have been subject to greater elaborative rehearsal. In the *recency effect*, words from the end of the list are recalled because they are still being supported by maintenance rehearsal.

Maintenance rehearsal enables the listener or reader to store linguistic material short term. The purpose does not seem to be to support word recognition. Instead, we need to retain the verbatim form of an utterance in order to deal with sentences where it is difficult to impose a semantic or syntactic pattern until we reach the end. Maintenance rehearsal is critical to parsing sentences that are long or complex, have a non-standard word order or have difficult thematic relationships (in the form, for example, of a Passive verb).

Elaborative rehearsal plays an important part in learning situations (including rote learning). The greater the number of repetitions, it is believed, the greater the probability of successful storage. Evidence of this is found in an increased primacy effect when extra time is allowed for mastering a word list.

What is the form in which linguistic material is stored while it is being rehearsed? Researchers have investigated the question by asking subjects to remember lists of words – a process demanding elaborative rehearsal. They have discovered that successful recall declines when a list features words that take a long time to say. This happens regardless of whether the list is in spoken or written form, suggesting that written material is *recoded* into some kind of phonological form when it is held in store. Likewise, the phenomenon of **'inner speech'** during reading (the impression of a voice in the head) suggests that a phonological form also features in maintenance rehearsal. Rehearsal is thus generally represented as involving a phonological mechanism (in Baddeley's model a *phonological loop*) which handles both spoken and written input.

It may seem odd that written material needs to be recoded. One explanation is that information stored in phonological form is more robust; another is that it interferes less with the reading process.

Because rehearsal is phonological in form, simple tasks which involve speaking aloud (reciting numbers or even just repeating the word *the*) interfere with it. This effect, known as **articulatory suppression**, is widely used in research into rehearsal.

See also: **Working memory**

Further reading: Baddeley (1997); Gathercole and Baddeley (1993)

REPAIR₁

A means of redressing a breakdown of understanding. Several possible repair strategies are available to a listener in order to draw attention to such a breakdown. They include: facial expression and other paralinguistic signals, repair formulae such as *Sorry?*; requests for clarification; waiting for amplification. The speaker's response will depend upon whether the failure of understanding is believed to be *perceptual* or *conceptual* in origin.

REPAIR₂ (also SELF-REPAIR)

An adjustment or correction added to an utterance by a speaker as a result of **self-monitoring**. Repairs commonly correct speech errors; but they might also rephrase part of an utterance to make it more precise, more appropriate or easier to understand.

Not all speech errors are repaired; but speakers seem to be especially sensitive to those that might cause problems for a listener. A stress placement error which also involves a change of vowel quality (*laGOON → LAgoon*) is treated as more disruptive (and is repaired much more often) than one that does not (*TURbine → turBINE*). It is not clear whether speakers judge that the second type of error does not pose a sufficient threat to comprehensibility, or whether they fail to notice it at all.

The distance between a problematic item and its repair varies considerably. In a *covert repair*, indicated by a pause or an editing expression (*er, I mean*), potential trouble may even be detected before the item is uttered. In *overt repairs*, the interruption might take place while the problematic item is being uttered (i.e. within the word), immediately after it or after a delay of one or more words. The most common situation is the second, followed by the third. Where there is a delayed repair, it often occurs at a phrase boundary. This may reflect the fact that self-monitoring is more active later in a phrase or may reflect a wish by the speaker to complete a planned phrase before interrupting the flow. Certainly, repairs appear to be structured syntactically so as to make it as easy as possible for the listener to continue to follow the utterance.

A distinction is made between repairs that are marked prosodically by a change in pitch, loudness and/or duration and those that are not. Here, type of repair is a factor. Just over half of error repairs are marked, but relatively few rephrasing ones.

See also: **Self-monitoring**

Further reading: Levelt (1989: Chap. 12)

REPRESENTATIONAL CODES

There is evidence that **working memory** can retrieve information from **long-term memory** (LTM) in the form of sensory (visual or auditory) codes as well as in the form of semantic codes. Researchers have therefore suggested that LTM representations include images and verbal symbols; but they have encountered great difficulty in determining what form they might be stored in. Some have argued that stored visual and auditory images are not exact representations, but are generated by abstract propositions, to which we do not have direct access. Others have claimed that images are stored in their own right, because they include spatial information which cannot be accounted for abstractly. Support for the second position comes from studies which suggest that the time taken to scan a mental image depends upon how far into the image one has to imagine oneself. Brain imaging research also appears to support this position, showing signs of brain activity in areas known to be used in vision when a task demands visual imagery.

RESEARCH METHODS: APPROACHES

Psycholinguistics employs a wide range of research methods and draws upon various types of data.

☐ *Naturally occurring data,* both written and spoken. Corpora of **Slips of the Tongue** have afforded insights into the process of assembling speech. Recordings of natural spoken language provide material for discourse analysis, which can offer insights into the planning and execution of connected speech. Recording also enables researchers to examine the effects upon language of damage to various parts of the brain and to classify the characteristics of speech impediments. In studying language acquisition, fixed microphones are widely used to collect samples of child language at random or at regularly timed intervals.

☐ *Observational.* The approach might involve the keeping of research notes or diaries. This kind of case study has proved especially fruitful in studying first language acquisition.

☐ *Theory-driven.* An obvious example is the use of **Chomskyan theory** as a framework for analysing language acquisition data – a method especially favoured by those on the linguistic rather than psychological wing of the field. They examine the productions of first language acquirers and the *grammaticality judgements* of second language acquirers for evidence of underlying universal **principles** of language or for the setting of language-specific *parameters.*

☐ *Neuropsychological.* Physical evidence is sought of how activity within the brain correlates with language. Current **brain imaging** techniques permit researchers to observe changing states within the brain by monitoring electrical currents or the flow of blood.

☐ *Experimental.* The most commonly used approach, especially in investigating language processing. It permits the researcher to control the many variables which are present in linguistic encounters and to focus upon one aspect of performance. It also enables findings to be tested across a wide range of subjects. Typically, experiments in psycholinguistics focus upon small-scale effects, from which larger conclusions may be derived. See **Research methods: experimental.**

☐ *Computer modelling.* Researchers in **Artificial Intelligence** construct models which attempt to simulate *natural language processing.* A 'strong' rationale would suggest that there are important parallels between the way the mind works and the operations of a computer. A more generally accepted view is that, by modelling language processes, the experimenter can gain insights into the analytic and decision-making processes in which a human being engages.

RESEARCH METHODS: EXPERIMENTAL

The most widely adopted approach in psycholinguistic research is to gather evidence experimentally. An issue is the extent to which a study under experimental conditions can claim to be investigating the natural use of language.

It is important to specify whether a particular research method taps in to language processing **on-line** (as it is actually occurring) or whether it involves some kind of subsequent decision-making. If the latter is the case, then the experiment is said to be **post-perceptual**: it measures the outcome of the process (e.g. what the subject reports they heard) rather than the process itself (the act of listening). Experimenters also have to beware of *task effects*: a task that requires subjects to recall something they read an hour ago involves not just reading skill but memory as well.

A wide range of experimental methods has been devised, many specific to psycholinguistics.

□ One group involves *measuring how long it takes a subject to respond* to a stimulus. The advantage of this kind of method is that it taps into on-line performance with no decision-making intervening. The simple tasks that are set are often distractions. They enable the experimenter to measure the effects of a particular condition (for example, sentence ambiguity) upon the subject; but the subject is not aware of the true goal of the experiment and can be assumed to be processing the material normally.

Reaction times (also referred to as *response times* and *response latencies*) are usually expressed in milliseconds. Examples of reaction time (RT) tasks are:

- *Phoneme/word monitoring.* The subject presses a button whenever they hear a particular phoneme or word in a recorded text. Their response is slower when the phoneme or word coincides with, for example, semantic or syntactic ambiguities in the text. This enables the experimenter to measure the increased demands which these ambiguities make upon **working memory**.
- *The naming task.* The subject reads words aloud. The time (*naming*

latency) is measured from the presentation of each word to the onset of the voice.

- *Lexical decision*. The subject presses a button whenever they encounter an actual word rather than a non-word. This task can provide evidence of: (a) how readily different types of word are recognised; (b) how strongly other attention-demanding operations interfere with word recognition.
- *Word spotting*. Subjects hear sequences of sounds which may or may not have actual words embedded in them. They press a button when they identify a word. The task is used to investigate how subjects segment connected speech into words.

These methods provide more than just reaction time data. The experimenter can also record how many items were missed or wrongly identified.

An alternative way of measuring reaction times is to present sentences word-by-word or phrase-by-phrase on a monitor. As a subject finishes reading each display, they press a key for the next, and the time between key strokes is measured. Equipment is also available which tracks the **eye movements** of a subject reading a text; this enables researchers to measure fixation times and regressions of the reader's eye.

☐ A similar group of methods involve *detection tasks* in which *subjects have to determine whether a feature is present and/or where it is located*. The researcher might record which features remain undetected or the distance between the actual and perceived position of a feature. Examples are:

- *Click location*. Subjects hear sentences with a click in them, and indicate where they believe the click occurs. The click may be perceived in the wrong place because of the influence of syntactic structure.
- *Phoneme restoration*. Subjects hear sentences from which a phoneme has been excised. They often cannot hear the gap.

☐ Other methods test subjects' *interpretation of linguistic input*:

- *Shadowing*. Subjects listen to a cassette recording, and repeat what they hear as closely after the speaker as possible. Shadowing provides insights into spoken language perception, particularly through the errors that subjects make.
- *Gating*. A piece of recorded speech is sliced into sections or 'gates'. Subjects hear the first section and write down what they think they

hear. Then they hear the first and second sections together and add to or revise their first impression. They continue to report on chunks of increasing size.

- *Masking.* Subjects hear sentences with background noise or read sentences where the text is partly masked. They report what they understand. A similar task asks subjects to report *faint speech* in the form of sentences played at the borders of audibility. The data obtained is post-perceptual.

☐ A further set of experimental methods is used to investigate *lexical storage and lexical access*. It includes:

- *Word association.* A traditional task for investigating how words are stored in semantic networks. Subjects are given a word and asked to record or write down the first word that comes into their heads.
- *'Tip of the Tongue'.* The experimenter gives a definition of an obscure word and asks the subject to name the word. This gives rise to many nearly accurate responses, which are compared with the correct one, so as to provide insights into what happens when we search for words.
- *Priming.* A word is presented to a subject, followed shortly afterwards by another believed to be associated with it. If there is a lexical association, the second word will be detected more rapidly. Priming experiments often incorporate the lexical decision task (see above).

☐ Methods used to investigate *working memory* include:

- *Recall.* Subjects remember as many words as they can from a list.
- *Repetition.* Subjects repeat digits, words or non-words after the experimenter. This forms the basis of various *span* tests, in which the number of items for repetition becomes longer and longer until the subject reaches a limit, a measure of their memory capacity.

☐ An ingenious set of methods has been designed to deal with the difficulty of acquiring information from *pre-linguistic infants*. The techniques exploit the fact that infants quickly become bored when they are presented with stimuli that are repetitive. They include the *high amplitude sucking* (HAS) *procedure* and the *operant headturn procedure*. See **language acquisition: research methods**.

See also: **Gating, Priming effect, Shadowing, Verbal report**

Further reading: Gernsbacher (1994: Chaps 1–2); Grosjean and Frauenfelder (1996); Jusczyk (1997: Appendix)

RESTRUCTURING

A sudden insight which leads to a reorganisation of existing knowledge structures. The change may occur as a result of acquiring important new knowledge or through reflection on experience.

The term 'restructuring' has especially been applied to second language learning. A learner at an interim stage of knowledge is said to employ an *interlanguage* (IL), a partial version of the target language with its own internal consistencies. One hypothesis suggests that acquiring new grammatical information causes the learner to completely reorganise the set of relationships upon which their IL is based, rather than simply adding new elements.

Further reading: McLaughlin (1987: 136–8)

RHYME

Tests with children have found a correlation between reading difficulties and insensitivity to rhyme. The finding indicates the importance of rhyme in enabling young readers to trace analogies between written forms in English (LIGHT and FIGHT). Evidence from identical twins suggests that insensitivity to rhyme may be an inherited phonological deficit.

RIME

In the spoken form of a monosyllabic word, the *nucleus* (vowel) plus the *coda*: i.e. the sequence /ed/ in HEAD or /ɑːm/ in FARM. British commentators often distinguish *rime* referring to a syllabic constituent from the word *rhyme* referring to phonological similarity.

A word's rime appears to be an important characterising feature. In the '*word-blending*' task, subjects show a preference for outcomes which conserve a rime. Thus, asked to combine BARK and TURN to form a third word, they prefer B+URN to BAR+N. Rime appears to be more influential than *digraphs* (e.g. -EA- in BEAN) in determining the preferred pronunciation of a non-word.

See also: **Neighbourhood**

SAVANT

An individual who is severely mentally impaired, but shows exceptional gifts, often in painting or music. A savant has been discovered who possesses similar gifts for language. Christopher was diagnosed as brain-damaged early in life and has to live in care; yet he is able to translate from, and communicate in, some 16 languages. This is taken by some commentators to demonstrate that there is a dissociation between linguistic and general cognitive abilities; and that language is a separate **modular** faculty.

See also: **Modularity₁, Specific language impairment, Williams Syndrome**

Further reading: Smith and Tsimpli (1995)

SCAFFOLDING

The support afforded by an adult to a developing child, by way of stimulating its interest in a task, orienting it towards appropriate goals, highlighting salient features of a task and demonstrating relevant strategies. Scaffolding plays an important part in assisting a child to advance into its *Zone of Proximal Development*, the difference between what it can achieve by its own problem solving and what it can achieve in collaboration with adults.

The term is sometimes used in first language acquisition to refer to a form of adult input which provides an infant step by step with the material upon which to build utterances. Example (C: Child; A: Adult):

C: Boat (*pointing to paper*).
A: Draw a boat.
C: Draw boat.
A: You want to draw a boat?
C: Want draw boat.

The term 'scaffolding' is used for similar techniques employed in **foreigner talk** and in foreign language teaching.

See also: **Social-interactionism**

SCHEMA THEORY

A *schema* (plural: *schemas* or *schemata*) is a complex knowledge structure which groups all that an individual knows about or associates with a particular concept. The term, much used in discussion of comprehension theory, was introduced by Bartlett (1932) and extended by many commentators since.

As an example, an adult in Western society has a schema for RESTAURANT which entails: waiters/waitresses – a meal (not a snack) – a meal eaten on the premises – a main course with optional first course and dessert – menus – a bill – a chef (unseen) – cutlery – glasses – napkins etc. This begins as *episodic* knowledge based on individual experiences of restaurants, but turns into *semantic* knowledge as the individual's experience of restaurants grows.

When a reader encounters the word RESTAURANT, they access this schematic knowledge. It enables them to build a richer context than a writer provides; indeed, the writer can assume that the schema is shared with the reader, and is thus spared the need to go into excessive detail. Schematic knowledge also enables the reader to anticipate events and ideas which might occur later in the text and to relate incidents in the text to what happens in normal life.

Schemas which supply background knowledge to the interpretation of a text are sometimes referred to as *content schemas*. The reader's ability to draw upon one may depend upon having a clearly established context for the text in question. A well-known experimental passage described how to use a washing machine but the schema could not be accessed without the assistance of an explanatory title.

Studies of reading and listening sometimes refer to *formal schemas*, which reflect previous experience of a text type or genre. Thus, in reading a scientific paper, we expect it to contain an abstract, a review of the literature, a presentation and analysis of data etc. This type of schema also provides expectations about style and register.

As well as referring to long-term knowledge structures, the term 'schema' is sometimes used more specifically to refer to the *meaning representation* that a reader or listener builds up while processing a particular piece of discourse. We approach a text with certain expectations about what it will say, which we derive from the title or from the purpose of the text; these enable us to develop a text-specific schema even before we read. As we read, we revise and add to the initial schema.

Schemas vary from one language user to another, and can be modified *ad hoc* to deal with a current situation. There are said to be three ways in which they can be changed. *Tuning* involves small adjustments made temporarily in order to confront immediate needs. *Accretion* modifies a schema gradually but permanently as new information is acquired or as repeated examples of contrary evidence accumulate. Thus, a child might have to adjust its category of DUCK to exclude birds that it has come to recognise as belonging to the category SWAN. *Restructuring* occurs when a sudden insight or new piece of knowledge leads to a radical reorganisation of existing knowledge structures.

Associated with **schema theory** are two other types of stored knowledge. A *frame* (Minsky, 1977) is a schema with optional slots. The frame for SHIP provides us with the information 'large – means of transport – floats on sea – manned by sailors'. We then use information from the text we are reading in order to fill empty slots relating to purpose (warship vs ferry vs merchant ship), power (diesel vs steam vs sail), colour, destination etc. If the information is not provided, we fill the slots with default values. In the absence of further information, our slots for SHIP would probably be filled out with passengers, a funnel and a dark colour rather than guns, sails or bright red.

A *script* (Schank and Abelson, 1977) is a sequence of activities associated with a stereotypical situation. A RESTAURANT script entails a particular ritual (W = waiter, C = customer): W greets C – C asks if there is a table – W shows C to the table – W presents menu – W asks what C wants to drink – C orders first two courses of meal. Scripts provide a framework for many everyday events, and permit speakers and writers to adopt a kind of shorthand. If we read *Helen ate in a restaurant*, we can supply for ourselves the details of what happened without having to have them spelt out.

See also: **Listening: higher-level processes, Reading: higher-level processes**

Further reading: Greene (1986: Part 1)

SEARCH MODEL

A model of **lexical access** in which stored words are examined *serially* (one item after another) in order to find a match for a word in the signal. Search models assume that evidence in the input first enables the processor to narrow down the search to a subset of the words in the lexicon; items in that subset are then examined until a match is achieved. In Forster's *search model* (1979), words are arranged in 'bins' by similarity of form and by **modality** (spoken vs written). A bin is selected for search, and within the bin the words that are reached first are those that are the most frequent (they are said to be 'higher' in the bin).

A different type of search model is Becker's (1979) *verification model*, which further limits the subset of words to be searched by employing semantic criteria (items associated with a particular context) as well as orthographic (items similar in form to the target).

See also: **Lexical access**

Further reading: Forster (1990)

SECOND LANGUAGE ACQUISITION (SLA)

Language teachers were once swayed by an argument that the most natural way of acquiring a second language was to emulate the process of first language acquisition. However, modern practice reflects a realisation that the two situations are very different. Compared with an infant acquiring its first language, an adolescent or adult acquiring a second:

- has less time for learning;
- is cognitively developed – possessing concepts such as causality or aspect;
- is primed by experience to seek for patterns in data and so responds to input analytically;
- already has a first language, which provides a lens through which the second is perceived;
- has access to a language of explanation, and is therefore capable of understanding (even if not applying) theoretical explanations;
- is accustomed to expressing their personality in L1, and may find their limited powers of expression in L2 a chastening experience;
- has pragmatic experience of a range of social circumstances in L1 and extensive world knowledge.

SECOND LANGUAGE ACQUISITION: APPROACHES

☐ *Linguistic.* In the linguistic tradition, research and analysis are usually based on the assumption that the acquisition of our first language is supported by an innately acquired **Universal Grammar** (UG). In this context, six different positions can be adopted in relation to second language (L2) acquisition:

- The L2 learner retains access to the same UG as was available for L1.
- UG supports L1 acquisition only, and is then lost. The process of L2 acquisition is therefore very different.
- UG supports L1 acquisition only, but L2 acquisition is able to model itself upon residual traces of our experience of acquiring L1.
- UG survives until early adolescence and then decays. There is thus a **critical period** for second language acquisition.
- Universal **principles** are retained and continue to guide L2 acquisition. However, the user's *parameters* are adjusted to L1 values and therefore need to be re-set to L2 values.
- Universal linguistic criteria (perhaps based on **markedness**) determine which linguistic concepts are the easiest to acquire and which are the most difficult.

One research approach is *theory-driven*: with researchers applying L1 linguistic theory (usually Chomskyan) to second language learning and use. Researchers often ask subjects to make L2 *grammaticality judgements*, which are said to tap in to their competence. A second approach is *observational*, with researchers obtaining longitudinal evidence of the order in which particular areas of L2 syntax are acquired and the variants which the learner employs at different stages. The data is then compared with patterns of L1 acquisition and interpreted in a framework of grammatical theory and of concepts such as *parameter-switching*.

☐ *Cognitive.* A theoretical assumption is adopted that language is part of general cognition. It is therefore valid to trace parallels between the techniques adopted by a second language learner and those employed in acquiring other types of **expertise**. Cognitivist accounts of second language acquisition (SLA) cover both acquisition (how learners construct a representation of L2) and use (how they employ their knowledge of L2 in order to communicate).

There has been discussion of the relationship between *explicit knowledge* gained in the form of L2 instruction and *implicit knowledge* gained by acquisition in an L2 environment. The former is likely to provide linguistic information in an **analysed** form, while linguistic information that is acquired naturalistically is often in the form of unanalysed **chunks**. A similar contrast exists between circumstances where accuracy is a requirement and the use of L2 may therefore be subject to careful **control** – and others where fluency is called for and it is desirable to aim for a high degree of **automaticity**.

If linguistic information is initially acquired in explicit/controlled form, then it has to be reshaped in order to support spontaneous spoken performance in the target language. A case has been put for treating second language acquisition as a form of skill acquisition not unlike learning to drive or becoming an expert chess player. Anderson's **ACT** models, which account for how expertise is acquired, have been applied to language learning.

Much attention in SLA research has been given to *transfer*, the effect of the native language upon performance in L2. Early accounts of transfer drew upon **behaviourist** theory. Language use was depicted as habitual behaviour, with the habits of the first language having to be replaced by those of the second. Current models treat the issue in terms of the relative cognitive demands made by L2 as against those made by L1. These might reflect the extent to which a grammatical feature is *marked* in one language but not the other. Or it might reflect differences between languages in the importance attached to linguistic cues such as word order, inflection or animacy.

Another approach considers L2 acquisition in terms of the way in which the learner's language develops. At any given stage, a learner is said to possess an *interlanguage*, an interim form of self-expression which is more restricted than the native-speaker target but may be internally consistent. Longitudinal studies have examined changes in interlanguage: for example, the different forms used to express the interrogative or negative. Most learners appear to proceed through similar stages; an explanation is found in the relative difficulty of the cognitive operations involved rather than in constraints imposed by UG.

Some commentators have suggested that SLA involves continual **restructuring** in which knowledge structures are reorganised in order to accommodate new linguistic insights. The *Multi-Dimensional Model* sees restructuring as part of a developmental process in which two important cognitive factors determine a learner's performance. The first is the developmental stage that the learner has reached, development being represented as the gradual removal of limitations upon the linguistic structures that the learner is capable of forming. The second is the extent to which each individual engages in a process of simplification, reducing and over-generalising the L2 grammar so as to make it easy to handle.

Another line of research has concerned itself with the learner as an active participant in the learning process. A non-native speaker's chief goal in L2 communicative contexts is to extract meaning, but the question arises of whether they also have to specifically '*notice*' (direct attention to) the form of the words that is used in order to add to their own syntactic repertoire.

A further area of study that is relevant to psycholinguistics considers the way in which second-language learners handle communicative encounters, and the strategies they adopt in order to compensate for their incomplete knowledge of the lexis and grammar of the target language. There has been interest in the **communication strategies** adopted in spoken production, but rather less is known about the strategies employed in extracting meaning from written or spoken texts.

See also: **Communication strategy**

Further reading: Ellis (1994); Gass and Selinker (1994); Mitchell and Miles (1998); Ritchie and Bhatia (1996)

SEGMENT₁ (n.)

A part of the speech signal that is recognised as a single phoneme. The phoneme is identified on the strength of the co-occurrence of certain phonetic *features* (voicing, nasalisation etc.).

SEGMENT₂ (vb.)

To divide connected speech into sections which correspond to words in the lexicon. The process is referred to as **lexical segmentation**.

SELECTIVE ADAPTATION

The adjustment of a language user's categories (especially perceptual categories) as a result of repeated exposure to a stimulus. When a listener is exposed repeatedly to the same sound, their acoustic feature detectors become fatigued. Their perceptual boundaries then become shifted in a way that disfavours the sound being heard. For example, extended repetition of the syllable /ba/ desensitises a listener to the features which characterise /b/, and, straight afterwards, they manifest a perceptual bias in favour of /p /.

SELF-MONITORING

The process of checking one's own language productions to ensure that they are: (a) accurate in terms of syntax, lexis and phonology; (b) appropriate in terms of register; (c) at an acceptable level of speed, loudness and precision; (d) likely to be clear to the listener/reader; and (e) likely to have the desired rhetorical impact.

It seems unlikely that a speaker can focus on all these criteria simultaneously. Indeed, many speech errors (possibly over half) are not repaired. It is difficult to say whether a particular error has not been detected or whether the speaker felt that it was not worth interrupting the flow of speech to deal with it. However, the balance of evidence suggests that self-monitoring is selective. Research has found that speakers are more aware of errors that are closely linked to the prevailing context or to the task in hand. Speakers also identify with the listener in that they are more likely to correct an error that is likely to impair understanding than one that is not.

Furthermore, the attention committed to self-monitoring seems to fluctuate during the course of an utterance: errors are detected and repaired much more often when they occur towards the end of a clause. This finding suggests that the weight of attention during the early part of the unit of utterance is directed towards executing the speech plan, but that, once the plan is running, the speaker has spare attentional capacity for evaluating the output.

Evidence from repairs indicates two different points at which self-monitoring occurs. A speaker engages in *pre-articulatory editing*, when they check if their speech plan has been correctly assembled before putting it into effect. They also scan their speech while it is being uttered. *Editor theories* propose that the first kind of self-monitoring takes place at each successive stage of planning (syntactic, lexical, phonological, articulatory). However, this would impose an enormous processing burden. Other commentators have concluded that the prearticulatory editor does not operate at all levels of planning but only at a late stage before production. This view is supported by evidence from experiments in which subjects are coaxed into uttering taboo words.

Levelt (1989) suggests that the two types of self-monitoring involve similar processes, two *perceptual loops*. In the first, the speaker attends to *internal speech* (a 'voice in the head' in the form of a *phonetic plan* which is the outcome of speech planning). In the second, they attend to *overt speech*. Both operations feed in to the same speech comprehension system as is used for processing the speech of others. This account faces the objection that the errors detected in a speaker's own speech are often different in kind from those detected in the speech of others. However, this may be due to the different goals of the speaker, who wishes to ensure that the forms of language produced conform to a plan, and the listener, for whom errors of form are secondary to the extraction of meaning.

See also: **Planning: speech, Repair₂, Speech production**

Further reading: Levelt (1989: Chap. 12)

SEMANTIC NETWORK

A representation of the way in which concepts are related to each other, showing the connections in terms of nodes and links.

The first such model, the *Hierarchical Network Model* (Collins and Quillian, 1969), attempted to represent not simply the links between lexical items but also the features which characterised each item. It was based upon relations of *hyponymy*, and consisted of a hierarchical structure with a node for ANIMAL at the top and nodes for **basic level** items such as BIRD and FISH below it. Below BIRD were subordinates such as CANARY or OSTRICH. Attached to each node were the attributes (*properties*) associated with it. These attributes were only stored at the highest possible level. Thus, features such as *has skin, can move, eats, breathes* were stored at the level of ANIMAL not that of BIRD – though BIRD shared them by implication since it was dominated by the ANIMAL node.

This model gave rise to a theory of *semantic distance*. It was hypothesised that it would take longer to confirm the truth of the 'category statement' *A canary is an animal*, than it would *A canary is a bird*, because the process involved crossing two nodes (CANARY → BIRD → ANIMAL) rather than one. A similar result was expected with 'property statements' such as *An ostrich has skin* since, again, two nodes would have to be traversed in order to access a property which was not that of the ostrich alone but associated with animals as a whole. Both assumptions were supported by evidence. In addition a *category size* effect was recorded: the larger the size of the category, the more time was needed for the search.

The Hierarchical Network Model was criticised on various aspects of its design; and it was also found that the model's predictions did not always hold true. The model was revised (Collins and Loftus, 1975), and based instead upon the principle of **spreading activation**. It now represents the way in which exposure to a lexical item enhances the recognition of other words associated with it. The effect is represented in terms of an electrical impulse running between connected items. This more recent model is no longer hierarchical; instead, there is massive interconnection. As before, concepts are represented as nodes, but now properties too can form nodes: CHERRY is linked to RED and RED to ORANGE and GREEN. The distance between concepts represents the strength of the connection between them: CANARY would be connected closely to SINGS but not closely to SKIN. The model thus accords with recent **connectionist** approaches to language processing.

See also: **Lexical storage, Propositional network, Spreading activation**

Further reading: Reeves *et al.* (1998: 196–202)

SENSATION

The unanalysed experience of sound reaching one's ear or visual patterns reaching one's eye. An important distinction is made between sensation and **perception**, the operation of analysing the stimulus.

SENSORY MEMORY

A briefly retained record of a stimulus in its raw form. Divided into:

□ *Iconic memory*. A short-lived imprint on the mind of an exact visual image – including the image of words encountered in reading. The trace may be retained for about a quarter of a second without being categorised (e.g. matched to letters). An alternative view is that the image is processed for about half a second, enabling perceptual faculties at different levels to determine first location (e.g. letter order) and then identity.

☐ *Echoic memory.* A short-lived verbatim memory of a piece of speech. Echoic memory may last for at least 2 seconds. It has been suggested that it consists of two phases – a sensory one of about a quarter of a second and a longer one with the information categorised phonetically, which lasts another 3–4 seconds. Echoic memory appears to last rather longer than iconic. Recall of the last digit in a list is significantly better when the list is presented in spoken form than when it is presented in written – suggesting that we do indeed retain a brief 'echo' of what has just been said.

See also: **Verbatim recall, Working memory**

Further reading: Kellogg (1995: Chap. 2)

SHADOWING

An experimental method (Marslen-Wilson, 1973) in which subjects are asked to repeat what a speaker says as soon as possible after hearing it. It has been shown that listeners are able to repeat back what they hear at a **latency** (response delay) of as little as 200 to 250 milliseconds, or approximately the length of a syllable in English. The finding demonstrates that processing takes place **on line** (while the signal is being received) rather than being suspended until the end of a clause or sentence. What is more, subjects spontaneously correct errors of grammar or pronunciation in what they hear, suggesting that they often recognise the words in question before they are actually complete.

Even shorter (*close shadowing*) latencies have sometimes been reported, but these should be treated with some caution, as findings are often based on shadowing relatively slow read-aloud speech rather than natural speech.

SHORT-TERM MEMORY

A memory store in which information is briefly retained for the purpose of a current piece of processing. The information may come from external sources (e.g. a visual or spoken stimulus) or may have been withdrawn from the more permanent store in **long-term memory**. The term **working memory** is often preferred to short-term memory because it emphasises the fact that this component of memory does not simply store information but also processes it.

See also: **Working memory**

SIGN LANGUAGE

A language employed by those with impaired hearing, whose modality is the use of gesture rather than sound. Sign language is based on three components: the place where the sign is made, the shape and angle of the hand(s) and the movement of the hand(s).

Historically, many sign languages evolved naturally within the communities that use them. This has given rise to a distinctive American Sign Language (ASL), British Sign Language (BSL), Australian Sign language and so on. It has also meant that *Sign* is an independent linguistic system. It is not simply a translation of speech into gesture in the way that writing is a translation of speech into script. ASL and BSL differ from standard dialects of English in a number of ways, particularly in the way they mark syntactic relations. They do not employ suffixed inflections: there are no specific signs for *-ed*, *-ing* etc. They do not have articles and sometimes modify a lexical sign in situations where English would use function words.

Current thinking stresses the importance of equipping children early with a means of self-expression in the form of Sign. Fluent signers thus acquire competence in a first language which has no spoken or written form. When they later acquire English as a second language, they have to master not only a different linguistic system but also two new modalities (speech and writing).

Sign is of psycholinguistic interest for a number of reasons:

☐ *Sign originally developed naturally and independently.* The situation has been compared with the way in which creoles develop from pidgins. The outcome of both processes is a fully-fledged language which appears to have been acquired on the basis of incomplete input. This lends support to **nativisation** theory, which holds that, in the absence of linguistic input, an innate biological programme drives the acquisition process.

Concrete evidence of how Sign develops was obtained when Nicaragua set up its first educational programme for deaf learners in 1980, with instruction based on lip-reading. Lacking any formal sign system, the learners communicated with each other outside the classroom by means of simple miming gestures (*homesigns*) which they had used at home to hearing relatives. Gradually these developed into a set of signs which the whole community shared and recognised.

Some ten years later, a new intake of deaf students arrived, learned the sign system of the older ones and greatly amplified it with a number of syntactic features including markers of word class and verb agreement and a procedure for pronoun reference. Thus, a new sign language emerged in two generations of learners, just as the **creolisation** model would predict.

There is some evidence that there may be a **critical period** for sign language acquisition. Those who acquire Sign young appear to make fewer mistakes of form while they are learning. An older age of acquisition seems to limit ultimate attainment, with a greater likelihood of grammatical inaccuracy and of problems in sentence recall.

☐ *Sign uses a different modality from that of conventional languages.* If it could be shown that the acquisition of Sign is markedly different from that of speech, it would challenge the notion that language acquisition is supported by a universal innately acquired mechanism. It would also suggest that language is part of general cognitive processing (and thus affected by the modality in which it operates) rather than a separate **modular** faculty. The current state of evidence indicates certain strong similarities between the acquisition of signing by children of deaf parents and the acquisition of spoken language, but there are also differences. Both hearing and deaf children **babble** vocally; but there is said to be a higher incidence of manual 'babbling' among deaf children with deaf parents. There is evidence that many deaf children acquire their first sign words earlier than children acquiring spoken language; however, this may be due to the fact that signing demands less precise motor control than speaking. Whereas hearing children manifest a sudden **vocabulary spurt** at a certain stage in their development, vocabulary acquisition among signers tends to be more gradual. On the other hand, there are some striking similarities in the content of these early vocabularies, which are nearly identical across the two groups. There are also similarities in the way in which conceptual meanings (e.g. the notion of DOG) become over-generalised. One might expect that signs which are *iconic* (i.e. related in some visual way to the entity they refer to) would be easier to master than those which are purely symbolic; but they do not appear to be acquired ahead of others.

There appears to be a relatively consistent order of acquisition for the forms of signing just as there is in phonology, though there is some variation. Of the three aspects of sign form, hand position is mastered the most readily and hand shape gives the most difficulty.

The resemblances between the two acquisition routes become particularly striking at the *two-word stage*. Deaf children learn to combine words just as their hearing peers do. They appear to discover the same semantic relationships – and do so in roughly the same order.

☐ *Sign has a different linguistic structure from English.* If children have been taught Sign first, they effectively come to English as a second language. When they write, their errors of syntax and spelling are often indistinguishable from those of a foreign learner. Their writing manifests features which may derive from structural differences between Sign and English. They often have serious difficulties with function words (articles, pronouns, prepositions, auxiliary verbs) and with inflectional suffixes. In reading, they are easily fazed by non-standard word orders (*Mary was contacted by John*). Word order is flexible in Sign; but signers seem to expect English to adhere quite strictly to its standard SVO (Subject-Verb-Object) sequence. In sum, there is some evidence that performance in the second language (English) is constrained by *transfer* from the first (Sign) despite the difference of modalities. On the other hand, some of these errors are also found with non-signing deaf learners.

See also: **Creolisation, Critical period, Deafness, Nativisation hypothesis**

Further reading: Bonvillian (1999); Klima and Bellugi (1979); Strong (1988)

SIGNAL DETECTION THEORY

A theory that the processor responds differently to different states of a signal. In a phenomenon known as *phoneme restoration*, subjects report hearing a phoneme that has been excised from a recording and replaced with a cough. However, they might be responding differently from how they would respond if the phoneme were present but masked by the cough. By statistically comparing subjects' ability to distinguish between these two states, it is possible to calculate a signal detection parameter d'. The closer d' is to zero, the more likely it is that the two states have been perceived in the same way. A second statistic, beta, represents other factors that may have biased the listener.

SLIPS OF THE EAR

Errors of misperception by a listener, which provide insights into how the speech signal is processed and how words are recognised in connected speech.

The data can be analysed at phoneme level, with the proviso that it is difficult to determine to what extent top-down lexical effects (the knowledge of whole words that nearly fit the signal) may have led to a particular interpretation. With consonants, three types of error occur: *deletions* where no consonant is heard, *additions* where a consonant is inserted for which there are no cues in the signal and *substitution* where the reported consonant resembles the target one. Most consonant errors are word-initial. Since words are processed **online**, a mistake in this position is more likely to lead to a wrong match at word-level. Plosives are the most liable to be misinterpreted – supporting the findings of **confusability** studies. So far as vowels are concerned, those in stressed syllables are much less prone to misinterpretation than those in unstressed.

Slips of the Ear are useful in providing insights into how listeners determine where word boundaries lie in connected speech. When listeners misplace boundaries, they tend to insert them between a weak syllable and a strong – suggesting that segmentation is influenced by the predominant **SW (strong–weak) pattern** which characterises English rhythm. This finding from naturalistic Slips of the Ear is supported by similar evidence from slips induced by the *faint speech* method, which involves playing anomalous sentences at a level just above the subject's hearing threshold. What both sources of data show is the vulnerability of weakly stressed function words, which may be misheard or attached to preceding strong ones.

Although there is a well-established corpus of Slips of the Ear, there are some problems in relying upon it as data. The slips are not usually audio-recorded, which means that the written record we have is dependent upon the observer's analysis of the situation and limited in terms of contextual information. It is difficult to determine if any part was played by ambient **noise**, regional accent or by context (the absence of disambiguating information or the presence of misleading information). A major question is how representative the slips are, and how many others may have occurred without the listener heeding them. It is also possible that some apparent Slips of the Ear may in fact have originated in **Slips of the Tongue**. Finally, it is not always easy to determine with certainty the cause of a slip. These difficulties are admitted by researchers, but the corpus is large enough for some general conclusions to be reached.

See also: **Lexical segmentation, Speech perception, SW (strong–weak) pattern**

Further reading: Bond (1999)

SLIPS OF THE PEN (AND KEYBOARD)

Small-scale errors of writing, which provide insights into the writing process – at *motor* level, at the level of **lexical retrieval** and even at **planning** level.

☐ *Motor errors* result from a failure in the signal that the brain sends to the hand or in the contact between hand and keyboard. A striking feature of motor errors (e.g. *the → teh*) is how recurrent they are in the output of some individuals. Typing is an activity that demands a great deal of conscious control at the outset, but that gradually becomes *proceduralised* into a set of automatic keystroke sequences – particularly for frequent words such as *the*. A characteristic of highly automatic procedures is that they are difficult to reverse, even though the wrong procedure may have been acquired. An interesting area of speculation is whether motor errors simply reflect the configuration of the keyboard (T and E on the same line, H a line lower) or whether certain keystroke sequences are more difficult for the brain–hand partnership to acquire.

Motor errors in handwriting also show the effects of automatisation. When a string of letters is very frequent, the letters may be inadequately formed or may run into each other because of reduced attention and/or the greater speed of execution. One feature of rapid handwriting is the uncompleted letter, where, for example, the writer makes the upstroke of a *b* but fails to complete the letter and forms an *l*.

☐ *Sub-lexical errors.* A writer might replace a string of letters with another that occurs frequently in other words. One explanation is that sequences of finger movements are chunked by the writer, and that, in signalling the word to be typed, the brain has selected the wrong **chunk**. Example: *details → detials, existence → existance*.

☐ *Phonologically based errors.* Around 20 per cent of slips of the keyboard involve the substitution of a word that sounds similar to the target one. Examples are: *there → their, could → good, you are → your, than → that, too → to*.

Especially striking in Hotopf's (1983) data is the substitution of *28* for *20A*. Slips like these provide evidence of the part played by phonology in writing, with writers using **'inner speech'** in order to store a clause while it is being written. It is much rarer to find words replaced by others that are similar in form but not pronunciation (e.g. *there → these*).

268

☐ *Errors affecting function words.* Function words are especially prone to typing errors. This might be a further reflection of the importance of phonology (the low salience of these words in speech). Or it might be that the writer processes function words at a lower level of attention than content words – perhaps as a result of their high frequency. Frequently one function word is substituted for another (*for → of*); or a function word is duplicated (*Saw the the movement*).

☐ *Forward planning.* A further type of Slip provides evidence of the way in which a writer plans ahead, storing words in a **buffer** ahead of executing them. The result is anticipatory errors such as *difference intelligence tests* or *neighbourshoods*. In other examples, a feature is transferred between two words, indicating that the two form part of the same stored chunk: e.g. *using bothing approaches*.

See also: **Writing**

Further reading: Fromkin (1980); Garman (1990: 230–6); Hotopf (1983)

SLIPS OF THE TONGUE (SOT)

Speech errors by normal speakers which provide insights into: (a) how we store and retrieve lexical items; and (b) how we assemble speech. Most errors are collected during normal conversation, but the data is sometimes supplemented by errors which are induced under laboratory conditions. Evidence from selection errors is often supported by evidence from **Tip of the Tongue** (TOT) experiments. There are two main types of SOT:

☐ *Selection errors,* where there is a problem in retrieving a word from the lexicon. It might involve the substitution of one word for another (*castanets → clarinets*) or it might result in words or non-words which are *blends* of two related items (*expect + suppose → expose; shout/yell → shell*).

This type of error provides insights into how items are stored in the lexicon and how they are retrieved. The substituted word is often linked to the target by similarity of form or by similarity of meaning; sometimes both seem to be involved. Selection errors thus demonstrate that both meaning and form play a part in the way we associate words in our minds and the way we retrieve them when we need them.

In terms of meaning, the substituted word is often an antonym of the target or from the same lexical set. In terms of form:

- *Beginnings and endings* of words are often correct, and thus seem to be important cues in retrieving words. This is sometimes called the *bathtub effect*: the important parts of the word are like a bather's head and feet sticking out of the water.
- The *stressed syllable* of a word is more likely to be correct, especially if the word is a short one. In addition, the *stress pattern* of the target word is often retained, and may be a characterising feature.
- The *number of syllables* is often correct. When it is wrong, there seems, in English, to be a tendency towards a three-syllable substitute word.

☐ *Assemblage errors,* where the appropriate lexical item is retrieved but is not produced correctly: example, *caterpillar → patter-killer.* Or a whole string of words is planned but is delivered in the wrong syntactic order. By identifying different types of assemblage error, we can identify stages in the process of constructing an utterance and the order in which they seem to occur. Assemblage errors provide insights into:

- Choosing a syntactic structure that fits the target verb;
  Example: *She swore me to secrecy → She promised me to secrecy*
- Fitting words into a syntactic frame;
  Example: *one spoon of sugar → one sugar of spoon*
- Attaching inflections;
  Example: *she slants her writing → she writes her slanting*
- Assignment of lexical stress;
  Example: *moBILity → mobilITy*
- Phonetic planning for articulation.
  Example: *fight very hard → fart very hide*

One finding from assemblage SOTs is how robust the syllable is. Individual phonemes become dislocated, but they end up in the same syllabic position (beginning-middle-end) as in the target. This suggests that the syllable may be an important unit of planning.

SOT data is not easy to obtain. To be sure of the context in which slips occur, they should ideally be recorded. However, slips are not frequent in speech; indeed one of the remarkable things about speech is that it is so error-free.

Some slips are difficult to categorise in terms of what the speaker's intention was and of how that intention failed. It is also important to distinguish between Slips of the Tongue and *malapropisms* (e.g. *bubonic plague* → *blue bonnet plague*) which are due to the speaker's ignorance of the correct term.

See also: **Speech production, Tip of the Tongue**

Further reading: Aitchison (2003); Fromkin (1973, 1980); Whitney (1998: 272–84)

SOCIAL-INTERACTIONISM

Approaches to first language acquisition which emphasise the parts played by the child's environment, its social instincts, its pragmatic needs and its relationship with the carer. Those who take this position do not necessarily deny the existence of an innately endowed capacity for language. But they maintain that genetic factors, if they exist, are insufficient on their own to ensure that language develops. Nor is simple exposure to language enough. What is important is the interaction, both linguistic and non-linguistic, which derives from the child's need to communicate.

It is argued that **child directed speech** (CDS) is not as impoverished as Chomsky suggests. The modifications that are made to adult speech (slow rate, repetitions, set phrases, simple syntax and heightened intonation patterns) appear to assist the child in decoding what is said. In response to the **nativist** assertion that children do not receive feedback on ill-formed utterances, social-interactionists claim that correction is often indirect. Without specifically correcting a child, parents show puzzlement, *recast* utterances or give responses that exemplify the correct form. There is also evidence that carers grade their language sensitively, increasing sentence length and complexity as the child gets older in response to evidence of the child's linguistic development.

A child's language does not develop faster in proportion to the level of input by the carer. But there appears to be a correlation between speed of acquisition and the *pragmatic* content of CDS – in particular, the extent to which, through questions, directives, acknowledgements and references to the child's activities, the adult invites interaction by the child.

Social-interactionist views stress the importance of the infant's relationship to its environment. One aspect is the familiarity of certain objects and events which ensures that there is a repetitive and even a ritualistic quality to much of the language that is used. Interaction with the principal carer (especially in the form of play) also follows predictable sequences; and it is through play that semantic relationships such as the agent/object distinction are said to become manifest. The carer plays an important role in interpreting new events as they arise.

☐ *Vygotsky,* the Russian psychologist, has greatly influenced social-interactionist thinking. He stressed the connections between speech, thought and interaction. For him, the early stages of a child's language are characterised by *egocentric speech,* utterances which include what for an adult would be private thoughts. As the child becomes more aware of its social context, a distinction is made between ideas directed at others and ideas directed at oneself. Vygotsky saw the child's development as a progress from dependency to independence. The adult offers support (termed **scaffolding** in more recent accounts) which is gradually withdrawn as a task becomes more familiar and as the child becomes more practised.

☐ *Jerome Bruner,* in the Vygotskyan tradition, places great importance on carer–child interaction. For him, the linguistic relationship between carer and infant begins with the establishment of *joint reference,* the carer using various techniques to focus the child's attention on an object or event. Mother and infant then develop a set of *standard interactional routines* where the infant knows what to expect and references are to familiar surroundings. Bruner does not accept that the young child has to develop for itself a set of relationships with the world around it; he asserts that they mainly derive their awareness of reality through the mediation of others. He is critical of the notion that a child has to distinguish between the public world and the private, which he suggests owes too much to Western culture. Similarly, he challenges the established wisdom that the child lacks a **theory of mind**, the ability to identify with the point-of-view of others, and suggests that this capacity may be innate. He is willing to accept that some semantic aspects of language may be innate. But also innate is a set of responses to human behaviour which permit the infant to derive the rules of language from experiencing it in use.

☐ *M.A.K. Halliday's* functional account, based upon observation of his son Nigel, views language acquisition as fuelled by the child's need to express certain basic pragmatic concepts. Even at a pre-linguistic stage, the child may employ *proto-language* for this purpose, using certain sounds consistently to express simple needs and feelings. The child's first utterances, according to Halliday, fulfil four basic functions. There is then a gradual increase in the range of meanings which the child learns to express within these areas, even if the forms used are not those of adult language. The child also becomes aware of the nature of interpersonal discourse: it engages in exchanges which resemble dialogue, and thus finds its way towards the expression of attitudes and wishes and the use of syntactic features such as the interrogative. In a third phase, the child's functional repertoire gradually comes to resemble that of an adult.

See also: **Child Directed Speech, Functionalism, Vygotskyan**

Further reading: Bruner (1983, 1985: Chap. 4); Cattell (2000: Chaps 7–8); Halliday (1975); Owens (2001)

SPEAKING *see* **Speech production**

SPEAKING RATE

The speed (usually measured in syllables per second) at which a speaker speaks, with pauses and hesitations included. Distinguished from **articulation rate**, the rate when pauses have been discounted. Speaking rate often correlates quite closely with the amount of pausing. So what appears to the listener to be faster speech may not in fact be articulated faster but may simply have fewer and shorter pauses.

Speaking rate varies considerably between speakers and within the speech of a single speaker. A normal rate for English is probably around 200 words a minute, or 5 to 5.5 syllables a second, but a great deal depends upon the type of speech event.

See also: **Articulation rate, Normalisation, Pausing**

SPECIAL CIRCUMSTANCES (also EXCEPTIONAL CIRCUMSTANCES)

An umbrella term for general factors which may adversely affect language development. It includes:

- studies of the effects of **deafness** or **blindness** upon language;
- comparative studies of language development in **twins**;
- studies of language **deprivation**;
- studies of developmental language **disorders** where some aspect of linguistic processing is impaired.

SPECIES SPECIFICITY

The notion that language is unique to the human race and that other types of **animal communication** differ markedly from it in terms of form and content. The issue is not whether other species can acquire speech; they do not have the appropriate vocal apparatus. It is whether they are cognitively capable of acquiring or using a complex symbolic system such as language.

There are four main ways in which species specificity can be investigated:

☐ *Design features.* We can determine exactly what characterises language and then establish if those features are present in other forms of animal communication. Here, Hockett's **design features** have provided a valuable benchmark. While some of the features are present in animal communication, it is clear that no form has more than a very few.

☐ *Brain structure.* If a human being has some kind of genetically transmitted capacity for language, then we might expect to find evidence of it by comparing the human brain with those of other primates. However, attempts to locate a specific locus for an innate language faculty have not been successful, and evidence from brain imaging suggests that the operations associated with language are widely distributed throughout the brain. It was once suggested that *lateralisation* (the dominance of one hemisphere of the human brain) might be related specifically to our possession of language. However, other species including birds and frogs have been shown to possess a dominant hemisphere (usually the left) associated with vocalisation or rapid auditory processing but clearly not with language. Attention has therefore focused on those areas of the human brain which are larger relative to the whole organ than they are in other primates. But perhaps most critical of all is the much greater control that the human brain is able to exercise over the operation of the larynx. This enables us to co-ordinate breathing and **vocalisation** and is an important factor in the ability to produce speech.

☐ *Evolutionary history.* If the human brain is indeed configured in a way that supports language, we need to explain how this state of affairs evolved in one particular species. Except for physiological evidence from hominid remains, hard facts are difficult to obtain. However, there are a number of theoretical positions on how language was first triggered:

- a serendipitous conjunction of events (social, physiological, cognitive);
- a gradual evolution of the human brain which came to differentiate it from that of other species; this possibly included the evolution of an innate language-specific mechanism in the brain;
- developments in human physiology (particularly in relation to the position of the larynx) which permitted the species to make the sounds of speech;
- a gradual evolution of early speech sounds into a sophisticated system which mapped on to established cognitive operations peculiar to the species;
- the social needs of human beings once they had formed settled communities which demanded a sophisticated system of transmitting information. Possibly connected with this, the development in humans of a **theory of mind** absent in other species.

An important insight provided by the evolutionary perspective is the *cost-benefit* notion that language comes at enormous cost in terms of the areas of the brain that have to be devoted to it and the bodily functions (e.g. supply of oxygen) that sustain such complex brain operations. It may be that other species did not evolve language because it would have limited their capacity to perform well in other areas.

☐ *Teaching other species to use language.* Unambiguous evidence that a chimp can acquire a complex form of language would challenge **nativist** theories. The hypothesis of an innate human language faculty might have to be rejected in favour of a view that acquiring a language depends entirely upon input or that language maps on to established cognitive operations which human beings share with other primates. Alternatively, it would have to be accepted that the innate language mechanism is not specifically human. Chimps might share the mechanism in some form, but lack a genetically transmitted trigger which activates it as part of the normal process of maturation.

There has been some limited success in training chimps and other primates to acquire simple semantic categories. However, it may not be appropriate to base hard and fast conclusions on the ability of other species to acquire a system which is quintessentially a product of the human mind and not of their own.

See also: **Animal communication, Brain: human vs animal, Chimp studies, Design features, Evolution of language**

Further reading: Aitchison (1998); Deacon (1997)

SPECIFIC LANGUAGE IMPAIRMENT (SLI)

A condition in which a child who appears otherwise normal fails to acquire language like its peers. These children sometimes have restricted vocabularies or make relatively basic errors of grammar. They may show problems of comprehension as well as problems of production: finding it difficult to follow the utterances of others or to put thoughts into words. In particular, they seem to have difficulty in sustaining a contextual framework for a conversation. What is striking is that this linguistic deficit cannot be clearly linked to low intelligence or cognitive impairment. It appears to affect language but not other faculties.

Some researchers believe that the condition provides convincing evidence that language is **modular** and distinct from other forms of cognition. Others take the view that the underlying causes are most likely cognitive or perceptual.

Early research into SLI sought a link with hearing difficulties caused by *otitis media with effusion* (OME), a disorder of the middle ear which causes some hearing loss. This view is no longer generally held, and more recent commentators have suggested that SLI may result from a deficit in the child's ability to recognise recurring patterns such as inflections in the language it encounters.

Those who adopt a **nativist** view maintain that innate grammatical components within **Universal Grammar** are defective or absent in SLI sufferers. An important study of three generations of a family (Gopnik, 1990) suggested that about half of them suffered severely from SLI and thus that the condition might be genetic. These individuals performed quite well on general grammaticality judgement tasks but their language lacked many important inflectional markings such as number, gender and verb endings. The initial conclusion drawn (the *'feature-blindness' hypothesis*) was that their representation of grammar lacked an important component which enables others to recognise and acquire inflectional morphology. However, it was later suggested that SLI sufferers adopt a strategy of learning exemplar by exemplar instead of recognising that inflectional marking can be derived by rule. This means that they have difficulty in using inflections because the process of retrieving them makes heavy demands on memory. A strong version of this hypothesis is, however, difficult to square with evidence that SLI sufferers sometimes over-generalise inflectional endings (*goed*), showing that they have some awareness of the system.

A contrary view attributes the absence of inflections in the language of SLI sufferers to inadequate perception. It finds a cause in the low salience of grammatical morphemes, which (in English) are weakly stressed and short in duration. English-speaking children suffering from SLI have been compared with Italians whose language has more perceptible inflectional markings. The Italian children showed a more extensive use of inflection and a preference for the more salient feminine articles *la* and *una* rather than the masculine *il* and *un*.

However, there are some reservations about the perceptual account. First, SLI appears to affect written as well as spoken language (though it could be that children simply do not write inflections because they do not perceive them). Second, no correlation has been established between the perceptual prominence of a feature and the likelihood that it will be absent from the speech of an SLI sufferer. If anything, the appearance of a particular inflection or functor seems to be determined by its grammatical function: final *-s* is more likely to be used for a noun plural than to mark possession or Present Simple Third Person. Children with SLI also have difficulty with inflections and functors that are not phonologically weak, such as irregular past tense forms and direct object pronouns. Finally, there is the argument that, if a perceptual deficit affects the recognition of certain inflectional features, there should be an impact upon wider syntactic knowledge (for example, the recognition of word classes).

A third possibility is that SLI may not be a unitary disorder but the result of a combination of several different forms of language impairment which are present to different degrees in different sufferers. Clinically based accounts have suggested a number of subtypes representing the symptoms which appear to co-occur in cases of SLI and of **autism**.

See also: **Autism, Disorder, Modularity₁, Savant, Williams Syndrome**

Further reading: Bishop (1997); Fletcher (1999); Gopnik *et al.* (1997)

SPEECH CODE

A term used in some accounts of reading for the phonological form in which written words are processed in the mind. There are two different types of speech code. One is *pre-lexical* and potentially assists in the identification of a word. The other is *post-lexical* and serves as a way of briefly retaining, in phonological form, the wording of a text.

SPEECH MODE₁

A distinctive type of listening engaged in when the stimulus is human speech or resembles human speech, rather than (say) music. There is evidence that listeners maintain a sharp dichotomy between sounds that are processed as speech and those that are not, so that we cannot hear natural speech in terms of its acoustic characteristics (buzzes, hisses etc.).

Switching into speech mode is highly automatic and not under the listener's control. It is triggered by the acoustic properties of the signal, regardless of whether the listener is expecting to hear speech or not. However, if natural speech is manipulated to extract some of its features (e.g. voicing cues and harmonic structure), neutral listeners perceive it as electronic sounds, while those who have been briefed to expect a 'strange' piece of language perceive it as speech. Once the latter have engaged in the speech mode, it is difficult for them to reverse it.

The existence of this speech mode is sometimes cited as evidence that language is special and distinct from other cognitive operations (see **modularity₁**).

SPEECH MODE₂

The co-ordination of muscles in the vocal tract, laryngeal system and/ or respiratory system when they are used for the purposes of speech. This is markedly different from the co-ordination of the same muscles when they are serving other functions (chewing, swallowing and breathing).

SPEECH PERCEPTION: AUTONOMOUS VS INTERACTIVE

As with reading, there has been controversy as to whether speech perception operates on a **bottom–up** principle, with features built into phonemes, phonemes into syllables, syllables into words – or whether an **interactive** account is the more correct one. The clash is between those who argue that an **autonomous** process (one level of processing at a time) streamlines decision making and those who argue that an interactive process enables multiple sources of evidence to be considered at once. See **modularity₂**.

Two considerations are critical:

- Top-down effects do not derive simply from contextual cues but can also take the form of, for example, lexical knowledge. For example, a listener's knowledge of the existence of the word CIGARETTE might mean that they do not perceive the error when a speaker says SHIGARETTE. This is a top-down effect: from higher unit (word) to lower unit (phoneme).
- A distinction must be made between the general effects of context upon understanding, which are not disputed; and the question of whether (for example) we actually, *at the time of listening,* believe that we have heard a particular sound because of our knowledge of higher-level features.

One can distinguish at least four views:

a. The *autonomous view* that neither lexical knowledge nor sentence context affect how we perceive sounds; they form later parts of the listening process.
b. The *bottom-up priority* view that some perceptual evidence is necessary before we bring in lexical or semantic information.
c. The *lexical effects* view that knowledge of words affects how we perceive the sounds of speech but that sentence context does not.
d. A full *interactive view* that all sources of information influence the way in which we perceive speech.

Several findings favour an interactive account:

□ The *Ganong effect.* Ganong (1980) presented listeners with synthesised variants of plosive sounds: for example a range which extended from a core value of [g] to a core value of [k]. He spliced them on to endings which created either a word or a non-word (example: GISS vs KISS). He established the point (see **categorical perception**) at which the listener might normally be expected to switch from reporting one sound to reporting the other, and found that it shifted when a potential word was involved. Thus, on the GISS/ KISS continuum, the perception of [g] would change earlier than normal to a perception of [k]. This suggested that knowledge of a word affects processing at the lower level of phoneme perception. Ganong's findings have since been questioned. The original experiment was repeated, using a more natural speech sample, and the effect was not found. It may be that the Ganong effect only obtains when degraded stimuli are involved.

□ *Sentence context*. Garnes and Bond (1976) constructed 16 synthetic stimuli which varied by degrees from BAIT to DATE to GATE. They inserted them into constraining sentence contexts such as '*Check the time and the . . .*', and asked subjects to report what they heard. Where there was a good exemplar of /b/, /d/ or /g/, subjects identified the target words accurately, even when they made no sense ('*Check the time and the gate*'). But where the exemplars were not good ones, subjects were influenced by the sentence context.

□ The *phoneme restoration effect*. Warren (1970) replaced a phonetic segment in certain words (e.g. the [s] in the word *legislature*) with a coughing sound. When the words were presented in sentences, subjects could not accurately indicate where the cough occurred. They heard the whole word *legislature* (with the [s] restored) and the cough as a background noise. This appeared to demonstrate top-down effects of word knowledge upon processing at phonetic level. Another experiment showed phoneme restoration effects that were apparently due to sentence context. Presented with sentences such as a and b, subjects restored the phoneme that was appropriate to the context.

a. *It was found that the *eel was on the orange.*
b. *It was found that the *eel was on the shoe.*
    [* indicates location of cough]

The problem with many of the experimental tasks used to investigate this issue is that they are **post-perceptual**. They do not tell us what subjects thought *at the time of processing* but only what they reported afterwards. An 'autonomous' advocate might argue that the listener hears that the phoneme is missing, but restores it at a later (but separate) stage of processing.

This was tested in a further series of phoneme restoration experiments which checked whether subjects could distinguish between sentences where noise replaced a phoneme and those where noise accompanied it. If they could not, then it would suggest that their perception was indeed affected by top-down influences. The researcher (Samuel, 1990) concluded that lexical knowledge does affect phoneme recognition. But he also found (contrary to the *eel findings) that sentence context does not.

See also: **Interactive activation, Modularity₁, Top-down processing**

Further reading: Harley (2001: 224–8)

SPEECH PERCEPTION: PHONEME VARIATION

It has proved difficult for listening researchers to account for our ability to identify the sounds of speech. This is because realisations of a given phoneme vary enormously.

☐ *Non-linearity.* The spoken signal does not consist of a string of phonemes in the way that written language consists of a string of letters. In any token of the word [kæt], there is no precise boundary for the sound /k/: *co-articulation* blends it into the succeeding /æ/, and the /æ/ blends into the /t/.

☐ *Non-invariance.* Co-articulation also means that there is no standard form for any given phoneme. The articulation of a vowel can range over a wide *vowel space.* Similarly, the place of articulation of a consonant such as /k/ varies greatly anticipating the vowel that is to follow it (compare /k/ in KILL with /k/ in CUT). Researchers have studied the cues that are physically present in the speech stream, but have failed to find any combination of features that uniquely serve to characterise a given consonant. They conclude that listeners recognise a consonant partly through the co-occurrence of several *phonetic features* (not always the same ones), but in particular through the shape of the *formant transition* which links a consonant to the following vowel.

☐ *Speaker variation.* There is enormous between-speaker variation. Every speaker has a distinctive voice: our *articulators* (mouths, jaws, tongues, teeth) vary greatly in size, shape and position. Many speakers have regional accents. There are important differences in pitch between the voices of men and the voices of women and children. We speak at different rates with different degrees of emphasis and with different idiolectal features. Researchers are interested in how we manage to *normalise* (adjust) to the voice and speech rate and accent of a wide range of individuals – and what kind of representation we match our perceptions against. We continually make fine judgements based upon rate of articulation: our judgement of how rapidly the speaker is articulating may even influence which phoneme we hear.

☐ *Within-speaker variation.* There is variation within the speech of a single speaker. For example, speech rate may vary enormously according to mood, auditor and communicative purpose, as may the degree of assimilation.

A number of theories have attempted to account for phoneme recognition. One approach has been to link speech perception with speech production. An early example is *Motor Theory*, based on the hypothesis that, in processing speech, we relate what we hear to our own experience of forming the same sounds. The theory faces problems in accounting for how we manage to interpret the speech of a speaker with a different regional accent, and how learners of a foreign language succeed in categorising sounds that they are not yet capable of making. A similar link between production and recognition is made in Stevens' (1960) *analysis-by-synthesis* model. Here the assumption is that we identify (analyse) phonetic features in the input, then use our competence as speakers to synthesise them.

A second set of proposals suggests that, given its amorphous nature, the phoneme might not be a unit of processing at all. The idea is supported by evidence from illiterate Portuguese subjects who had difficulty in performing phoneme-based tasks; this suggests that phonemic awareness may be a product of literacy rather than vice versa. Some commentators have proposed a larger, more stable unit of processing such as the syllable. The assumption is that listeners match spoken input against a stored set of all the syllables of their language. However, a more efficient unit might be the *demi-syllable* (in the word *cat*, /kæ/ and /æt/) which would require fewer forms to be stored (the estimate for French is about 2000).

Alternatively, a direct match might be made between phonetic features in the signal and the stored representation of words in the mind, without needing to convert the features into phonemes. A phonetic feature detector would examine auditory values over a short time-slice, and would detect the presence or absence of particular features on the basis of the evidence available. This information could then be compared with entries in the lexicon, where the spoken word would be stored in the form of a cluster of features which distinguished it from all others. This is the basis of Stevens' (1986) *LAFF* (Lexical Access from Features) model. In an alternative 'direct' model, Klatt's (1986) *LAFS* (Lexical Access from Spectra), words are stored instead in the form of spectral patterns which represent the transitions between their phonemes.

A third set of solutions focuses upon **phonological representation**. Because phonemes (and indeed words) are so variable in connected speech, there is obviously no possibility of making an exact one-to-one match between the word form that we hear and a template in our mind. Whatever is stored therefore has to allow for variation. It might be that the phonological form of a word takes the form of an idealised **prototype** to which a sequence of sounds in the signal can be matched on the basis of an approximate fit. It might be that the stored form of the word is **underspecified**, consisting only of those features which are sufficient and necessary to identify it. Or it might be that we are capable of storing multiple exemplars of a particular word (all those that we have come across), thus enabling us to form a match between the form we hear and any one of a large number of stored variants.

A final, radical solution to the 'non-invariance' problem proposes that we do not package the signal into linguistic units at all but divide it up into equal sections determined by time. This is the approach adopted by the most well-known computer simulation of listening. **TRACE**, a connectionist model, processes the signal in small *time-slices* which are independent of phoneme, syllable and word boundaries. Each time-slice is connected to those that immediately precede it, so the processor can combine evidence from current input with evidence from what has immediately gone before. This enables TRACE to deal with the way in which phonemic features overlap in time due to co-articulation. However, it faces the problem of adjusting to differences of speech rate between speakers.

See also: **Normalisation, Phonological representation, Unit of perception**

Further reading: Hawkins (1999); Nygaard and Pisoni (1995)

SPEECH PRODUCTION

Speaking, one of the most complex cognitive operations that human beings perform. A normal speech rate in English is around 150 words a minute. This means that a speaker retrieves two or three words per second from an everyday vocabulary of about 30,000. What is more, they continue to do so over very extended periods of time and with remarkable accuracy (about one slip per 1000 words).

Studies of the **pausing** and hesitation patterns of speakers provide insights into the way speech is planned and executed. Pauses in connected speech occur mainly at the ends of major syntactic units, usually clauses. This suggests that a major unit of planning is the clause or (often the same thing) the *phonological phrase*.

Research in speech production has aimed to identify the stages through which a speaker passes in assembling an utterance. Evidence has been sought in **Slips of the Tongue** (SOTs), inadvertent speech errors which, by showing us the system malfunctioning, can provide insights into the choices that a speaker makes. By examining a misplaced feature, it is sometimes possible to form conclusions as to the stage in the process when the feature was inserted into a partly assembled sentence. For example, in the SOT sequence *the forks of the prong,* the *-s* of *forks* is pronounced /s/ in conformity with the unvoiced nature of the /k/ at the end of *fork.* It must thus have been added after the transposition of *fork* and *prong* occurred.

Introspection and research have suggested that models of speech production need to incorporate the following stages:

☐ *A conceptual stage,* where the proposition that is to be expressed is identified, but in abstract form.

☐ *A syntactic stage,* where an appropriate frame is chosen, into which words are to be inserted. Evidence for this comes from SOTs such as *She promised me to secrecy,* where a syntactic frame seems to have been prepared for the word SWORE but the word PROMISED seems to have been substituted.

☐ *A lexical stage,* where a meaning-driven search of the lexicon takes place, supported by cues as to the form of the target word. Once the **lexical entry** for a word is accessed, information about the word becomes available (its sense, collocational potential, phonology and morphology).

☐ *A phonological stage,* where the abstract information gathered so far is converted into a speech-like form.

☐ *A phonetic stage,* where features such as assimilation are introduced, and instructions are prepared to the muscles that control the articulators.

In addition, a model of speech must allow for:

☐ A forward-planning mechanism at discourse level which (for example) determines which parts of the message are to receive informational focus by way of intonation.

☐ A **buffer** in which the whole of a planned clause can be held while the clause is being articulated.

☐ A monitoring mechanism which enables a speaker to check their own speech for errors or for lack of clarity.

This outline of components represents a considerable simplification.

First, uncertainty arises as to the exact relationship between syntax and lexis. Current grammar theory views the two as closely intercon-nected. If one chooses the word PUT as the **predicate** (central element) of an utterance, then with the word come important syntactic constraints on the structure to be used (PUT X + preposition *on/in/into* + Y) as well as semantic constraints on what can fit into the X and Y slots. These constraints are said to be part of the **lexical entry** for the word PUT. It therefore seems that the lexical and syntactic operations involved in constructing an utterance must be closely interconnected and mutually supportive. In Garrett's (1988) model of speech production, the situation is dealt with by bifurcation, with the two processes taking place in parallel.

It is also difficult to determine when certain features of connected speech are added into the plan. For example, lexical stress can only be marked once word forms have been retrieved from the lexicon. This means that sentence stress cannot be allocated until that moment, as it has to fall on the stressed syllable of one of the words. But surely the placing of sentence stress must be the outcome of an earlier decision at discourse level? A similar problem arises with the syntactic frame into which words are slotted. One might assume that it is already tagged for inflections such as -*ed* (past) or -*s* (plural). However, the *forks of a prong* example indicates that inflections are not added on until lexical items are already in place.

A favoured solution is to assume that in the early stages speech is assembled in an abstract *preverbal* form which has not yet been realised phonologically. We can thus mark a particular component of a proposition as due to receive semantic focus, without yet needing to specify the precise syllable that it will fall on. We can retrieve a lexical item in the form of an abstract *meaning code* without yet needing to attribute a phonological form to the word. And we can mark a position in a frame with some kind of abstract tag indicating that an inflection is needed ('past', 'plural') without yet specifying exactly what form the inflection takes. The inflection is given phonological shape only after the root has been inserted. Support for this version of events comes from the **Tip of the Tongue** experience where language users confidently state that a word exists and can specify the semantic range that it covers, but cannot retrieve its form. This suggests that a word's lexical entry falls into two parts, one related to form and one related to meaning.

Levelt (1989) has produced the most detailed model of speech production. It incorporates three major processes – conceptualising, formulating and articulating. The *Conceptualiser* chooses a particular proposition, selects and orders the appropriate information and relates it to what has gone before. The *Formulator* translates this conceptual structure into a linguistic one. It first engages in a process of *grammatical encoding* which builds an abstract syntactic structure. This is followed by *phonological encoding*, in which the syntactic structure is tagged for inflection and is then given phonological form. Other processes specify the form and duration of the syllables as they are to occur in connected speech and add rhythm and prosody. The outcome of these operations is a *phonetic* or *articulatory plan*, a representation of how the planned utterance is to be articulated. It is temporarily stored in an *articulatory buffer*. The *Articulator* then retrieves chunks of internal speech from the buffer, unpacks them into sets of motor commands and issues the commands to the muscles controlling the larynx, the articulators and the respiratory system.

See also: **Articulation, Buffer, Lexical entry, Pausing, Planning: speech, Self-monitoring, Slip of the Tongue, Speech: unit of processing**

Further reading: Levelt (1989)

SPEECH SIGNAL

The physical signal from which a listener constructs a message. Also referred to as the *acoustic-phonetic signal*: 'acoustic' referring to the sound waves which reach the listener's ear; while 'phonetic' refers to the speaker's perception of these waves in terms of *features* (+/− voiced etc.). The term *percept* is sometimes used when the signal is discussed from the point of view of a listener.

It is important to be clear whether the signal is being discussed from an *acoustic* point-of-view (in terms of what is physically present) or an *auditory* one (in terms of what the listener perceives). The volume of a sound (the degree of force behind it) is referred to as *intensity* (or *amplitude*) in an acoustic context but *loudness* in an auditory one. Intensity is measured in decibels (dB); whereas loudness is measured on a phon scale. The two are not the same: if two sounds have the same intensity but different frequency, listeners may perceive them as differing in loudness.

In an acoustic context, the term **frequency** is used for the high-low continuum (the effect of the tension and speed of vibration of the vocal cords), and is measured in vibratory cycles per second or Hertz (Hz). The term *pitch* is used for perceived frequency. However, again, the listener's perception of frequency does not relate in a simple way to a Hertz measurement: they would not find a sound at 500 Hz to be twice as high as one at 250 Hz. Pitch is measured in mels, on a scale that is logarithmic rather than linear. This reflects the fact that listeners are much more sensitive to frequency changes at lower levels. An increase in frequency from 20 Hz to 160 HZ corresponds to an increase in mels from 0 to 250; whereas the difference between 3120 Hz and 4000 Hz produces the same difference of 250 mels.

Human speech can be displayed on a computer in the form of a *spectrogram*. This shows the intensity of the signal at different levels of frequency and plots it against time. A simpler display is a *waveform*, which shows the amplitude of the signal over time. It is important to remember that this information is purely acoustic: a spectrogram shows the information that physically reaches the listener's ear; it gives us no indication as to which parts of this information the listener heeds.

Different parts of the signal may also vary in *perceptual prominence* or *saliency*. In general, more prominent syllables involve greater muscular effort on the part of the speaker. Stressed syllables in lexical words are perceptually more salient than unstressed function words. Important factors contributing to saliency are pitch movement, duration and loudness. Individual phonemes also vary in saliency, depending upon their *sonority* (vowels > nasals > fricatives > stops) and their duration.

Note that while a phone has a target frequency and amplitude, its resonant quality varies according to the size and shape of each speaker's vocal tract. Factors include not simply the variation in thickness of the vocal folds (especially as between men and women) but also the size, shape and position of the articulators: teeth, tongue, palate, nasal cavity etc.

See also: **Noise, Phonological representation, Speech perception: phoneme variation**

Further reading: Ball and Rahilly (1999); Fry (1979); Laver (1994); Pickett (1999)

SPEECH: UNIT OF PRODUCTION

A number of phonological units of analysis can be identified in connected speech. They include the *phonetic feature* (voicing, nasality etc.); the phoneme; the syllable; the rhythmic foot; the *phonological phrase*; the *intonational phrase*. It is difficult to determine which plays a primary role in the assembly of speech. The units cited are perceptual ones, which may not have the same relevance for a speaker as they do for a listener.

Empirical evidence for a unit of speech planning has been sought in pausing, in speech errors, in intonation patterns and in the gestures which accompany speech. There are conflicting findings; and a reasonable conclusion seems to be that different units are available at different levels of processing.

Pauses for planning have been shown to occur consistently at the ends of syntactic clauses, suggesting that the clause plays an important part. But even here the situation is not entirely clear. The boundary of a syntactic clause is often also the boundary of a phonological phrase or an intonational phrase. And the reasons for employing a unit of this size may be semantic rather than syntactic, deriving from the formation of a *predicate/argument structure*.

At the final, phonetic, stage of planning, the phoneme is an unlikely unit of analysis because it varies so much according to the context in which it occurs. Some commentators suggest that articulatory information is stored in the form of syllable-level operations. Further evidence for the importance of the syllable comes from **Slip of the Tongue** data, which shows that syllable structure is very robust. A sound that occurs at the beginning of a syllable is rarely transposed with one that occurs at the end.

See also: **Unit of perception**

SPREADING ACTIVATION

A process which speeds up the retrieval of lexical items that are associated with one that has just been seen or heard. The earlier word is sometimes said to *prime* the later one.

Spreading activation is automatic and not under the control of the language user. It is thus distinct from **top-down processing** where the wider context influences interpretation. It is subject to quite rapid decay, thus ensuring that too many items are not activated at one time.

The effects of spreading activation have been demonstrated for many types of semantic relationship including words that fall into the same lexical set (CHAIR–TABLE), antonyms (HOT–COLD), words which share functional properties (BROOM–FLOOR) and super-ordinate-hyponym pairs (BIRD–ROBIN). However, the strength of the effect may depend on the strength of the association: the co-hyponyms CAT and DOG are strongly associated but the similar co-hyponyms PIG and HORSE are not. A connectionist account would represent this in terms of connections between concepts which are strengthened the more they are used.

See also: **Activation, Priming effect, Semantic network**

STORY GRAMMAR

An attempt to represent the structure of a narrative text in terms of a set of rules. It was suggested that the surface forms of the simpler types of story derive from a single underlying deeper structure and that this structure plays an important part in the way we process such stories. A set of rewrite rules were proposed following the principles of early Transformational Grammar:

1   STORY → SETTING + THEME + PLOT + RESOLUTION
2   SETTING → CHARACTERS + LOCATION + TIME
3   THEME → GOAL
4   PLOT → EPISODE(S)
5   EPISODE → SUBGOAL + ATTEMPTS + OUTCOME
6   ATTEMPT → EVENT(S)
7   RESOLUTION → EVENT or STATE

The theory is based on the type of folk tale that is handed down orally; such stories are said to be memorable because of the way they are structured. There is a high degree of internal organisation; and a theme is established for the story quite close to the beginning. These two factors enable the reader or listener to slot information into a recognisable framework. However, even when a thematic sentence is presented late in the text, performance is better than when no theme is specified. This suggests that, at quite a late stage, readers remain able to *restructure* the information they hold.

The story grammar approach does not account adequately for more sophisticated fiction. However, it receives support from the kind of broad outline which readers give when asked to recall a story and from evidence that readers spend more time reading sentences which are high in the structure of a story and thus potentially thematic.

See also: **Reading: higher-level processing**

Further reading: Brown and Yule (1983: Chap. 3); Whitney (1998: 248–57)

STRATEGY

A technique adopted (a) in order to solve an immediate or long-term problem or (b) in order to achieve learning. In the context of language acquisition and use, it is important to distinguish two types:

☐ *Communication strategies* (see separate entry): techniques for overcoming obstacles to communication. Example: an aphasia patient suffering from vocabulary loss, a dyslexia sufferer, a child in the process of acquiring its first language or a foreign language learner might find it difficult to retrieve a certain word and might substitute an approximate alternative. Some commentators include communication strategies in a wider category of *strategies of use*. This also embraces *retrieval strategies* (ways of locating linguistic information in long-term memory), *rehearsal strategies* (mental dialogues in preparation for real-life encounters) and *cover strategies* (ways of concealing a lack of linguistic or general knowledge, perhaps by resorting to formulaic utterances).

☐ *Learning strategies:* techniques for committing linguistic information to memory. Example: the aphasic or L2 learner might form an association between a problematic word and a more familiar one that is similar in form. They might link PAIR with *pear*, and fix the connection in memory by forming a mental image of two pears. The aim would be to ensure that the difficult word was retrieved more easily in future.

There has been discussion as to the extent to which strategies are conscious and/or available to report. It has not been helped by the tendency of some commentators to conflate the two strategy types. One solution is to view learning strategies as often more *intentional* than communication strategies, given that the latter often represent an unpremeditated response to an immediate problem of communication.

See also: **Communication strategy**

Further reading: Cohen (1998); Faerch and Kasper (1983); Kasper and Kellerman (1997); O'Malley and Chamot (1990)

STROOP TEST

A task (Stroop, 1935) which demonstrates how hard it is to override a highly **automatic** language process (specifically, decoding in reading). Subjects are presented with a list of colour words written in different colours. They are required to call out not what the word says but what colour it is written in. They find the task difficult to accomplish because of interference from the form of the word, which maps automatically on to its lexical entry.

STUTTERING

A disorder of fluency. It varies considerably between sufferers but presents characteristics which give a sense of strain in the speaker. Symptoms include the repetition of phonemic segments, syllables or words (*c-c-computer, com-com-computer, got a-got a-got a brother*) and/or an extreme lengthening of segments or syllables (*af:::raid*). The most typical symptom is a blocking of the airflow, which results in long pauses, effortful speech and distorted facial expressions. There may be a greater than normal use of fillers such as *erm* or *oh* to cover, or sometimes anticipate, a gap. The general hesitancy of speech often leads to irregularities of rhythm and intonation and words may be stressed erratically or left incomplete. Sufferers are often aware of their limitations and may circumlocute or use general terms to avoid words that they anticipate will be difficult.

Stuttering thus involves more than difficulty in articulating particular words: there may also be disruption at the stages of phonetic and prosodic planning. The phenomenon has been interpreted in terms of *demands and capacities*: the demands made by speech upon the speaker's attentional, linguistic or motor resources exceed what the speaker is capable of.

A cognitive theory would link stuttering to listening and to **self-monitoring**. It suggests that there may be split-second delays in the auditory feedback mechanism linking ear, brain and vocal organs, which disrupt the encoding of speech. There have also been neurological explanations, which suggest that a particular type of brain configuration may be the cause or that chemicals within the brain may disrupt the transmission of information across *synapses*.

See also: **Cluttering**

Further reading: Crystal and Varley (1999); Dalton and Hardcastle (1989); Wingate (1988)

SUBVOCALISATION

Evidence of movement in the speech tract (either muscular or involving the articulators) while reading or writing is taking place. There is controversy over the exact contribution that subvocalisation makes to the reading process. It is possible that it supports the reader's subjective impression of an **inner voice**, but must be in some form of code, since articulating the words in full would be much slower than silent reading.

One view might be that subvocalisation is a relic of the way in which, as children, we acquired reading through the phonological system: certainly there is greater subvocalisation among novice readers than among more experienced ones. However, even with skilled readers, the phenomenon appears to increase as the difficulty of a reading task increases: there is evidence of greater subvocalisation with texts that are difficult to process and texts that are in a foreign language.

Experimental studies inhibited subvocalisation by playing unpleasant noises to readers when muscular activity reached a particular level. The consequence was a deterioration in levels of comprehension, suggesting that subvocalisation does indeed contribute to reading skill. However, an alternative interpretation of this finding is that it simply reflects the increased difficulty of reading in a way that (without subvocalisation) was unfamiliar.

See also: **Inner speech, Reading: decoding**

Further reading: Rayner and Pollatsek (1989)

SW (STRONG–WEAK) PATTERN

A rhythmic pattern in which a 'strong' syllable is followed by, or grouped with, a 'weak' one. In many accounts, 'strong' is taken to mean 'stressed relative to the following weak syllable'; but in some it is defined as bearing a full quality vowel rather than a weak one.

In metrical phonology and elsewhere, the pattern is recognised as a phonological unit (the SW *foot*) which is highly characteristic of English speech. A preference for the pattern appears to underlie phenomena such as *cliticisation*, where a weak syllable attaches itself leftwards to a strong one (*fish'n # chips, must've # done*).

Research suggests that English listeners divide up the speech stream into strong-weak units in order to determine where word boundaries are most likely to fall. This *Metrical Segmentation Strategy* is an effective one, since around 90 per cent of content words in running speech begin with a strong syllable.

From an early age, English-acquiring infants seem to be aware of the SW pattern (sometimes referred to in the literature as a *trochee*). American infants as young as nine months manifest a preference for SW words rather than those that follow other rhythmic patterns. The pattern may later assist them in the process of **bootstrapping** to locate words in connected speech.

The language that infants produce retains certain weak syllables from adult speech and omits others:

  giRAFFE → *raffe MONkey* → *Monkey baNANa* → *nana*

The parts which are retained seem to reflect a view of the typical word as SW in form. Gerken (1994) hypothesises that infants develop a *metrical template* which shapes the words that they produce.

See also: **Bootstrapping, Lexical segmentation**

Further reading: Jusczyk (1997)

SYMBOLIC REPRESENTATION

A form of representation in which there is no necessary connection between the sign that is used and the entity in the real world which it represents. Language is a good example of such a system.

A distinction is made between:

- *Iconic representation* where the sign depicts the referent (e.g. a circle to represent the sun);
- *Indexical representation* where the sign is associated in some way with the referent (e.g. a child with a satchel on a road sign for a school);
- *Symbolic representation* where the connection between sign and referent is arbitrary (e.g. red traffic light to mean STOP).

Some commentators suggest that, though we can train chimps to communicate in simple ways, they are unable to grasp the symbolic nature of language.

SYNAESTHESIA

A sensory impression associated with a lexical item but unconnected to its meaning. There are rare cases of language users who report that they associate shades of colour with many words, and appear to store the colours as part of their **lexical** entries for the words.

SYNTACTIC DEVELOPMENT

The gradual approximation of a young child's syntactic competence to that of the adult language user.

The rate at which syntax is acquired by infants varies greatly. But research has attempted to trace important similarities in the order in which structures are acquired. The problem is to determine precisely when a concept can be regarded as 'acquired'. Many children go through phases of **U-shaped development**, in which a form that has apparently been acquired (e.g. *went*) is rejected in favour of one that conforms to a rule (*goed*). This appears to be the result of an **over-generalisation** of a newly acquired rule. Similarly, it cannot be concluded from the first appearance of a particular form that the child has internalised the rule associated with it. Inflected words may be acquired as single units (*walked*, *toys*) well before the child extrapolates a generalisable rule from them ('add *-ed*', 'add *-s*').

Because of problems such as these, research into syntactic development is often longitudinal. The child's progress is assessed in relation to the length of its utterances. A measure known as the **mean length of utterance** (MLU) indicates the average number of morphemes in its productions at a given point. and is a more reliable indicator of progress than age.

Syntactic development can be monitored once the child begins to use two or more words together. Early multi-word productions have been described as *telegraphic speech* because they mainly contain content words, with few functors or inflections. These utterances were once believed to be constructed by means of a **pivot grammar** in which a fixed item had a second item attached to it; but the pattern proved not to be universal. Researchers went on to seek a richer interpretation, which took account of the meanings the child wished to express as well as the forms it used. It was suggested that three language functions were performed in the earliest stages of speech: *nomination* (naming), often marked by the combination of nouns and deictic terms, *recurrence* (coded by words such as MORE and ANOTHER), and *non-existence* (ALLGONE, NO). Several formal patterns were identified, including modifier + head (BIG DOGGIE), negative + X (NO BED), location (BOOK TABLE) and agency (DADDY HIT). Most of them served multiple functions: thus, NO + X was used for refusal, absence and denial.

Beyond the two- and three-word stages, observational evidence can be analysed by comparing the child's grammatical system to the adult norm. The absence of certain types of error is sometimes cited as evidence for an innate **universal grammar** which supports the acquisition process.

☐ *Word class.* Errors (e.g. attaching verb inflections to nouns) have proved to be very rare. Some commentators suggest that infants operate with innate adult categories of Noun and Verb. Others argue that infants are capable of mapping lexical items on to reality; they can distinguish quite early between objects (= nouns) and states/changes of state (= verbs).

☐ *Word order.* Children sometimes use a word order that is unusual in the language being acquired; but never an order that is impossible. They appear to recognise the importance of order very early if the language they are acquiring is heavily dependent upon it. Some commentators assert that children have an innate concept of subject and object. Others argue that children map sentence patterns on to reality. Thus, when an adult describes a picture or event using the form $X + verb + Y$ (*The rabbit is feeding the duck*), the child comes to recognise which sentence slots are occupied by agent and by patient.

☐ *Inflection.* It is generally assumed that the infant is more aware of word order than inflection. However, children acquiring highly inflected languages (Russian, Hungarian, Greenlandic Eskimo, Turkish, German) show great sensitivity to inflections at quite an early age, and may employ a range of them by the age of two. This finding challenges universalist notions, suggesting that infants respond to the specific features of the target language.

A second approach has been to track the development of a syntactic feature to see if children pass through similar phases in the forms they employ. The English negative and interrogative have been investigated in this way, and four stages of development have been identified.

A more semantically based approach asks how children conceptualise the forms they use. Early past tense forms (emerging at MLU 2.0–2.5) tend to be used mainly or entirely for completed events rather than states. The past tense is found with *telic* verbs (verbs which have a goal) but not with *atelic* ones. This, coupled with the evidence that *-ing* is used preferentially with durative verbs, suggests that infants distinguish *situation types* at a surprisingly early age.

The findings described so far have been mainly observational. It is also possible to research syntactic development by setting tasks which establish the extent of a child's syntactic knowledge. One technique has been to get young children to modify a non-word. For example, a child might be shown a picture of an animal described as a WUG, then invited to comment on a picture showing two of them. Infants as young as one year five months have shown themselves capable of distinguishing between *That's Dax* and *That's a dax*.

Comprehension tasks have been used with older children to check their understanding of more complex syntactic structures. It has been established, for example, that four year olds sometimes have difficulties in understanding *reversible* passives (*The boy was hit by the girl*), which they interpret in terms of the standard SVO order of English.

Several theories attempt to account for the way in which syntactic development follows similar patterns across infants. One nativist account (Radford, 1990) suggests that the **Universal Grammar** with which the child is born is a reduced version of the adult system. The system it is working with lacks certain branches of the tree structure of adult grammar which are acquired as the child matures. Hence the lack of function words and verbal inflections in the child's early speech. This enables the child to focus on acquiring lexically focused information.

Evidence of consistent patterns in syntactic development does not only support a nativist interpretation. It could equally reflect the different levels of cognitive difficulty involved in acquiring syntactic concepts. There might be an interplay of two factors: the relative complexity of the various language points and the current stage of development of the child's own cognitive capacities.

An alternative empiricist account is provided by **connectionist** computer programs which have accurately modelled exactly the kind of **U-shaped development** that a child goes through in acquiring past tense forms.

See also: **Cognitivism, Empiricism, Nativism, Social-interactionism**

Further reading: Clark (2003); Crain and Lillo-Martin (1999: Part 1); Foster (1990); Foster-Cohen (1999); O'Grady (1997); Owens (2001); Tomasello and Bates (2001: Part III)

SYNTACTIC PARSING

A stage in the processing of written or spoken language at which a syntactic structure is assembled from a string of words. Two problems arise in attempting to relate syntactic parsing to linguistic theory:

a. Linguistic theory attempts to describe how language is structured, not how a language user performs. It does not claim that the way in which it chooses to represent a linguistic system is **psychologically real** (a model of how the user's mind operates). Linguistics attempts to represent language *competence*, while psychology attempts to describe language *performance*.
b. Modern approaches to syntax are based upon hierarchies of phrases – reflecting the *structure dependency* that characterises all languages. But the psychological processes of reading and listening have been shown to be linear, with words decoded as they are perceived. A theory of parsing has somehow to square these two perspectives.

☐ *'Linguistic' approaches.* Early approaches to parsing took transformational grammar as a point of departure and attempted to establish that Chomsky's descriptive system represented what actually takes place in the mind of the language user. The primary role of parsing was seen as being to recover the deep structure of a sentence by reversing any transformations that might have gone into its creation. A *Derivational Theory of Complexity* (DTC) hypothesised that the more transformations there were, the more difficult it was for a listener or reader to process a sentence. A task in which subjects matched derived sentences to their deep structure form seemed to support the theory. However, there were many uncontrolled variables in the material. Later commentators dismissed the DTC theory on a number of counts: among them, the fact that listeners do not wait until the end of a sentence in order to begin processing it.

Researchers next tried to confirm the psychological reality of deep structure. '*Click experiments*' were devised in which listeners had to identify the location of a click inserted into sentences with differing deep structures. A click was inserted during the word *criminals* in:

a.   *[The corrupt police can't bear] [criminals to confess quickly]*
b.   *[The corrupt police can't force criminals] to confess quickly*

Subjects reported it as occurring before the word in sentence a. and afterwards in sentence b., suggesting that they had indeed constructed a representation based on deep structure. However, again there were problems of research design – not least the fact that subjects reported *post-perceptually* – a short time after hearing the click.

Much research into syntactic parsing still takes **Chomskyan theory** as its framework, and continues to seek for evidence of *d-structure* (deep structure) patterns underlying *s-structure* (surface structure) ones. In current theory, the concept of transformation has been replaced by one of *movement*. A sentence such as:

c.   *I wonder which book my cousin borrowed (t)*

is said to be the product of a movement rule which shifts the Noun Phrase *which book* leftwards from the position it originally occupied in deep structure. That position is marked in the example above by (t), showing where a *trace* of the NP remains. Researchers have suggested that the successful parsing of a sentence such as c. depends upon temporarily storing *which book* in memory until its deep structure position (t) is reached. Evidence from timed reading supports this theory: reading slows when a 'filler' such as *which book* is encountered, suggesting that demands on **working memory** do indeed increase at that point.

Another area of research influenced by Chomskyan theory seeks evidence of the setting of *parameters*, linguistic features which are adjusted according to the language which one acquires. One line of enquiry compares syntactic competence across speakers of different languages, by asking them to make *grammaticality judgements*. There has, for example, been interest in the processing of *wh-* interrogatives involving prepositions since languages vary widely in the degree to which they permit *preposition stranding* (*Who did he speak to?*) as against *pied piping* (*To whom did he speak?*).

Another line of enquiry attempts to establish when parameters become established in young language acquirers. There has been interest in **anaphor resolution**, particularly where it involves reflexive pronouns. At an early age, children have shown themselves much more successful in interpreting a sentence containing a reflexive (*Cinderella's sister points to herself*) than a similar sentence containing an ordinary pronoun (*Cinderella's sister points to her*).

☐ *The unit of parsing.* Experiments investigating **wrap up effects** demonstrate that it becomes difficult for subjects to report the verbatim form of a spoken utterance once a clause boundary has been passed. The conclusion is that meaning is 'packaged' clause by clause and that the actual words heard are then lost to memory since they are no longer required. There is also evidence from reading that the processing load on working memory is greatest at the end of a clause and that eye fixations are longer. These effects appear to reflect the reader's need to allocate additional attention to syntax. It thus seems that the clause boundary is the point at which syntactic decisions are made.

☐ *Linear processing.* But processing is not delayed until a clause is complete, as early parsing theory assumed. Indeed, experiments have established that both listening and reading take place **on line**, with the language user processing words as they are identified before going on to construct higher-level syntactic patterns from them. Parsing is therefore viewed as an *incremental* process.

Researchers in **Artificial Intelligence** have addressed the issue of how to combine linear processing at word level with the building of higher-level syntactic structures. They have devised computer programs known as **Augmented Transition Networks** (ATNs) which identify a series of points in the parsing of an utterance at which accumulated evidence can lead to a 'change of state' and thus a new direction for the processing. The points occur after each complete phrase and sentence as well as after each word, thus enabling syntactic structures to be built. While computer networks of this kind enable programs to process pieces of text, they are heavily dependent upon conventional sentence structures, and their top-down nature leads to many incorrect predictions and much backtracking.

☐ *Ambiguity.* Much parsing research has investigated how the language user deals with cases of **ambiguity** as typified by **garden path** sentences such as:

d. *The old man / the boats.* (slash indicates point of ambiguity)
e. *John remembered the answer / was in the book*

where the word class of a word and/or the syntactic structure of a sentence are unclear at a given point in the sentence but are subsequently resolved. Evidence suggests that a preferred analysis is chosen by the parser and later revised if necessary. There are several theories as to why a particular interpretation is preferred:

● *Syntactic.* The listener/reader exercises a preference for a *canonical*

(SVO) sentence structure. Alternatively, specific syntactic strategies are used, such as 'make an attachment to the clause that is currently being processed'.

- *Lexical.* The preferred reading reflects the argument structure of the current verb.
- *Semantic.* World knowledge indicates which interpretation is the most probable.

☐ *Syntactic vs semantic processing.* The discussion of ambiguity exemplifies a broader disagreement over the extent to which semantic criteria influence syntactic parsing. The major issue is whether parsing involves syntax and semantics together or whether a first pass analysis relies solely on syntax. Strong evidence for separate processes comes from studies of the brain. A negative **event–related potential** (variation in electrical activity) occurs 400 milliseconds after a semantic anomaly has been detected; but a very different positive ERP occurs 600 milliseconds after a syntactic anomaly. Evidence from readers' eye movements is also cited in support of a two–stage model. Subjects appear to be slowed down by sentences such as g below, where semantic evidence of animacy is available to help them, just as they are by f, where it is not.

f.   *The defendant examined by the lawyer was unreliable.*
g.   *The evidence examined by the lawyer was unreliable.*

See also: **Ambiguity: syntactic, Anaphor resolution, Augmented Transition Network, Derivational theory of complexity, Event-related potential, Garden path sentences, Wrap up effects**

Further reading: Aitchison (1998: Chaps 9–10); Harley (2001: Chap. 9); Pickering (1999)

SYNTHESISED SPEECH

Speech–like acoustic waves which have been artificially constructed by computer. The use of computer equipment enables an experimenter to construct a series of acoustic forms which cover the continuum from (say) a central version of [ba] to a central version of [pa]. These can then be played to subjects in order to determine at what point on the continuum their perception shifts categorically from one interpretation to the other. Synthesised speech also enables researchers to manipulate different acoustic cues in order to identify which ones are the most important in assisting listeners to identify consonantal phonemes.

Further reading: Denes and Pinson (1993: Chap. 10)

T-UNIT (also MINIMAL TERMINAL UNIT)

A main clause with all of its modifiers, including subordinate clauses. Mean length of T-unit is used as a measure of 'syntactic maturity' in writing, indicating how effectively a writer manipulates syntax. It has been reliably demonstrated that, as young learners proceed through school, their writing shows a gradual increase in the average number of words per T-unit and per clause. This is a better indicator than number of words per sentence. The measure has also been used to assess the effects of instruction upon writing performance and to compare the syntactic density of different types and genres of writing. However, evidence suggests that there may be considerable variation in length of T-unit even within the writing of a single individual. Variation is especially likely when an individual switches from one type of writing to another (e.g. from description to narration).

See also: **Writing: skilled**

TACHISTOSCOPE

A device used in reading research which enables an experimenter to control the amount of visual information which is supplied to the subject and the duration of exposure.

TASK DEMANDS

The different aspects of cognition that are involved in performing a task. An experimental task might be questioned if it does not simply test the process that it is intended to test, but also makes demands, for example, upon memory.

The term is also used when discussing the level of attention that a particular task requires. The more complex a task is, the greater the demands it makes upon **working memory**. Similarly, certain types of language task demand greater accuracy and clarity (compare a public talk with a conversation with a friend). They require a degree of **control** and thus place heavier demands upon the language user.

THEMATIC (THETA) ROLE

The semantic role of a constituent in a sentence. Consider the following sentences:

a. *Julie opened the door.*
b. *The key opened the door.*
c. *Paul fears wasps.*

In each, the first Noun Phrase is the syntactic subject. But in a. Julie is an *agent* (she performs an action). In b. the key is an *instrument*. In c. Paul is an *experiencer* (he undergoes an experience but does not do anything). Describing constituents in terms of their theta roles gets behind the surface form of a sentence to its underlying propositional content. Major theta roles include: Agent (actor) – Patient (human sufferer of action) – Theme (non-human sufferer of action) – Experiencer – Instrument – Beneficiary – Recipient – Location – Goal.

Theta roles have been incorporated into theories of speech production. An utterance is constructed around a central notion or **predicate**, which is often (but not always) a verb. When the speaker accesses a verb in their lexicon, they gain information about the syntactic frame which the verb usually requires: for GIVE, this might be V (_ NP_1, NP_2) as in *give Mary a present* or V (_ NP_2 *to* NP_2) as in *give a present to Mary*. Semantic information about *theta role constraints* then specifies which lexical items can fill the slots in the frame. With GIVE, NP_1 requires a Recipient and NP_2 requires a Theme. Further semantic information can extend the restrictions on potential fillers by specifying, for example, that NP_2 is usually inanimate and portable.

See also: **Argument structure, Predicate**

THEORY OF MIND

The ability to recognise that another human being has their own ideas and intentions, which may be distinct from one's own; the ability to conceptualise those ideas and intentions.

The possession of a theory of mind is said to be a prerequisite for language. It underpins the use of deixis, and the recognition that words like THIS, HERE and ME are employed from the standpoint of the speaker, not that of the listener. It is critical to the way in which speakers and writers determine the knowledge which they share with the listener/reader and the knowledge which is not shared and has to be explained. It enables a speaker/writer to anticipate responses and thus to shape their productions in a way that persuades or manipulates feelings. In addition, it plays an important part in activities such as story telling, which oblige the hearers to understand the beliefs, motivations and reactions of the characters involved.

There is disagreement as to whether the possession of a theory of mind is specific to human beings. Monkeys and most primates appear to lack the capacity. They are sometimes good at interpreting behaviour, but do not show themselves capable of identifying with the mind behind the behaviour. With chimps, the situation is less clear.

One reason that other species may not have developed this insight is that it appears to be costly in terms of the demands it makes upon brain capacity. Even human beings find it hard to conceptualise what is demanded by tasks which extend to the fifth order (*A thinks that B thinks that A thinks that B thinks that A thinks the world is flat*).

There are two main views as to how the theory of mind operates in human beings. One is that our understanding of other minds is part of a symbolic system, with certain rules of inference which enable us to understand the needs and feelings of others. This may or may not be innate. The other is that we use our own experience in order to simulate mentally what others think and feel.

Current evidence suggests that a theory of mind develops in infants between two and four years old. This poses a problem for accounts of language acquisition which rely heavily on the notion that children are driven to speak by a desire to communicate. They need to explain how the notion of communication can arise without the parallel notion of a mind distinct from one's own to which information is to be imparted.

See also: **Evolution of language, Social-interactionism**

Further reading: Bloom (2000: Chap. 3); Garnham and Oakhill (1994: 336–9)

THOUGHT AND LANGUAGE

A classical view (dating back to Aristotle) holds that thought is prior to language and that languages have developed the properties they have in order to express ideas. A contrasting view holds that we can only think logically and coherently because language assists us in doing so.

Both raise the question of the precise relationship between the linguistic form in which we express our ideas and the form in which they are stored in our minds. To what extent is language an external representation of thought and to what extent is it an entirely different code?

Behaviourist theory treated the mind as unknowable, and some of its exponents suggested that thought was nothing more than internalised speech. They cited evidence of electrical activity in the throat muscles when thinking was in progress, which they claimed was some kind of **subvocalisation**. This view was put to the test in a famous experiment in which curare was used to temporarily paralyse the muscular system of a volunteer; the volunteer nevertheless reported later that he was able to think and solve problems.

The relationship between thought and language has implications for theories of how the cognitive development of a young child affects the course of language acquisition. Here, several positions have emerged:

☐ *Cognition drives language.* Piaget saw the development of language as determined by the stages at which cognitive concepts are acquired. For example, the child could not refer to the absence of objects (CUP GONE) without having achieved the concept of *object permanence*.

☐ *Language and cognition are mutually supportive.* Vygotsky believed that in the early years of life speech and thought are independent. However, from the age of two onwards, pre-linguistic thought (= action schemas, images) begins to interact with pre-intellectual language (words treated simply as properties of the objects they denote). Gradually, 'thought becomes verbal and speech rational'. An important part is played by *egocentric speech*, which serves two functions: an internal one, where the child monitors and organises its thoughts and an external one, where it communicates those thoughts to others. The two are not fully differentiated until the child is about seven, when a distinction is made between public conversation and private thought.

☐ *Language is independent of general cognition,* though the two are closely linked. This view is critical to the thinking of Chomsky and others, who argue that language is a separate faculty which is innately acquired and which develops independently of the intellectual capacities of the individual.

☐ *The way thought is structured helps to shape language.* Like Chomsky, Pinker regards linguistic and cognitive development as distinct. But he represents language as mapping on to an abstract code specific to thought which he terms *mentalese*.

The thought vs language issue also embraces a long-standing discussion about how we perceive reality. Does the physical world fall into natural categories which all human beings readily recognise (a *realist* view)? Or do we see the world in terms of the categories that our language has taught us (a *constructivist* view)? The anthropologists Sapir and Whorf made strong claims for the latter position. *Linguistic determinism* holds that the characteristics of the language we speak determine the way in which we think and view the world. The theory was called into question by studies of **colour systems** across languages. Although languages divide up the colour spectrum in different ways, it was found that *focal points* (prototypical examples) for particular colours are not only shared by speakers of the same language, but are also shared across languages.

Other studies have tried to establish whether the ability to form particular concepts is influenced by the nature of a language's grammar. There is some evidence that Chinese speakers find counter-factual reasoning (*If I were rich, I'd buy a plane*) more difficult than speakers of some other languages; but it is difficult to be sure that this is specifically the result of linguistic rather than cultural or educational differences.

Currently, some credence is given to a weaker form of the *Sapir–Whorf Hypothesis* – namely that language can support or hinder performance on certain cognitive tasks. In an early experiment, subjects were shown visual symbols accompanied by two different descriptions (the same symbol might be described as a broom with one group and a gun with another). When subjects were later asked to draw the symbols, their versions matched the descriptions rather than the original drawings.

See also: **Colour systems, Linguistic relativity, Modularity$_1$, Piagetian stages of development, Vygotskyan**

Further reading: Garnham and Oakhill (1994: Chap. 3); Greene (1975)

TIP OF THE TONGUE (TOT)

A state in which a language user is aware of the existence of a particular word (perhaps a search for the word has been triggered by a *meaning code*) but cannot retrieve it from the lexicon.

Experimenters sometimes create the 'Tip of the Tongue' state artificially by providing subjects with definitions of obscure words and asking them to name the words. The task elicits responses which are inaccurate but bear resemblances to the target words; these provide insights into the criteria we use when searching the lexicon.

TOT evidence strongly supports similar evidence obtained from **Slips of the Tongue** (SOT), which indicates that certain aspects of a word are less likely to be misrepresented than others. Especially robust are the initial and final syllables, stressed vowels, the distribution of lexical stress and the number of syllables. These appear to be the kinds of cue which enable us to locate words; and they are therefore probably a feature of the way words are associated in the mind by form.

The TOT state demonstrates that it is possible to hold the meaning of a word in one's mind without necessarily being able to retrieve its form. This has suggested to commentators that a **lexical entry** falls into two distinct parts, one relating to form and one to meaning, and that one may be accessed without the other. In assembling speech, we first identify a given word by some kind of abstract meaning code and only later insert its actual phonological form into the utterance we are planning.

See also: **Slips of the Tongue**

Further reading: Aitchison (2003)

TONE LANGUAGES

Languages such as Thai, Mandarin and Cantonese which use pitch movement as a way of differentiating lexical items. For example, *ma* in Mandarin Chinese means 'horse' when said with a falling-rising tone but 'mother' when said with a level one. Besides using tone as the property of a word, these languages also employ it in intonation.

Prosody (stress, rhythm and intonation) appears to be handled by the right hemisphere of the brain. However, speakers of Thai have been shown to have a right ear (= left hemisphere) advantage for the processing of lexical tones. They also (like English speakers) show a left ear (= right hemisphere) advantage for the processing of intonational tones. Hence a *functionalist hypothesis* that it is the purpose served by a stimulus (lexical vs intonational) which determines which hemisphere handles it rather than the nature of the stimulus itself.

See also: **Brain: lateralisation**

TOP-DOWN PROCESSING

The influence of higher-level (conceptual) knowledge upon lower-level (perceptual) processing. The terms 'top-down' and 'bottom-up' are derived from computer science, where they refer respectively to information that is knowledge-driven and information that is data-driven.

'Top-down' is sometimes loosely used as a synonym of 'contextual'. However, strictly speaking, it refers not to a single level of processing but to a *direction of processing*. Suppose the knowledge that a given word exists can be shown to affect the way we hear the sounds in that word. This can be described as a top-down effect, because knowledge at word level is influencing processing at a lower (phoneme) level. Similarly, the way in which speech or writing is planned can be described as a 'top-down' process since it begins with large, conceptual units (propositions) and ends with small, perceptual ones (words in the speaker's mouth or on the writer's page).

For this reason, the term '*higher-level processing*' is often preferred when describing the use of contextual information, as against *lower-level* decoding operations. Or a distinction is made between *conceptual* and *perceptual* processes.

The term 'top-down' is also sometimes used to refer to theories of reading or listening which hold that contextual information plays a more important part than perceptual. Again, this is misleading as it implies that a choice has to be made. Even 'top-down' accounts have to include at least some perceptual evidence. The issue is to establish how the two information sources interact and which one predominates in case of conflict.

There are conflicting views. Some commentators claim that top-down information is only used for checking bottom-up. Some argue for *bottom-up priority*, with contextual evidence only invoked once sufficient bottom-up evidence has become available. Their case is based partly on the fact that bottom-up processing is more automatised than top-down, and therefore faster; and partly on the argument that too many sources of information impede rapid decision making. Other commentators favour a fully **interactive** model of listening or reading, contending that both sources of evidence are available throughout. They argue that it is more efficient to have all the information available at one time.

It is important to make a distinction between two different purposes for invoking contextual knowledge in listening and reading:

- To *compensate* for gaps in understanding. In the case of the weak reader, the gaps might reflect weak decoding skills. In the case of the second language learner, they might be the result of a limited vocabulary or grammar or the inability to recognise known words in connected speech.
- To *enrich* the meaning interpretation of what has been read or heard by bringing in world knowledge, knowledge of the discourse so far etc.

The second purpose characterises the more skilled listener/reader and the more advanced language learner. They have achieved a degree of **automaticity** in the way they decode language, which frees working memory resources and makes them available for considering the wider contextual implications of what is being read or heard.

See also: **Context effects, Listening: higher-level processes, Reading: bottom-up vs top-down, Reading: higher-level processes, Speech perception: autonomous vs interactive**

TRACE

A leading computer simulation of spoken word processing (McClelland and Elman, 1986). TRACE is a **connectionist** model which operates on three different levels, corresponding to phonetic features, phonemes and words. It first encodes an incoming speech signal, not in terms of discrete phonemes or syllables but by dividing it into extremely short *time slices* which record the values of seven different acoustic features at any given moment. A series of phoneme units then samples this data for evidence that a given phoneme is present. The evidence upon which a phoneme unit draws covers three time-slices at a time, but the unit is linked, in all, to eleven consecutive slices. In this way, TRACE's architecture takes account of the way in which features specifying different phonemes overlap in time (the *non-linearity* problem).

There is also a lexical level, containing a bank of units for each word in the lexicon. Each bank samples the phonemic data for evidence of the presence of its particular word. Like the phoneme units, the word units receive information from three time-slices at a time; and, also like the phoneme units, they are connected to, and continue to monitor, preceding time-slices. Though a word boundary may have been crossed, the lexical banks still have access to information which the system extracted before the boundary occurred. This enables the model to deal with the '*right-context*' problem: the fact that many words cannot be confidently identified until well after their offsets.

However, TRACE's critics suggest that its time-slice solution is bought at the cost of an extremely complex structure. The entire set of lexical units has to be duplicated every third time-slice. In the original TRACE format, there were only 211 words in the program's lexicon; to simulate a typical listener they would have to be expanded to at least 30,000, all of which would need to be matched repeatedly against the input.

TRACE is a highly **interactive** model, with a continuous flow of information between its levels in both bottom-up and top-down directions. Evidence for a unit at one level lends support (**activation**) to a unit at a higher level but reduces support for competing units at the same level. Thus, evidence of /w/ at phoneme level would boost the activation of the word WORK, but scale down the activation of the competing phoneme /v/. This interactive structure enables TRACE to deal with misheard or mispronounced input. If there is a less than perfect match (e.g. if the model encounters a word like SHIGARETTE), the incoming evidence continues to build up activation for the most likely fit.

TRACE has performed impressively in lexical recognition tasks. But some reservations have been raised in relation to its ability to simulate the process of **lexical segmentation**.

See also: **Connectionism, Interactive activation, Speech perception: phoneme variation**

Further reading: Ellis and Humphreys (1999: 343–7); Harley (2001: 233–7)

TRADING RELATIONS

A mechanism which allows the listener to identify a particular phoneme by weighing the cues for and against its presence in the signal. A clear articulatory cue that the phoneme is [p] might thus cancel out a more ambivalent timing cue which suggests that it is [b]; and vice versa (see **cue trading**).

TURING TEST

A possible solution to the issue of whether a computer can ever be regarded as 'thinking'. The test proposed by Turing, the early computer scientist, envisaged a human being communicating indirectly with a computer. If they cannot determine from its answers whether they are communicating with a computer or another human being, then we should concede that the machine can think. The value of this idea is that it dispenses with philosophical issues relating to the nature of thought, and treats intelligence in terms of the way it functions.

TWINS

If language is genetically transmitted, then its development is likely to be markedly similar in twins who are 'identical' or *monozygotic* (products of a single egg). There is considerable evidence that this is the case. However, it is not easy to factor out other variables such as shared intelligence and the fact that the twins share the same home environment. More evidence is needed on language acquisition in the rare cases of twins who have been separated early in life.

Another area of study compares language acquisition by twins with that by singletons. There is strong evidence that early language development in twins is often delayed. In only about 35 per cent of identical twins and 40 per cent of fraternal twins does the onset of language occur at the normal time; and the language of twins tends to fall behind that of their peers during the third year of life.

The most convincing explanations relate to the circumstances of being a twin. It may be that twins feel less need to communicate with others because of their close mutual bonding. Some researchers report evidence of a secret language between twins (*cryptophasia*) consisting of sounds and words which are unintelligible to others. In the early stages, this supplants the need for socialised language. Or it may be that carers find it harder to divide their attention and time between two infants. Observation suggests that there is less verbal interaction per individual twin than a single child receives. Furthermore, carers are less able to assist meaning construction by monitoring and directing the child's attention when there are two children involved.

It is not clear whether the language acquired by twins is different as well as delayed. However, it may be that, because of their situation, twins develop faster than other children in their use of certain discourse skills such as the ability to take turns and the ability to monitor third-party exchanges.

Further reading: Mogford (1993a)

TYPING

Studies of typing patterns offer insights into the last (motor) stage of the writing process when a PC is in use. Average typing speed is seven to eight strokes per second; but evidence of the way in which typists execute their writing plans comes from the regularity of the finger strokes and the duration of the intervals between them. The following conclusions have been reached:

☐ In terms of rhythm, the unit of typing seems to be the word rather than the phrase or sentence.
☐ Intervals between strokes are greatest at the beginnings and ends of words.
☐ Intervals between strokes are longer for letter strings which occur infrequently.
☐ Syllable boundaries appear to have some effect; the frequent sequence *-th-* is typed faster in PATHETIC than in PORTHOLE.
☐ Performance declines with nonsensical letter strings, but not with non-words that bear a resemblance to existing ones.

The evidence may offer insights into the way in which words are retrieved from the brain, or insights into the typing process itself. Typing is clearly an activity that demands a great deal of conscious control at the outset, but that gradually becomes *proceduralised* into a set of automatic keystroke sequences, particularly for very frequent words such as THE. It may be that the keystrokes made by a typist are stored as an independent set of procedures (hence the faster performance with more frequent letter sequences). Or it may be that they are linked to an orthographic representation of each word, or even to a phonological representation.

See also: **Slips of the Pen, Writing**

Further reading: Garman (1990: 234–6)

U-SHAPED DEVELOPMENT

A process in first and second language acquisition where a syntactic feature appears to have been acquired but is later used or formed incorrectly. Often quoted is a finding that many children use the correct irregular past tense forms in English (*went, fell*) but then go on to use incorrect forms in *-ed* (*wented, goed, falled*). In due course, the correct form is restored.

Initial mastery of language may well be holistic: the child acquiring inflected words as individual units without recognising the system that links, for example, *walked* to its stem *walk*. Similarly, irregular forms such as *broke* or *went* are probably first acquired as if they were simple items of vocabulary. However, at some stage, the child comes to recognise that morphology is rule-governed. Its reaction is then to *over-generalise* the rules it has extrapolated ('for past tense, add *-ed*'), replacing irregular forms with regularised ones. In time, evidence from adult speech leads it to restrict the application of the *-ed* rule and to reinstate the irregular forms.

A **connectionist** computer program has simulated the trial-and-error learning of regular and irregular past tense forms in English. The learning process manifested exactly the kind of U-shaped development that has been observed naturalistically.

See also: **Over-generalisation, Syntactic development**

UNDERSPECIFICATION

A theory that it is not necessary for all the characteristics of a linguistic unit to be stored in the mind, but only those which serve to uniquely characterise it. The concept is especially applied to the **phonological representation** which enables a language user to recognise the sounds of a language.

Early generative phonology represented the phonemes of a language in binary form, indicating the presence or absence of certain acoustic features ($+/-$ consonantal, $+/-$ nasal etc.). A basic underspecification could restrict this to the $+$ features (those that are actually present). But among those features would still be some which are redundant: for example, if a consonant is nasal, it must also be voiced. It is therefore possible to reduce the specification further by eliminating all features which can be inferred from others by means of a rule.

Underspecification of this kind provides an economical account of how we store phonology in the mind. By reducing the importance of non-essential cues, it also streamlines the process of recognising phonemes and thus compensates to some extent for the fact that phonemes vary greatly from one context to another in terms of the phonetic features that compose them.

At syllable level, underspecification enables the listener to ignore any information in the acoustic signal which is not contrastive. For example, it has been shown that distinctions between nasalised and non-nasalised vowels are not represented phonologically for an English listener since they do not serve to differentiate words. However, they do form part of the phonological representation of a Bengali speaker since Bengali possesses vowels of both types.

See also: **Phonological representation**

Further reading: Crystal (1997); Goldsmith (1995: 13–18)

UNIQUENESS POINT

The point at which a spoken word becomes distinct from all others. Some accounts of spoken word recognition such as **Cohort Theory** adopt the premise that words are often recognised before their offsets, i.e. before the whole word has been uttered. As more and more of a word is heard, an initial set of likely word matches is narrowed down until, at the uniqueness point, a single match is identified.

The hypothesis derives from evidence that some listeners are capable of **shadowing** (repeating back running speech) at delays of around a quarter of a second behind the speaker. This is approximately the length of a syllable in English, suggesting that listeners are capable of *early recognition* of words before the phonetic information is complete. It has also been shown that *co-articulatory* information in vowels enables listeners to anticipate syllable endings before they hear them. According to some commentators, recognition is also supported by evidence from the general context.

'Early recognition' offers an account of how word boundaries are identified in connected speech. Having recognised a word early, the listener can anticipate its offset and this provides a marker for the onset of the word that follows.

However, evidence from a statistical analysis of the lexicon suggests that many words do not, in fact, have an early uniqueness point. Luce (1986) found that, with frequency weighting, only 39 per cent of

English words in normal speech are unique before their offsets, and only another 23 per cent at offset. Many sequences that appear to constitute monosyllabic words may prove instead to be the initial syllables of polysyllabic ones, while 94 per cent of two-phoneme words and 74 per cent of three-phoneme words are potentially part of a longer word. Luce's figures are probably an under-estimate since they do not take full account of suffixation (RUN is potentially the first syllable of RUNNING).

Experimental findings have also cast doubt upon the view that recognition is tied to a word's uniqueness point. In the **gating** task, subjects are presented with progressively longer sections of input and asked to record their impressions of what they hear. This has shown that about half of low-frequency monosyllabic content words are not identified until after the word has finished – on the strength of subsequent phonetic (and possibly syntactic and semantic) information. Words are more likely to remain unrecognised at offset if they are of short duration, occur early in an utterance or are functors. Overall, late recognition is quite common, and often takes the form of two words being recognised simultaneously. This presents a challenge to the view that we always process utterances linearly, from '*left to right*'; it suggests that much processing is *retroactive*.

See also: **Cohort Theory, Lexical segmentation, Shadowing**

Further reading: Luce (1986); McQueen *et al.* (1995)

UNIT OF PERCEPTION (UNIT OF PROCESSING)

A unit into which the raw features of speech are automatically 'packaged' at an early *pre-lexical* stage – i.e. before any match is sought with words in the lexicon.

Traditional accounts of language processing tend to assume that the listener identifies phonemes from phonetic cues in the speech signal. However, this is difficult to square with the fact that the features which make up individual phonemes are highly variable in connected speech. There is also evidence that our awareness of the phoneme may only be achieved as a result of alphabetic literacy.

One proposed alternative is that the signal is processed exactly as it is received, without being analysed into any intermediate units. In these *direct access* models, phonetic features (+ nasals, + consonantal etc.) are the evidence that is used for making word matches.

Another proposal is that there is a unit of processing which is larger than the phoneme, and therefore less variable. Suggestions have included the syllable, the demi-syllable and the *diphone* (a combination of two adjoining phonemes). The advantage of the syllable or demi-syllable is that there is a restricted number in any language (the estimates for French are 6000 and 2000 respectively). There is also evidence that infants become aware of the syllable as a unit in speech at an early stage of linguistic development. However, although the syllable is more robust than the phoneme, it is still subject to variation through **accommodation** (assimilation, elision, resyllabification etc.). More importantly, there are languages such as English where the syllable boundary is not always clearly marked: the sound /m/ in a word such as LEMON is *ambisyllabic* in that it does not clearly form either the end of the first syllable or the beginning of the second but seems to participate in both. This makes it difficult to divide some English words into clear syllabic units.

The rival claims of phonemes and syllables as 'units of perception' have been hotly argued. An early study obtained faster detection times for syllables than for phonemes, suggesting that words were primarily analysed syllabically and only afterwards broken into phonemes. However, this finding was later widely questioned. A subsequent study demonstrated faster results for disyllabic words than for syllables, suggesting that the size of the unit was a factor in the results achieved. Further studies followed, some supporting the syllable and some not. But a criticism that is levelled against many of them is that they provide evidence of how subjects *identify* a syllable in connected speech rather than how (at an earlier and more automatic stage) they *perceive* it.

A more sophisticated method explored the assumption that, if the syllable were indeed the basic unit of perception, the same time would be taken to recognise the difference between PID and PIT (third phoneme divergent) as the difference between PID and BID (first phoneme divergent). The results did not support this hypothesis, and the researchers concluded that, if speech is 'packaged' by English listeners, it is into units smaller than the syllable. An alternative view holds that the listener has several units of analysis available to them. The unit that is employed is determined by the nature of the task they are performing and by the attentional demands that the task makes upon them.

See also: **Lexical segmentation, Phonological representation, Speech perception: phoneme variation**

Further reading: Norris and Cutler (1988); Nygaard and Pisoni (1995)

UNIVERSAL GRAMMAR (UG)

The term is used in two ways:

a. A mechanism which is innate in human beings and which sensitises an infant to the features which characterise all languages, thus giving it a head start in the process of acquiring its own. Some accounts see UG as part of a *maturational* process, with awareness of the characteristics of language gradually unfolding as the child develops. Others assume that it is fully present, **hard-wired**, from the start, but that the child is not able to take full advantage of it because of its limited cognitive development.

b. The linguistic content of such a mechanism, a set of phonological, syntactic and lexical features which are shared by all languages. The content of UG falls into two categories: *principles* which are true universals, occurring in all (or nearly all) languages, and *parameters*, which are universal to the extent that they occur across languages in one form or another. An example of the latter is the *pro-drop parameter* which specifies whether a language employs an obligatory subject pronoun (*She speaks English*) or is able to omit it (*Parla inglese*). Another example is seen in the fact that languages with a standard VO (verb + direct object) word order make use of certain syntactic patterns which differentiate them sharply from those with an OV (direct object + verb) order. These patterns constitute a set of '*If... then*' features – meaning that if a language has one, it is likely to manifest most or all of the others.

There are two broad approaches to the quest for evidence of universals. The Chomskyan approach is based upon putting to the test a detailed theoretical model. Researchers might ask adult subjects to make *grammaticality judgements*, deciding whether a particular string of words is or is not acceptable. These judgements are said to tap in to *competence* and are preferred to evidence of actual speech production, which would reflect *performance*. An alternative *typological approach* examines evidence across many languages in order to trace similarities.

There is a broad measure of agreement that the following are universal:

● some lexical categories (noun and verb);
● *structure-dependency*;

316

- phrases containing a head of the same type as the phrase;
- a phrase structure consisting of *Specifier, Head* and *Complement*.

UG theory accepts that languages may deviate to some degree from the universal pattern. A language user's competence is said to consist of a *core grammar* of universal principles and parameters and a *periphery* of features specific to the language in question, which cannot be explained by reference to UG. They might be survivals from an earlier stage of the language, loans from other languages or fixed idioms. The relationship between core grammar and periphery is best described as a cline, with central UG characteristics defined as *unmarked* and features that fall outside UG as progressively more and more *marked*. When acquiring a language, the child comes to recognise that some features of the target language do not conform to the criteria specified by UG, and have to be mastered by a process which is independent of the normal acquisition route.

Chomsky himself recognises that cognitive constraints such as short-term memory restrictions may have an impact upon performance, limiting what the child is capable of achieving with its innately acquired UG. For example, the absence of a subject pronoun in much early English speech might indicate a parameter setting which initially favours a pro-drop pattern; but it might equally well indicate a cognitive inability to process more than two words. A useful distinction has been made between *language acquisition*, which is supported by UG, and *language development*, in which cognitive factors play a part.

See also: **Chomskyan theory, Language acquisition: theories, Language universals, Markedness, Principles and parameters**

Further reading: Cook and Newson (1996)

VERBAL REPORT

A widely used experimental method, which asks subjects to report on a linguistic process in which they are engaged. The data provided by subjects is often referred to as a *protocol*.

Verbal report may be *concurrent*, the reporting taking place when the subject is actually engaged in a task, or *retrospective*, where the reporting occurs immediately after the task. The choice is sometimes determined by the process under investigation (for example, it is virtually impossible for a subject to report concurrently on listening) or on the kind of data that a researcher wishes to obtain. Concurrent report provides clearer, and often more detailed, insights; however, the act of reporting may distort the natural process of (say) reading or writing. One solution is to ask subjects to pause at regular intervals and to report what is uppermost in their mind; another is to leave them free to report when they feel they have encountered a problem or a potential solution.

Although the method provides useful insights into **on-line processing**, it has some drawbacks. What is reported may vary considerably from subject to subject, according to the importance attached to different aspects of the process. Subjects tend to describe processes as rather more systematic than they actually are; while some subjects lack the necessary *metalanguage* to analyse their experience accurately.

See also: **Research methods: experimental**

Further reading: Ericsson and Simon (1993)

VERBAL TRANSFORMATION EFFECT (VTE)

An effect which occurs when the same word is repeated over and over again to a listener for a period of several minutes. The subject reports hearing words phonologically similar to the one being spoken. The longer the experiment continues, the greater the number of variants that are reported. The subject may also report that the word appears to have lost its meaning: to have become like a non-word to which **lexical access** cannot be gained. This effect of *semantic satiation* may be due to accessing the lexicon repeatedly (and automatically) each time the word is heard.

The VTE does not seem to occur when it is the subject who is repeating a word. But it does when a subject listens to a recording of their own speech. This suggests important differences between speech perception and the **self-monitoring** that takes place during speaking.

VERBATIM RECALL

The ability to reproduce the exact words used in an utterance. Accurate verbatim recall is relatively short-lived, with auditory input decaying faster than visual. After a brief interval, subjects are able to report the propositional content of a sentence they have just heard or read, but find it difficult to reproduce its surface form. Presented with a paraphrase of the original, they may identify it as featuring the exact words which they encountered. They may also claim to recognise sentences containing inferences which they themselves have added and which were not present in the original utterance.

It thus appears that listeners and readers jettison surface form as soon as possible in favour of a more easily stored conceptual representation. Verbatim recall drops markedly at clause and sentence boundaries, suggesting that the process of packaging the signal into syntactic units takes place at these points. It may be that the actual words are no longer necessary once the syntactic unit has been constructed. Or it may be that syntactic processing places such heavy demands upon **working memory** that it has to abandon its verbatim record of the words.

There is evidence that the ability to recall exact wording is influenced by the nature of the message. Asked to identify utterances from an informal seminar 30 hours earlier, a group was quite accurate in recognising those which had a high *interactional* content in the form of humour, personal criticism etc.; but rarely correct when more *transactional* (i.e. neutral informative) information was involved. But note that this finding (like many others in this area) tests the ability to recognise utterances when they are repeated rather than the ability to recall the words unprompted.

Of course, there are many cases where individuals do indeed succeed in recalling long sequences of verbatim text: for example, actors learning lines or Muslim children studying the Koran. The important factor here seems to be that the task focuses attention specifically on verbatim content rather than on general meaning. Recall of the exact words of a passage is more accurate when subjects are advised in advance that they will have a memory test.

Some commentators claim that we do not have a memory store for verbatim language. They suggest that, when necessary, we reconstruct (*regenerate*) the wording of a message by identifying words in the lexicon which have been encountered recently and thus retain some residual level of **activation**. Our ability to do this comes to an end once the activation has finally decayed. Support for regeneration theory comes from evidence that a recently activated word is sometimes substituted for another that is close in meaning.

There is evidence that subjects recall function words less accurately than lexical ones. This may be because functors receive less attention during processing than lexical words or because they are stored and processed separately. On the other hand, the finding is also consistent with a regeneration account. Many functors occur very frequently.

Their activation is therefore less likely to be noticed. Or it may be that the difference between their activated and non-activated state is relatively small, due to their high probability of occurrence.

See also: **Rehearsal, Syntactic parsing, Wrap up effects**

Further reading: Potter and Lombardi (1990); Singer (1990: 41–7)

VOCABULARY ACQUISITION

The construction of a system of vocabulary by a child as part of the process of acquiring a first language. Research studies the increase in vocabulary size and the rate at which it occurs. It also examines the underlying semantic development: for example, the way in which the child learns to form *conceptual categories* and the way in which meaning associations are built up between the words that are acquired.

The child first has to recognise the word as a linguistic unit, since there are few gaps between words in connected speech. Their attention may be drawn to the existence of syllables, which are identifiable by *steady-state* periods (i.e. vowels) at the centre of each. They then notice and store recurrent chunks of language which are associated with a particular context. They gradually deconstruct these chunks, isolating perceptually salient sections and recurrent sub-sequences. This *holistic* learning style appears to be adopted by a majority of children; but a minority adopt a *localistic* style, in which they build individual words into chunks.

Late in its second year (though there is much variation), a child has mastered 50 to 100 words. It may understand four times more words than it produces; but it is also likely to produce certain words without fully understanding what they signify. The first 50 words tend to be mainly nouns, which are frequent in the speech of carers and easily matched to physical objects. However, this may depend upon **learning style**: a minority are said to acquire a wider range of word classes, especially verbs.

At some point, most children manifest a **vocabulary spurt**, where the rate of acquisition of new words increases suddenly and markedly. From then until about six years old, the average rate of acquisition is estimated to be five or more words a day. Many of the new words are verbs and adjectives, which gradually come to assume a larger proportion of the child's vocabulary. The vocabulary acquired during this period partly reflects frequency and relevance to the child's environment. **Basic level** terms are acquired first (DOG before

ANIMAL or SPANIEL), possibly reflecting a bias towards such terms in **child directed speech**.

The initial 'acquisition' of a word entails its use in a very limited range of contexts. It is only over an extended period of time that a child comes to recognise a word's full range of senses and comes to establish a system of associations between the word and other items in the lexicon.

Children appear to need minimal exposure to a new word form (sometimes just a single occurrence) before they assign some kind of meaning to it; this process of *rapid mapping* appears to help them to consolidate the form in their memory. In the early stages, mapping is exclusively from form to meaning; but it later also takes place from meaning to form, as children coin words to fill gaps in their vocabulary ('spooning my coffee'; 'cookerman' for a chef).

Four important issues arise:

☐ *Word-object relationship*. How does a child recognise, for example, that the word DOG refers to the whole animal rather than its tail and to a whole class of animals rather than to a specific exemplar? See **mapping**.

☐ *Concept formation*. The range of meaning first assigned to a word may not coincide exactly with the adult one, though it often overlaps with it. There is then a process in which the concept associated with a word is constantly adjusted as the child encounters more and more exemplars of it. Instances of **over-extension** or *under-extension* of the adult meaning are frequent.

☐ *Word associations*. Connected with concept formation, but less studied, are the relationships between words that the child builds. It needs, for example, to establish complex patterns which link words such as BIG and LARGE but which also differentiate them. Newly acquired words appear to be stored in a very systematic way, as is seen in substitution errors (e.g. the word *spoon* used instead of FORK).

☐ *Cognitive development*. A different line of research has examined the order in which items of vocabulary are acquired, and has attempted to match the findings to the child's cognitive development. The kind of cognitive constraints that need to be considered include attention span and memory as well as world knowledge and ability to handle concepts. Thus, the over-extension of items at the one-word stage may reflect the child's inability to separate object and event (*ball* = THROW) but may equally reflect processing limitations due to working memory.

See also: **Bootstrapping, Concept formation, Mapping, Over-
extension, Vocabulary spurt**

Further reading: Aitchison (2003: Chaps 16–17); Barrett (1995); Bloom (2000);
Clark (1993, 1995); Dromi (1999); Gleitman and Landau (1994); Griffiths (1986);
Kuczaj (1999); Neisser (1987); Tomasello and Bates (2001: Part II)

VOCABULARY SPURT (also VOCABULARY BURST, VOCABULARY EXPLOSION)

A sudden rapid increase in the vocabulary produced by a child, which
usually begins during the second half of the second year of life. At the
time the spurt occurs, the child usually has a productive vocabulary of
around 50 to 100 words; this may rise to as many as 350 to 500 over a
relatively short period of time. While many of the new words are
nouns, the spurt results in a much higher overall proportion of verbs
and adjectives in the child's vocabulary than before.

The precise cause of the spurt is unknown. One explanation is that
the child has suddenly become aware that language functions as a
symbolic system. This might take the form of a *naming insight*, where
the child comes to fully appreciate the link between objects and the
names attached to them. A second view links the spurt to
developments in cognition, particularly in the child's ability to
categorise objects. A third finds an explanation in the development of
the child's articulatory skill, while a fourth suggests that there may be
some kind of bottleneck which needs to be passed before referential
vocabulary can expand. This last view has been supported by evidence
from **connectionist** computer simulations of the learning of words,
which have manifested a spurt like that observed in real life.

However, no theory entirely fits the data, and the concept of a
vocabulary spurt remains somewhat controversial. One reason is that a
sudden increase in vocabulary is not universal. In some infants,
vocabulary develops in a series of short bursts; in some, the
development is gradual and continuous. It has also proved difficult
to pinpoint the moment at which, in a given child, the increase begins;
this would seem to cast doubt upon the theory of a sudden insight into
the nature of language. Finally, account has to be taken of the complex
relationship between comprehension and production; it may be that
many of the words that feature in the spurt have been 'acquired' much
earlier and stored for future use.

See also: **Learning style, Vocabulary acquisition**

Further reading: Bates *et al.* (1995: 103–7); Bloom (2000: Chap. 2); Clark (2003: 81–8); Dromi (1999)

VOCALISATION

The uttering of a stretch of sound. Sometimes, more narrowly, the use of the vocal cords to produce a voiced sound.

One type of human vocalisation is *reflexive* and, like the calls of many mammals, difficult to suppress. An example is laughter. By contrast, speech is *voluntary*. Though it is a highly automatic set of motor behaviours, it can be modified and turned on and off at will. This is possible because it is regulated by the *cortex* of the human brain. The calls of other species are mainly controlled by *subcortical* areas and are thus, like human laughter, difficult to inhibit. The cortical areas of most mammals do indeed control movement of the oral muscles; but the purpose is mainly to regulate eating and grooming.

At birth, the human *larynx* begins quite high, preventing food from entering the windpipe of the new-born child. It gradually moves downwards, however, to occupy a lower position than in other species. This enables us to produce a much wider range of sounds. The lowered larynx was not present in early *homo erectus*, suggesting that, if language existed at that stage of evolution, it was much more limited, particularly in the range of vowels.

Humans have a much greater degree of voluntary control over the sounds produced in the larynx than do other species. They also possess the ability to co-ordinate breathing and speaking. Separate systems control the reflexive behaviour involved in breathing and swallowing and the voluntary behaviour involved in the articulation of speech.

See also: **Articulation, Evolution of language**

Further reading: Deacon (1997); Lieberman (1998)

VOICE RECOGNITION

Human beings appear to have a remarkable capacity to store the voices of others in **long-term memory**, and to recognise them when they are heard again. This despite the fact that **verbatim recall** of a given utterance lasts a relatively short period of time. A single sentence appears to be sufficient for later recognition to occur; a longer utterance does not greatly increase the likelihood that a voice will be recognised. The recognition of familiar voices is extremely durable, and subjects have achieved an impressive 30 per cent accuracy in naming famous speakers who they have not heard for 50 years. However, recall of unfamiliar voices is much less reliable: after an hour, recognition may drop to 24 per cent and after 24 hours to zero. Voice recognition in legal evidence must thus be treated with caution.

See also: **Normalisation**

VYGOTSKYAN

The ideas of the Russian psychologist Lev Vygotsky (1896–1934) cover several areas:

☐ *Thought and language.* For Vygotsky, thought and language are mutually supportive. Thought exists prior to language, and there is initially a separation between the two; but, during three phases of language acquisition, their different functions become established:

- Phase 1: Before the age of two, pre-linguistic thought (action schemas and images) becomes linked to pre-intellectual language in the form of babbling. 'Thought becomes verbal and speech rational.'
- Phase 2: From two to seven, the child does not distinguish clearly between private thoughts and public conversation. Both are expressed externally in *egocentric speech*. Speech thus serves as a means of imposing patterns upon thought.
- Phase 3: From seven onwards, thought becomes internalised. The thinking aloud of the previous phase continues in the form of '*internal speech*', the voice in the head which plays a role in reading, in writing and in the **rehearsal** of items which need to be memorised.

☐ *Concept formation.* Vygotsky suggested that the way in which children learn to categorise the world around them followed three phases.

- Phase 1: The child puts together disparate objects in a heap to form a *syncretic* relationship. A group of objects is created at random; the group then becomes defined by its spatial proximity.
- Phase 2: The child begins to think in *complexes*, associations based upon concrete relationships between objects, rather than simply its own impressions. At this stage, Vygotsky identified what he terms a

chain complex: a child used QUAH (= quack) for a duck on a pond, then any liquid including milk, then a coin with an eagle on it, then any round coin-like object. Each new item that is added has something in common with a previous member of the category.

- Phase 3: The child moves from grouping objects on the basis of maximum similarity to grouping them on the basis of a single attribute (e.g. roundedness or flatness). When a trait (or *potential concept*) has been identified, it now becomes stable and established.

☐ *Cognitive and linguistic development*. Vygotsky saw human behaviour as closely related to the social environment in which it developed. He suggested that, for the developing child, there was always a potential area of skill and knowledge (a *Zone of Proximal Development* (ZPD)) just ahead of what it could currently achieve. Vygotsky argued that a child is enabled to enter the next ZPD as a result of communicative interaction with its carers, who provide step-by-step support for the learning process. The concept of a ZPD has been invoked in discussion of both first and second language acquisition.

See also: **Scaffolding, Social-interactionism, Thought and language**

Further reading: Vygotsky (1934/1962)

WILLIAMS SYNDROME

A genetic condition in which sufferers show signs of cognitive impairment, yet their language competence appears to be relatively unaffected. The symptoms are the reverse of those associated with **specific language impairment**, where individuals of normal intelligence fail to achieve full linguistic competence.

Williams sufferers are often talkative and highly gregarious. They exhibit major cognitive deficits in the form of poor problem-solving skills and impaired spatial reasoning, and may have IQs as low as 50. Yet their early vocabulary and speaking skills are rated as above average. They are often verbally adept at repeating information and telling stories; though they experience problems in analysing language at thematic level.

WS has been linked to imbalances in brain structure, with a reduction of some areas of the brain but a sparing of the *cerebellum* and *frontal lobes*. Some commentators cite the Syndrome as evidence of a dissociation between language and other cognitive abilities, and thus as support for the notion that language is a separate, **modular** faculty. An alternative view is that the intelligence of Williams sufferers is splintered in a manner that spares the processes most critical to language development.

See also: **Modularity₁, Savant, Specific language impairment**

Further reading: Bellugi *et al.* (1993); Deacon (1997)

WORD PRIMITIVE

The most basic form in which a word is represented in the mental lexicon. The major issue is whether derivational inflections like UN- or -NESS constitute word primitives and are thus stored in lexicon separately from the roots to which they are attached.

See also: **Morphology: storage**

WORKING MEMORY

A component of memory which holds short-term information for the purposes of performing a current process. It is distinguished from **long-term memory** (LTM), which stores information permanently or for long periods. The information in working memory may come from external sources (as with linguistic input that is being processed) or it may be retrieved from LTM and held temporarily for present use. The term 'working memory' is often preferred to **short-term memory** on the grounds that this component does not simply store information but also processes the information it holds.

Working memory (WM) is said to have *limited capacity*. It is limited (a) in terms of what it can store; and (b) in terms of the amount of processing it can undertake.

Limitations on storage capacity mean that it is under pressure:

- to *chunk* information (combining smaller units into larger ones). An eight-digit phone number is better remembered as 83-42-76-18 instead of 83427618;
- to shed *verbatim* information and replace it with abstract propositions (one complete idea instead of a number of words);
- to transfer important information to LTM before it decays.

Limitations on processing mean that complex tasks make heavy demands upon WM resources because they require high levels of attention. Syntactically complex sentences may even exceed our attentional capacity: hence the difficulty of processing a multiply-embedded sentence like *The man the cat the dog chased bit died*.

The limited capacity of WM explains the relevance of developing processes which are **automatic**. They make fewer demands upon WM than **controlled** processes, leaving capacity spare for other operations. A reader who is able to decode words automatically instead of painfully deciphering them has spare resources of attention to allocate to achieving a richer understanding of what is being read.

WM capacity varies between individuals. This may reflect

- how much information an individual is able to store;
- how rapidly information decays when held in an individual's store;
- how much information an individual is able to **rehearse** (repeat in the mind as a way of retaining it in memory).

The most detailed model of WM (Gathercole and Baddeley, 1993) consists of a *central executive* which determines how much attention to allocate to a particular processing task. It also co-ordinates activity within WM and controls the transfer of information from other parts of the cognitive system (including from LTM). The executive regulates two dependent components or *slave systems*, which are responsible for short-term processing and for maintaining material in memory. One, the *visuo-spatial sketchpad*, deals with non-verbal material which is visual or spatial in form. The other, the *phonological loop*, handles verbal information.

The phonological loop is able to briefly store a phonologically encoded record of spoken language. However, the store has a very limited capacity, and the traces decay quickly (in 1–2 seconds). If we wish to retain what we have heard, we have to make use of a *rehearsal mechanism* which enables us to review it in our minds, thus preventing the verbatim form of words from fading. Rehearsal involves subvocal repetition of the material; hence the 'voice in the head' that subjects sometimes report when doing a memorisation task. Its main role in speech processing appears to be to ensure that a listener retains the surface form of an utterance for long enough to *parse* it syntactically.

The second function of the rehearsal mechanism is to convert written words into phonological code. This enables them to be rehearsed and fed into the phonological store in the same way as spoken words. It may seem curious that visual words are not stored in the visuo–spatial sketchpad. However, there is considerable evidence of a phonological basis to the way written language is processed and committed to memory.

See also: **Attention, Automaticity, Embedded processes model, Long-term memory, Phonological working memory, Rehearsal**

Further reading: Gathercole and Baddeley (1993)

WRAP UP EFFECTS

Effects which mark the point at which the reader or listener constructs a higher-level *meaning representation* and no longer retains the verbatim form (the actual words) of a clause or sentence.

The clause appears to be an important unit of processing in reading and listening (and indeed in speaking and writing, where whole clauses are held in a **buffer** ready for production). When listeners are presented with two consecutive sentences, their ability to recall the actual words they have heard begins to decline at the end of the first sentence. It seems that henceforth the actual words are no longer available in **working memory**. It may be that the effort of imposing a syntactic structure on the string of words is so demanding that WM can no longer hold on to verbatim text as well. Or it may simply be that the words are no longer needed and efficiency demands that they be dropped.

Similar 'wrap up' effects have been demonstrated in reading. When subjects have to press a space bar in order to bring up the words of a text on a computer screen, they slow down at clause and sentence boundaries. The more clauses a sentence contains, the greater the slowdown at syntactic boundaries – suggesting that it takes longer to integrate each new chunk as the mental representation becomes more and more complex.

Note that sentence wrap up effects do not demonstrate that processing is delayed until the end of the clause. Processing takes place **on-line** (as the stimulus is received). Wrap up effects occur when it becomes necessary to impose a pattern on what has been processed.

See also: **Syntactic parsing, Verbatim recall**

Further reading: Singer (1990: 41–7)

WRITING

The writing process is usually represented as falling into a number of stages:

☐ *Macro-planning*. The writer assembles a set of ideas, drawing upon world knowledge. The writer establishes what the goal of the piece of writing is to be. This includes consideration of the target readership, of the *genre* of the text (earlier experience as a reader may assist) and of *style* (level of formality).

☐ *Organisation*. The writer provisionally organises the ideas, still in abstract form, (a) in relation to the text as a whole and (b) in relation to each other. The ideas are evaluated in terms of their relative importance, and decisions made as to their relative prominence in the text. The outcome may be a set of rough notes.

☐ *Micro-planning*. The writer shifts to a different level and begins to plan conceptually at sentence and paragraph level. There is constant reference back to two sets of criteria: to decisions made at earlier stages and to the way in which the text has progressed so far. Account is taken of the overall goals of the text; of the organisational plan and the direction in which the text is currently tending; and of the content of the immediately preceding sentence or paragraph. At this stage, the writer needs to give consideration to whether an individual piece of information is or is not shared with the reader (a) by virtue of shared world knowledge or (b) as a result of earlier mention in the text.

☐ *Translation*. The propositional content that has been assembled undergoes a process of conversion from abstract to linguistic form. The extent to which the exact language of the text is anticipated appears to vary from writer to writer and from task to task. At times, a fully formed sentence may be constructed. At times, the information to be stored appears to be in the more abbreviated form of key words, of a set of codes to lexical items not yet fully accessed or of a syntactic frame into which such retrieval codes have been inserted. The information is stored in a *writing buffer*, ensuring that, while executing the first part of the sentence, a writer is aware of how to complete it. The material in the buffer appears to be phonological in form. Hence the often-reported experience of a 'voice in the head' while writing. There are a number of possible explanations for this. It may be that a spoken trace is more robust than a written one. Or it may be that future content stored in phonological form is less likely to interfere with the process of putting words on to the page in visual form.

☐ *Execution.* The writer begins the physical process of writing. Moto-neural signals from the brain direct the hand and pen in making letter shapes which are so well practised that they and the between-letter movements that link them have become highly *automatised*. Writing with a keyboard operates similarly: a letter cue produces a highly automatised finger response. Finger movements are also stored in sets which represent regularly occurring sequences such as THE.

Mistakes of execution sometimes demonstrate that the material in the writing buffer is in phonological form. Up to 20 per cent of Slips of the Keyboard are phonologically related to the target word, with educated writers substituting, for example, *their* for *there* or even *28* for *20A*.

With experienced writers, it is sometimes execution that begins the whole writing process rather than prior planning. The experience of putting words on to a page or screen appears to trigger a kind of writing mode, which enables the writer to loop back into planning and organisation as the text develops.

☐ *Monitoring.* Self-monitoring while writing is a complex operation at many different levels. At the lowest, it involves checking the accuracy of spelling, punctuation and syntax. At a higher level, it involves examining the current sentence to see how clearly it reflects the writer's intentions and whether it fits into the developing argument structure of the text. Because monitoring is so demanding, it is subject to attentional constraints. Writers seem to focus on one level at a time. While actually producing text, heed might be paid to lower-level features, with higher-level ones reserved for a later editing stage.

☐ *Editing and revising.* Current views of writing treat the process as a recursive rather than a linear one, and place emphasis upon the importance of *drafting* and redrafting. After monitoring generally while writing, a writer will return to aspects of the text which he/she feels to be unsatisfactory and revise them. The intervention may come after a sentence, after a paragraph or after the whole text has been written. Particular consideration is given to rhetorical issues, not least whether an appropriate degree of formality has been achieved. Studies of redrafting by skilled writers suggest that many of the revisions that are made are at lexical level and represent adjustments to ensure that the right tone is set for the target reader. Monitoring, editing and revising are thus feed-back processes which can impact upon any of the previous stages, causing the writer to revise a macro-plan, to reword translated text or to correct an error of execution.

The most quoted model of writing (Hayes and Flower) identifies two distinct components of the process which are external to it: the writer's long-term memory (including knowledge of topic, text type and reader) and the immediate *task environment*. The latter includes the *rhetorical problem* (consideration of topic, readership and current exigencies), which directs writing decisions. It also includes the text produced so far, against which writing decisions have to be matched

The Hayes and Flower model aims to give a general account of the writing process. However, it has been criticised for its apparent assumption that the process remains similar across different writers and across different writing tasks. In particular, it does not allow for the major differences that may exist between skilled and less-skilled writers.

See also: **Buffer, Inner speech, Typing, Writing: skilled, Writing system**

Further reading: Bereiter and Scardamalia (1987); Hayes and Flower (1980); Kellogg (1994)

WRITING: SKILLED

Studies have suggested that less-skilled writers pay less attention to higher-level operations – i.e. to the planning and monitoring aspects of text production. They produce less elaborated pre-writing notes, they concern themselves primarily with generating text rather than making time to consider goals and rhetorical implications; and they are often unable to handle major revisions of a text which involve reorganising content.

This has given rise to a distinction (Bereiter and Scardamalia) between two different types of writing. In *knowledge-telling*, less-skilled or less-experienced writers confine themselves to identifying what they know of a topic and putting it down as it occurs to them. In effect, the first piece of information that is written down generates what comes next. The texts produced are coherent (the approach works well for narrative) but lacking in organisational structure. By contrast, in *knowledge-transforming*, a writer repeatedly reviews and reorganises material in a problem-solving way. Issues of content are identified, considered and resolved in a content *problem space* while problems with rhetoric (style, readership, etc.) are similarly dealt with in a rhetorical problem space.

Research into skilled writing has studied how children learn to co-ordinate and sequence the many components of the skill – in particular how they learn to store linguistic material before executing it. Early learners focus heavily on the process of forming letters, to the extent that they often mouth syllables as they write them. This would appear to leave few attentional resources for forward planning. However, after about two years, they begin to mouth whole strings of words, suggesting that forward planning is now an option. From the age of ten onwards, there is a close correlation between what children expect to write and what they actually produce. This suggests that they have acquired the capacity to co-ordinate planning and execution. Occasional adult-like errors of execution suggest that, when there are conflicting demands, a primary concern is to maintain words in the buffer rather than (as previously) focusing on form.

Further insights have been obtained by comparing the different processing demands of speech and writing. The child who begins to write has already developed an executive system which co-ordinates the different components of the speaking process. But this system is an interactive one which is heavily dependent upon *production signalling* in the form of responses by interlocutors. In acquiring writing, the child has to learn new procedures in which additional language is generated from the text itself rather than from outside prompting.

See also: **Buffer, Orthography, Writing, Writing system**

Further reading: Bereiter and Scardamalia (1987); Kellogg (1994); Scardamalia and Bereiter (1987)

WRITING SYSTEM

A method of representing language visually. Three main types of writing system are used by the world's languages, though no language's orthography provides an exact example of one of these systems.

- *alphabets*: with a symbol for each phoneme of the language;
- *syllabaries*: with a symbol for each syllable of the language;
- *logographic systems*: with a symbol for each word of the language.

The first two are based upon the phonology of the language, and the third upon the language's lexical system. However, it is not necessarily true that writing in a logographic script involves a direct mapping from a concept to a word shape. For example, about 90 per cent of Chinese characters consist of two parts: a radical followed by a phonetic element. It seems likely that, when recalling a character, a Mandarin writer is influenced in part at least by the phonology of the word. Furthermore, any mainland Chinese writer educated from 1958 onwards has some phonological awareness through having done their first writing in *pinyin*, a phonemic representation of Mandarin based upon the Roman alphabet.

Is the process of employing a logographic system different in psychological terms from that of employing a phonologically based one? Japanese has a mixed orthography, with lexical items written in logographic *kanji* characters but inflections and function words written in simpler *kana* characters which represent syllables. Evidence suggests that the two systems do involve two different types of processing. In cases of senile dementia, the ability to produce *kanji* characters is usually lost well before the ability to produce *kana*. This may mean that the phonologically based *kana* is the more robust; but it may simply reflect the fact that Japanese children acquire *kana* characters first.

Clearly a logographic system makes great demands on the writer's memory store – though apparently Chinese writers can manage with a minimum of only about 2000 characters. With a phonological system, a writer has the advantage of a prior knowledge of the spoken word, from which spellings can sometimes be guessed. However, at a pre-literate stage, children may not be sensitive to the individual sounds which make up the words in their language. Evidence from adult Portuguese illiterates suggests that we only learn to recognise the individual phonemes of our language as a result of learning an alphabet.

An interesting case is presented by an alphabetic script such as Arabic which depends chiefly upon the representation of consonants. Part of the writer's representation must take the form of semantic links between words, since the same letter string represents: 'books', 'he wrote' and 'it is written'. A consonantal system of this kind is clearly fast in execution, since not all sounds are represented; but it is a system that throws up ambiguities which the reader has to resolve by reference to context.

See also: **Grapheme–phoneme correspondence rules, Graphotactic rules, Orthography**

Further reading: Coulmas (1989); Harris and Coltheart (1986)

ZIPF'S LAW

A finding (Zipf, 1935) that any piece of text will contain a very small number of high-frequency word forms and a large number of low-frequency word forms. A second observation was that words with higher text frequency are shorter in length.

BIBLIOGRAPHY

BACKGROUND READING

General

Altmann, G. (1997) *The Ascent of Babel*, Oxford: Oxford University Press.
Field, J. (2003) *Psycholinguistics: A Resource Book for Students*, London: Routledge.
Libben, G. (1996) 'Psycholinguistics: The Study of Language Processing', in W. O'Grady, M. Dobrovolsky and F. Katamba (eds), *Contemporary Linguistics: An Introduction*, London: Longman, pp. 438–63.
Whitney, P. (1998) *The Psychology of Language*, Boston, MA: Houghton Mifflin.

Specific

Aitchison, J. (1998) *The Articulate Mammal*, 4th edn, London: Routledge.
—— (2003) *Words in the Mind*, 2nd edn, Oxford: Blackwell.
Baddeley, A. (1982) *Your Memory: A User's Guide*, London: Sidgwick & Jackson.
Cattell, R. (2000) *Children's Language: Consensus and Controversy*, London: Cassell.
Chiat, S. (2000) *Understanding Children with Language Problems*, Cambridge: Cambridge University Press.
Dobrovolsky, M. (1996) 'Animal Communication', in W. O'Grady, M. Dobrovolsky and F. Katamba (eds), *Contemporary Linguistics: An Introduction*, London: Longman, pp. 625–63.
Ellis, A.W. (1993) *Reading, Writing and Dyslexia: A Cognitive Analysis*, Hove: Psychology Press.
Foster-Cohen, S. (1999) *An Introduction to Child Language Development*, Harlow: Longman.
Hale, S. (2003) *The Man who Lost his Language*, London: Penguin.
Henderson, J. (1999) *Memory and Forgetting*, London: Routledge.
Kellogg, R.T. (1995) *Cognitive Psychology*, London: Sage Publications.
Lieberman, P. (1998) *Eve Spoke*, London: Picador.
Oakhill, J. and Beard, R. (eds) (1999) *Reading Development and the Teaching of Reading*, Oxford: Blackwell.
Obler, L.K. and Gjerlow, K. (1999) *Language and the Brain*, Cambridge: Cambridge University Press.
Pinker, S. (1994) *The Language Instinct*, London: Penguin.
Smith, N. (1999) *Chomsky: Ideas and Ideals*, Cambridge: Cambridge University Press.
Ungerer, F. and Schmid, H.J. (1996) *An Introduction to Cognitive Linguistics*, London: Longman.

REFERENCES

Aitchison, J. (1996) *The Seeds of Speech: Language Origin and Evolution*, Cambridge: Cambridge University Press.

—— (1998) *The Articulate Mammal*, 4th edn, London: Routledge.

—— (2003) *Words in the Mind*, 2nd edn, Oxford: Blackwell.

Altmann, G. (1990) 'Lexical Statistics and Cognitive Models of Speech Processing', in G. Altmann (ed.), *Cognitive Models of Speech Processing: Psycholinguistic and Computational Perspectives*, Cambridge, MA: MIT Press, pp. 211–35.

—— (1997) *The Ascent of Babel*, Oxford: Oxford University Press.

Anderson, J.R. (1983) *The Architecture of Cognition*, Cambridge, MA: Harvard University Press.

—— (1990) *Cognitive Psychology and its Implications*, New York: W.H. Freeman.

Archibald, J. (1996) 'Second Language Acquisition', in W. O'Grady, M. Dobrovolsky and F. Katamba (eds), *Contemporary Linguistics: An Introduction*, London: Longman, pp. 503–39.

Baddeley, A. (1982) *Your Memory: A User's Guide*, London: Sidgwick & Jackson.

—— (1997) *Human Memory: Theory and Practice*, Hove: Psychology Press.

Ball, M.J. and Rahilly, J. (1999) *Phonetics: The Science of Speech*, London: Arnold.

Balota, D. (1994) 'Visual Word Recognition: The Journey from Features to Meaning', in M.A. Gernsbacher (ed.), *Handbook of Psycholinguistics*, San Diego, CA: Academic Press, pp. 303–58.

Baron-Cohen, S., Leslie, A.M. and Frith, U. (1985) 'Does the Autistic Child Have a "Theory of Mind"?', *Cognition*, 21: 37–46.

Barrett, M. (1995) 'Early Lexical Development', in P. Fletcher and B. MacWhinney (eds), *The Handbook of Child Language*, Oxford: Blackwell, pp. 362–92.

Bartlett, F.C. (1932) *Remembering*, Cambridge: Cambridge University Press.

Bates, E., Dale, P.S. and Thal, D. (1995) 'Individual Differences and their Implications for Theories of Language Development', in P. Fletcher and B. MacWhinney (eds), *The Handbook of Child Language*, Oxford: Blackwell, pp. 96–151.

Bates, E. and Goodman, J.C. (1999) 'On the Emergence of Grammar from the Lexicon', in B. MacWhinney (ed.), *The Emergence of Language*, Mahwah, NJ: Erlbaum.

Bates, E. and MacWhinney, B. (1982) 'Functionalist Approaches to Grammar', in E. Wanner and L. Gleitman (eds), *Language Acquisition: The State of the Art*, Cambridge: Cambridge University Press, pp 173–218.

Becker, C.A. (1979) 'Semantic Context and Word Frequency Effects in Visual Word Recognition', *Journal of Experimental Psychology: Human Perception and Performance*, 5: 252–9.

Bellugi, U., Marks, S., Bihrle, A. and Sabo, H. (1993) 'Dissociation Between Language and Cognitive Functions in Williams Syndrome', in D. Bishop and K. Mogford (eds), *Language Development in Exceptional Circumstances*, Hove: Psychology Press, pp. 177–189.

Bereiter, C. and Scardamalia, M. (1987) *The Psychology of Written Composition*, Hillsdale, NJ: Erlbaum.

Berlin, B. and Kay, P. (1969) *Basic Color Terms: Their Universality and Evolution*, Berkeley, CA: University of California Press.

Bhatia, T.K. and Ritchie, W.C. (1996) 'The Bilingual Child: Some Issues and

Perspectives', in W.C. Ritchie and T.K. Bhatia (eds), *Handbook of Second Language Acquisition*, San Diego, CA: Academic Press, pp. 569–645.

Bialystok, E. (1990) *Communication Strategies*, Oxford: Blackwell.

Bickerton, D. (1990) *Language and Species*, Chicago, IL: University of Chicago Press.

Birdsong, S. (ed.) (1999) *Second Language Acquisition and the Critical Period Hypothesis*, Mahwah, NJ: Erlbaum.

Bishop, D. and Mogford, K. (eds) (1993) *Language Development in Exceptional Circumstances*, Hove: Psychology Press.

Bishop, D.V.M. (1997) *Uncommon Understanding: Development and Disorders of Language Comprehension in Children*, Hove: Psychology Press.

Bloom, L. (1973) *One Word at a Time*, The Hague: Mouton.

Bloom, P. (2000) *How Children Learn the Meanings of Words*, Cambridge, MA: MIT Press.

—— (2001) 'Roots of Word Learning', in M. Bowerman and S.C. Levinson (eds), *Language Acquisition and Conceptual Development*, Cambridge: Cambridge University Press, pp. 159–181.

Boden, M.A. (1979) *Piaget*, London: Fontana.

Bond, Z. (1999) *Slips of the Ear: Errors in the Perception of Casual Conversation*, San Diego, CA: Academic Press.

Bonvillian, J.D. (1999) 'Sign Language Development', in M. Barrett (ed.), *The Development of Language*, Hove: Psychology Press, pp. 277–310.

Bowerman, M. and Levinson, S.C. (eds) (2001) *Language Acquisition and Conceptual Development*, Cambridge: Cambridge University Press.

Braine, M.D.S. (1963) 'The Ontogeny of English Phrase Structure: The First Phase', *Language*, 39: 1–13.

Brown, G. (1990) *Listening to Spoken English*, 2nd edn, Harlow: Longman.

—— (1995) *Speakers, Listeners and Communication*, Cambridge: Cambridge University Press.

Brown, G. and Yule, G. (1983) *Discourse Analysis*, Cambridge: Cambridge University Press.

Brown, R. (1973) *A First Language: The Early Stages*, Cambridge, MA: Harvard University Press.

Bruner, J. (1983) 'The Acquisition of Pragmatic Commitments', in R.M. Golinkoff (ed.), *The Transition from Prelinguistic to Linguistic Communication*, Hillsdale, NJ: Erlbaum, pp. 27–42.

—— (1985) *Child's Talk: Learning to Use Language*, New York: Norton.

Burgess, A. (1962) *A Clockwork Orange*, New York: W.W. Norton.

Bybee, J. (2001) *Phonology and Language Use*, Cambridge: Cambridge University Press.

Cacciari, C. and Glucksberg, S. (1994) 'Understanding Figurative Language', in M.A. Gernsbacher (ed.), *Handbook of Psycholinguistics*, San Diego, CA: Academic Press, pp. 447–78.

Caplan, D. (1992) *Language: Structure, Processing and Disorders*, Cambridge, MA: MIT Press.

Carroll, D.W. (1999) *Psychology of Language*, 3rd edn, Pacific Grove, CA: Brooks Cole.

Cattell, R. (2000) *Children's Language: Consensus and Controversy*, London: Cassell.

Chiat, S. (2000) *Understanding Children with Language Problems*, Cambridge: Cambridge University Press.

Chomsky, N. (1959) 'Review of Skinner's *Verbal Behavior*', *Language*, 35: 26–58.

—— (1965) *Aspects of the Theory of Syntax*, Cambridge, MA: MIT Press

—— (1986) *Knowledge of Language: Its Nature, Origin and Use*, New York: Praeger.

Clark, E. (1993) *The Lexicon in Acquisition*, Cambridge: Cambridge University Press.

—— (1995) 'Later Lexical Development and Word Formation', in P. Fletcher and B. MacWhinney (eds), *The Handbook of Child Language*, Oxford: Blackwell, pp. 393–412.

—— (2001) 'Emergent Categories in First Language Acquisition', in M. Bowerman and S.C. Levinson (eds), *Language Acquisition and Conceptual Development*, Cambridge: Cambridge University Press, pp. 379–405.

—— (2003) *First Language Acquisition*, Cambridge: Cambridge University Press.

Clark, J. and Yallop, C. (1990) *An Introduction to Phonetics and Phonology*, Oxford: Blackwell.

Cohen, A. (1998) *Strategies in Learning and Using a Second Language*, Harlow: Longman.

Cohen, G. (1989) *Memory in the Real World*, Hove: Erlbaum.

Cohen, G., Kiss, G. and Le Voi, M. (1993) *Memory: Current Issues*, Buckingham: Open University.

Collins, A.M. and Loftus, E.F. (1975) 'A Spreading-Activation Theory of Semantic Processing', *Psychological Review*, 82: 407–28.

Collins, A.M. and Quillian, M.R. (1969) 'Retrieval Time from Semantic Memory', *Journal of Verbal Learning and Verbal Behavior*, 8: 240–7.

Cook, V. and Newson, M. (1996) *Chomsky's Universal Grammar: An Introduction*, 2nd edn, Oxford: Blackwell.

Coulmas, F. (1989) *The Writing Systems of the World*, Oxford: Blackwell.

Cowan, N. (1999) 'An Embedded-Processes Model of Working Memory', in A. Miyake and P. Shah (eds), *Models of Working Memory*, Cambridge: Cambridge University Press.

Craik, F.J. and Lockhart, R.S. (1972) 'Levels of Processing: A Framework for Memory Research', *Journal of Verbal Learning and Verbal Behavior*, 11: 671–84.

Crain, S. and Lillo-Martin, D. (1999) *An Introduction to Linguistic Theory and Language Acquisition*, Oxford: Blackwell.

Cruttenden, A. (1986) *Intonation*, Cambridge: Cambridge University Press.

Crystal, D. (1997) *A Dictionary of Linguistics and Phonetics*, 4th edn, Oxford: Blackwell.

Crystal, D. and Varley, R. (1999) *Introduction to Language Pathology*, 4th edn, London: Whurr.

Curtiss, S. (1977) *Genie: A Psycholinguistic Study of a Modern-day 'Wild Child'*, London: Academic Press.

Cutler, A. (1989) 'Auditory Lexical Access: Where Do We Start?', in W. Marslen-Wilson (ed.), *Lexical Representation and Process*, Cambridge, MA: MIT Bradford, pp. 342–56.

—— (1990) 'Exploiting Prosodic Possibilities', in G. Altmann (ed.), *Cognitive Models of Speech Processing: Psycholinguistic and Computational Perspectives*, Cambridge, MA: MIT Press, pp. 105–121.

—— (1996) 'Prosody and the Word Boundary Problem', in J.L. Morgan and K. Demuth (eds), *Signal to Syntax*, Mahwah, NJ: Erlbaum, pp. 87–99.

Cutler, A. and Mehler, J. (1993) 'The Periodicity Bias', *Journal of Phonetics*, 21: 103–8.

Dalton, P. and Hardcastle, W.J. (1989) *Disorders of Fluency*, 2nd edn, London: Whurr.

Daneman, M. and Carpenter, P.A. (1980) 'Individual Differences in Working Memory and Reading', *Journal of Verbal Learning and Verbal Behavior*, 19: 450–66.

De Houwer, A. (1995) 'Bilingual Language Acquisition', in P. Fletcher and B. MacWhinney (eds), *The Handbook of Child Language*, Oxford: Blackwell.

Deacon, T. (1997) *The Symbolic Species*, London: Penguin.

Denes, P.B. and Pinson, E.N. (1993) *The Speech Chain: The Physics and Biology of Spoken Language*, 2nd edn, New York: W.H. Freeman.

Derwing, B.L. and Baker, W.J. (1986) 'Assessing Morphological Development', in P. Fletcher and M. Garman (eds), *Language Acquisition*, 2nd edn, Cambridge: Cambridge University Press, pp. 326–338.

Dingwall, W.O. (1998) 'The Biological Bases of Human Communicative Behavior', in J.B. Gleason and N.B. Ratner (eds), *Psycholinguistics*, 2nd edn, Fort Worth, TX: Harcourt Brace, pp. 51–105.

Dobrovolsky, M. (1996) 'Animal Communication', in W. O'Grady, M. Dobrovolsky and F. Katamba (eds), *Contemporary Linguistics: An Introduction*, London: Longman, pp. 625–63.

Donald, M. (1991) *Origins of the Modern Mind: Three Stages in the Evolution of Culture and Cognition*, Cambridge, MA: Harvard University Press.

Dromi, E. (1999) 'Early Lexical Development', in M. Barrett (ed.), *The Development of Language*, Hove: Psychology Press, pp. 99–131.

Eckman, F.R. (1977) 'Markedness and the Contrastive Analysis Hypothesis', *Language Learning*, 27: 37–53.

Ellis, A.W. (1993) *Reading, Writing and Dyslexia: A Cognitive Analysis*, Hove: Psychology Press.

Ellis, N. (ed.) (1994) *Implicit and Explicit Learning of Languages*, London: Academic Press.

Ellis, R. (1985) *Understanding Second Language Acquisition*, Oxford: Oxford University Press.

—— (1994) *The Study of Second Language Acquisition*, Oxford: Oxford University Press.

Ellis, R. and Humphreys, G. (1999) *Connectionist Psychology: A Text with Readings*, Hove: Psychology Press.

Elman, J.L., Bates, E.A., Johnson, M.H., Karmiloff-Smith, A., Parisi, D. and Plunkett, K. (1996) *Rethinking Innateness*, Cambridge, MA: Bradford MIT Press.

Ericsson, K.A. and Simon, H.A. (1993) *Protocol Analysis: Verbal Reports as Data*, 2nd edn, Cambridge, MA: MIT Press.

Faerch, C. and Kasper, G. (eds) (1983) *Strategies in Interlanguage Communication*, Harlow: Longman.

Fay, W.H. (1993) 'Infantile Autism', in D. Bishop and K. Mogford (eds), *Language Development in Exceptional Circumstances*, Hove: Psychology Press, pp. 190–202.

Fitzpatrick, J. and Wheeldon, L.R. (2000) 'Phonology and Phonetics in Psycholinguistic Models of Speech Perception', in N. Burton-Roberts, P. Carr and G. Docherty (eds), *Phonological Knowledge: Conceptual and Empirical Issues*, Oxford: Oxford University Press, pp. 131–59.

Fletcher, P. (1999) 'Specific Language Impairment', in M. Barrett (ed.), *The Development of Language*, Hove: Psychology Press, pp. 349–371.

Fletcher, P. and Garman, M. (eds) (1986) *Language Acquisition*, 2nd edn, Cambridge: Cambridge University Press.

Fletcher, P. and MacWhinney, B. (eds) (1995) *The Handbook of Child Language*, Oxford: Blackwell.

Fodor, J. (1983) *The Modularity of Mind*, Cambridge, MA: MIT Press.

Forster, K.I. (1979) 'Levels of Processing and the Structure of the Language Processor', in W.E. Cooper and E.C.T. Walker (eds), *Sentence Processing: Psycholinguistic Studies Presented to Merrill Garrett*, Hillsdale, NJ: Erlbaum.

Forster, K. (1990) 'Lexical Processing', in D.N. Oscherson and H. Lasnik (eds), *An Invitation to Cognitive Science, Vol. 1: Language*, Cambridge, MA: MIT Press, pp. 95–131.

Foster, S.H. (1990) *The Communicative Competence of Young Children*, Harlow: Longman.

Foster-Cohen, S. (1999) *An Introduction to Child Language Development*, Harlow: Longman.

Fromkin, V. (ed.) (1973) *Speech Errors as Linguistic Evidence*, The Hague: Mouton.

—— (ed.) (1980) *Errors in Linguistic Performance: Slips of the Tongue, Ear, Pen and Hand*, New York: Academic Press.

Fry, D.B. (1979) *The Physics of Speech*, Cambridge: Cambridge University Press.

Gallaway, C. and Richards, B. (eds) (1994) *Input and Interaction in Language Acquisition*, Cambridge: Cambridge University Press.

Gallaway, C. and Woll, B. (1994) 'Interaction and Childhood Deafness', in C. Gallaway and B. Richards (eds), *Input and Interaction in Language Acquisition*, Cambridge: Cambridge University Press, pp. 197–218.

Ganong, W.F. (1980) 'Phonetic Categorization in Auditory Word Perception', *Journal of Experimental Psychology: Human Perception and Performance*, 6: 110–25.

Garman, M. (1990) *Psycholinguistics*, Cambridge: Cambridge University Press.

Garnes, S. and Bond, Z.S. (1976) 'The Relationship Between Semantic Expectation and Acoustic Information', in W. Dressler and O. Pfeiffer (eds), *Proceedings of the Third International Phonology Meeting*, Innsbruck: Phonologische Tagung.

Garnham, A. (1985) *Psycholinguistics: Central Topics*, London: Routledge.

Garnham, A. and Oakhill, J. (1994) *Thinking and Reasoning*, Oxford: Blackwell.

Garrett, M.F. (1988) 'Processes in Language Production', in F.J. Newmeyer (ed.), *Linguistics: The Cambridge Survey III: Psychological and Biological Aspects*, Cambridge: Cambridge University Press, pp. 69–96.

Garrod, S.C. and Sanford, A.J. (1994) 'Resolving Sentences in a Discourse Context: How Discourse Representation Affects Language Understanding', in M.A. Gernsbacher (ed.), *Handbook of Psycholinguistics*, San Diego, CA: Academic Press, pp. 675–98.

Gass, S.M. and Selinker, L. (1994) *Second Language Acquisition: An Introductory Course*, Hillsdale, NJ: Erlbaum.

Gathercole, S.E. and Baddeley, A. (1993) *Working Memory and Language*, Hove: Erlbaum.

Gerken, L.A. (1994) 'A Metrical Template Account of Children's Weak Syllable Omissions from Multisyllabic Words', *Journal of Child Language*, 21: 565–84.

Gernsbacher, M.A. (1990) *Language Comprehension as Structure Building*, Hillsdale, NJ: Erlbaum.

—— (ed.) (1994) *Handbook of Psycholinguistics*, San Diego, CA: Academic Press.

Gernsbacher, M.A. and Foertsch, J.A. (1999) 'Three Models of Discourse

Comprehension', in S. Garrod and M. Pickering (eds), *Language Processing*, Hove: Psychology Press, pp. 283–99.

Giles, H. and Coupland, J. (eds) (1991) *The Contexts of Accommodation: Dimensions of Applied Sociolinguistics*, Cambridge: Cambridge University Press.

Gimson, A.C. (1994) *An Introduction to the Pronunciation of English*, London: Arnold.

Gleitman, L.R. (1990) 'The Structural Sources of Verb Meanings', *Language Acquisition*, 1: 3–35.

Gleitman, L. and Landau, B. (eds) (1994) *The Acquisition of the Lexicon*, Cambridge, MA: MIT Press.

Glenberg, A.M., Kruley, P. and Langston, W.E. (1994) 'Analogical Processes in Comprehension: Simulation of a Mental Model', in M.A. Gernsbacher (ed.), *Handbook of Psycholinguistics*, San Diego, CA: Academic Press, pp. 609–40.

Glushko, R.J. (1979) 'The Organization and Activation of Orthographic Knowledge in Reading Aloud', *Journal of Experimental Psychology: Human Perception and Performance*, 5: 674–91.

Gold, R.M. (1967) 'Language Identification in the Limit', *Information and Control*, 16: 447–74.

Goldsmith, J. (1995) 'Phonological Theory', in J. Goldsmith (ed.), *A Handbook of Phonological Theory*, Oxford: Blackwell.

Golinkoff, R.M., Hirsh-Pasek, K. and Hollich, G. (1999) 'Emerging Cues for Early Word Learning', in B. MacWhinney (ed.), *The Emergence of Language*, Mahwah, NJ: Erlbaum.

Goodman, J.C. and Nusbaum, H.C. (eds) (1994) *The Development of Speech Perception: The Transition from Speech Sounds to Spoken Words*, Cambridge, MA: MIT Press.

Goodman, K. (1967) 'Reading: A Psycholinguistic Guessing Game', *Journal of the Reading Specialist*, 6: 126–35.

Gopnik, M. (1990) 'Feature Blindness: A Case Study', *Language Acquisition*, 1: 139–64.

Gopnik, M., Dalakis, J., Fukuda, S.E. and Fukuda, S. (1997) 'Familial Language Impairment', in M. Gopnik (ed.), *The Inheritance and Innateness of Grammars*, New York: Oxford University Press, pp. 111–40.

Goswami, U. (1999) 'Phonological Development and Reading by Analogy: Epilinguistic and Metalinguistic Issues', in J. Oakhill and R. Beard (eds), *Reading Development and the Teaching of Reading*, Oxford: Blackwell, pp. 174–200.

Goswami, U. and Bryant, P. (1990) *Phonological Skills and Learning to Read*, Hove: Erlbaum.

Gough, P.B. and Wren, S. (1999) 'Constructing Meaning: The Role of Decoding', in J. Oakhill and R. Beard (eds), *Reading Development and the Teaching of Reading*, Oxford: Blackwell, pp 59–78.

Greenberg, J.H. (1966) 'Some Universals of Grammar with Particular Reference to the Order of Meaningful Elements', in J.H. Greenberg (ed.), *Universals of Language*, 2nd edn, Cambridge, MA: MIT Press, pp. 73–113.

Greene, J. (1975) *Thinking and Language*, London: Methuen.

—— (1986) *Language Understanding: A Cognitive Approach*, Part I, Milton Keynes: Open University.

Grice, H.P. (1975) 'Logic and Conversation', in P. Cole and J.L Morgan (eds), *Syntax and Semantics 3: Speech Acts*, New York: Academic Press, pp. 41–58.

Griffiths, P. (1986) 'Early Vocabulary', in P. Fletcher and M. Garman (eds), *Language Acquisition*, 2nd edn, Cambridge: Cambridge University Press.

Grosjean, F. (1980) 'Spoken Word-Recognition Processes and the Gating Paradigm', *Perception and Psychophysics*, 28: 267–83.

—— (1982) *Life with Two Languages: An Introduction to Bilingualism*, Cambridge: Cambridge University Press.

—— (1985) 'The Recognition of Words After Their Acoustic Offsets: Evidence and Implications', *Perceptions and Psychophysics*, 34 (4): 299–310.

—— (1996) 'Gating', *Language and Cognitive Processes*, 11: 597–604.

Grosjean, F. and Frauenfelder, U. (eds) (1996) 'A Guide to Spoken Word Recognition Paradigms', *Language and Cognitive Processes*, 11: 553–699.

Grosjean, F. and Gee, J. (1987) 'Prosodic Structure and Spoken Word Recognition', *Cognition*, 25: 135–55.

Hale, S. (2003) *The Man who Lost his Language*, London: Penguin.

Halliday, M.A.K. (1975) *Learning How to Mean: Explorations in the Development of Language*, London: Arnold.

Hamilton, H. (1994) *Conversations with an Alzheimer's Patient*, Cambridge: Cambridge University Press.

Hansen, L. (2001) 'Language Attrition: The Fate of the Start', *Annual Review of Applied Linguistics*, 21, pp. 60–73.

Harley, T. (2001) *The Psychology of Language*, 2nd edn, Hove: Psychology Press.

Harris, M. and Coltheart, M. (1986) *Language Processing in Children and Adults*, London: Routledge & Kegan Paul.

Hawkins, S. (1999) 'Looking for Invariant Correlates of Linguistic Units: Two Classical Theories of Speech Perception', in J.M. Pickett (ed.), *The Acoustics of Speech Communication*, Needham Heights, MA: Allyn & Bacon, pp. 198–231.

Hayes, J.R. and Flower, L.S. (1980) 'Identifying the Organization of Writing Processes', in L.W. Gregg and E.R. Steinberg (eds), *Cognitive Processes in Writing*, Hillsdale, NJ: Erlbaum, pp. 3–30.

Henderson, J. (1999) *Memory and Forgetting*, London: Routledge.

Hintzman, D.L. (1986) 'Schema Abstraction in a Multiple-Trace Memory Model', *Psychological Review*, 93: 411–28.

Hockett, C.F. (1963) 'The Problem of Universals in Language', in J.H. Greenberg (ed.), *Universals of Language*, Cambridge, MA: MIT Press.

Hoffmann, C. (1991) *An Introduction to Bilingualism*, London: Longman.

Horwitz, E.K. and Young, D.J. (1991) *Language Anxiety*, Englewood Cliffs, NJ: Prentice Hall.

Hotopf, W.N. (1983) 'Lexical Slips of the Pen and Tongue: What They Tell Us About Language Production', in B. Butterworth (ed.), *Language Production. Vol. II: Development, Writing and Other Language Processes*, London: Academic Press.

Hurford, J.R., Studdert-Kennedy, M. and Knight, C. (eds) (1998) *Approaches to the Evolution of Language*, Cambridge: Cambridge University Press.

Ingram, D. (1989) *First Language Acquisition*, Cambridge: Cambridge University Press.

—— (1999) 'Phonological Acquisition', in M. Barrett (ed.), *The Development of Language*, Hove: Psychology Press, pp. 73–97.

Jackendoff, R. (1987) *Consciousness and the Computational Mind*, Cambridge, MA: MIT Press.

Johnson, K. and Mullenix, J.W. (1997) *Talker Variability in Speech Processing*, San Diego, CA: Academic Press.

Johnson-Laird, P. (1983) *Mental Models*, Cambridge, MA: Harvard University Press.

Jusczyk, P. (1997) *The Discovery of Spoken Language*, Cambridge, MA: MIT Press.

Just, M.A. and Carpenter, P.A. (1987) *The Psychology of Reading and Language Comprehension*, Newton, MA: Allyn & Bacon.

Kahneman, D. (1973) *Attention and Effort*, Englewood Cliffs, NJ: Prentice Hall.

Kasper, G. and Kellerman, E. (1997) *Communication Strategies*, Harlow: Longman.

Katz, J.J. and Fodor, J.A. (1963) 'The Structure of a Semantic Theory', *Language*, 39: 170–210.

Keil, F.C. (1987) 'Conceptual Development and Category Structure', in U. Neisser (ed.), *Concepts and Conceptual Development*, Cambridge: Cambridge University Press.

Kellogg, R.T. (1994) *The Psychology of Writing*, New York: Oxford University Press.

—— (1995) *Cognitive Psychology*, London: Sage Publications.

Kintsch, W. (1988) 'The Use of Knowledge in Discourse Processing: A Constructive-Integration Model', *Psychological Review*, 95: 163–82.

—— (1994) 'The Psychology of Discourse Processing', in M.A. Gernsbacher (ed.), *Handbook of Psycholinguistics*, San Diego, CA: Academic Press, pp. 721–40.

Klatt, D.H. (1986) 'The Problem of Variability in Speech Recognition and in Models of Speech Perception', in J. Perkell and D. Klatt (eds), *Invariance and Variability in Speech Processes*, Hillsdale, NJ: Erlbaum.

Klima, E.S. and Bellugi, U. (1979) *The Signs of Language*, Cambridge, MA: Harvard University Press.

Kolinsky, R. (1992) 'Conjunction Errors as a Tool for the Study of Perceptual Processing', in J. Alegria, D. Holender, J. Morais and M. Radeau (eds), *Analytic Approaches to Human Cognition*, Amsterdam: North Holland, pp. 133–49.

Kuczaj, S.A. II (1999) 'The Development of a Lexicon', in M. Barrett (ed.), *The Development of Language*, Hove: Psychology Press, pp. 133–159.

Labov, W. (1973) 'The Boundaries of Words and Their Meaning', in C-J.N. Bailey and R. Shuy (eds), *New Ways of Analyzing Variation in English*, Washington, DC: Georgetown University Press, pp. 340–373.

Landau, B. and Gleitman, L.R. (1985) *Language and Experience: Evidence from the Blind Child*, Cambridge, MA: Harvard University Press.

Laver, J. (1994) *Principles of Phonetics*, Cambridge: Cambridge University Press.

Lenneberg, E.H. (1967) *Biological Foundations of Language*, New York: Wiley.

Lesser, R. and Milroy, L. (1993) *Linguistics and Aphasia*, Harlow: Longman.

Levelt, W.J.M. (1989) *Speaking*, Cambridge, MA: MIT Press.

Libben, G. (1996) 'Brain and Language', in W. O'Grady, M. Dobrovolsky and F. Katamba (eds), *Contemporary Linguistics: An Introduction*, London: Longman, pp. 416–37.

Lieberman, P. (1998) *Eve Spoke*, London: Picador.

Luce, P.A. (1986) 'A Computational Analysis of Uniqueness Points in Auditory Word Recognition', *Perception and Psychophysics*, 39: 155–8.

Luce, P., Pisoni, D. and Goldinger, S. (1990) 'Similarity Neighbourhoods of Spoken Words', in G.T.M. Altmann (ed.), *Cognitive Models of Speech Processing: Psycholinguistic and Computational Perspectives*, Cambridge, MA: MIT Press, pp. 122–47.

Lund, N. (2001) *Attention and Pattern Recognition*, London: Routledge.

Lyons, J. (1970) *Chomsky*, London: Fontana.

Macnamara, J. (1969) 'How Can One Measure the Extent of One Person's Bilingual Proficiency?', in L. Kelly (ed.), *Description and Measurement of Bilingualism*, Toronto: University of Toronto Press.

Marcus, G.F. (1996) 'Why Do Children Say "Breaked"?', *Current Directions in Psychological Science*, 5: 81–5. Reprinted in D. Messer and J. Dockrell (eds) (1998) *Developmental Psychology: A Reader*, London: Arnold.

Markman, E.M. (1990) 'Constraints Children Place on Word Meanings', *Cognitive Science*, 14: 57–77.

—— (1994) 'Constraints on Word Meaning in Early Language Acquisition', *Lingua*, 92: 199–227. Reprinted in L. Gleitman and B. Landau (eds) (1994) *The Acquisition of the Lexicon*, Cambridge, MA: MIT Press.

Markman, E.M. and Hutchinson, J.E. (1984) 'Children's Sensitivity to Constraints on Word Meaning: Taxonomic versus Thematic Relations', *Cognitive Psychology*, 16: 1–27. Reprinted in D. Messer and J. Dockrell (eds) (1998) *Developmental Psychology: A Reader*, London: Arnold.

Marslen-Wilson, W. (1973) 'Linguistic Structure and Speech Shadowing at Very Short Latencies', *Nature*, 244: 522–3.

—— (1987) 'Functional Parallelism in Spoken Word Recognition', *Cognition*, 25: 71–102

—— (1999) 'Abstractness and Combination: The Morphemic Lexicon', in S. Garrod and M. Pickering (eds), *Language Processing*, Hove: Psychology Press, pp. 101–119.

Marslen-Wilson, W., Tyler, L.K., Waksler, R. and Older, L. (1994) 'Morphology and Meaning in the English Mental Lexicon', *Psychological Review*, 101: 3–33.

Maxim, J. and Bryan, K. (1994) *Language of the Elderly*, London: Whurr.

McClelland, J.L. and Elman, J.L. (1986) 'The TRACE Model of Speech Recognition', *Cognitive Psychology*, 18: 1–86.

McClelland, J.L. and Rumelhardt, D.E. (1981) 'An Interactive Activation Model of Context Effects in Letter Perception. Part 1. An Account of the Basic Findings', *Psychological Review*, 88: 375–407.

McLaughlin, B. (1987) *Theories of Second Language Learning*, London: Arnold.

McQueen, J. and Cutler, A. (1998) 'Morphology in Word Recognition', in A. Spencer (ed.), *The Handbook of Morphology*, Oxford: Blackwell, pp. 406–27.

McQueen, J.M., Cutler, A., Briscoe, T. and Norris, D. (1995) 'Models of Continuous Speech Recognition and the Contents of the Vocabulary', *Language and Cognitive Processes*, 10: 309–31.

McShane, J. (1991) 'The Origins of Representations', *Cognitive Development*. Reprinted in D. Messer and J. Dockrell (eds) (1998) *Developmental Psychology: A Reader*, London: Arnold.

Menn, L. and Stoel-Gammon, C. (1995) 'Phonological Development', in P. Fletcher and B. MacWhinney (eds), *The Handbook of Child Language*, Oxford: Blackwell, pp. 335–359.

Miles, T.T. (1993) *Dyslexia: The Pattern of Difficulties*, 2nd edn, London: Whurr.

Miller, G.A. (1990) 'Linguists, Psychologists and the Cognitive Sciences', *Language*, 66: 317–22.

Miller, G.A. and Nicely, P. (1955) 'An Analysis of Perceptual Confusions Among Some English Consonants', *Journal of the Acoustical Society of America*, 27: 338–52.

Miller, J. (1990) 'Speech Perception', in D. Osherson and H. Lasnik (eds), *An*

Invitation to Cognitive Psychology: Vol. 1, Language, Cambridge, MA: MIT Press, pp. 69–93.

Mills, A. (1993) 'Visual Handicap', in D. Bishop and K. Mogford (eds), *Language Development in Exceptional Circumstances*, Hove: Psychology Press, pp. 150–164.

Minsky, M. (1977) 'Frame System Theory', in P.N. Johnson-Laird and P.C. Wason (eds), *Thinking: Readings in Cognitive Science*, Cambridge: Cambridge University Press.

Mitchell, D.C. (1994) 'Sentence Parsing', in M.A. Gernsbacher (ed.), *Handbook of Psycholinguistics*, San Diego, CA: Academic Press, pp. 375–409.

Mitchell, R. and Miles, F. (1998) *Second Language Learning Theories*, London: Arnold.

Mogford, K. (1993a) 'Language Development in Twins', in D. Bishop and K. Mogford (eds), *Language Development in Exceptional Circumstances*, Hove: Psychology Press, pp. 80–95.

—— (1993b) 'Oral Language Acquisition in the Prelinguistically Deaf', in D. Bishop and K. Mogford (eds), *Language Development in Exceptional Circumstances*, Hove: Psychology Press, pp. 110–13.

Morgan, J.L. and Demuth, K. (eds) (1996) *Signal to Syntax*, Mahwah, NJ: Erlbaum.

Morton, J. (1969) 'Interaction of Information in Word Recognition', *Psychological Review,* 76: 165–78.

Myers, F.I. and St Louis, K.O. (1992) *Cluttering: A Clinical Perspective*, London: Whurr.

Neisser, U. (ed.) (1987) *Concepts and Conceptual Development*, Cambridge: Cambridge University Press.

Nelson, K. (1973) *Structure and Strategy in Learning to Talk*, 2nd edn, Cambridge, MA: MIT Press.

Newport, E.L. (1990) 'Maturational Constraints on Language Learning', *Cognitive Science*, 14: 11–28.

Norris, D. and Cutler, A. (1988) 'The Relative Accessibility of Phonemes and Syllables', *Perception and Psychophysics*, 43: 541–50.

Nusbaum, H.C. and Goodman, J.C. (1994) 'Learning to Hear Speech as Spoken Language', in J.C. Goodman and H.C. Nusbaum (eds), *The Development of Speech Perception: The Transition from Speech Sounds to Spoken Words*, Cambridge, MA: MIT Press, pp. 299–338.

Nygaard, L.C. and Pisoni, D.B. (1995) 'Speech Perception: New Directions in Research and Theory', in J.L. Miller and P.D. Eimas (eds), *Speech, Language and Communication*, San Diego, CA: Academic Press, pp. 63–96.

O'Grady, W. (1997) *Syntactic Development*, Chicago, IL: University of Chicago Press.

O'Malley, J.M. and Chamot, A.U. (1990) *Learning Strategies in Second Language Acquisition*, Cambridge: Cambridge University Press.

Oakhill, J. and Beard, R. (eds) (1999) *Reading Development and the Teaching of Reading*, Oxford: Blackwell.

Oakhill, J. and Garnham, A. (1988) *Becoming a Skilled Reader*, Oxford: Blackwell.

Obler, L.K. and Gjerlow, K. (1999) *Language and the Brain*, Cambridge: Cambridge University Press.

Owens, R.E. (2001) *Language Development: An Introduction*, 5th edn, Needham Heights, MA: Allyn & Bacon.

Paap, K.R., Newsome, S., McDonald, J.E. and Schvanevelt, R.W. (1982) 'An

Activation-Verification Model for Letter and Word Recognition: The Word Superiority Effect', *Psychological Review,* 89: 573–94.

Palmer, F.R. (1981) *Semantics,* 2nd edn, Cambridge: Cambridge University Press.

Paradis, M. (1986) 'Foreword', in J. Vaid (ed.), *Language Processing in Bilinguals: Psycholinguistic and Neurolinguistic Perspectives,* Hillsdale, NJ: Erlbaum.

Paribakht, T.S. and Wesche, M. (1997) 'Vocabulary Enhancement Activities and Reading for Meaning in Second Language Vocabulary Acquisition', in J. Coady and T. Huckin (eds), *Second Language Vocabulary Acquisition,* Cambridge: Cambridge University Press, pp. 174–200.

Pawley, A. and Syder, F.H. (1983) 'Two Puzzles for Linguistic Theory', in J.C. Richards and R.W. Schmidt (eds), *Language and Communication,* London: Longman, pp. 191–226.

Pearce, J.M. (1997) *Animal Learning and Cognition,* Hove: Psychology Press.

Perfetti, C. (1985) *Reading Ability,* New York: Oxford University Press.

—— (1999) 'Cognitive Research and the Misconceptions of Reading Education', in J. Oakhill and R. Beard (eds), *Reading Development and the Teaching of Reading,* Oxford: Blackwell, pp. 42–58.

Peters, A. (1983) *The Units of Language Acquisition,* Cambridge: Cambridge University Press.

—— (1995) 'Strategies in the Acquisition of Syntax', in P. Fletcher and B. MacWhinney (eds), *The Handbook of Child Language,* Oxford: Blackwell, pp. 462–482.

Piattelli-Palmarini, M. (1980) *Language and Learning: The Debate between Chomsky and Piaget,* Cambridge, MA: Harvard University Press.

Pickering, M.J. (1999) 'Sentence Comprehension', in S. Garrod and M. Pickering (eds), *Language Processing,* Hove: Psychology Press, pp. 123–54.

Pickett, J.M. (ed.) (1999) *The Acoustics of Speech Communication,* Needham Heights, MA: Allyn & Bacon.

Pinker, S. (1994a) 'How Could a Child Use Verb Syntax to Learn Verb Semantics?', *Lingua,* 92: 377–410.

—— (1994b) *The Language Instinct,* London: Penguin.

—— (1997) 'Evolutionary Biology and the Evolution of Language', in M. Gopnik (ed.), *The Inheritance and Innateness of Grammars,* New York Oxford University Press, pp. 181–208.

Posner, M.J. and Raichle, M.E. (1994) *Images of Mind,* New York: Scientific American Library.

Potter, M.C. and Lombardi, L. (1990) 'Regeneration in the Short-term Recall of Sentences', *Journal of Memory and Language,* 29: 633–54.

Premack, D. (1986) *Gavagai! Or the Future History of the Animal Language Controversy,* Cambridge, MA: MIT Press.

Premack, D. and Premack, A. (1983) *The Mind of an Ape,* New York: W.W. Norton.

Radford, A. (1990) *Syntactic Theory and the Acquisition of English Syntax,* Oxford: Blackwell.

Rayner, K. and Pollatsek, A. (1989) *The Psychology of Reading,* Englewood Cliffs, NJ: Prentice Hall.

Reeves, L.M., Hirsh-Pasek, K. and Golinkoff, R. (1998) 'Words and Meaning: From Primitives to Complex Organization', in J.B. Gleason and N.B. Ratner (eds), *Psycholinguistics,* 2nd edn, Fort Worth, TX: Harcourt Brace, pp. 157–226.

Ritchie, W.C. and Bhatia, T.K. (eds) (1996) *Handbook of Second Language Acquisition*, San Diego, CA: Academic Press.

Robertson, S.I. (2001) *Problem Solving*, Hove: Psychology Press.

Romaine, S. (1995) *Bilingualism*, 2nd edn, Oxford: Blackwell.

—— (1996) 'Bilingualism', in W.C. Ritchie and T.K. Bhatia (eds), *Handbook of Second Language Acquisition*, San Diego, CA: Academic Press, pp. 571–604.

Samuel, A.G. (1990) 'Using Perceptual Restoration Effects to Explore the Architecture of Perception', in G. Altmann (ed.), *Cognitive Models of Speech Processing: Psycholinguistic and Computational Perspectives*, Cambridge, MA: MIT Press, pp. 295–314.

Sanford, A.J. and Garrod, S.C. (1981) *Understanding Written Language: Explorations of Comprehension Beyond the Sentence*, Chichester: John Wiley.

Savage-Rumbaugh, E.S. and Lewin, R. (1994) *Kanzi: The Ape at the Brink of the Human Mind*, New York: Wiley.

Scardamalia, M. and Bereiter, C. (1987) 'Knowledge Telling and Knowledge Transforming in Written Composition', in S. Rosenberg (ed.), *Advances in Applied Psycholinguistics, Vol. 2*, Cambridge: Cambridge University Press, pp. 142–175.

Schank, R.C. and Abelson, R.P. (1977) *Scripts, Plans, Goals and Understanding*, Hillsdale, NJ: Erlbaum.

Schiff-Myers, N. (1993) 'Hearing Children of Deaf Parents', in D. Bishop and K. Mogford (eds), *Language Development in Exceptional Circumstances*, Hove: Psychology Press, pp. 47–61.

Seliger, H.W. (1996) 'Primary Language Attrition in the Context of Bilingualism', in W.C. Ritchie and T.K. Bhatia (eds), *Handbook of Second Language Acquisition*, San Diego, CA: Academic Press, pp. 605–26.

Shillcock, R. and Bard, E. (1993) 'Modularity and the Processing of Closed Class Words', in G. Altmann and R. Shillcock (eds), *Cognitive Models of Speech Processing*, Hove: Erlbaum, pp. 163–86.

Simpson, G.B. (1994) 'Context and the Processing of Ambiguous Words', in M.A. Gernsbacher (ed.), *Handbook of Psycholinguistics*, San Diego, CA: Academic Press, pp. 359–74.

Singer, M. (1990) *Psychology of Language*, Hillsdale, NJ: Erlbaum.

—— (1994) 'Discourse Inference Processes', in M.A. Gernsbacher (ed.), *Handbook of Psycholinguistics*, San Diego, CA: Academic Press, pp. 479–516.

Singleton, D. (1989) *Language Acquisition: The Age Factor*, Clevedon: Multilingual Matters.

Skinner, B.F. (1957) *Verbal Behavior*, New York: Appleton–Century–Crofts.

Skuse, D.H. (1993) 'Extreme Deprivation in Early Childhood', in D. Bishop and K. Mogford (eds), *Language Development in Exceptional Circumstances*, Hove: Psychology Press, pp. 29–46.

Slobin, D. (1970) 'Universals of Grammatical Development in Children', in G. Flores d'Arcais and W.J.M. Levelt (eds), *Advances in Psycholinguistics*, Amsterdam: North Holland, pp. 175–208.

—— (1973) 'Cognitive Prerequisites for the Development of Grammar', in C.A. Ferguson and D.I. Slobin (eds), *Studies of Child Language Development*, New York: Holt, Rinehart & Winston.

—— (1982) 'Universal and Particular in the Acquisition of Language', in E. Wanner and L. Gleitman (eds), *Language Acquisition: The State of the Art*, Cambridge: Cambridge University Press, pp. 128–72.

—— (1985) 'Crosslinguistic Evidence for the Language-Making Capacity', in D.I. Slobin (ed.), *The Crosslinguistic Study of Language Acquisition: Vol. 2. Theoretical Issues*, Hillsdale, NJ: Erlbaum, pp. 1157–249.

Smith, F. (1971) *Understanding Reading: A Psycholinguistic Analysis of Reading and Learning to Read*, New York: Holt, Rinehart & Winston.

Smith, N. (1999) *Chomsky: Ideas and Ideals*, Cambridge: Cambridge University Press.

Smith, N. and Tsimpli, I. (1995) *The Mind of a Savant: Language Learning and Modularity*, Oxford: Blackwell.

Snow, C. (1986) 'Conversations with Children', in P. Fletcher and M. Garman (eds), *Language Acquisition*, 2nd edn, Cambridge: Cambridge University Press, pp. 363–75.

—— (1995) 'Issues in the Study of Input', in P. Fletcher and B. MacWhinney (eds), *The Handbook of Child Language*, Oxford: Blackwell, pp. 180–94.

Springer, S.P. and Deutsch, G. (1997) *Left Brain, Right Brain*, 5th edn, New York: W.H. Freeman.

Stanovich, K.E. (1980) 'Toward an Interactive-Compensatory Model of Individual Differences in the Development of Reading Fluency', *Reading Research Quarterly*, 16: 32–71.

Stein, B.S. and Bransford, J.D. (1979) 'Constraints on Effective Elaboration: Effects of Precision and Subject Generation', *Journal of Verbal Learning and Verbal Behavior*, 16: 769–77.

Stemberger, J.P. (1998) 'Morphology in Language Production: With Special Reference to Connectionism', in A. Spencer (ed.), *The Handbook of Morphology*, Oxford: Blackwell, pp. 406–27.

Stevens, K.N. (1960) 'Towards a Model of Speech Recognition', *Journal of the Acoustical Society of America*, 32: 47–55.

—— (1986) 'Models of Phonetic Recognition II: A Feature Based Model of Speech Recognition', in P. Mermelstein (ed.), *Proceedings of the Montreal Satellite Symposium on Speech Recognition*, Twelfth International Congress on Acoustics.

Stevenson, R.J. (1993) *Language, Thought and Representation*, Chichester: John Wiley.

Strong, M. (ed.) (1988) *Language Learning and Deafness*, Cambridge: Cambridge University Press.

Stroop, J.R. (1935) 'Studies of Interference in Serial Verbal Reactions', *Journal of Experimental Psychology*, 18: 643–62.

Styles, E. (1997) *The Psychology of Attention*, Hove: Psychology Press.

Swinney, D. (1979) 'Lexical Access During Sentence Comprehension: (Re)-consideration of Context Effects', *Journal of Verbal Learning and Verbal Behavior*, 5: 219–27.

Taft, M. (1979) 'Lexical Access via an Orthographic Code: The Basic Orthographic Syllable Structure (BOSS)', *Journal of Verbal Learning and Verbal Behavior*, 18: 21–39.

—— (1981) 'Prefix Stripping Revisited', *Journal of Verbal Learning and Verbal Behavior*, 20: 289–97.

Taylor, I. and Taylor, M.M. (1990) *Psycholinguistics: Learning and Using Language*, Englewood Cliffs, NJ: Prentice Hall.

Thiery, C. (1978) 'True Bilingualism and Second-language Learning', in D. Gerver and H. Sinaiko (eds), *Language Interpretation and Communication*, New York: Plenum Press.

Tomasello, M. and Bates, E. (eds) (2001) *Language Development: The Essential Readings*, Oxford: Blackwell.

Tomasello, M. and Brooks, P.J. (1999) 'Early Syntactic Development: A Construction Grammar Approach', in M. Barrett (ed.), *The Development of Language*, Hove: Psychology Press, pp. 161–90.

Towell, R. and Hawkins, R. (1994) *Approaches to Second Language Acquisition*, Clevedon: Multilingual Matters.

Ungerer, F. and Schmid, H.J. (1996) *An Introduction to Cognitive Linguistics*, London: Longman.

Valian, V. (1996) 'Input and Language Acquisition', in W.C. Ritchie and T.K. Bhatia (eds), *Handbook of Child Language Acquisition*, San Diego, CA: Academic Press, pp. 497–530.

van den Broek, P. (1994) 'Comprehension and Memory of Narrative Texts: Inferences and Coherence', in M.A. Gernsbacher (ed.), *Handbook of Psycholinguistics*, San Diego, CA: Academic Press, pp. 539–88.

Van Dijk, T.A. and Kintsch, W. (1983) *Strategies of Discourse Comprehension*, New York: Academic Press.

Vygotsky, L. (1934) *Thought and Language*, trans. E. Hanfman and K. Vakar, 1962 edn, Cambridge, MA: MIT Press.

Warren, P. (1999) 'Prosody and Language Processing', in S. Garrod and M. Pickering (eds), *Language Processing*, Hove: Psychology Press, pp. 155–188.

Warren, R.M. (1970) 'Perceptual Restoration of Missing Speech Sounds', *Science*, 167: 392–5.

Weinreich, U. (1968) *Languages in Contact*, The Hague: Mouton.

Wesche, M.B. (1994) 'Input and Interaction in Second Language Acquisition', in C. Gallaway and B. Richards (eds), *Input and Interaction in Language Acquisition*, Cambridge: Cambridge University Press, pp. 219–249.

Whitney, P. (1998) *The Psychology of Language*, Boston, MA: Houghton Mifflin.

Wingate, M.E. (1988) *The Structure of Stuttering: A Psycholinguistic Analysis*, New York: Springer Verlag.

Wingfield, A. and Titone, D. (1998) 'Sentence Processing', in J.B. Gleason and N.B. Ratner (eds), *Psycholinguistics*, 2nd edn, Fort Worth, TX: Harcourt Brace, pp. 227–274.

Wittgenstein, L. (1958) *Philosophical Investigations*, trans. G.E.M. Anscombe, 2nd edn, Oxford: Blackwell.

Wray, A. (2003) *Formulaic Language and the Lexicon*, Cambridge: Cambridge University Press.

Yeni-Komshian, G.H. (1998) 'Speech Perception', in J.B. Gleason and N.B. Ratner (eds), *Psycholinguistics*, 2nd edn, Fort Worth, TX: Harcourt Brace, pp. 107–156.

Yuill, N. and Oakhill, J. (1992) *Children's Problems in Text Comprehension*, Cambridge: Cambridge University Press.

Zipf, G.K. (1935) *The Psycho-biology of Language: An Introduction to Dynamic Philology*, Cambridge, MA: MIT Press.

INDEX

Page numbers in **bold type** indicate a complete entry on the topic. Names of researchers are restricted to those who are closely identified with a particular concept.

abstract words 159
access code **1**, 160
access *see* lexical access
accommodation (phonetic) **1–2**, 156, 315
accommodation (interpersonal) **2**, 115
accretion 255
accuracy **2**, 16
achievement behaviour 66
acoustic 286
acoustic cue **3**, 82
acoustic feature 209
acoustic-phonetic signal 286
acquired disorder 92
acquired dyslexia 95, **98–9**
acquisition **3**
ACT models **4–5**, 107, 224, 258
action potential 43
activation **5–6**, 41, 44, 64, 67, 73, 78, 102, 138, 151, 159, 165, 190, 200, 218, 222, 235
Adaptive Control of Thought **4–5**
addition 267
additive bilingualism 33
Adjacency Parameter 220
affective signal 140, 228
affective state 25
affixation 184, 326
age of arrival 81
age of child 144
ageing **6–7**, 86
agnosia **7**

agrammatism **7–8**
AI **21–23**, 26, 223, 226, 248–9, 299
algorithm 179, 223
alphabet 332
alphabetic approach 238
Alzheimer's disease 86
ambiguity 78, 299
ambiguity: lexical **8**; local 9; standing 9; syntactic **8–11**
ambiguity resolution **8–11**; 78
ambisyllabicity 1, 315
amplitude 286
anacrusis 140
analogy 197, 238
analogy effect 124, 127
analogy model **11**
analogy theory 95, 189
analysed knowledge 142
analysis **11–12**, 258
analysis-by-synthesis 282
analytical style 111, 142, 148
anaphor 12, 220 ; deep 13; surface 13
anaphor resolution **12–14**, 114, 164, 174, 242, 298
Anderson, J.R. 4–5
animacy 68
animal communication **14–15**, 274
animals 44–45
anomia 17
anti-mentalist 62
anxiety 2, **15–16**, 34
aperiodic 191

aphasia **16–17**, 49, 87, 152, 183, 201
apraxia **18**
Arabic writing 333
architecture 179
argument 175, 218, 225
argument structure 10, **18**
artibrariness 91
articulation **18–20**, 42
articulation rate **20–21**, 82, 192, 203, 273
articulator 18, 104, 281
Articulator 286
articulatory buffer 286
articulatory gesture 18
articulatory learning theory 205
articulatory plan 19, 216, 286
articulatory rehearsal 211
articulatory setting 20
articulatory suppression **21**, 246
artificial grammars 127
Artificial Intelligence **21–23**, 26, 223, 226, 248–9, 299
assemblage error 270
assimilation 2, 140, 209
association **23–24**
association strength 219
associative complex 71
associative stage 4,107
ASTM test 211, 243
ATN **26**, 299
attention (focus) 2, **24**, 112
attention (capacity) 15, **24–5**, 28, 128, 207, 327
attentional dyslexia 98
attic children 88
attrition **25–6**, 33
attunement theory 205
auditory 286
auditory masking 171
auditory nerve 125
auditory perception 204, 278–83
Auditory Short Term Memory 211, 243
auditory theory 19
Augmented Transition Network **26**, 299
autism **27**, 180
automatic 6, **28**, 51, 107, 141, 152, 166, 202, 218, 232, 234, 241, 243, 258, 291, 327, 330

automaticity *see* automatic
autonomous **29,** 150, 151, 181, 278–80
autonomous stage 4, 107
autonomous view 278–9
autonomous vs interactive **278–80**
avoidance behaviour 66

babble: reduplicated 29 variegated 29
babbling **29**, 37, 84, 141, 144, 208, 265
baby talk 54–55, 134
back propagation 23, 75
back tracking 236, 241
backward inference 129
backward masking 171
Baddeley, A. 211, 327
balance theory 35
balanced bilingualism 33
balanced homonym 8
band-pass filter 113, 136
basic level **30**, 70, 168, 261, 320–1
basilar membrane 125
bathtub effect 158, 270
behaviourism **30–31**, 59, 62, 103, 146, 258, 304
Berlin, B. and Kay, P. 65
best fit 202, 222
best match 191
between-levels 138
bilingualism **31–35**, 87
bin 256
Binding Principles 220
biologically triggered behaviour **35–6**, 185
bioprogram 79
bird calls 36
birdsong **36**
blend 269
blindness **36–8**, 39, 273
bonobo 57
bootstrapping **38–40**, 54, 63, 213, 293
borrowing 35
BOSS 1
bottle-neck hypothesis 233
bottom-up **40–42,** 77, 137, 181, 204, 232–4
bottom-up priority 41, 65, 77, 152, 279, 307
bottom-up view 278

bottom-up vs top-down **232–4**
bound root 1
bounding node 220
Bounding Parameters 220
brain 16–17, **42–50**, 86
brain: human vs animal 274
brain evolution 104
brain growth 45
brain imaging **45–46**, 49, 80, 108, 118, 248
brain lateralisation **46–48**, 80, 227, 274, 306
brain localisation **48–50**, 103
Branching Parameter 220–1
breathing 45, 323
bridging inference 129, 177
brightness masking 171
broad class transcription **50**, 132
Broca's aphasia 16–17
Broca's area 48, 118
Bruner, J. 272
buffer 19, **50–51**, 203, 212, 269, 284, 328
bundle of features 229

candidate 67, 151, 222
candidate search space 131–2
canonical sentence structure 9–10, 299–300
capacity theories 24–5, **51**, 326
carer correction 186
caretaker talk 54–55, 134
CAT scanning 46
cataphora 14
catastrophic view 105
categorical knowledge 142
categorical perception **51–54**, 81, 105, 206
categorisation 322
category 37, 65, 70–2, 106, 214, 320
category size effect 262
central dyslexia 98
central executive 175, 327
cerebellum 42, 44
chain complex 71, 197, 325
chain shift 209
chaining 31
characteristic features 230
child directed speech 37, 39, **54–55,** 60, 80, 84, 103, 134, 186–7, 271, 321
child grammar **55–6**, 145
Child Language Data Exchange System 144
CHILDES 144
chimp studies **56–7**, 275
Chinese writing 333
Chomsky, N. 31, **57–60**, 89, 304
Chomskyan 57–60, 147, 185, 230, 248
chunk 4, 11, **60–61**, 107, 111, 113, 116, 142, 148, 158, 188, 236, 258
chunking **60–1**, 268, 326
clang response 23
Clark, E. 168
class-inclusion statement 178
clause 283, 288, 328
clause boundary 215, 319
click experiments 297–8
click location 250, 297–8
cliticisation 292
close shadowing 263
closeness of fit 64
closure 123
cluttering **61**
co-articulation 18, 82, 209, 291, 314
cocktail party effect 24
coda 252
code: access **1**, 160; phonological 217, 327–8; speech (in reading) 132–3, **277**; storage 176, **247**
code-mixing 34
code-switching 26, 34
codification 162
co-evolution 105
cognition **61–2**, 93
cognitive approaches (SLA) 257–8
cognitive development 213, 321, 325
cognitive difficulty 296
cognitive psychology **62**
cognitive system 165
cognitivism **63–4**, 146, 147
coherence 129
Cohort Theory **64–5**, 67, 122, 152, 155, 313
collective monologue 214
Collins, A.M. and Quillian, M.R. 261
colour systems **65–6**, 105, 162, 305
commisurotomy 47
common underlying proficiency 35

communication strategy **66–7**, 259, 290

comparison model 112

compensation 234

compensatory use of context 308

competence 59, 186, 221, 297, 316

competition 41, **67–8**, 117, 151, 184, 189

Competition Model **68–9**

competitor 5

complete feedback 90

complex 324

componential analysis **69**

composed 166

composition 4

compound bilingualism 32

comprehension monitoring 240

computer modelling 248–9

computerised axial tomography 46

concept **69–70**, 169, 229

concept formation **70–2**, 198, 324

conceptual category 320

conceptual core 229–30

conceptual information 232–4

conceptual processing 41, 307

conceptual vs perceptual 163, 240

conceptualisation 215

Conceptualiser 285–6

concrete operational stage 214

concurrent articulation 133

concurrent report 317–18

conditioning 30

conduction aphasia 17

confusability **72–3**, 267

connected speech 156–8, 285

connectionism 5, 23, 62, **73–6**, 103, 106, 124, 138, 147, 159, 179, 188, 190, 198–9, 200, 214, 262, 308, 312, 322

constraint-based approach 9

Construction-Integration model 173

constructivist view (inference) 130, 177

constructivist view (vs realist) 305

content schema 240, 254

context 68, **76–7**, 139, 152, 163, 232–4, 239, 241, 254, 278–80, 307–8

context-bound 70

context effects 6, **77–8**

context-free 70

continuation 123

continuity hypothesis 29

continuity theory 187

contralateral relationship 42

contrast 228

contrast principle 70, 168

control *see* controlled

controlled 4, 12, 107, 134, 141, 166, 232, 258, 301, 327

conventionality principle 70, 168

convergence 2

cooing 144

co-ordinate bilingualism 32

co-ordinative structures 19

core grammar 170, 317

corpus callosum 42

correspondence hypothesis 90

cortex 42, 44, 323

cortical dementia 86–87

cost-benefit 275, 303

co-text 76

cover strategy 290

covert repair 247

creole 55, 79

creolisation **79**, 185, 265

critical period 36, 47, **79–81**, 84, 87, 206, 257, 265

cross-linguistic 34–5

cross-modal priming 219

cryptophasia 310

cue strength 68, 82

cue trading **82**, 309

cultural factors 229

cultural transmission 91

Cutler, A. 157

cycle 74–5

d′ 266

d-structure 58, 298

data collection 248

deaf parent **83–84**

deafness **83–85**, 265, 273

decay 218

decentration 214

decibel 286

declarative knowledge 2, 107, 141, 166, 175–6

declarative memory 4

decoding 28, 138–9, 167, 232–4, 241, 243
decoding: reading **234–6**, 292
decomposition model 183–4
deductive 148
deep anaphor 13
deep dysgraphia 97
deep dyslexia 99, 100
deep reading 244
deep structure 58, 298
defining features 71, 230
degradation effect 153
degraded 139, 190, 234, 244
deixis 37, 195, 302–3
delay **85–86**, 92
deletions 267
demands and capacities 291
demarcative stress 158, 160
dementia **86–7**, 139
demi-syllable 210, 282, 315
denativisation 185
density, neighbourhood 189
deprivation 47, 80, **87–9**, 273
depth of processing **89**
derivational theory of complexity (DTC) **89–90**, 297
desensitisation 53
design feature 14, **90–1**, 274
developmental disorder 92
deviance **85–86**, 92
dichotic listening 47, **91–2**, 179
digit span 211, 243
digraph 124, 189, 252
diphone 315
direct access 314
direct procedure 238
directed thinking 223
discontinuity hypothesis 29
discourse analysis 248
discourse comprehension 173
discreteness 91
discrimination net 238
disorder **92–4**, 273
displacement 14, 91
distributed processing 76
distributed representation 124, 200
divergence 2
domain 81
domain-specific 32, 181
dominance test 34

dominant bilingualism 33
dominant sense 78, 152
double storage 118
Down's Syndrome **94**, 180
drafting 330
dual route **94–5**, 124, 235
duality of patterning 91
Dugum Dani 65
duplex perception **95–6**
duration 287
dysarthria **96**
dysgraphia 93; acquired **96–7**; developmental **97–8**
dyslexia 93, 197; acquired **98–9**; developmental **99–101**
dysphasia **101**

E-language 126
ear canal 125
Ear, Slip of the **266–7**
eardrum 125
early recognition 314
echoic memory 175, 263
echolalia 27, 37, **101**, 145, 214
editing 330
editing expression 247
editor theories 260
effect **101**; lexical 153; position 216–7; priming 218
effort after meaning 172
egocentric speech 146, 272, 304, 324
egocentric thought 214
elaboration **101**, 176
elaborative inference 130, 135, 177
elaborative rehearsal 245
electrical stimulation 45
elision 2
embedded processes model **101**, 176
emphasis 228
empiricism 76, **103–4**, 146, 185–7
encapsulated 150, 181
encoding 167
encoding specificity hypothesis 167
enemy 188
episodic knowledge 254
episodic memory 166
equivalence class 131
ERP **103**
error reduction 75
ESB 45

event related potential 46, **103,** 300
evoked potential 46
evolution of language **103–5**, 274–5
exceptional circumstances 93–4, 273
excitatory 5, 43
excitatory connection 74
execution 330
exemplar models **105–6**, 140, 166, 209, 230
expected class size (ECS) 132
experimental data 248
experimental methods 143–4, **249–252**
expert system 22, **106–7**
expertise 4, 21, 62, **107–8**, 166, 178, 223, 257
explicit focus 13, 113, 174
explicit knowledge 12, 139, 142, 258
explicit learning 127
expressive aphasia 17
expressive learning style 148, 320
eye contact 215
eye movements **109–10**, 231, 250
eye-mind hypothesis **108–9**, 127
eye-voice span 232

F_0 117–8
F_1, F_2, F_3 116
facilitatory 5
facilitatory connection 74, 138, 200
faint speech 251, 267
family resemblance **110**, 121
feature analysis theories 202
feature detection 171
feature mask 171
feature, phonetic 259, 282, 286
feature-blindness hypothesis 276
feral children 87
field dependency **111**
figurative language **111–12**, 178
filled pause 203
filter (attention) 24, **112–3**
filter (acoustic) 72, **113**
filter theory 24
finite-state 149, 186
first fixation 109
first language acquisition 3 *see* language acquisition
fis phenomenon 206
fixation 109, 232, 243

flexibility test 34
fluency 4, 16, 60, 93, **113**
fluent aphasia 17
fluent phase 215
fMRI 46
focal point 65, 305
focus **113–4**
focus of attention 102
Fodor, J. 181
foot 287–8
foregrounding 78, **113–4**
foreigner discourse 114
foreigner talk 55, **114–5**, 134–5, 253
formal operational stage 214
formal schema 240, 254
formant 96, **115–6**
formant transition 116, 281
form-based priming 219
formulaic **116,** 142
formulaic speech 60, 87
formulation 216
Formulator 286
forward inference 130
forward masking 171–2
fossilisation **116–7**
fovea 110
frame 255
frequency (acoustic) **117–8**, 286–7; band 117, 136; fundamental 117; range 84
frequency (of occurrence) 5, 22, 67, **117**, 189, 229, 256
frequency attenuation 219; effect 153, 165
frequency of neighbourhood 189
friend 188
frontal lobe 42
function 120
function words 49, **118–9**, 236, 269, 319–20
functional approach **120**, 272–3
functional core hypothesis 71
functional disorder 92
functional load **119**
functional resonance magnetic imaging 46
functionalism **120**, 272–3
functionalist hypothesis 306
fundamental frequency 117

fuzzy boundary **121**

Ganong effect 279
garden path 9, **121**, 227, 299
gate 122
gating **122,** 250–1, 314
gaze duration 109
General Problem Solver 223
generative 31, 57–8
Genie 88
genre 254, 329
Gerken, L-A. 38, 293
Gernsbacher, M.A. 174, 242
Gestalt 62, **122–3**
Gestalt style 148
given / new **123**, 129, 141, 228
Gleitman, L. 39
goal state 223
Gold's theorem 186
Goodman, K. 232–4
goodness of fit 72, **123,** 209, 229
gossip view 103
government and binding 58
GPC rules 11, 94, **124**, 196, 235
GPS 223
grammatical encoding 286
grammaticality judgement 59, 85, 143,
    221, 248, 257, 298, 316
grapheme 196
grapheme-phoneme correspondence
    11, 94, **124**, 196, 235
graphotactic rules **124–5**
gyri 42

habituation 205
Halliday, M.A. K. 120, 272–3
handedness 47
hard-wired **125**, 182, 187, 316
HAS Procedure 251
Head Parameter 220
headturn preference procedure 144
hearing 125
hearing aid 84
hemisphere 42, 44, **46–8**
hemisphere, left 80
hemisphere, right 227
Hertz 117, 286
hesitant phase 215
hesitation 203
heuristic 179, 223–4

heuristic function 120
Hierarchical Network Model 261
hierarchical structure 149
high-amplitude sucking procedure 52,
    143, 251
higher level processing 6, 41, **126**,
    307–8; in listening **163–5**; in read-
    ing **240–1**
highly interactive 75, 181
high-pass filter 113, 136
Hockett, C. F. 90–1
holistic style 111, 148, 320
holophrastic speech 145
homesign 79, 185, 264
homo erectus 323
homonymy 78, 152, 168, 261
hypothesis testing **126**

IAC 73
iconic memory 175, 262
iconic representation 265, 293
ideal speaker-hearer 59
identification function 229–30
idioms 209
If …then features 316
If…then rules 224
I-language **126**
imageability **126–7,** 153
imaginative function 120
immediacy of interpretation **127**
implicational universals 147
implicit focus 113–4, 174
implicit knowledge 139, 141–2, 258
implicit learning **127–8**
'impoverished' 134
incidental learning 127, **128**
incidental task 142
incoherence model 111
indeterminacy **128–9,** 177
indexical 14, 209
indexical information 191
indexical representation 213, 293
indirect task 142
inductive learning 4, **129**, 142, 148
inference 114, **129–30**, 142, 173, 225,
    239, 240, 242
inflection 49, 68, **194–5**, 295
information focus 140, 228
information processing 62, **131,** 150,
    224

information value 131
informationally encapsulated 182
informative function 120
informativeness 119, **131–2**, 160
inhibitory 5, 43, 219
inhibitory connection 74, 138
initial state 223
initial teaching alphabet 238
innateness: phonology 208
inner ear 125
inner speech 51, 93, **132–4,** 235, 245, 268, 292
inner voice 51, 93, **132–4**, 235, 245, 268, 292
input **134–5**
input systems 181
instance models 105–6
instantiation 112, **135,** 178, 242
instrumental function 120
intake **135–6**
integration 163, 173–4, 176, 218, 232–3, 240, 242
integrative inference 129
intelligibility **136**
intensity 84, 136, 286
intentional 290
intentional learning 128
interaction 271–2
interaction models 112
interactional content 319
interactional function 120
interactional view: reading/listening **136–7**
interactive 41, 77, 151, 152, 181, 201, 235–6, 237, 278–9, 307, 309
interactive activation **137–8**
Interactive Activation and Competition model 73
interactive compensatory hypothesis 67, **138–9,** 234
interchangeability 90
interface view **139**
interference task 216–7
interlanguage 252, 258
internal speech **132–4**, 261, 324
intonation 39, **139–41,** 208
intonation group 140
intonational phrase 140, 227, 287–8
intraverbal response 31
involuntary activities 42

isolation point 122
Itard, J.M. 87–8

Japanese 53, 68
Japanese writing 333
jargon aphasia 17
joint reference 272
Johnson-Laird, P. 174, 177
juncture pause 203

Kanzi 57
Katz, J. and Fodor, J. 69
Keyboard, Slip of the **268–9**
kinesic feature 200
Kintsch and Van Dijk
knowledge **141–2**
knowledge-telling 331
knowledge-transforming 331–2

L1 **143**
L2 143
LAD **143**, 187
LAFF 282
LAFS 282
language acquisition 36–8, 38–40, 60, 60–1, 83–84, 84–85, **143–7**, 303, 317
language acquisition device **143**, 187
language attrition **25–6**
language development 317
language disorder 93
language loss 6–7, 25
language universals **147,** 162
langue 59
larynx 15, 104, 323
late closure 10
latency **148,** 249, 263
lateralisation 44, **46–48,** 80, 100, 104, 274, 306
learnability 91
learning plateau 117
learning strategy 290
learning style 64, **148**
learning theory 75, 106, **149**
learning: deductive 148; explicit 127; implicit **127–8**; incidental 128; inductive 129, 148; intentional 128
left-branching 221
left-to-right processing **149**, 314
legal 212

lemma 154–5
length effect 153
length of run 113
Lenneberg, E. 80
'less is more' 56–57, 64, 81, 146, **149–50**
letter-by-letter reading 98
levels of processing 40–41
levels of representation 131, 137, **150–1**, 201, 224
Levelt, W. 154, 228, 285
lexeme 117
lexical access 5, 67, 78, 117, 118, 135, **151–3**, 165, 201, 203, 232, 234, 255–6, 318
Lexical Access from Features 282
Lexical Access from Spectra 282
lexical bias effect 205
lexical decision 219, 250
lexical effect 101, **153–4**
lexical entry 140,151, **154–5**,161, 201, 284–5, 294, 306
lexical knowledge 53, 279–80, 307
lexical probability 222
lexical recognition **155–6**
lexical retrieval 87, 156, 268
lexical route 94, 124, 235
lexical segmentation 65, 68, **156–8**, 259
lexical storage 75, **158–60**
lexical stress 140, 157–8, **160–1,** 270
lexical vs sentence stress 285
lexicalist view 10
lexicon 1, 5, 64–5, 158, **161**, 165
lexigram 56
linear segmentation 156
linearity 186
linguistic approaches (SLA) 257
linguistic competence 165
linguistic determinism 65, 69, 162, 305
linguistic relativity 147, **161–2**
link 226
listening 64–5, 156–8, **163–5**, 191–2, 205–8, **278–83**, 286–7, 314–5
literacy 85, 204–5
lobes 42
local ambiguity 9
localisation **48–50**
localistic learning style 320

location-programming 19
logical bootstrapping 40
logical inference 129
logogen **165**, 201
logographic system 197, 332
long term memory 4, 21, 102, 165–7, 175–6, **247**, 263, 323, 326
'look and say' method 237
loudness 136, 286
lower-level processing 41, **167**
low-pass filter 113, 136

Machiavellian intelligence view 104
macro-planning 215, 329
macro-proposition 173, 225
maintenance rehearsal 245
malapropism 270–1
mand 31
mandatory 182
mapping 70–2, **167–9,** 321
marked *see* markedness
markedness **169–70**, 221–2, 257, 258, 317
Markedness Differential Hypothesis 170
Marslen-Wilson, W. 64
masker 171
masking **170–2**, 251
mathetic function 120
maturation 63, 80, 146
maturational process 316
maturational theory 187, 205
McClelland, J.L. and Elman 75, 308
McClelland, J.L. and Rumelhardt, D.E. 138
McGurk effect **172**
mean length of utterance 145, **172,** 294
meaning code 285, 305
meaning construction **172–4**
meaning postulate **175**
meaning representation 163, 224, 234, 254, 328
means-ends 213
medulla 42
mel 287
memory **175–6**: echoic 263; iconic 262; long term **165–7**; phonological **211–2**; short term **263**; sensory **262–3**; working **326–8**

memory demands 301
Memory Focus model 174
memory restrictions 317
mental lexicon **161**
mental model 128, 135, 174, **176–7**, 177, 225
mental representation 13, 101, 119, 130, 173, 176, **177**
mentalese 187, 305
meronym 129
metacognition 61–2, **178**
metaphor 111–12, **178**
Metrical Segmentation Strategy 157, 293
metrical template 38, 293
micro-planning 215, 329
micro-proposition 225
migration **179**
minimal attachment 10, 300
minimal pair 207
minimal terminal unit 301
minimalism 58
minimalist view 130, 177
miscue analysis 231–2, 233
mixing 32
MLU 145, **172**, 294
modality **179**, 237, 265
model 21, **179**
modularity (independent language faculty) 61, 93–4, 105, **180**, 213, 253, 265, 276–7, 278, 326
modularity (levels of processing) 137, 201, **181–2**, 278
monitoring space 6, 108, 163, 164, 173, 233, 234, 240, 242, 246, **260–1**, 284, 291, 318, 330
monitoring comprehension 163, 173, 240
monozygotic 310
mora 157
morpheme studies 194
morphology 154, 169, **182–4,** 194–5, 326: acquisition **182–3**; storage **183–4**
Moses illusion 174
motherese 54–55, 134
motivation 25
motor activity 42, 268
motor area 45
Motor Theory 282

movement rule 58–9, 199, 298
Multi-Dimensional Model 258–9
multiple trace 72, 106, 192, 209, 283
multi-store model 175
multi-word stage 145
mutism 27
mutual exclusivity assumption 70. 168

N400 103
naming insight 322
naming latency 249–50
naming task 249–50
nativisation hypothesis 79, **185**, 264–5
nativism 36–7, 55, 60, 82, 103, 104, 146, 147, 149–50, 180, **185–8**, 193, 194, 271, 275, 276
natural order 194
natural language processing 248
naturalistic acquisition 142, 258
naturally occurring data 248
necessary inference 129
negative evidence 186
neglect dyslexia 98
negotiation of meaning 115
neighbour 68, 238
neighbourhood **188–9**
Neighbourhood Activation Model 189
neighbourhood effect 95, 153
neoteny 104
network model 159
neural network 62, 73, **190**
neurolinguistics **190**
neuron 43, 73
neuropsychological data 248
node 226
noise 136, **190–1**, 191, 244
nomination 294
non-existence 295
non-fluent aphasia 17
non-interface view 139
non-invariance 281
non-linearity 281, 308
non-semantic reading 99
non-word repetition 211
no-overlap assumption 71
normalisation 106, **191–2**, 202, 207, 209, 281
Norris, D. 157
noticing 25, 135, 259
novice 108

nucleus 140, 252
Null Subject Parameter 220

object permanence 63, 145, 213, 304
observational methods 143, 248, 257
occipital lobe 42
OME 276
one-word stage 145
on-line processing 164, **192–3**, 217, 232, 121, 122, 149, 263, 267, 298–9, 318, 328
on-line task **193**, 249
ontogeny 104, 188
opaque orthography 95, 124, 196–7, 237
openness 91
operant headturn procedure 144, 251
operating principles 63, **193–4**
operator 223
order of acquisition 84, 85, 182, 186, **194–6**, 208
organic disorder 92
orthographic coding **196**
orthographic representation 154
orthographic stage 239
orthography **196–7**
ossicles 125
otitis media with effusion 276
over-extension 71, 169, **197–8**, 321
over-generalisation 4, 76, **198–9**, 294, 312
over-regularisation **198–9**
over-regularisation error **199**
overt repairs 247
overt speech **261**

P600 **103**
parafoveal 231
parafoveal preview 110
paralinguistic feature (vocal) 199
paralinguistic feature (visual) 199–200
parallel distributed processing 23, 76, 190, **200**
parallel processing 41, 73, 151, **201**, 224
parameter 60, 143, 170, 187, 196, **220**, 257, 298, 316
parameter setting 220
parameter switching 257
paraphasia **201**

parentese 54–55 *see* child directed speech
parietal lobe 42
Parkinson's disease 86
parole 59
parsing **297–300**
past tense 49, 75–6
path 223
pattern masking 171
pattern matching 119, 161, **202**
pattern recognition **202,** 209
pausing 113, 140, **202–4**, 215, 283
PDP 23, 76, 190, **200**
Pen, Slip of the **268–9**
percentage of information extracted (PIE) 132
percept 286
perception **204,** 262
perceptual bootstrapping 40
perceptual hypothesis 277
perceptual information 232–4
perceptual loop 261
perceptual magnet effect **204**
perceptual processing 41, 234–6, 240
perceptual prominence 287
perceptual saliency 182, 287
perceptual space 204
perceptual span 110
Perfetti, C. 233
performance 59, 186, 297, 316
performance disorder 93
peripheral auditory system 125
peripheral dysgraphia 96, 98
peripheral dyslexia 98
periphery 170, 317
personal function 120
PET 46
phon 286
phoneme 314–5
phoneme awareness 207
phoneme discrimination 51–54
phoneme monitoring 249
phoneme recognition 72–3, 204–5
phoneme restoration 250, 266, 280
phoneme variation **281–3**
phonemic paraphasia 201
phonetic context 53
phonetic feature 259, 281, 282, 286, 287–8
phonetic plan 19, 50, 261, 286

phonetic planning 270
phonics method 237
phonological awareness **204–5**, 237, 333
phonological bias technique **205**
phonological code 217, 327–8
phonological development 29, 84, 141, **205–9**
phonological dysgraphia 97
phonological dyslexia 95, 98, 99
phonological encoding 286
phonological loop 211, 246, 327
phonological phrase 283, 287–8
phonological recoding 239
phonological register 206
phonological representation 106, 154, 191, **209–11**, 230, 234, 282, 312–3
phonological route 133
phonological working memory 164, **211–212**
phonotactic cue 156
phonotactic rules **212–3**
phylogeny 104, 188
physiological problems 93
Piaget, J. 63, **213–4**, 304
pidgin 55, 79, **214**
pied piping 221, 298
Pinker, S. 39, 304–5
pinna 125
pitch 117, 286–7
pivot grammar **214–5**, 294
planning 15, 268–9, 332: speech 203, **215–6**, 283; writing **216**
planum temporale 100
plasticity 47
Plato's problem 103, 185
polarised homonym 8
polysemy 78, 152
position effect 101, **216–7**, 245
positron emission tomography 46
post-lexical 235, 277
post-perceptual 182, **217**, 249, 280
potential concept 325
poverty of stimulus 54, 60, 186
pragmatic content 271
pragmatic system 120
pre-articulatory editing 260
pre-assembled 60
predicate **217–8**, 225, 302
predicate / argument structure 218

predictability **218**, 233, 244–5
predictive inference 130
prefix 1, 184, 326
prefix-stripping 184
pre-frontal area 44
pre-lexical 235, 277
prelinguistic stage 144
pre-operational stage 145, 214
preposition stranding 221, 298
pre-text 51
prevarication 91
preverbal form 285
preverbal message 215
primacy effect 176, 216, 245
primary accent 140
primary stress 160
priming 159, 218, **218**, 251, 288
principles 60, 170, 187, 219–222, 257, 316
principles and parameters **219–222**
prioritisation 193
probabilistic 123, 156, **222**
probabilistic knowledge 142
probability 22, 189, **222–3**
problem space 223, 332
problem-solving 22, 62, 179, 214, **223–4**
procedural knowledge 22, 141, 166, 176, 224
proceduralisation 4, 107, 166, 268, 311
processing **224–5**: autonomous 29; bottom-up 40–42; conceptual 126; higher-level 126, 163–5, 240–1; interactive 181–2; lower-level 167; modular 181–2; perceptual 234–6, 281–3; top down 307–8; top down vs bottom up 232–4, 278–80
pro-drop language 220
Pro-drop Parameter 170, 220, 316
production memory 4
production rules 107, 224
production signalling 332
Projection Principle 220
property 261
proposition 163, **225**
propositional information 173, 240
propositional meaning 177
propositional network **226**
proprioceptive feedback 19
prosodic bootstrapping 38

prosody 10, 121, 139–40, 164, **226–9**;
and repair 247
Prosody Generator 228
protocol 317
proto-language 272
prototype 65, 71–2, 166, 198, 204,
209, 222, 229–30, 283,
Prototype Theory 123, 202, **229–30**
proto-words 120
pseudo-affix 1
pseudo-prefix 184
pseudo-word superiority effect 153
psychologically real 59, 90, **230–1**, 297

rapid mapping 169, 321
Rapid Serial Visual Presentation **231**
rationalism 103
Reaction Time 148, 218, 249
reading **231–244**: bottom up vs top
down **232–4**; decoding **234–6**;
higher-level processes **240–1**; recursiveness in 244; skilled **241–3**
reading ability 212
reading aloud 134, **231–2**
reading development 99–100, 133,
204–5, **236–40**
reading span **243**
reading span test 211–2
reading speed **243–4**
real time 192
realist 305
recall 251
recall cues 135
recast 271
recency effect 176, 216, 245
receptor neurons 125
recoding 245–6
recognition point 122, 156
recurrence 294
recursiveness 163, **244**
redundancy 114, 232, **244–5**
referential representation 176–7, 177
referential style 148, 320
reflectiveness 91
reflexive 323
reflexive production 208
reflexive pronoun 14
regeneration theory 319
regression 109, 231, 233, 236
regression hypothesis 7

regulatory function 120
rehearsal 21, 89, 107, 164, 166, 176,
211, 243, **245–6,** 324, 327
rehearsal mechanism 327
rehearsal strategy 290
reinforcement 30
reiterant speech 161
relevance 239
remaking the message 136–7, 164
repair strategy 115
repair (understanding) **246**
repair (self-repair) **246–7**, 260
repetition 251
repetition priming 165, 219
representation 223
representational code **247**
research methods **143–4, 248–252**
response buffer 165
response latency 249
response time 249
restructuring 126, **252**, 255, 258, 289
resyllabification 2
retrieval *see* lexical access
retrieval cue 152, 166
retrieval strategy 290
retroactive processing 314
retrospective report 317
reversible passive 90, 296
rhetorical problem 331
rhyme **252**
rhythm 207
right-branching 221
right-context 309
rime 11, 95, 188, 238, **252–3**
risk-avoider 66, 148
risk-taker 66, 148
Rosch, E. 229
rote learning 245
RSVP **231**
rule-and-memory model 198

s-structure 58, 298
S/N ratio 136, 190
saccade 109, 232, 236, 243
salience imbalance 112
saliency 287
Sapir-Whorf Hypothesis 161, 305
savant 180, **253**
scaffolding 54, **253**, 272
schema 76, 164, 166–7, 240, **254–5**

schemata 254
script 196, 255
search 223
search model 1, 151, 201, **255–6**
second language acquisition 3, 81, 221–2, **256–9**
second language learning 212
secondary stress 160
second-language vocabulary acquisition 160
segment (phoneme) **259**
segment (into words) **259**
segmentation **156–8**
selection 176
selection error 269
selection restrictions 111
selective adaptation **259–60**
selective processing 174
self-monitoring 6, 108, 164, 234, 240, 242, 246, **260–1,** 291, 318, 330
self-repair **246**
semantic association 288–9
semantic bootstrapping 39–40
semantic distance 261
semantic knowledge 254
semantic memory 166
semantic network 226, **261–2**
semantic paraphasia 201
semantic priming 219
semantic processing 300
semantic satiation 318
semanticity 91
sensation 204, **262**
sense relations 288–9
sensitive period 80, 88
sensori-motor stage 145, 213
sensory memory 165, 175, **262–3**
sentence context 280
sentence mode 140, 227
separate development hypothesis 32
sequential bilingualism 32
serial position effect **216–7**
serial processing 151, 201, 224, 255–6
shadowing 250, **263,** 313
shallow reading 244
shape bias 71
shared knowledge 303
shifting process 174
shigarette problem 64
short term memory 175, **263**, 326

Shortlist 138
sight vocabulary 237
Sign **264–6**
sign language 56, **264–6**
signal detection theory **266**
simultaneous bilingualism 32–3
simultaneous masking 171
simultaneous translation 48
situation type 296
situational model 176–7, 177
skilled reading **241–3**
skilled writing **331–2**
Skinner, B.F. 30–31
SLA **256–9**
slave system 327
SLI **276–7**
Slip of the Ear **266–7**
Slip of the Keyboard **268–9**
Slip of the Pen **268–9**
Slip of the Tongue 152, 158, 183, 215, 248, 267, **269–271,** 283, 306
Slobin, D. 193
social interactionism 103, 146, 120, **271–2**
sonority 287
SOT **269–271**
span tests 251
spandrel view 105
speaker variation 281
speaking 18–20, 208–9, 215–6, 228, **283–6, 287–8,** 323
speaking rate 20, 202, **273**
'special circumstances' 93–4, **273**
specialisation 91
species specific 14, **274–5,** 303
specific language impairment 180, 182, **276–7,** 325
spectrogram 115, 287
speech buffer 51, 212
speech code 132–3, **277**
speech disorder 93
speech mode (listening) 82, 96, **278**
speech mode (vocalising) 20, **278**
speech perception 20–21, **205–8, 278–83**
speech planning **215–6**
speech production 18–20, 208–9, 228, **283–6, 287–8,** 323
speech signal **286–7**
spontaneous usage 91

spreading activation 5, 77, 87, 130, 152, 159, 218, 262, **288–9**
stages of acquisition 144–6
stages of development (Piaget) **213–4**
stages of syntactic development 294–6
standard interactional routines 272
standing ambiguity 9
standing feature 200
Stanovich, K.E. 67, 234
steady-state 38, 116, 207, 320
stimulus-response 30
story approach 238
story grammar **289**
strategic competence 66
strategy 224, 259, **290:** communication 66–67; compensatory 66
strategy of use 290
strength of connection 73
stress: demarcative 158; lexical 157–8; primary 160; secondary 160; sentence 139–41, 226–9
stress-based 157
stressed syllable 270
strong-weak pattern **292–3**
Stroop test 28, 34, 167, 234, **291**
Structure Building Framework 174, 242
structure dependency 58, 91, 186, 220, 297
stuttering 61, 93, **291**
style 329
subcortical areas 323
subcortical dementia 86
Subjacency Principle 220
sub-lexical route 94, 124, 235, 237
subordinate bilingualism 32
substitution 267, 269
subtractive bilingualism 33
subvocalisation 133, **292**, 304
successive bilingualism 32–3
suffix 184, 326
sulci 42
surface anaphor 13
surface dysgraphia 96
surface dyslexia 95, 98, 100, 199
surface structure 58, 298
SW pattern 38, 207, 267, **292–3**
Swinney, D. A. 78, 181
syllabary 332
syllable 18, 207, 209, 270, 288, 315

syllable-based 157
symbolic representation 14, **293**
symbolic reference 213
symbolic sense 213
synaesthesia **294**
synapse 43
syncretic relationship 324
syntactic bootstrapping 39
syntactic boundary 140, 203
syntactic development **294–7**
syntactic parsing 9. 59, 147, 224, 227, 239, 241–2, **297–300**
syntactic probability 222–3
syntactic structure 154, 199, 270
syntactic vs semantic criteria 300
syntax vs lexis 285
synthetised speech **300–1**
system disorder 93
systematic variation 3

tachistoscope **301**
tact 31
target 218
task complexity 301, 327
task demands 3, **301–2**
task effects 249
task environment 331
taxonomic assumption 50, 168
telegraphic speech 83, 85, 145, 294
template theories 202, 209
temporal lobe 42
text structure 240
Thai 53
thematic role 13, 18, **302**
theory of mind 27, 272, 275, **302–3**
theory-driven 143, 248, 257
theta role *see* thematic role
thought and language **303–4,** 324
three-stage view 178
three-store model 131
time/intensity cue 84
time-slice 157, 283, 308
Tip of the Tongue 7, 251, 269, 285, **305–6**
tone group 140
tone language 139, **306**
Tongue, Slip of the **269–71**
tonic accent 139–41, 226–9
top-down 40–41, 75, 77, 137, 152, 181, 232–4, 279, 288, **307–8**

top-down view 232
topic 112
TOT **305**
total acceptance point 122
TRACE 75, 138, 157, 283, 298, **308**
trace 58
trading relations 82, **309**
transactional 319
transcortical aphasia 17
transfer 170, 258, 266
transformational rules 58, 89
transitional 38
transitional probability 22, 223
translation 329
transparent orthography 95, 196–7
tree diagram 220–1
trochee 293
tune 140
tuning 255
T-unit **301**
Turing test **310**
turn taking 91, 140, 203, 227
twins 252, 273, **310–11**
two-word stage 145, 265–6
type assumption 70
typing **311**
typology 147, 316

UG *see* universal grammar
under-extension 169, 198, 321
under-specification 209, 283, **312–3**
uniqueness point 65, 122, 155, **313–4**
unit 200
unit of parsing 299; of perception **314**; of representation 209; of segmentation 156; of speech processing 282, **314–5**; of speech production **287–8**
unitary language hypothesis 32
universal grammar 55, 60, 79, 80, 115, 143, 147, 170, 187, 193, 194, 220, 257, 296, **316–8**
universal markedness 169
universal theory 205
unmarked *see* markedness
U-shaped development 3, 76, 195, 198, 294, **312**

vague boundaries 70

variable 248
variation 154
vehicle 112
verbal efficiency theory 233
verbal report **317–18**
verbal transformation effect **318**
verbalism 37
verbatim form 245, 263, 326, 328
verbatim recall 119, **318–20,** 323
verification model 256
Victor 87–8
visual masking 171
visual perception 204
visuo-spatial sketch pad 327
vocabulary acquisition 85, 159–60, 212, **320–2**
vocabulary burst **322**
vocabulary explosion 120, **322**
vocabulary spurt 145, 213, 265, 320, **322**
vocal tract 287
vocal-auditory channel 90
vocalisation 15, 45, 274, **323**
'voice in the head' 132–4, 329–30
Voice Onset Time 51–53, 82, 244
voice recognition **323–4**
voluntary 323
VOT 51–53
vowel harmony 157
vowel quality 157, 161
vowel space 281
VTE **318**
Vygotsky, L. 71, 146, 272, 304, **324–5**

Wada injections 47
waveform 287
weight of connection 75
Wernicke's aphasia 16–17
Wernicke's area 48
white noise 190–1
whole object assumption 70, 168
whole word method 231, 235–6, 237
Williams Syndrome 180, **325–6**
win-stay lose-shift assumption 126
within-levels 138
within-speaker variation 281
word / non-word effect 153
word association **23–24,** 251, 321
word boundaries 213

word class acquisition 295
word coinage 321
word mask 171
word monitoring 249
word order 49, 68
word order acquisition 295
word primitive 183, **326**
word shape recognition 236
word skipping 110
word span 211
word spotting 250
word stress 1
word superiority 138, 153
word-blending task 252
working memory 4, 6, 21, 51, 102, 133, 163, 165, 175, 211–12, 217, 232, 241–3, 247, 263, 301, **326–8**, 328
working memory capacity 24–5, 28, 107, 141
world knowledge 10, 165, 173, 225, 240
wrap up effects 110, 163, 299, **328**
WRAPSA model 207
writing 51, 216, 311, **329–33**
writing acquisition 97
writing buffer 51, 329, 332
writing system 196, **332–3**
Wundt, W.M. 62

Zipf's law 334
Zone of Proximal Development 253, 325